THE POTENTATES

THE POTENTATES:

 TWO CENTURIES OF AMERICAN LIFE
A Bicentennial Series
Harold M. Hyman, Leonard W. Levy, Editors

Business and Businessmen in American History

BEN B. SELIGMAN

The Dial Press, New York, 1971

ALSO BY BEN B. SELIGMAN

Main Currents in Modern Economics: Economic Thought Since 1870
Poverty as a Public Issue (editor)
Most Notorious Victory: Man in an Age of Automation
Permanent Poverty: An American Syndrome
Aspects of Poverty (editor)
Economics of Dissent
Molders of Modern Thought (editor)

Library of Congress Catalog Card Number: 74–131169

Printed in the United States of America

Designed by Larry Alexander

First Printing

CONTENTS

Mammon led them on—
Mammon, the least erected spirit that fell
From Heaven; for even in Heaven his looks and thoughts
Were always downward bent, admiring more
The riches of Heaven's pavement, trodden gold,
Than aught divine or holy else enjoyed
In vision beatific.

—JOHN MILTON, *Paradise Lost,* Book I

What is business? . . . Business is bargaining, buying and selling, and producing goods and services for sale. Business is the struggle for wealth. Business is the system of social cooperation by mutual exchange. And— since part of a definition consists in knowing what a thing is not—business is not charity or benevolence. . . .

—JOHN MAURICE CLARK, *Social Control of Business*

To Theresa Wolfson Wood

THE POTENTATES

PREFACE

Doubtless this book will disturb many of its readers. A history of business in America, its basic premise is that a businessman's primary concern is profit-making. To be sure, the specific manner in which profit has been sought has always reflected the economic, political, and social circumstances of the time: the freebooting behavior of a Jay Gould was not likely to be duplicated in a later period when, at least publicly, many insisted that profit-making be subjected to a measure of public scrutiny. Nevertheless, the occasional outcries of venality, or demands for a greater sense of "responsibility" by business, or insistence on "stewardship," merely redirected modes of profit-making. Certainly nothing happened to reduce or curtail it.

However, the argument that business should be more "responsible" often evades the central issue in America's major institution—business cannot survive without profit. When "responsibility" and profit clash, it is profit that invariably wins out. Businessmen have been perfectly willing to demonstrate their responsibilities in dealing with certain critical social issues—e.g., employment in the ghetto—provided the profit-and-loss statement was not jeopardized. I recall a group of bankers assuring me not long ago that they would be happy to provide loans at favorable rates of interest to inner-city marginal enterprises (surely an important way of creating jobs) so long as someone else, presumably the Government, insured them against loss. From a business standpoint, such views are understandable.

The search for profit, then, is accepted as axiomatic for business. All other motivations seem to me to be secondary, or offered as apologies intended to rationalize the major thrust, or as mere constructs for the development of an ideology of business. Of course, what an appropriate level of profit—a proper rate of return—might be, always has been subject to debate. On this point, the businessman has been likely to have views at odds with those groups —workers, consumers, suppliers, and stockholders—with whom he maintains relationships. By and large, as this narrative underscores, the businessman's conception has prevailed. Had such not been the case there would have been little to tell of the building of great fortunes, of the rise of the Rockefellers, du Ponts, and Mellons, or of the new rich and super-rich.

In relating the story of American business there is no point in waxing indignant after the fashion of the muckrakers, or those who gleefully repeated

1

Theodore Roosevelt's fulminations against the "malefactors of great wealth." The past is to be evaluated, it seems to me, only in terms of the mores and conventions of the particular period under study. It is not very helpful to criticize men in history for being what they were, except insofar as one may wish to judge them for not having weighed alternatives that might have been available to them. In any case, the antics of eighteenth-century and nineteenth-century businessmen are now more likely to be viewed with a kind of wry admiration than with anger. If there is a moral to be drawn from the history of American business it would be proper to place whatever inner meaning it has in the setting of particular periods of time, unless it be to voice a few cautionary words about contemporary affairs, on the theory that leopards do not change their spots. Hence, I have sought to treat past events in American business with some measure of bemusement, and even detachment. One does not contemn what preceded the present; rather one seeks to explain one's antecedents.

Thus, comprehending old realities imposes on us the obligation to evaluate them in their setting. At this point I part company with recent fashions in American history. I may be criticized for this act of *lèse-majesté;* some may even charge that such chastisement as may be inflicted on me is justified by the very act of trespassing on other disciplines. Yet, given the opportunity to tell a story, there may be some value in bringing to the recitation a fresh viewpoint—that of an economist who is less than fully enchanted by the virtues of our civilization.

A great debate now rages among historians as to the sort of men who have filled the pages of business history. All too often today the historian offers a view of the past that is too clean and gilt-edged. Sordid episodes in the history of the businessman are frequently minimized and the antics of nineteenth-century financiers and promoters have become quaint tales in the annals of capital accumulation. Critical examinations of the careers of businessmen are rejected because they "rob the people of their heroes" and insult the folk memory of great men. Allan Nevins, for example, makes Henry Ford a genius of industrial productivity and places very little stress on the sort of factory totalitarianism with which he achieved high output. Julius Grodinsky converts Jay Gould into a giant of railroad construction although his business career was strewn with the wreckage of road after road. Any suggestion that there exists a close correspondence between economic motivation and political action is said to reflect an archaic view of society. History, in the view of these writers, becomes a celebration of national greatness and a source of "hope and faith, if not charity."

Those who have attacked such writers as Henry Demarest Lloyd, Matthew Josephson, and Gustavus Myers employ curious *ad hominem* arguments for the most part. These critics of business are said to be either Marxists or muckrakers or agrarian progressives, as though such characterizations wipe

clean the slate of predatory behavior of post-Civil War businessmen. What
those business careers do suggest is an overwhelming drive to make money
without much regard for the social by-products or what economists call "external diseconomies." If what was done may sometimes be described as creative
destruction, it was often more destructive than creative.

To take at face value the pronouncements of business leaders, as one
respected historian does, is to be gulled into a peculiar kind of benevolent
acceptance of the more sordid, and perhaps more hilarious, episodes in business
history. Certainly it would be difficult to discern the quality of creativity in the
career of Daniel Drew, and historians who wish to rewrite the chronicles of the
nineteenth century would have to go to great lengths to find creativity in the
machinations of Jim Fisk. Indeed, if present day benefit-cost analysis were
applied to that period in our history, the ratio would be somewhat less than
unity. Rather than grant absolution for the sake of capital accumulation, let us
look at the record. If "folk heroes" are not to be critically studied, then it is
history itself that is diminished. The speculators and financiers helped build an
economy, to be sure, but at what cost? The capitalist worked as rapidly as he
could, for there was only one lifetime in which to gather the dollars. The
"robber baron" grasped whatever he could reach, and his reach was longer and
surer than others'. He gave no quarter and he seldom asked for any. Significantly, the shape of the economy was altered, pointing the way to a capitalism
that was to be dominated by industrialist and financier.

While the narrative offered here is a continuous one, it suggests certain
major features in given periods. Thus, despite the obvious pattern of mercantilist regulation that dominated the Colonial period, the businessman then was
determined to carve out for himself a successful career pretty much as he
pleased. He was creating an age of individualism that persisted well beyond
the Civil War. Yet, overlapping the characteristics of early business firms, and
indeed stemming directly from them, was the viewpoint of the business master,
a potentate who was to build a private fortune without regard to the effect
that his actions might have on society. He did what he pleased with the economy and with his environment, and he shaped for years to come the structure
of American society.

Not all the masters were solely interested in making money by creating
and manipulating a "paper economy," to employ David T. Bazelon's apt
phrase; some believed that great wealth could be achieved by making goods
and providing services that people could use—producing automobiles, telephones, electric lights, radios, and gunpowder—and selling them. They were
Makers. As the economy and its technology evolved, new ways of engaging
in business were developed, and the old Masters and Makers were displaced by
a new breed of businessmen—the Procurators. Like the ancient Roman officials, they were ostensibly representatives; however, the nature of the changing
business system was such that they came to rule it, and they rule it today.

In saying all this, I do not wish to create the impression that strict dividing lines are to be drawn between the various periods of business history. Masters began to evolve in the age of the individualist, and there were Makers when the Masters were thriving. Moreover, many Masters prospered in the age of the Makers, as evidenced by the career of Andrew Mellon. And the Procurators could clearly trace their origins to the period before World War I. In this sense, business history, like all history, is but a seamless web; nevertheless, it seems helpful to try to outline a pattern, however vague and inchoate it may be, if only to focus on the central concerns of a period.

Any writer is indebted to sundry persons—in the past and in the present —for ideas and insights. In my case, there is a major obligation to all the writers listed in the bibliography from whom I have drawn the material for this book. One may attribute to them whatever small merit, but not whatever major fault, remains in the book. I am especially grateful to a number of colleagues, historians all, who consented to read parts of the manuscript. They have been more helpful than they know: our discussions on matters of interpretation constituted a series of seminars in which I was the student. There were agreements and differences; such differences as remain are entirely due to the stubbornness of one who still believes that America is predominantly an acquisitive society. My thanks and gratitude go to Professors Milton Cantor, Melvyn Dubofsky, Mira Wilkins, and Howard Quint. I should also like to express my thanks to Professor William A. Davis, not only for a critical reading of several chapters but for graciously allowing me to utilize unpublished materials based on the papers of William Constable. I am also grateful for typing assistance to Barbara Fifield as well as to my wife, who, incidentally, maintained her role as perceptive reader and severe critic.

BEN B. SELIGMAN

Amherst, Massachusetts

PART ONE

By the end of the Middle Ages, those in power had learned enough to realize that a strong economic policy was necessary to foster the growth of a nation, and out of this realization came Mercantilism. This was the policy under which the early American businessman had to function, however much he disliked guidance from London. Yet given the great distance from the mother country, it was not too difficult for him to disregard the directives that flowed from England and to engage in business according to his own definition of what was proper. Such was the spirit that formed the Individualist, the businessman who was ready to seize a continent and to shape it to his own needs.

When he could no longer tolerate interference from the metropolitan center in London, he simply broke away, entirely sincere in his rage for liberty. But in the beginning that liberty meant identification with his own self-interest, an identification that threatened nothing less than anarchy. Some persons, motivated in part by nationalistic sentiments, recognized the threat and determined to meet it. And so a constitution was written and a new nation established.

Yet an important motive for replacing the Articles of Confederation was a deep concern for the future of commerce: there was a sense of chagrin that business should have to be conducted under hampering conditions. Economic considerations played a significant part in the ensuing contest of wills. Moreover, the Founding Fathers avoided a democratic system as we might define it: they were hostile to popular rule, and feared that a

The Individualists

democracy would attack "accumulated property." Thus the motives of the
Founding Fathers appear to have been a compound of group interest plus
nationalistic impulses, mixing personal concerns and "statecraft" in uncertain proportions.

While it is difficult to unscramble this mixture, the fact is that eighteenth-century America was governed in the main by the upper strata of
society; there were clashes of interest; the wealthier were more likely to
support the Constitution; and there were elements of the conspiratorial in
the whole complex of circumstances that led to the founding of the nation.
(It was strange that the Treasury Building should burn just as the Federalists were forced out of power, destroying most of the records that might
have revealed what they had done for more than a decade.)

And so the terms for a business civilization were set. But perhaps not
entirely so, for North and South were moving in different directions, one
toward industrialism, the other toward a manorial system based on chattel
slavery. In many ways the difference was critical, for not only was it economic, but social and cultural as well. America was on the verge of becoming two nations, and conflict between North and South seemed inevitable.
And after the fighting there was bitterness, a bitterness that has remained
to the present. But after 1865 there was no question what the rules of the
game were to be—the opening of a continent and a roaring surge toward
success, with the devil taking the hindmost.

CHAPTER 1 Colonial Origins of Business

By the end of the Elizabethan era, England, with its surplus profits gathered by a new middle class, was ready to burst the last bonds of feudalism. The merchant capitalist had prepared the ground for conquering and exploiting a new world, creating bold new ways for accomplishing his aims. Initially, enterprising Englishmen thought to get around the new continent somehow to reach the wealth of Cathay. Unable to accomplish that objective, they chose the second-best course—robbing the treasure fleets of Spain. Colonization for gain was a kind of afterthought, almost an accidental one, to be achieved mainly through the formation of joint-stock companies. These companies were cooperative ventures of merchants that brought together large blocs of capital in order to gather in even larger quantities of capital, mainly from overseas.

Membership in the companies was not limited to merchants—even a nobleman could buy into them and claim a share of the proceeds. Organization of the Moscovy Company (1555) and the Levant Company (1592) had resulted in substantial gains for their investors. The East India Company, founded in 1600, eventually evolved into the largest and most powerful company of them all. With the discovery and exploration of the New World, attention shifted across the Atlantic. It seemed that colonization now offered the English businessman unbounded opportunities.

In 1584, Sir Walter Raleigh, the beneficiary of a grant from Elizabeth I, planted the first American colony at Roanoke Island in Virginia. Hopes were high, and it was expected that this venture, the first of many, would make Englishmen the "lords of navigation." However, the logistics for supplying the colony with its wherewithal were too difficult for it to succeed. Like all the early settlers, those in Roanoke had all sorts of problems with the Indians, and by 1590 the colony had disappeared.

In 1606, James I granted a charter for colonizing the New World to the Plymouth Company. A colony was tried at the Kennebec River in New England, and another at Jamestown, in Virginia, in 1607. The first slaves on American soil were owned by Jamestown settlers, who used them as house servants, but slavery was not to become important for another hundred years. In 1619, Jamestown began exporting tobacco to England; the trade flourished from the first, in spite of the violent objections of James I, who thought it to be "a filthy weed." There was never a time, however, when the British Government refused the revenue derived from the import duties imposed on tobacco.

What sort of men peopled the first colonies? Often they were soldiers of fortune, like Tom Vierney, scion of a respectable English family, who had previously sought quick wealth in Flanders, France, Sweden, and Barbados. Many were just on the edge of gentility, often second sons deprived of inheritance and unwilling to try hard work at home. They preferred a mercenary career for some other government in the hope that one day Lady Luck would smile on them so radiantly that they would magically become lords of a manor. Or they might be gay blades like Thomas Morton, who set up a trading post at Mount Wollaston where sporting opportunities, especially with young Indian squaws, were plentiful. "Young Pilgrims probably found an occasional surreptitious visit . . . as stimulating, and ultimately as exhausting, as their descendants do a trip to New York," comments a present-day historian. In 1627, Morton set up a May Pole, "drinking and dancing aboute it many days togeather, inviting the Indean women for their consorts, dancing and frisking togither . . ."

Yet underlying the venturesomeness was the age-old urge for profit and wealth. It became a major motive for colonization. To be sure, there were those who sought a greater measure of freedom for thought and religion, or who were driven by the hope of somehow discovering a better life, but in the main the British colonies were business ventures. Even where philanthropy provided impetus, as with Oglethorpe and Penn, there were commercial elements at play; why should profit be disdained while creating a New Arcadia?

In time the colonists were able to evolve forms of work that were not quite like those of England. Where conditions were similar to England's, as in the northern colonies, the structure of the economy was also similar. However, in the South, new modes of production were created, and they shaped the economy. The plantation system of the southern colonies permitted the production of cash crops with a limited supply of labor. At first the words "plantation" and "colony" were synonymous, but the former revealed more clearly a settlement's roots in the profit-making expectations of some company back home. The colony was simply the "industrial" outpost of a group of merchant adventurers in London.

Tobacco soon became a staple export, with the planters' investment heavily committed to it. By the middle of the eighteenth century, two hundred ships were employed in the the tobacco trade. Rice from Georgia and South Carolina was shipped to Holland, Germany, and Portugal. North Carolina became a source of naval stores and ships' masts, and by 1767 there were some fifty saw mills along the Cape Fear River. Charleston served as the chief port, with English merchants acting as agents for American planters and shippers. Often the home country agent was also a "factor," financing the Colonial planter, and thereby placing the latter in financial bondage to English interest. Try as they might, however, the colonists could not relieve the burden of debt, despite Colonial legal action, as in Virginia, where the Assembly in effect nullified contracts that were disadvantageous to the planters.

English merchants took the tobacco, rice, and indigo, and sent in return luxurious clothing, home furnishings, and wine. The Colonial middle class was virtually nonexistent, for manufacturing and trade were discouraged under the mercantilist regime of Britain. Hence the successful planter was able to form the basis of a local aristocracy in the South, tied by the invisible strings of credit to his agent, factor, and British merchant. Credit was the lubricant of exchange: land, tools, and slaves might be pledged for a loan while mercantilist monopoly saw to it that profit flowed in adequate quantities across the Atlantic.

Moneylending in the South was controlled largely by French Huguenots who had been excluded from industry. They became planters' agents, shipping tobacco overseas and lending money to the planters. One Gabriel Manigault achieved ownership of numerous ships and fourteen thousand acres of land. Upon his death the value of his estate was equivalent to $845,000.

Slowly the factors and agents became merchants also. William Claiborne came to Virginia in 1621 and built for himself a prosperous business at Kent Island. He was shrewd enough to realize that moving goods was the life of trade, and he did not hesitate to employ rumor and intrigue to achieve his aims. In 1649, Peter Force described a worthy "Captain Matthews, an old planter of above thirty years' standing." Wrote Force, "He hath a fine house and all things answerable to it; he sowes yeerly store of Hempe and Flax, and causes it to be spun; he keeps Weavers and hath a Tan-house . . . [and] forty Negro servants . . . and selleth [wheat] at four shillings the bushell; kills store of Beeves and sells them to victual the ships when they come thither. . . . he is worthy of much honour. . . ."

Some Englishmen thought a manorial system would offer the greatest opportunity for gain. After all, that would mean simply transplanting the most aristocratic forms of wealth from the home country. In a sense, there would be no innovation. Lord Baltimore planned his colony of Maryland as a collection of large feudal estates. Any "gentleman" who would transport five men to America was offered five thousand acres of land. Yet in the first forty years of Maryland's existence only sixty such manors were established. Despite the hopes that the colony would blossom into a society for their lordships, Maryland became quite democratic. Tenants passed local ordinances, and politically Maryland was very much like a New England town. The Toleration Act of 1649 attracted many oppressed Protestant sects to the colony, and with a good climate, fertile soil, and usable waterways, a firm foundation for the growth of the economy was laid. As elsewhere in America, indentured servants were Maryland's first source of manpower, but the open spaces, providing land to all who wanted it, undermined the manorial system. Soon the lords of the manor began to behave like Virginian planters, but in the hinterlands the small independent farmer prevailed.

Farther north, in the Massachusetts Bay Colony, the inhabitants were also mainly farmers with small holdings. But lacking a staple crop such as tobacco, and dependent largely on their own labor, New Englanders turned to timber, furs, fisheries, and some rudimentary manufacturing. When the French and the Indians arrived at their borders, they turned to the sea for a livelihood. Within a century and a half, Puritans and Pilgrims had evolved a society of status in which the topmost spot was occupied by the merchant.

Such was the diverse New World milieu from which the merchant classes of England hoped to extract profits through trade. It did not matter whether the head of state was a King or a Protector. Both were equally interested in commerce. Disturbed by the vigorous competition of the Dutch, who were cutting rates on ocean freight, the English began in 1645 to pass a series of laws that were intended to enforce the use of English bottoms for English imports. These statutes were reinforced by the Navigation Act of 1651, and under Charles II territorial expansion in America moved rapidly to widen the Englishman's field of operation.

Colonization meant dividends for investors at home, either through the exploitation of overseas resources, or through trade with the colonists. English merchants wanted trade to be controlled, that is, monopolized for the home country. And so more Navigation Acts were passed by Parliament in 1660 to reserve to Englishmen all the fruits of commerce with the colonies.

By the latter part of the seventeenth century the settlements were no longer experimental. Sugar, tobacco, furs, lumber, fish, and naval stores were sold to home-country merchants who were eager to receive the goods. A day in Boston was filled with activity. Ships from many countries were coming to harbor, taverns did a good business with visiting seamen, and "boys and girls [were] sporting up and down the streets, between freshly painted houses." Even the King and his courtiers saw merit in trade: Charles II did not mind the gains he could make from the sale of Negro slaves to the colonists, a business that had been granted to the Royal African Company in 1672.

No sooner had the colonists established an economy along the eastern coastline than they began to push westward. A hunger for land led to explorations along the Kentucky River in 1751. In 1775, a promoter, Richard Henderson, bought western land from the Indians, called it Transylvania, and dreamed of millions to be made. The exhausting régime of tobacco culture meant expansion if shipments to England were to be kept up. The consequence was bickering with London, for the home country— driven by its own imperial reasons—had forbidden movement into the West. Nevertheless, land speculation became almost as important a way of wealth as shipping or staple crops.

Of course, speculation required lawyers, and they were eminently successful, so much so that they conceived themselves to be patroons, and lived lavishly. They took their hospitality most seriously. In the late eighteenth century, William Walton habitually proffered the most sumptuous banquets for all sorts of important people in his three-story house on Pearl Street in New York. When John Adams was entertained there in 1774, he was taken aback by the opulence, splendor, and lack of good breeding. New Yorkers, said Adams, "talk very loud, very fast, and all together."

The Colonial businessman really didn't overwork himself: he could always employ others to seek out pelts and do the dirty work. More challenging was writing a contract that might defraud the Indians of their land, as did Frederich Philipse of New York, who "took away" 205,000 acres by simply changing a clause after the agreement had been signed. And if the fur trade suffered from French and Indian predations, the British army could establish their claims for Englishmen. Land speculation was a New York art; in that colony land was available for private sale rather than obtained through assignment, as in New England. Hence, Robert Livingston could purchase 2,600 scattered acres, call them contiguous, and obtain another 175,000 acres for which he paid nothing.

Colonial trade had now become important. The plantation system in New England had failed, and quick returns for the settlements' English backers were simply not forthcoming. And so colonists, particularly in the North, had to turn to the fur trade, fishing, and commerce.

But the Puritan clergy wanted to keep the practices of the old country; just price, guild regulations, and all the other restrictions of the fourteenth- and fifteenth-century town seemed to them quite proper. It was not surprising that John Oldham should be driven from Plymouth because he violated Puritan notions and was too unscrupulous to be tolerated. Yet more and more Bible interpretations were modified to favor a turn to trade; thus the Puritan could reconcile his religion and his business.

There were honest businessmen like John Hull, a Boston goldsmith who would not indulge in speculation, giving fair treatment and expecting fair treatment in return. He imported English goods, exported furs, owned land, bred horses, lent money, and dealt in mortgages. He was a cautious man, for whom religion and business were identical. When Robert Keayne sold his wares in a time of shortage at what the traffic would bear, he was criticized and fined by the colonists for overcharging. Called a sinner, and harshly castigated, his only defense was that he had followed Calvinist precepts. Thomas Morton was to lay his eventual downfall to the Pilgrims' dislike of mirth, but it was in fact his trading methods that brought him into conflict with the authorities: he bought pelts with firearms and taught the Indians how to use their new acquisitions.

Farming, of course, remained the backbone of the Colonial economy. The farmer literally "mined" the soil. He believed that land was without limit, and if the fertility of one tract gave out, he simply moved westward. Land, in effect, became a commodity like any other, and one could "deal" in it. This attitude was in sharp contrast to that of the English yeoman, who looked upon land as an inheritance to be carefully guarded. For the American, on the other hand, investment in land was a gamble for future gains. It was not surprising that agriculture was to assume the quality of pioneering, moving ever westward, and drawing surplus population to it.

Fur trappers moved in advance of the farmer and land speculator. The nobility and the wealthy of Europe demanded furs; they were ready to pay for America's ample supply, which was gathered by trappers directly or through trade with the Indians, who were always happy to have the cheap manufactured goods or the rum that the traders could offer. Profits were great: between 1631 and 1666, Plymouth sent £30,000 worth of furs to England, and by 1770 the fur trade had reached a level more than four times that of the previous century. Unfortunately, the business was usually in the hands of riffraff and scoundrels, who were not above cheating the

Indians and using rum as an aid in concluding transactions. It was to be expected that this traffic would generate hostilities with the Indians. The white trader felt that justice was really on his side, and the possiblility that the business might lead to total war with the Indians did not trouble his conscience. The white American believed that he was invulnerable and that he could take from nature whatever he wanted.

New Englanders explored all of their waterways, thinking the rivers ran up to the Great Lakes, so avid were they in the search for fur-bearing animals. When the Dutch began to move into Connecticut (they had come up as far as Hartford), William Pynchon, who had begun trading in Roxbury in 1632, quickly established himself at Springfield, Massachusetts. Just above the navigation head of the Connecticut River and on the road from Massachusetts to Albany, it was a strategic location for fur trading. Pynchon handled beef, corn, and pork, and he shipped goods by way of Hartford and Boston to London. In return he obtained sugar, textiles, and manufactures. The grandson of an Elizabethan yeoman who had attained the status of gentleman, Pynchon sold his holdings in England to start again in New World fur trading. His selection of Springfield was a shrewd one, for from that point he could easily control all trade in the region. He set up branch posts manned by loyal agents, and by the sixteen-fifties he was able to export some fourteen thousand pounds of beaver skins worth eight shillings a pound. Eminently successful, he became an important figure in Springfield, and employed his power for "the betterment of man" and his own estate.

When the fur trade in New England started to decline, the old families settled down to undertake roles as landed aristocracy. Trading posts became retail stores as trade shifted from furs to farm goods. Some merchants tried their hand at shipping iron ore, but the economy could not support that any more than it could sustain trapping. Fishing and shipping had to come to the rescue, opening opportunities for those who preferred mercantile affairs. The early businessman discovered that kinship ties were enormously helpful, for through relatives in England he could feel safe in his exports and be sure that he would get what he needed in return. The merchant became a man of consequence, controlling local affairs, even if he couldn't control Colonial affairs. With his profits he bought land, the traditional form of wealth, and the one that came closest to allowing him to behave like a lord.

Within 150 years New England had been converted by trade into a kind of entrepôt. Since specie was lacking, profits were converted into overseas credits. Trade was triangular or quadrangular, making up for the lack of specie. As contacts with the merchants of the West Indies were developed, fish was often used as an item of export. Samuel Maverick of the Bay Colony sent whale oil to Bristol and clapboards to Spain, and obtained wine to sell to England for credits. In 1644 merchants turned to the Caribbean for the third leg of their shipping ventures. The following year slaves were entered on the books as an item of commerce. By 1660, sugar from Barbados was brought in for the rum distillers of New England, completing the three-sided flow—rum, sugar, and Negroes.

The demand for fish was also high, and became an important field of activity for the Colonial businessman. The Grand Banks of Newfoundland had been a source of fish for Europeans since 1500, and it was there that the Colonial fisherman sought his catch. Early in the seventeenth century, Captain John Smith was urging that fisheries be established. By 1641, fishing began to match trading and shipping in importance. The early immigrant who had wanted to become a planter went to sea instead for his livelihood. His product consisted of mackerel, bass, lobster, herring, sturgeon, haddock, crabs, oysters, and the omnipresent cod. By 1641, New England was exporting large quantities of cod, and by 1700, there were four thousand men and six hundred ships engaged in the trade. By 1776, the catch of fish was worth $7,000,000 a year. Nantucket became the center of whaling, supplying oil, ambergris, and materials for candles. So important did fishing become that well into the twentieth century the "sacred cod" was hung in the hallways of the Massachusetts Great and General Court.

Many family fortunes were thus founded. But trade without specie had no stopping point, and one bad shipment could spell trouble. Realized profits from fishing and furs went into land, often sight unseen. Land holdings became a way of measuring status—besides, there might always be timber and more furs. This was not unreasonable, for New Hampshire had long supplied masts for the King's Navy: a contract with the British Government became a most desirable document for many a New England merchant.

Meanwhile, there were other European powers seeking to gain a hold in America—also for reasons of profit. Holland had been a powerful trading nation. It began to colonize the New World in 1618 when it concluded a treaty with the Iroquois Indians. Operating through the Dutch West India Company, Holland established colonies in 1624 on Manhattan Island and at what is now Albany. The control of New Amsterdam was highly centralized, and the settlements were little more than trading posts for obtaining fur pelts. In fact, the pattern for the future fur trade was established by the Dutch West India Company: it exchanged rum and guns for skins, a policy that resulted in frequent warfare with the Indians, which went on long after Peter Stuyvesant had surrendered to the English in 1664. To encourage migration, large grants of lands were offered to patrons who exercised baronial power. Ordinary settlers were mere tenants. The system, however, was not successful: only one, Kilaen van Rensselaer, was able to build his own "empire." But smaller grants, called "bouweries" or farms, were also available; these were usually worked by indentured servants.

Religious reasons for settlement governed further south. George Fox, the founder of the Quaker sect, had thought of a colony in the New World in the sixteen-sixties, but not until William Penn joined the Quakers was the dream realized. In 1680 Penn petitioned Charles II for a grant, and with the political influence he had earned from being active in the Restoration, his plea was successful. Charles gave Penn a proprietary charter stipulating that the Navigation Acts were to be enforced in the new colony. Penn proceeded with his "Holy Experiment": he selected a site—Philadelphia—and established a frame of government. Many of those who migrated were Welsh and German, and most of them were artisans as well. Relationships with Delaware and New Netherlands created few problems. As a true peace-loving Quaker, Penn insisted on paying the Indians for their land.

The early Quakers were a pious group; they collected books and built fine formal gardens. Yet they were not averse to the fruits of business. Isaac Morris, for example, emigrated to Philadelphia in 1693 to become a leading merchant. Anthony Morris emigrated in 1682 at the age of twenty-eight, purchased two hundred acres of land in New Jersey, moved to Philadelphia, and opened one of the first American breweries. Prolific and proper, the Morrises were to provide leaders for every Philadelphia institution for over two hundred years.

At first Penn offered large tracts of land in the hopes of creating large estates, but it was the farmer and the merchant who moved into the colony. When Penn was forced to return to England, he was accused by the colonists of being a harsh landlord. The conflict with the settlers continued after his death in 1718; there were quarrels over paper money, quitrents, and taxes. Finally, in 1764, the colonists asked Benjamin Franklin to go to London to have the charter removed.

Up to 1700, the colonists had occupied the narrow coastal strip and the river valleys. By 1763, they had cleared the land for a hundred miles inland. Colonists moved to western Massachusetts and up the Hudson Valley to move along the Mohawk or across the Susquehanna. Little wonder, for few farmers fertilized their soil, and its depletion forced them after a while to move elsewhere. The land around Philadelphia, New York, and Boston was worn out. In 1747 Jared Eliot supposed that soil depletion was the cause of wheat crop failures. Nevertheless, land values increased near these cities, for the populations there kept growing. The Colonies began to make grants of land to persons whose only intent was speculative profit. As in New York, such large grants, often of ten thousand acres, severely inhibited farming: it was simpler to go elsewhere to farm land in fee simple, rather than be a tenant of an absentee landlord.

Thus, land policy from 1700 to 1755 hastened the rapid settlement of the hinterland. But what was sold went to middlemen in a hurry to resell; careful surveys were notoriously lacking, and disputes over boundaries were intense enough to last for generations. The unrest over land led to an armed insurrection in the Kennebec area of Maine.

For some merchants British policy appeared too paternalistic, but it was a policy sustained by a perpetual trade deficit and in perennial need of specie. Timber and iron for the navy had come from the Baltic and had to be paid for in specie. Similarly, gold paid for the tea, specie, and silk that the new British affluents demanded from the Far East. Hence, a favorable balance of trade had to be developed with the Colonies. The West Indies and South European trade brought to the North American Colonies specie that then flowed to England to pay for goods from there. New England merchants complained continually about the lack of specie, but for England the trading system was essential. The Baltic trade was difficult enough; all that English merchants could offer for the timber and iron was textiles. Moreover, there were always the Dutch, who were formidable rivals. The British tried to find Colonial sources for goods they had been getting from Baltic countries, but they could not get enough timber to fill their needs. The chief sources of supply were still Danzig, Riga, and Memel, and to do business there they needed specie to complete the balance of trade.

Although the home country's trade might be in overall balance, the colonists were quite unhappy. Prosperous conditions generally prevailed before 1772, but that held true only so long as credit was available, for trade activity far exceeded specie supplies. The crash in that year sharply curtailed credit, portending a serious economic problem for the colonists. For the period 1701 to 1710, the Colonies exported virtually the same amount as they imported, but from 1761 to 1770, imports were twice as great as exports. Little wonder that the Colonial businessman felt he was beginning to go under.

Yet he carried on, establishing trade routes that covered half the world. Not only did he have a coastwise trade at home, but overseas he traded American products for fish, rum, and slaves. He carried on his affairs in the seaport towns and along the rivers. Here there were wharves, warehouses, country houses, and shipyards. Nearby were the shops where all sorts of goods were available for sale. One could generally buy hardware, food, and books in one place, although some shops specialized in high-priced luxury imports. The wealthier merchant might open a store in another town, heralding the chain store of the future. Cabinetmakers and silversmiths had their own shops, and alongside them one could always discover the coffeehouse and the tavern where one learned of the latest events of the day. The town was a place where traders could gather to dream up new things to sell, such as warming pans for ladling molasses in the West Indies.

Colonial society depended on the merchant, who in the final analysis dominated it. Despite a rather primitive economy, the merchant did well and he was aware of his growing status. He might be a Thomas Hancock, who started as an apprentice in 1720 and became one of Boston's wealthiest merchants forty years later. Hancock was a wholesaler, retailer, importer, banker, and landlord all in one. He acquired his own ships, which ventured as far as Portugal and Spain. His store, located near Faneuil Hall, contained a general assortment of English and Indian goods as well as "choice Newcastle coals and Irish butter." Perhaps half the sales consisted of dresses, cloth, ribbons, and shoe buckles. Hardware and rum were also important items. In one corner there were stationery and books, and in the other salt and leather. Transactions were based on credit and duly recorded in the books of account. The indebted customer was obliged to return, much as miners or tenant farmers in later decades were tied to the company store. The arrival of a boat from Britain signaled brisk activity in the shop, and the merchant would advise everyone with handbills and press notices. If the Bohea tea did not suit "the ladies' taste, they might return the tea and receive their money again."

Hancock gradually turned toward wholesaling, providing country traders with imported goods. He was "glad to supply" the village stores with all sorts of items, and was willing to extend credit where that was needed. Or he might outfit itinerant peddlers with wares to hawk to back-country housewives. There were customers in Kennebec, Barnstable, Lyme, Danbury, and Long Island. They might even come all the way to Boston, New England's major city, with fifteen thousand inhabitants. Hancock might spend time at the Town House with captains of coastwise ships that took his goods up the Connecticut River. His customers often paid with goods in kind, but he could be harsh toward delinquents, who in their turn were quick to complain when shipments arrived from Boston in poor condition. Hancock had interests in all sorts of ventures, collecting rents, hiring out indentured servants, and caring for the needs of new arrivals. On occasion he would enter into partnership ventures to import pork or butter and then distribute them. He held a 5 per cent share in iron mines, and tried his hand at copper extraction and paper-making, but these efforts were unsuccessful, for they were fifty years too early.

Hancock was typical. The merchant bought and sold domestically and overseas, either for himself or as a part of a side venture (or in modern parlance, a syndicate). The ships that carried his wares were apt to be his own, and they included fishing craft, whalers, and coastwise vessels, as well as those that could cross the Atlantic to England and the Mediterranean. His business was both wholesale and retail; the merchant could get to be as rich as Thomas Boyleston, who was worth about $400,000 at the time of the Revolution.

Hancock's nephew, John, inherited everything but was not nearly as astute as his uncle, and the estate did not increase under his aegis. John had been a smuggler in his youth, and he was fated to be called that for the rest of his life. In fact, the House of Hancock had initiated its smuggling activities under Thomas, but it was John who was to become known as the "prince of contraband traders." At the very moment of the Battle of Lexington, John Hancock was being defended by John Adams in a lawsuit brought to impose a heavy penalty on him for alleged smuggling. On one occasion Hancock tried to bribe customs officials, and when that failed he simply used a gang of thugs to lock up the guard and unload his ship. Known as a profligate and disliked by most of the leading Bostonians, John is best remembered for his oversized signature on the Declaration of Independence.

Peter Faneuil was also the beneficiary of an inheritance from an uncle. He became a commission merchant, charging usurious rates of interest for credit, shook down his fellow townsmen, and built himself a Hall that still stands today. Much of the Faneuil fortune came from extensive ventures in the slave trade, an activity that the family would later try to forget.

James Brown of Providence also ran a general store and operated distilleries and shipping enterprise. His four sons tried to monopolize candle manufacturing, but that did not last long. The Browns resisted British monopoly, however, so it was all a matter of whose ox was being gored. The family became one of the longest-lived business dynasties in America and gave their name to a great university.

And there was William Pepperell, a tycoon from Maine, who inherited a prosperous fishing business, but preferred to harvest trees for masts and ships. His own fleet roamed to Europe and the West Indies partaking in the three-cornered trade of the day, bringing enough profits to enable Pepperell to buy into land. He was a leading citizen—rewarded by the Crown with a baronetcy—and he lived well.

Despite the growth of trade, many settlements complained about their inability to obtain merchandise. As late as 1770, Colonel Landon Carter noted bitterly that he would have to sit in the dark if the candles he had ordered from Norfolk did not arrive on time. Merchants hurled diatribes at their agents and factors, both here and abroad, and even George Washington found a shipment of cloth to have been "eaten to a honey comb by moths." But merchants and lawyers soon dominated colonial society. By 1760 wealthy mercantile families had primacy of place in the large cities. In addition to the Faneuils, Hancocks, and Boylestons of Boston, there were the Whartons and Morrises of Philadelphia and the Livingstons and Lows of New York. They had been able to escape most of the restraints of the mercantile system, and were content to be suppliers of raw materials and recipients of manufactured goods from England.

When the Navigation Acts of 1660 allowed the colonists to have their own ships, the merchants found another lucrative outlet. Mercantilist regulations might hamper the export of certain goods, such as grain, and might restrict Colonial manufacturing, but in the main the Colonies prospered. To be sure, restrictions were annoying, but most of the time they were simply ignored.

The long and irregular Colonial coastline, the distance from England, the inefficient administration at the ports, and the venality of customs officials allowed the Colonial merchant and shipper to do pretty much as he pleased. Many a cargo would go directly to Holland or Germany, and then come back to the Colonies without stopping in England. Shipbuilding itself began as early as 1631, and by 1660 the laying of keels was a thriving activity in Gloucester, Boston, and Salem. The Navigation Acts of 1651, restricting trade to English and Colonial bottoms, provided an important fillip to the trade. By the end of the seventeenth century, ships from New England were the important carriers out of coastal cities to England and Europe. Massachusetts became a maritime colony and Boston became the entrepôt for the West Indies. More than that—New England's ships brought copal from Zanzibar, rubber from Brazil, sandalwood from Hawaii, and pelts from the British Northwest, as well as coffee and pepper and linseed oil and slaves.

The shipper might even engage in smuggling. A favorite item in this trade was molasses from the West Indian islands controlled by France and Holland. The English authorities often looked the other way, since the suppression of smuggling would have crushed Colonial commerce and upset the British balance of trade. Connived at by many an official, the contraband business developed an aura of respectability. As the historian Arthur M. Schlesinger has remarked: "The truth was that the income of many wealthy families in the North—yea, the prosperity of whole provinces—depended on a trade which was approved by a robust public opinion but forbidden by parliamentary statute."

The smugglers' scent for profit was keen: they did not hesitate to supply food to the French in America when warring with the British. Peter Faneuil was said to have shipped foreign brandy in false rum casks and smuggled Barcelona handkerchiefs "as coolly as he took snuff in the streets of Boston." If caught, the smugglers could hire the best lawyers to plead for them, nor were they above attempting to bribe the court. They opposed search warrants, and in Massachusetts harassed officers of the crown with common-law suits. Their muttering grew louder when the King's minister, William Pitt, insisted on compliance with the law. The majority of American merchants were well aware of what was going on, and perhaps a fourth of the signers of the Declaration of Independence accepted smuggling as a mark of normality.

Not far removed from smuggling was piracy and privateering. The latter was a legitimate activity pursued in time of war and supported by the greatest of sovereigns. Sometimes a sea captain would be reluctant to give up privateering at the end of a war, thereby running the risk of being hanged as a pirate from the highest yardarm in His Majesty's Navy. Pirates enjoyed "working" the Caribbean area, for the Spanish galleons that plied those waters might be transporting gold and silver from Mexico or Peru.

Nor did the English Government mind if its citizens preyed on Spanish ships. Officials in the English Colonies were apt to be deaf when charges of piracy were leveled: too many local merchants were in cahoots with the pirates, for it was one way of obtaining goods rather cheaply. In fact, the pirates were likely to look upon themselves as just another sort of tradesman. Charleston was visited often by pirates, and Newport is to be credited for receiving as a citizen a privateer turned pirate when Captain Tom Tew returned to reimburse the owners of his ship. He was grateful to them for starting him in business, and he was happy to settle down as one of Newport's first millionaires.

At times privateering produced its wry episodes. In the West Indian trade, Rhode Island shippers would supply their captains with two sets of papers as a means of evading capture. And so when Thomas Hazard sailed from the West Indies with a valuable cargo, he threw overboard one set of papers when he was chased by a privateer out of Boston. Much to his chagrin he found himself taken to Charleston as a prize. He had disposed of the wrong papers. Or the captain might have in his possession two flags or false bills of lading. Beginning in 1700, the Government clamped down on unlawful activities at sea. Smuggling was not only an evasion of the law but hurt the revenue intake, and ordinary business was becoming too good to be spoiled by piracy. Besides, such methods were unreliable for steady capital accumulation.

Industry developed slowly in the Colonies; the base of the economy remained primarily agricultural. There was no adequate medium of exchange, and the absence of an indigenous banking system narrowed the sources of liquid capital. Machinery and equipment were scarce, and in a mercantilist society dominated by a metropolitan center, the growth of industry in the Colonial outposts was apt to be frowned upon. Yet there were some beginnings in furniture, wheels, farm equipment, foodstuffs, cloth, and leather. To be sure, many of these items were made at home, but manufacture for sale was not lacking. Furs, fish, and timber were put through a primitive kind of processing. Barrels and staves, for example, were significant items; between 1763 and 1766 Virginia exported 100,000 hogsheads of tobacco for which the containers were supplied domestically. Shipbuilding became important, stimulated not only by the demand for ships for fishing and the coastwise trade, but also by the lower costs of construction in the Colonies. In 1714 only two out of the 170 ships sailing from Boston were built outside the Colonies. And the shipbuilding industry meant naval stores—pitch, tar, resin, turpentine, and hemp. At the mercy of the Swedish Tar Company, Britain understandably encouraged America to produce naval stores. Besides, it was an opportunity for some farmers to engage in "moonlighting," by no means an exclusively modern phenomenon.

Iron ore, of course, was found in virtually all the Colonies. John Winthrop, Jr., established the first permanent forge at Lynn, Massachusetts, in 1643. With imported skilled workers and English capital he was able to produce eight tons of pig iron a week. Furnaces began to spread throughout the colonies, and by 1775 they were producing one-seventh of the world's supply of iron. Active in the industry were Peter Hasenclever, Alexander Spotswood, and Heinrich Stiegel. Building materials, of course, had to be obtained locally; however, cheap methods of providing granite for building had not yet been discovered. (That was to await the nineteenth century, when improved techniques for splitting stone were devised to bring the price of hewn granite into line with the increased demand.) Eventually, granite became a profitable item for export.

But a growing economy, albeit one at so primitive a level, needed manpower, and there was little to be had. One solution was the importation of indentured servants, individuals who contracted to work for a period of years in return for their passage to America. Recruiting agents were employed by merchants who specialized in the sale of indentured-servant documents, much as baseball players' contracts are negotiated today. The agents would hire drummers, or salesmen, to go through the towns of Germany and England peddling voyages to America and spreading leaflets glorifying the new land. The business, however, was shot through with fraud. Germans, tired of years of war, were told that in America one had but to stand with mouth open and food would drop in like manna. The ships were jammed full of immigrants, and often the mortality rate during passage was half the voyagers. Food rations were small and the quality abominable. When typhus broke out aboard ship, it was called "Palatine fever." The conditions were not much better than those in the slave trade, except that the servitude was generally limited to seven years. But the merchants had no hesitation in selling the contracts for husbands and wives to different persons, nor did they balk at separating children from their parents. The trade in young girls threatened to become a trade in prostitution.

Another source of manpower was the criminal of the old country. In the sixteen-sixties, English justices could sentence a convict to any overseas colony for at least seven years. Such persons became known as "His Majesty's Seven Year Passengers." The dregs of English society were thus exported to the Colonies—the unemployed, paupers, murderers, rapists, shoplifters, arsonists, and horse thieves, with an occasional sprinkle of political prisoners. It has been estimated that some fifty thousand criminals were shipped to America during the Colonial period. In Maryland, half the indentured servants were products of England's system of justice. They were all characters out of Hogarth, and some plied their former trades here. Yet the business of transporting criminals was quite profitable, for while the merchants of flesh might pay £3 a head for the right to transport a criminal, they could get anywhere from £9 10s. to £25 a head in the Colonies for the contract. In time the only thing the colonists could do in self-defense was to bar entry to criminals over the opposition of contractors engaged in transporting England's castoffs.

A far better business was the slave trade. It made millionaires in England and in New England. Shipowners, distillers of rum, and manufacturers of cloth and trinkets all profited. Slaves helped stimulate the production of plantation crops in the Colonies by providing needed labor, but the trade kept the growers continuously in debt. In Africa, the slave trade impelled the chieftains of some tribes to use every device they could think of to supply human cargos for English, Dutch, and Portuguese ship captains. If kidnaping and selling off debtors were insufficient, there were always raids and tribal wars. The slave trade became the plunder of a continent serving the gods of Mammon on both sides of the Atlantic.

The Portuguese had initiated the slave trade in the fifteenth century, but it was the English who carried it to the most profitable levels of business. A monopoly was granted to the Royal African Company in 1672, but the trading in Negro slaves became so profitable that by 1698 competition had become too keen to be contained. Indentured servitude could barely meet the manpower needs of the Colonies, and besides, it was easier to engage in kidnaping in Africa than in Liverpool. The Negro was a better and cheaper worker, and his visibility made it easier to establish property rights in him. He could be kept for life, together with his wife and all his children. And the women could also work, besides being breeders.

Planters were careful with pregnant slaves. Richard Cartin advised his overseer in 1759 not to force "Breeding wenches when with child upon any service or hardship that will be injurious to them & that they have every necessary when in that condition that is needful for them . . ." In the eighteenth century, the average annual transport of slaves to America totaled 30,000 a year. Jamestown was honored with the first Negro slave in 1619; by 1760 there were 400,000 in the Colonies, three-fourths of them in the southern provinces. There were also slaves on the large estates along the Hudson River. Only small holdings kept slavery in New England at a minimum. Yet the Puritan ethic did not prevent the New Englander from employing the slave trade as a source of handsome profits.

The slave trade was the key leg of a triangular system. Rum was shipped to West Africa, where it was swapped for slaves. The next exchange was in the West Indies, where the human cargo was sold for £14 to £21 each, with a third of the price taken in molasses and the rest in specie. Molasses then went to the Colonies to be distilled into more rum. The middle passage to the West Indies was utterly dreadful. If a Negro took ill, he was simply dumped overboard in order to avoid "spoiling" the rest of the cargo, which was crowded below deck and in chains. The net profit on a modest-sized ship could be £500 or thereabouts. Money from the slave trade could buy a peerage. Some of the leading families in Newport could count slave traders among their progenitors.

The colonists wanted slaves: Britain did not have to impose the slave system on them. Colonial merchants like the Pepperells, Cabots, Faneuils, and Belchers were ready to supply human chattel for a profit. In England, the African trade was said to be a "divinely contrived system" that brought a favorable balance of trade. Slave merchants could be found in Boston, Salem, and New York; but for Newport, the very basis of prosperity was rooted in slavery. It was a business conducted by the best elements of society, and one that was apt to arouse the theologians to the finest rationalizations of the Puritan ethic.

To be sure, there were a few whites who dared to ask whether slavery was either profitable or efficient. George Washington was convinced that the peculiar institution would eventually disappear. But Patrick Henry thought that life would be most inconvenient without a Negro slave, though it is true that he foresaw the end of "this lamentable evil." In any case, abolition in the eighteenth century seemed quite unthinkable, for the planters were in debt to English merchants, and they needed a cash crop to pay off that indebtedness. And for the sort of cash crops the South could produce—tobacco, rice, indigo (and later cotton)—cheap gang labor seemed necessary.

These were the essentials of the Colonial class structure: despite the attempt to recreate the manorial system, it was the merchant who quickly rose to the top, and soon a wide gap separated him from the artisans and the land-hungry poor who made up the rest of the populace. The Colonial merchant was a man of leisure. The hours between one and four were spent at the tavern, where he could imbibe rum with his peers. He was "privileged, brightly buckled, and buttoned," and might be well bedecked with diamonds. His most strenuous form of exercise was banqueting, interspersed with numerous toasts of wine. He lived well, with a mansion in Boston and a country home in some outlying town. Feasts, dances, and pleasure cruises were not unknown. Swords were worn around the waist and quickly unsheathed when the bearers were not accorded proper obeisance by lower-class persons. The latest fashions for the merchants' women were imported from London. A few merchants might be energetic and sweep out their stores on occasion. But mainly a merchant's effort was limited to risk-taking and displaying a sharp nose for profit. He connived and jockeyed and, barred from the even tenor of middle-class development by mercantilist regulation, he smuggled, privateered, and dealt in slaves.

The planters in the southern colonies were closest to becoming an aristocracy: in any case they believed themselves to be aristocrats. They assumed the style of the cavalier, took part in politics, and sent their children off to Oxford and Cambridge. But they were still *nouveau riche*, descendants of merchants, shippers, and indentured servants. They demanded obeisance from everyone else because they had all the wealth and therefore supposedly all the talent.

This was the Colonial social and economic experience. It was based on the exploitation of natural resources and the acquisition of political knowledge that was "to sweep half a continent into independence and summon into being a governing class capable of sustaining it."

CHAPTER 2 Businessmen in a New Nation

As the group with wealth and power, merchants were perforce dominant in Colonial society. They formed a virtual aristocracy and were leaders in philanthropy and politics. They held their fortunes in land, houses, and securities (in which investments ran as high as £10,000), living in comfort very much like their peers in London. By the late eighteenth century, their homes were built of brick, a luxury for the Colonial period; merchants often had their residences above their stores without suffering any loss of status in the community. In addition to a town house, the merchant might have a "country house" to which to escape during the hot summers. There were Negro slaves to serve as footmen and housemaids, and the wealthier merchant might have his portrait painted by a local artist. Wigs were imported from England to make certain that these powdered head-coverings fitted properly. The merchant's club was the coffeehouse, and while many of the first generation did not have a college education, prosperity encouraged them to send their sons to Harvard or Yale.

By the time of the American Revolution there were many such affluent merchants, chiefly in urban centers or river towns. The merchant was a leisured "capitalist" and a "gentleman" who frequently married into the families of other merchants. In New York, the van Cortlandts and the Rutgerses were related, as were the Ludlows and the Alsops; in Philadelphia, it was the Willings, the McCalls, and the Shippers who were tied by marriage; and in Massachusetts, the Hutchinsons, Olivers, and Shirleys.

Shipping became a major industry and a major source of surplus capital, stemming from legal as well as illegal enterprises. The merchants of New York, Newport, Boston, and Philadelphia vied with each other for trade. Some cities had distinct advantages: New York, for example, could draw on a hinterland that supplied wheat, and Philadelphia was well situated for exporting tobacco. Real estate—farmlands, buildings in town, houses—was a favorite investment for surplus capital. Joseph Galloway of Philadelphia claimed that he obtained £500 a year from one house. Whatever manufacturing had developed was primitive and crude. Important also was "personalty," investments secured by paper obligations, such as notes and mortgages. Phineas Bond, a Philadelphia lawyer, reported in 1776 an investment in such paper of almost £1,800, no small sum for the time. With a lack of banking and with most companies still operating on an *ad hoc* joint-venture basis, the merchant perforce became the banker for his community. The Colonial mind, however, was still mainly agrarian, and it was not infrequent for the merchant to face public hostility, especially on the issue of paper money. As a major creditor, the merchant was likely to be more cautious than his customer on this matter. Yet he didn't mind the circulation of paper money, provided it was issued with a good measure of circumspection.

The depression of the seventeen-sixties had upset the whole Colonial credit structure. Merchants were still hampered by the perennial shortage of specie. The development of the coastwise trade was an attempt to get out of the ensuing economic morass. Some merchants thought that importing luxuries such as wines would help. The art of smuggling was developed to a high pitch: tea and bolts of cloth were brought through customs in molasses kegs, and hemp and textiles came in as herring. Wines and handkerchiefs were buried in salt. The visible product usually bore little or no duty. During one period the Newport distilleries used up 14,000 hogsheads of molasses, but only 2,500 hogsheads had gone through customs. One customs collector "earned" 6,000 Spanish dollars, although his salary was but £100 for the year.

By the late seventeen-sixties the Colonial merchant sensed what it was that he had to accomplish, and he did not hesitate to call in the lower orders of society to help him demonstrate against Crown regulations. But many merchants did not want a show of force, and so there was an unavoidable split on the sort of political action that was to be undertaken. The older, and richer, merchants had their investments in loans, securities, and rentals; they did not relish political strife.

But the smaller merchants, and the artisans, were bearing the burden of the depression, and they were becoming restless. Moreover, the home country was demanding that the Colonies provide more revenue, further straining the ties that had existed for so long. A sugar act, passed in 1764, attempted, among other things, to control smuggling; then currency regulations, at first limited to New England, were extended to all the Colonies. The Stamp Act gave the Sons of Liberty good cause to wreck the stamp offices, thus making the law virtually inoperable. London backed down and the colonists toasted George III. But there was still need for revenue, and

Britain imposed the Townshend Acts, taxing a variety of goods. Sam Adams, a combination of Colonial mercantilist and ideologue, became a leading spokesman for the colonists. At first he had no more thought of independence than the average colonist—he simply wanted London to keep its hands off the Colonies. Schuyler and Livingston, among the leading New York merchants, insisted that the old order had to be restored. London was again forced to back down: all but one of the Townshend Acts were repealed. But the colonists began to feel that the business of America was its own business, and by 1773 the sentiment for going it alone had become fairly strong.

This sentiment was reinforced that year with London's decision to grant the East India Company a virtual monopoly on the marketing of tea in America. There had always been a tax on tea: John Adams did not mind drinking the brew (it was America's favorite beverage); he merely hoped that his cup had been smuggled in from Holland. Up to this time, tea had been generally sold at auction in London. Merchants in the Colonies had developed a fairly involved marketing structure, and the act giving a monopoly to the East India Company threatened to destroy it. Further, the monopoly threatened to depress prices, since the company had a seven-year supply on hand which it was anxious to reduce. In 1774, fearing that the situation would be a precursor to other monopolies, the American merchant reacted rather violently and undertook a series of "tea parties" of which the famous Boston affair was but one. Paul Revere and Lendall Pitts, and no doubt John Hancock and Sam Adams, among other Bostonians, whooped it up disguised as Indians and dumped the Boston shipment into the harbor. London was quick to react with punitive measures. But the colonists also reacted. Then came Lexington and the war for life, liberty, and property.

The businessman, however, had been a law unto himself for too long; he could not suppress a taste for profit despite patriotic precepts. When conflict came, he was ready to take advantage of all the gainful opportunities it offered. He still operated pretty much alone, or in concert with partners, acting as wholesaler, retailer, shipper, and banker. Transactions were conducted on a basis of personal relationships, kinship, and trust. Nevertheless, business was a kind of conspiratorial game.

Handled through agents, all deals were matters of high security and secrecy. Mutual commitment and involvement generally insured the completion of a purchase or sale. Trading with the enemy was not so heinous an affair: it even had a certain respectability. As a fact of economic life, such trading was a law of nature. Some merchants argued that England's need to buy overseas would drain her "treasure" and enrich America. Joseph Jones of Virginia feared that the agricultural surplus would become intolerable unless it was sold to others—among them England. The individual states vied with each other for prisoner-of-war camps because the English Government sent specie to the prisoners. And there was enough demand for English goods that American merchants did not disdain importing them: the profit was good despite high prices. Where did these goods come from? From Nova Scotia or the West Indies or Amsterdam: these places did a splendid wartime business with Americans.

Merchants who helped provision the armies of General Washington did well: they mixed private and public business in about equal proportions. It was common for merchants holding public office to be engaged in secret deals with others selling to the Government. In 1778 Samuel Chase used confidential information, obtained as a member of the Continental Congress, to corner the market in flour, a commodity needed by the French fleet that was coming into Philadelphia. Later he became a judge, only to be impeached. John Brown, of Providence, delayed building frigates for the Government while he was busy getting out ships for private purposes. Yet none of these men believed that they were engaging in immoral practices, for such were the ways of Colonial business.

Massachusetts business suffered very little during the war; the illicit trade with Nova Scotia was centered there. Elias Derby noted that he made 100 per cent profit on cocoa and sugar imports, and 150 per cent on linens and cottons. It was better than privateering. If trade did slacken in 1778, that was due to a temporary lack of goods. Massachusetts merchants began to produce gunpowder and clothing for the army. The firm of Otis and Andrews became "collectors of clothing" for the Continental Army: their "emoluments were considerable." Thomas Cushing was in private business, but he found time to contract for beef shipments to Washington's soldiers. John and Andrew Cabot made a sizable fortune by privateering. Joseph Peabody, also a privateer, was well received by the merchants of Alexandria, to whom he sold his booty. Afterward he wrote a book of maxims, illustrating the higher morality, thus setting a model for Andrew Carnegie about a hundred years later. Benedict Arnold and John Livingston secretly proposed to four New York businessmen that they each hide goods worth £10,000 to £30,000, which could then be sold when the British had been ejected from the city. In return for a guarantee of protection Arnold and Livingston asked for a mere two-thirds share. A similar plan was suggested by Arnold to General Sullivan, who was on the attack in Rhode Island. In 1778 and 1779, the Amorys had an interest in at least twenty ventures. Providence, Rhode Island, was no longer a place that could supply only pickled oysters: under the stimulus of war it developed a far-flung commerce.

To be sure, many merchants took an active part in the war. They had a large stake in the outcome, for liberty, property, and the right to engage in business in one's own way were all synonymous. Many rejected the belief that property should be sacrificed to patriotism, and foresaw that when freedom had been won, the businessman would set out to create a society in his own image. It was an image that represented a reaction to prewar times. In the past he could only rage as England insisted that he buy his molasses in the West Indies. And so the desire for profit led him first to violate the law and later to break with the British.

During the war, the American businessman carried on his affairs as though the fighting—directed by the Continental Congress—had been all for his benefit. Supplies were withheld from the Army to force prices up; and if the troops were without food, clothing, and ammunition, his attitude suggested not so much that he didn't care as that he was more concerned with the condition of his coffers. Moreover, the individual state governments were unlikely to enforce the law against him.

More important, of course, was the fact that those controlling the government—such as it was—would not tax themselves enough to pay for the war. The major part of the cost of the conflict was defrayed with paper notes (all of which were virtually repudiated) and by bonds, later funded into the national debt to be liquidated by indirect taxes. Gouverneur Morris (not related to Robert Morris) had opposed paper money in New York in 1769; but in 1775 he was a strong advocate of fiat currency. He proposed an issue of $2,000,000 to be repaid in seven years. It was a clear way of avoiding taxation. The heaviest losers were the soldiers of the Continental Army, who were paid in paper money. No wonder they became restless after Yorktown.

Some businessmen were more than enthusiastic about the Revolutionary cause: William Gray, a wealthy Boston merchant, marched off to Lexington, and Haym Solomon lent money to the government when it was in dire straits, money which was never repaid. One merchant pledged all his property in support of the war, for, said he, everything would be worthless if the Americans were to lose. But in the main, business support of the war was mixed. There were Tories in Norfolk, and most of New York's merchants were Loyalist. Any number of them were trading with British merchants. Robert Walpole, son of the English statesman, headed a ring of businessmen who smuggled arms to the Americans, and British capital outfitted American privateers who made sport with Loyalist ships. When

Admiral Rodney of the English Navy captured St. Eustatius, in the Dutch West Indies, London merchants set up such a roar of indignation at this interference with their trade—most of it with American rebels—that the Admiral had to give up his loot. And later on, in 1812, American merchants reciprocated for their British cousins by maintaining trade, again through St. Eustatius.

Robert Morris was at the center of wartime trade, but he could not, or would not, distinguish his private affairs from his public responsibilities. Born in Liverpool, he migrated to America to become a leading Philadelphia merchant.

Philadelphia was quite a gay place, where a man of means could always obtain his gin and wine. Luxury was an expression of high public taste. American seaports were opened to everyone by the commercial declaration of independence in April, 1776. The Dutch, Swedes, and French were delighted to trade with the Americans, and American agents traveled overseas to represent Boston and Philadelphia merchants. The big business, however, was provisioning the army. As Superintendent of Finances for the Continental Congress, Robert Morris offered associates and friends many an opportunity to obtain contracts. Jeremiah Wadsworth and Nehemiah Hubbard served their apprenticeships, as it were, under Morris, who devised the method of contracting for supplies. Profits in the port of St. Eustatius rose sevenfold as American agents scrambled for arms and ammunition and an appropriate commission. Wadsworth arranged to have a frigate built, allocating to himself a 5 per cent fee. Dr. William Shippen, head of the Hospital Department, sold hospital supplies for his own profit.

Morris was taken into partnership by Thomas Willing, who supplied the family background that Morris lacked. It was rumored that the firm of Willing and Morris made twelve thousand pounds one year on powder deliveries to the Continental Congress. The complex relationships between the merchants of the day suggests a large measure of cooperation among them. When Morris went along with Silas Deane in a privateering venture, the ship was to be outfitted by British factors, but Morris and his friends displaced them, again using the Dutch port of St. Eustatius. William Bingham, a Morris associate, was the Congressional agent in the West Indies from 1775 to 1780. He took half the profit and commission on all trade handled for Willing and Morris. The latter's partnerships and ties with other merchants and agents were wondrously complicated. Involved were David Parker, Jeremiah Wadsworth, John Church, William Duer, Tench Tilghman, and others. Wadsworth and Church were partners; Tilghman was a close friend of Alexander Hamilton. But Hamilton was Church's brother-in-law, and a friend of Gouverneur Morris. Hamilton and Church had married into the Schuyler family, which was tied to the Livingstons, van Rensselaers, and van Cortlandts. It was a fairly tight society.

Morris became the financial power in America. According to one historian, his influence was greater than J. P. Morgan's in a later era. Morgan would have had to be the Secretary of the Treasury, and in control of Tammany Hall as well, to match Morris' power. When the Continental Congress offered Morris the post of Superintendent of Finances, he exacted a high price—the unqualified right to run his own business affairs at the same time, absolute control of provisioning personnel, and sole authority to contract for the army. Later he helped found the Bank of North America in Philadelphia and made Thomas Willing its perpetual president. The bank was intended to cement the ties between the wealthy and the government. The Congress invested $254,000 in cash. Morris obtained $146,000 from friends and then lent the government $1,200,000 in bank notes. He imported wines and other luxury goods and sent ships to the Orient. Morris was active also in the new three-cornered trade in which American hardware and clothing were shipped to the Pacific Northwest for furs to be exchanged for goods from China, Japan, and India. And, like most other merchants, he tried his hand at land speculation. For this caper he sold short on government securities, and when prices of the latter went up, he landed in a debtors' jail. General Washington was happy to receive Morris's wife while he tried to straighten out his affairs. By the time of the Constitutional Convention, Morris, worth about $200,000, was the richest man in America. It is frequently said that Morris financed the revolution: however, as E. J. Ferguson has demonstrated, it was the other way around—the revolution financed Morris.

A new breed of businessman was in the making. Adventurous, always hustling, and unconcerned that the future brought no certainty, he was ready to pursue all opportunities for the single objective of making a profit. Ruthlessness was a common attribute; businessmen were anxious to dispose of the last vestige of mercantilist regulation in order to create the conditions of life in a virgin continent. But those conditions were to be of their own making. William Constable once instructed a supercargo, or shipper's agent, to feed the ship's crew substandard food and to abuse them mercilessly, all to encourage desertions in Caribbean ports, with replacements by foreign sailors who could be paid less.

A noteworthy career was that of Jeremiah Wadsworth, son of a Hartford minister. Young Wadsworth inherited two thousand pounds, thus starting with a fair inheritance, some property, and a good background. In 1775 he was appointed Commissary of Supplies for Connecticut and soon began to buy goods for the Continental Army. In 1778 he was elevated to Commissary General for all the Continental forces, earning as a commission one-half of 1 per cent of all money spent and received. Although this was not exorbitant by comparison to others, his earnings did cause some resentment. He was not above diverting money to his own purposes and failing to replace it.

While in public office he had engaged in some transactions on his own behalf, and in association with General Nathanael Greene and Silas Deane. He had the frigate *Trumbull* built and earned himself a 5 per cent commission. Wadsworth's great coup was a contract with the French forces, but they had to reject some of his shipments. In 1779 he resigned under pressure and went into business for himself, venturing into privateering, insurance, and the handling of bills of exchange. By 1783 he possessed $41,000 in specie. He became an important man in New York.

His sometime associate, Silas Deane, the son of a blacksmith, was a Yale graduate and a practicing lawyer in Wethersfield, Connecticut. A suitable marriage to a wealthy widow enabled him to gain a foothold in commerce. Through his second wife he established a connection with the Saltonstalls. Soon after joining the Continental Congress in 1774, he allied himself with commercial interests. And we must not forget Daniel Parker, who became so involved in the intricacies of private and public business that he fled the country in 1784 to escape his creditors. He had in his possession some public funds and forty thousand dollars worth of securities: the sum was sufficient to renew speculative ventures overseas.

William Bingham penetrated the highest social circles of Philadelphia with a fortune stemming from privateering and land. An admirer of the British system of banking, he commended it to Alexander Hamilton as a model for America. To satisfy his wife's aristocratic tastes, he imported luxuries from England, copied English architecture for his own residence, and gave the first masquerade ball in Philadelphia. Eventually he achieved his social ambitions by marrying off one daughter to a French count and another to a scion of the Barings of London. He was now a member of the aristocracy, if only by marriage. John Church, operating under the name of "Carter," came to America as the war started and was quickly appointed Commissioner of Accounts. Marriage secured his position in Newport. His handling of army purchasing helped line his pockets. But such actions were no different from the business behavior of Oliver Phelps of Granville, Massachusetts, or Daniel Parker of Watertown, or James Watson or Peter

Colt. They all mixed public service with private transactions, and they were all successful enough to become great postwar capitalists.

The admixture of business and patriotism was common throughout the states. In the Hudson Valley a great deal of such trade went through the hands of Philip Schuyler, a major general in the Continental Army from 1776 to 1779. Schuyler was accused of outright peculation, but he was cleared by Congress. Yet even Robert Morris complained that Schuyler's commissions were twice what he was accustomed to paying. Schuyler evidently did so well that he could pay off his debts in 1781 in specie. Any transaction these men could latch on to was grist for their profit mill. Morris' plan to achieve economy and efficiency by pitting one contractor against another came to a sad end. In several instances the government was left holding an empty bag.

The close relationship of business and politics during those years is perhaps best exemplified in the career of William Duer. A native of England, he inherited a modest fortune, including some property in the West Indies. Securing a contract to supply masts to the British Navy, he came to New York in 1768 to obtain the necessary timber. He acquired a tract of land in the upper Hudson Valley for this purpose, and built himself a mansion, a grist mill, and a snuff mill; he became an American citizen when the Revolution broke out. However, Duer refused an army commission for fear of losing his West Indian estates. He did lend assistance, though, by becoming one of the Continental Army's principal suppliers—at the usual commission. In one transaction for thirty thousand bushels of grain, he paid himself fifteen thousand dollars. Duer was allied with Robert Morris, but he was so full of guile that on several occasions he was able to take even that astute man on a wild-goose chase.

Duer was involved in the notorious Scioto speculations. As early as 1783, Washington had recommended that the veterans of the war be paid in western lands. However, this was difficult, since ownership of the land was in dispute between the states. A number of businessmen formed the Ohio Company to buy as much land as they could, no doubt for speculation. But Congress refused to sell at their offering price. Duer believed that the price could be jacked up—by his own inimitable methods. Upon reaching an agreement with several other businessmen over an oyster dinner in Brooklyn, Duer began to lobby among Congressmen to purchase several million acres at a dollar an acre, and he finally got the contract, after some underhanded deals. He served briefly in the Government as Assistant Secretary of the Treasury and learned enough of Hamilton's funding plans to encourage his friends to buy heavily in depreciated securities. Eventually, the Scioto scheme blew up and Duer landed in a debtors' jail. According to some historians, the speculative antics of Duer and his friends had much to do with the Panic of 1792.

A protracted war and paper money only meant inflation. By 1778 one dollar in specie brought twenty paper dollars. In Philadelphia, stockings were four hundred dollars a pair. The Continental Congress might ask the states to deal with the problem, but they were concerned only with helping themselves. The Army began to pay for its supplies with paper certificates, adding to the accumulation of debt. A great cry went up from the populace against the "monopolists." Pelatiah Webster, a leading Philadelphia merchant, tried to explain that paper money was not the cause of the people's troubles: they were all due to the circumstance of the war. The Reverend William Gordon assured everyone that "The nature of the time must unavoidably make goods dearer . . ." Price advances could not be attributed to extortion by the merchants, who were in fact helping the Army to obtain its supplies. It was evident that most of the states and Congress could not manage a fiat currency. Yet some states were fairly successful in controlling the supply of money, thereby contributing to their own economic growth. But on the whole the inadequacy of specie, banks, and the "sanctity of contract" produced chaos.

The demand that prices be fixed by law was too strong to be resisted, and a number of states undertook such action. Even Samuel Chase defended price-fixing. But General Greene, who conducted his own business as a sideline, held that price-fixing was motivated by a desire "to have the property of a few at a less value." By 1778 the Continental Congress recommended the abandonment of price laws, for they were creating more trouble than they were worth. More paper money was issued: it was the only way to finance the war.

To Benjamin Franklin paper money was a "wonderful machine," for it paid and clothed the troops and then paid itself off by depreciating away. (He did not add that the soldiers wound up with nothing.) Franklin has been described as the most civilized American produced in the Colonies. Initially, like most Americans, he accepted the precepts of British imperial rule. It was only later that he changed his mind. In Philadelphia he achieved high status as a successful publisher and printer: during his career he found time to learn four languages and to help found the Philadelphia Library and the American Philosophical Society. He also made a sizable fortune through his printing and publishing business. *Poor Richard's Almanac,* issued annually for three decades, earned more for Franklin than his job-printing enterprise. To insure a supply of paper he sold rags to mills whose establishment he had fostered. Earnings were obtained from paper sales to other printing enterprises. He did not hesitate to pick up new type, just in at the wharves from London, with a wheelbarrow to get it to his shop quickly. He embodied all the middle-class virtues of a nascent business civilization. For Franklin "time was money," a perfect bourgeois aphorism. If a man pursued industry and frugality, God would take care of the rest. Such were the attributes that were later embodied in the legend of the self-made man who by his own enterprise and abstinence could create the capital required for great undertakings. Franklin retired early from business to spend his time on amateur scientific inquiries, politics, and land speculation. For a while he was associated with Thomas Wharton (whose name now graces a school of business in Philadelphia) and was involved in various land companies seeking grants in the Ohio Valley. To Franklin the open spaces of the West promised a future greatness.

The wealthy colonials survived the war quite well. Class distinctions had not been much disturbed. Many merchants were less upset by depreciation per se than by the legal-tender laws that required them to accept currency at face value. However, a number of such laws were being repealed. The fishing industry of the Northeast had been virtually closed down while the fighting was on, but it recovered quickly in the postwar years. The merchants' wealth suffered little depletion. Gouverneur Morris' claim that merchants had been impoverished by the war was simply unfounded. Even the treatment of wealthier Loyalists was not so harsh: only in New York were they roughly handled. John Worthington survived to become Springfield's town moderator in 1778. The greatest attrition of merchants occurred in Boston and New York, but enough old-timers remained to provide continuity to the quality of business life. John Langdon of Portsmouth, helped by the war to accumulate his fortune, gave a bridge to the town in 1786; Joseph Cutts was fortunate enough to acquire the confiscated property of Sir William Pepperell; and Stephen Girard began to acquire his enormous fortune during the war.

The Colonies became sovereign states. They retained in the main the same political structure to which they had been accustomed, except for the eradication of a few feudal remains, such as primogeniture and the established church. The franchise was broadened somewhat, although property and money were still the chief qualifications for voting in most states. When Maryland wanted to provide a government that promised to be quite democratic, it was the notorious Samuel Chase who led the fight against it. The Continental Congress had not been strengthened: it still had to appeal to the states to accomplish what any government needed to do. The commercial interests discovered that fresh difficulties were cropping up.

Trade discrimination among the states developed, and each state levied duties on goods imported from the others. There were figuratively fifty-seven varieties of money in circulation, and boundaries between the states were in continual dispute. New York and Vermont were embroiled in a border fight, and Connecticut and Pennsylvania each laid claim to the same land. The infant manufacturing industries were strangled in their cribs by British dumping, and there was no national tariff to protect newborn industries. By 1785 a depression was well on its way. Advocates of the printing press as a way of solving monetary shortages won majorities in seven of the state legislatures in 1786. Rhode Island defied Congress on taxes, and Alexander Hamilton thought the Army ought to be used to enforce Congressional actions. For the merchant aristocracy, these decades —known to historians as the "Critical Period"—bordered on chaos, and eventually they determined to do something about it.

The Articles of Confederation, a loosely drawn compact among the states, reflected the American fear of a centralized government. After a while some of the states did not even bother to send representatives to the Congress. America was not a nation: Congress had as much power as the onetime colonists would have liked to give to Britain. But nationalist sentiment for a stronger government was beginning to germinate. To Hamilton, as well as Madison, the Articles were little more than a treaty and worth about as much. A critical deficiency, Hamilton noted, was control of the purse strings by the individual states. The Articles vented a "rage for liberty," and this was anathema to him. It became evident to these men, as well as to others of like mind, that more attention had to be given to the rights of property. After all, these were essentially the same as the rights of man.

And so, a fairly clean-cut political struggle developed: on one side were arrayed those of inherited wealth, together with wealthy merchants, speculators, former privateers, and army contractors; on the other were small farmers, such artisans as there were, tax delinquents, purchasers of Loyalist property who wanted to pay with depreciated money, and those hampered by lack of reliable currency. All were middle-class, but some were well off and many were hurting. Merchants and traders seemed to be advocating fewer restraints on business. William Bingham became an outspoken advocate of untrammeled laissez faire. However, in New York and Massachusetts, the new aristocracy tightened its control. Some of the states authorized the establishment of banking institutions: in Philadelphia, the

Bank of North America had become the first quasi-public bank. Pelatiah Webster thought that a national government that would include a chamber of merchants from the chief towns would be a splendid idea. Such a chamber would advise the government on trade and be in charge of revenue. It would give dignity and safety to trade, argued Webster. The result would have been as though the Treasury and the Department of Commerce today were to be handed over to the U.S. Chamber of Commerce.

Many arguments took place during the Critical Period over the question of western lands. The issue represented primarily a struggle between the commercial and landed groups, or as one historian has put it, between expansionism and self-government. Some thought that America should surrender its claims to western lands in return for help from Spain. The majority sentiment, however, favored expansion. Land speculators, deeply involved in the issue, fought each other bitterly for control of vast parcels. The Ordinance of 1784, which projected ten new states as soon as there were enough people in the territory, seemed for a while to resolve the political debate. But soon efforts were made to alter the Ordinance. Land speculators had had their "money nerve" affected: they wanted congressional control of western lands so that they might dip into the public trough. In 1787, 5,000,000 acres in Ohio were sold at sixty-seven cents an acre; Oliver Phelps and Nathaniel Gorham acquired 6,000,000 acres in New York at a very low price. Even Europeans were anxious to place their surplus capital into American lands.

For many of the aristocrats, the lands beyond the Appalachians promised to become a source of tribulation. They wanted a society based on hierarchy and tied to British tradition. The West could bring only tumult. In the end, the expansionists won. And for them the issue illustrated their argument that the general political system had revealed serious flaws. The sentiment for a stronger government developed apace, especially among merchants. Ironically, their economic philosophy was derived from Sir James Steuart rather than from Adam Smith. Steuart, the last of the mercantilist writers, had advocated, among other things, a strong state with strong central government. Tench Coxe, a Philadelphia merchant of nationalist sentiments, urged at the very least a "balanced" state. Coxe was quite close to Hamilton and others of the upper strata, although he himself never achieved the income he believed he was entitled to by ancestry and position.

In the beginning, Alexander Hamilton, like many others, did not seek a complete break with Britain. He advocated, rather, a kind of federation akin to what was later to become Commonwealth status: like most eighteenth-century political writers, his vision of the body politic stemmed from the order established by God and nature. After the war, he advocated close commercial ties with Britain. Hamilton's attitude toward the "mob" was displayed rather early when he deplored a raid led by Issac Sears to kidnap a Loyalist clergyman. The people, said Hamilton, was a beast. Men were so depraved and selfish that only a strong government could hold them together. He was arrogant and impatient with those less quick than he. Hamilton simply wanted to be the first among equals. And his views were shared by most businessmen. Robert Morris had only contempt for the people and for popular government: *they* were motivated only by passion and greed! Yet Hamilton welcomed the war and served Washington well as an aide-de-camp. Though he believed he was defending the Revolution, he was, in the last analysis, defending the world of silk stockings and powdered wigs.

Hamilton was to pose the strongest and most persistent arguments for a centralized government. His proposal to consolidate and fund the state and national debts was well received by the business community and ultimately brought speculative profits to many. For example, Duer and Constable picked up securities in North Carolina and South Carolina, with a face value of $1,000,000, for about $100,000, actually investing but $20,000 of their own funds. The securities were then resold to a Dutch bank for $800,000, and the profit invested in British bonds. The interest from the latter was used to pay the interest due on the original securities to make them look good. The gain on this one transaction netted the two operators more than $600,000. One authority has estimated that this sort of pyramiding brought Duer a total profit of almost $5,000,000.

Some writers treat Hamilton's funding scheme as though it had been the only alternative to chaos. Since other refinancing methods might have been devised, such as a drastic scaling down of the debt, the entire solution suggests that Hamilton's views were somewhat less than godlike. Since the idea stemmed from the successful debt-funding in Britain after the Revolution of 1689, it was believed that such a financial step was an essential attribute of economic stability. For men of Hamilton's persuasion, funding created a debt rooted in patriotism. As it was, the patriotism turned out to be quite profitable. Hamilton's aristocratic views underpinned a curious lack of enthusiasm for his famous report of manufactures; it was almost a full year before he submitted it to Congress. Some of the leadership of the aristocracy openly feared manufacturing: to them the industrialist was just a notch above the artisan. Would the mechanics receiving bread from their employers, asked one, have respect for liberty? It was clear that a manufacturing class and a working class would threaten their conception of state and society.

Hamilton was a dashing young man who affected bold colors in clothes, and he was just as audacious in politics. He preferred the company of the rich and the wellborn, believing that great men made a nation great. He was also, no doubt, motivated by a deeply felt nationalistic urge. As a native of the West Indies, he did not identify with any particular state. His sympathies lay with wealthy merchants, bankers, and aristocrats. Although the seeds of sectional antagonisms had already been planted, Hamilton's proposals intensified them in the long run. Out of his schemes came that blight of American political life—the political party—and it was, ironically, his archenemy, Jefferson, who achieved unity for a short while. Hamilton looked upon the Electoral College system as a foolproof way of choosing men of ability and virtue. The "mob," he thought, should accept the Electoral College as a way of expressing the verdict of superior people. And he did not hesitate to try to manipulate the College for his own purposes in 1788, 1796, and 1800; among superiors, he knew what was best. To have Washington elected unanimously, he contrived to have New York's procedure for selecting electors changed; he tried to withhold votes from Adams, and sought to defeat Jefferson. John Jay, Governor of New York, refused to go along with the Hamiltonian scheme to keep Jefferson out of the Presidency.

Property, to Hamilton, meant a strong nation and the accumulation of capital. His model for a bank was the Bank of England, embellished by the ideas of John Law, the Scottish adventurer who had established the Royal Bank of France. Of course, economic independence was necessary to buttress political independence, and this implied a bank. After the war, Hamilton pressed his view that order was unattainable unless the government were reformed, with sovereignty transferred from the states to Congress. This view did not endear him to the general public, which feared the moneyed interests. But the bank would strengthen nationalist sentiment, and he became involved with his brother-in-law, John Church, and with Jeremiah Wadsworth in establishing a bank in New York.

Hamilton's political behavior was conditioned by the commercial and financial interests of the northern states and by a nationalistic purview. In pushing through their platform, these groups had in effect engineered a counterrevolution, and while they believed that they were defending the nation, they were really the aggressors against it. The powerful conservative element that evolved defeated legal-tender demands, sought bank charters, defended the property of former Tories, and helped suppress such outbreaks as Shays' Rebellion. In fact, fomentors of the Rebellion were used by conservatives searching for scapegoats. Rumors flew about that the enemy was within. Men of "principle and property" were shocked by Shay's outrage.

Conservatives also preferred that the burden of taxation be placed on the farmers: for them the principle of "equality of sacrifice" in taxation was absurd. Funding the debt gave them a store of fluid capital. Securities had been acquired at one-tenth to one-half the face value, so that the profit on funding the debt was enormous. By the time funding actually was carried out, only one-fourth of the outstanding securities were held by the original buyers. Financiers and speculators sent their agents all over the country with specie to buy huge numbers of securities at ten to fifteen cents on the dollar. In Massachusetts the state debt had become the property of a small number of persons. More than 80 per cent had gone into the hands of speculators, wealthy merchants, and their cohorts. In Maryland, the debt was owned by a little more than three hundred persons. When the Federal loan of 1790 was floated, it turned out that 7 per cent of the subscribers had taken 62 per cent of the total. In that year, a debt of over $12,000,000 was held by about three thousand persons: for almost a decade a market for the purchase and sale of these securities had been in full swing. There was enough ambition and common economic interest among the Hamiltonians to create a need for a revision of the Articles of Confederation.

The Continental Congress was stumbling along, a debating society in which the delegates from sovereign states could discourse on their views. All too often a quorum was lacking. Then in February, 1787, Virginia, at the suggestion of James Madison, sent a circular letter to the other states inviting them to a conference in Annapolis to discuss commercial issues, the major one being Virginia's discontent with Maryland's control of the Potomac. However, representatives of only five states appeared: northern merchant interests distrusted Virginia and did not believe that cavaliers were interested in the welfare of business. New York and Massachusetts, however, did come, disturbed as they were by the tariff wars between the states. Besides, it was rumored that actual revisions of the Articles would not be discussed. In any case, the states were too busy attacking one another with economic weaponry.

Hamilton appeared for New York, but without much hope that the conference's patchwork would succeed. He was eager to press for a constitutional convention. Those who did come to Annapolis were clearly nationalist-minded. They decided to call for a constitutional convention that would correct the defects of the Articles. Indeed, the Boston Chamber of Commerce had written to Constable urging that a convention be called. The appeal was worded with circumspection (otherwise it would have gone unheeded) and was directed to the state legislatures, rather than to the Congress: this would make it easier to get the "right" sort of delegations to the Convention. This was the beginning of what amounted to a *coup d'état*.

All the states except Rhode Island sent delegates to the Convention, many with instructions to go no further than a revision of the Articles of Confederation. They did not, however, reckon with the nationalist politicians, who, in any case, had the support of most of the merchant and commercial interests. At first, the Continental Congress ignored the Annapolis resolution, but when the states appointed their delegations, it was sanctioned, partly because Washington had been elected a delegate by Virginia. When the delegates convened in Philadelphia in 1787, Benjamin Franklin was there, well on in years, but neither John Jay nor Thomas Jefferson nor Sam Adams appeared. Patrick Henry refused to come because he "smelled a rat." Washington appeared in his role as "Father of his Country."

Washington's very imperiousness was enough to hold recalcitrants in line. He fancied himself an aristocrat. When Gilbert Stuart came to do his portrait while he was President, the painter tried to get Washington to relax a bit. Evidently the President's stern mien was not altogether a matter of keeping his dentures in place. "Now, sir," said Stuart, "you must let me forget that you are General Washington and that I am Stuart the painter." Replied Washington coldly, "Mr. Stuart need never feel the need of forgetting who he is or who General Washington is." Only such a man could have served as chairman of the Constitutional Convention.

James Madison, erudite and bookish, took the only notes later available. The delegates straggled into Philadelphia as the Convention dragged on for months. They were destined to become the "Founding Fathers," regarded as demigods of a sort. But they were assuredly not; they were practical men, experienced in business, law, and politics. The Convention comprised a mixed group with mixed views, but most of the delegates were convinced that the Articles had failed. Many were also convinced that the states had become useless as political entities. But they had all come to protect their own interests. Although the Declaration of Independence had spoken of popular government, policies in the states were set by men of wealth. Although tradesmen of the lower middle class sat in a number of state legislatures, they took their cues from lawyers, merchants, and the wealthy. If the Constitutional Convention was a cross section, it really sliced only the upper layers of American society. All the delegates were aware of the ultimate purpose: otherwise they would not have compromised so often.

And so shippers, merchants, aristocrats, and their lawyers could write a document that would establish a strong central government, one in which the rights of the lower orders were not terribly important. Hamilton would have preferred that the states become administrative districts of the national government, but he did not speak up too often, and indeed he soon left the Convention. The general sentiment viewed the common man as a creature of passion to whom many evils could be traced. The delegates argued about credentials and house rules, and the Virginia Plan versus the New Jersey Plan, and established a rule of secrecy. Some thought a national bank would be a good idea, but suspected that it would have to be achieved indirectly. The various interests worked out deals and compromises, and in the end the writing of the document was given over to a Committee on Detail and to Gouverneur Morris, who had a fine flair for penmanship.

Morris took liberties with the text, introducing ambiguities and shading meanings on the ground that a certain gracefulness of language was desirable. He even inserted a clause that had been rejected by the Convention; seeking to protect the Bank of North America, he wanted to prohibit the states from "impairing contracts." The clause was to have enormous consequences. At one point he inserted a semicolon that would have altered the meaning of the general welfare clause enough to give Congress virtually unlimited power. It was caught in time.

Some of the delegates held stock in companies seeking to profit on speculation in western lands. Their agents were picking up securities destined to be funded under the national government. The new Stock Exchange in New York was doing a lively business in government securities. When the funding went into effect under the Constitution, speculators gained at least $40,000,000. When the bill to fund the securities was momentarily stalled, Robert Morris, now a senator, became angry and confused (a savage contemporary description of the senator depicted him as widening his nostrils and flattening his nose like the head of a viper whenever business interests were at stake), and the other speculators in Congress were panic-stricken as they had visions of security prices collapsing. When it came time to consider a bill through which the Federal Government would assume the debts of the states, a bill that was at first defeated in the House, the business interests of the North were delighted to work out a political deal handing over the site of the future capital of the nation to Virginia and Maryland in return for their profits.

Were there "classes" in those days? Perhaps not in the modern sense, but in 1765 Cadwallader Colden spoke of four groups in Colonial society— landed proprietors, lawyers, merchants, and small farmers and artisans. The distinctions were based on the reactions of these groups to the political and economic questions of the time. Especially in the North, the first three tended to coalesce—socially, economically, and politically. They were the "ruling class," held together by a community of interest and by inter- marriage. Among leading New York families, for example, the Schuylers were not primarily a mercantile family, but they had cousins among the van Cortlandts, Livingstons, and DeLanceys, all in commerce. The Livingstons were frequently thought of as landed aristocracy, but there were at least a half dozen merchants among them. Lawyers were most likely to be sons of ministers or other lawyers, yet many were sons or brothers of businessmen. In short, landowners, merchants, and lawyers could be found in the best families. Among the businessmen there were sugar refiners, general mer- chants, distillers, ironmongers, and shippers, and they all wished to be known as gentlemen.

The Constitution consequently stemmed from a series of compromises over issues and details raised by conflicting economic interests. It was a document with which nascent manufacturer and merchant, shipper and creditor could live. The Federal Government was to control taxation, war, commerce, and the western lands. Money also was to be controlled by Congress. Ratification of the Constitution was indeed carried through by a minority. In fact, the whole procedure—bypassing the Continental Con- gress, going to the states, ratification by special conventions that could be more easily swayed than state legislatures, and the need for action by just nine of the thirteen states—represented a political coup, and for economic reasons. It was a document intended to advance the common economic interests of men of business. On the other hand, small debtors were clearly affected adversely by the new rules of the game. The delegates to the Constitutional Convention may have come from a variety of regions, but in the main they sought to escape the commercial chaos of the Articles and represented a demand for the protection of property. If a large number of delegates were lawyers, this fact hardly diminishes the influence of eco- nomic concerns, for whom did they represent?

Ratification went to the states, rather than to the Continental Congress, for with all the difficulties that Madison, Hamilton, and the others rec- ognized, it would still be the easier way. Several states had suffered so much from the turmoil of the Critical Period that they would probably ratify. For example, New Jersey was in fairly good condition, but it did need access to the port of New York, and it was being hampered by the import duties New York levied on its goods. Georgia wanted protection from the Indians, and in Connecticut there were enough problems to make the campaign for ratification a resounding success. Maryland's aristocracy felt it would be better off in a national union. However, Rhode Island resisted: there speculators were taking advantage of the situation if not helping to oppose ratification outright. In addition, New York, Virginia, and North Carolina might try to go it alone. Thus, with firm opposition expected from only four states, ratification might just squeeze through.

The tale of universal acceptance is but another part of the mythology of the Constitution. The likelihood was that a direct national vote on the proposed Constitution would have sent it down to defeat. The ratification procedure may have been republican, but it was something less than democratic. Urban artisans and inland farmers were not especially enchanted by the document, although nationalist sentiments among the plantocracy and business groups insured its ultimate adoption. Madison and Hamilton mounted an intensive campaign in favor of ratification, which culminated in the Federalist Papers. Most states had some sort of limitation on voting, and to imply that universal suffrage, as in New York, meant a broad decision by the populace is to ignore the nature of the voting process. There were numerous voluntary nonvoters, and many who might have expressed opposition to ratification simply followed their leaders. As it was, it took all of the eloquence of Alexander Hamilton to rout the antiratification forces in New York led by Clinton, who had his own economic reasons for opposing the Constitution.

The fact is that an "economic interpretation" of the Consitituion is still a meaningful one. The Founding Fathers fought each other for wealth and power and in the process were able to create a myth of the businessman's beneficence and political wisdom, a myth that was to be celebrated for more than a hundred years. Only when the noted historian Charles Beard dared to question that myth in 1913 did the patriot become disturbed. Perhaps Beard's use of the term "economic interpretation" was somewhat restricted, but this does not destroy the patent fact that economic concerns had great weight in the formation of the Constitution. In any case, James Madison was quick to acknowledge the strength of economic interests although noneconomic ones might be involved as well. In the words of John W. Burgess, the Founding Fathers had perpetrated a "peaceable revolution." John Adams, who was close to the event, remarked, "The Federal constitution was the work of commercial people in the seaport towns, of the slave holding states, of the officers of the revolutionary army, and the holders of property everywhere."

The Constitution set the conditions for a businessman's civilization. Hamilton's extreme views, which suggested something close to a constitutional monarchy, were abandoned, as was Madison's suggestion that the national government have a complete veto power over the states. There resulted, rather, what seemed to be a reasonable distribution of power between the Federal Government and the states. In the final analysis, the Constitution was a document that protected property in its various guises— securities, goods, and slaves. And perhaps events could be shaped in no other way.

The businessman, despite a wide diversity of interests, had time to partake of political life, and he made certain that he did so. Indeed, some members of the new aristocracy would have preferred a monarchy, so as better to enjoy their property in peace. In local affairs, it was quite clear who comprised the governing élite. Money established one's status, and visitors from Europe were quick to note that "the rich blockhead is more considered than the first magistrate."

CHAPTER 3 Federalists and Democrats

When it came to voting for representatives to the new Congress, only a minority went to the polls. In some states no more than 16 per cent of eligible voters participated in elections to the House of Representatives. And the men elected to office were generally of the same group that had engineered the Constitution. About half the new senators in the first Congress had been at the Constitutional Convention. Washington was President, and he had chosen Hamilton for Secretary of the Treasury, Edmond Randolph for Attorney General, and Henry Knox for Secretary of War. The one anomaly was Jefferson, who was asked to be Secretary of State, and his was the only voice that might speak out against an Administration dominated by Federalists. The Judiciary Act of 1789 established the Federal courts; their position was later reinforced by Chief Justice Marshall's decisions. The only concession made to popular sentiment was the Bill of Rights, the first ten amendments to the Constitution, protecting speech, press, assembly, and worship.

The men who made the Constitution were mainly out of the governing class, comprised of wealthy families whose members had climbed the economic and social ladder by speculation, privateering, smuggling, and in some instances "legitimate" business. They wanted America to have respectability, but only they were to be allowed access to that exalted state. Powdered wigs and silk hose were worn, even at the President's house. Washington, whose sense of dignity was almost royal, rode about in a coach drawn by four horses. Some persons thought he ought to be addressed as "His Majesty, the President." Mrs. Washington was appalled by the "filthy democrats." The Republican party was deemed to be little more than a gang of despicable Jacobins. If the new aristocrats were not entirely monarchist in feeling, they at least preferred ties with English nobility to brushing shoulders with the mobs of New York, Philadelphia, and Boston.

Merchants, bankers, and speculators lived well at the end of the eighteenth century. Robert Morris was not content until he had built a mansion that would have suited the taste of an English nobleman. Philadelphia was

the intellectual capital of the country. The Quakers were quickly overshadowed by a gay society that revolved around the President and his court.
Huge quantities of Madeira wine were consumed at the many parties and
dinners, and high society mixed with politics made a powerful potion. The
Federalist center was the home of Thomas Bingham, who as a senator
found a "goodly company of businessmen engaged in giving concrete application to the theory that those who owned the country ought to run it."

Business expansion proceeded apace. In New England, the poverty of
the land had forced men to take to the sea, and it was not long before they
began to explore the China trade which had been initiated by Robert Morris
in 1784. By 1789 some fifteen American vessels had arrived in Canton.
Now that the American businessman was no longer a British subject, trade
with China was seen as a substitute for the declining coastwise trade. New
England merchants tried to displace British ships that had once carried
cargo to and from Virgina. In the Chinese trade, the most common export
was ginseng, an herb easily grown in America but rare in the Orient, where
it was valued as an aphrodisiac. The return cargo usually consisted of tea, a
popular drink in the new country. Elias Derby owned no less than four of
the ships that went to Canton. Often a ship might itself be sold, along with
the cargo, and another acquired, all for a profit.

Patterns of business became more and more complicated. The foundations for a new triangular trade were laid when ships began to stop at the
Pacific Northwest, the Hawaiian Islands, or the Falkland Islands to pick up
lumber. The supercargo might exchange these in the Orient for sugar, silks,
saltpeter, spices, or drugs, items that were quite profitable in Boston or New
York. Involved in these activities were such families as the Lees, Higgin-
sons, and Jacksons—notable merchants of the time. When his ship arrived
in Canton, the American supercargo had to work through an agent, a *co-
hong*, who was apt to be the only Chinese with whom he would come in
contact. Often the return goods were sold in port at auction. Despite all the
uncertainty, the profit on a single cargo often came to 20 per cent. The
merchant, of course, had his hand in other endeavors as well—fishing or
some small manufacturing in which he might invest surplus capital.

John Jacob Astor, Thomas Smith, and John Clive Green took part in
building the China trade. In the eighteen-sixties Seth Low was importing
Chinese goods. Trading with Canton was quite a romantic affair, filled with
uncertainty, high costs, and the dangers of piracy. But it was worthwhile—
to judge by the profits that were earned—and though Canton was the only
port available to Westerners, a bit of smuggling could get by the Chinese
port authorities. John Cushing stayed on in Canton for thirty years as agent

for a Boston mercantile house, becoming the wealthiest foreign merchant in China. Tea and silk were in heavy demand in the United States; in return for these the Chinese took furs and sandalwood. William Sturgis, starting as a sixteen-year-old deck hand aboard a ship plying the China trade, became one of the wealthiest merchants of his day. He had learned to prefer the Spartan life of the sea, and even though he could well afford the amenities due a merchant prince, he refused to procure them. Many other Boston families could trace their fortunes to trade with China.

Salem had been for a long time a powerful rival to Boston. At the turn of the nineteenth century it was the sixth largest city in the nation. It had its merchant-shippers, mansions, wharves, and stores. An ample supply of capital had been accumulated in Colonial days. When Elias Derby died in 1799 he bequeathed his heirs an estate of a million dollars. Jerathmeel Pierce acquired enough in shipping to retire at the age of twenty-nine, build a three-story house, and live long enough to vote for Abraham Lincoln. There were barns, elegant stables, and formal gardens attached to the mansions of the merchants. Social life was arranged in a careful hierarchy, with the merchants and shippers on top, but in Salem everyone was concerned with the sea.

Shipbuilding had always been a major activity in Salem. Ships' keels were laid all along the Merrimac: over a thousand vessels had been built between 1793 and 1815. While the Boston shipyards were busily constructing ships for the navy, Salem concentrated on merchant carriers. Shipmasters sailing out of Salem were apt to follow the route of Vasco da Gama around Africa, rather than round the Horn, on the way to China. A cargo was put together by visits to southern ports and the West Indies to supplement what New England could supply, and the collection was sold at the Cape of Good Hope and in various ports throughout the East Indies. A Salem shipper was a peddler afloat, disposing of pottery, fish, ale, soap, lard, tobacco, and even small items of furniture. Goods would be turned over several times in a single voyage. An important stop was Madeira, where wine for the tables of the wealthy was obtained. For a while Salem became the world's chief entrepôt for pepper: by 1805 the largest part of American exports of pepper passed through the port.

In short, merchant-shipping was a major source of capital accumulation in America. For over two centuries this trade had flourished despite occasional setbacks, and it provided the basis for expansion into other areas. Trade in New York received a tremendous boost after the War of 1812, when the British dumped cloth and hardware into the port. Then came the Erie Canal to enable New York to outflank the mountains and reach into the hinterlands. Southern planters began to ship their cotton overseas via New York; the port could also draw on southern New England. The canal took textiles, sugar, and coffee westward and brought cotton, flour, tobacco, and naval stores eastward. After the war, regular sailings and punctual schedules created the ocean liner, initiated when Jeremiah Thompson established the Black Ball Line. In the eighteen-thirties steamships began to compete with fast packets.

James Chesterman, a journeyman tailor who made ready-to-wear garments for the laborers of the South and Southwest, added to the westward flow of goods. But most important was the cotton trade. Ships carried bales of cotton from southern ports first to New York and then to Europe, returning with freight and immigrants. Men like Anson Phelps, William Whitlock, Jr., and Elisha Hurlbut staked their fortunes on the cotton trade. Charleston, Savannah, Mobile, New Orleans, and New York thrived on it. Yet the business was quite speculative: fortunes were made and lost gambling on King Cotton. Coupled with this commerce was a lucrative coastwise trade linking Maine, Boston, Philadelphia, and Charleston. Lewis Rogers, a Virginian, grew wealthy shipping tobacco out of Richmond, and the House of Lorillard began its career during this period.

Piracy on the high seas had by no means been stamped out completely. In 1831 Charles Gibbs, scion of a respectable Rhode Island family, admitted killing over a hundred persons in a career of piracy. He was hanged.

Gradually New England moved toward manufacturing, and soon shipping was overshadowed. Newburyport, Marblehead, and Salem could not compete with Boston, which itself had some trouble keeping pace with New York. But one could always find an important and wealthy merchant in New England. Merchant banker George Peabody left his huge estate to libraries and museums. His partner and successor was Junius Spencer Morgan, whose son was to leave an indelible imprint on business in the United States.

By 1812, the shipper and ship ownership were being separated. The merchant was becoming more exclusively an importer-exporter. A sense of class began to grow: John Bromfield found it difficult to start in business because his mother was the daughter of a minister, not a merchant. The latter preferred to deal with overseas agents who were in some way related. Supercargos were often chosen from among ambitious young relatives. The merchant felt safer this way, for kinship ties were still rather strong. While there was a deep sense of mutual obligation between the shipper and his supercargo, the rule for everyone else was *caveat emptor*. A government, whether one's own or not, was in the same category as the ordinary customer. What today might be reported to the Better Business Bureau as outright fraud, was to a late eighteenth-century merchant nothing more than sharp business practice. The merchant might think himself a gentleman, but if lying brought profit, he did not hesitate. He often beseeched the Government to help him, but woe betide the Administration that endangered his welfare. The war with England in 1812 was to the merchant an utter abomination, for it played havoc with the life of trade.

William Duer, whom we have met earlier, was perhaps a prime example of the businessman at the end of the eighteenth century. Duer had been an assistant to Alexander Hamilton, but it was soon evident that the latter should have been more circumspect. If the Secretary of the Treasury had to be like Caesar's wife, the company he kept was not unlike that lady's friends. Duer, who was born in England, came to America to join the embattled colonists. He married well and lived in a style that befitted his wife's conception of her high social status. There were numerous servants in the Duer mansion, a coat of arms was affected, and fifteen different kinds of wine were served at dinner. Duer's business, primarily speculating in Government debt, was hardly beset with uncertainty, for it was conducted on the basis of tips from Government sources. As with Robert Morris, public office for Duer meant private gain. Hamilton chose him because he supposedly knew a great deal about public finance, but Duer had few scruples and not only did business for himself, but let his friends in on his lucrative game. Wanting to make himself the richest man in the United States, Duer speculated feverishly in Bank of United States scrip and in Government bonds while in office. He was finally forced to resign in 1790, but he did obtain a contract from the Army, only to have the Government discover a shortage of $238,000 in his account. Duer received his comeuppance in 1792 when he was caught in a squeeze play by rival groups: as the speculative frenzy collapsed, a mob was ready to hang him from the nearest tree.

However, some businessmen did seek their profits in the performance of a service. One was Frederic Tudor, who established an ice business to help Americans cool their food for preservation. The colonists had attempted to build ice houses but in the main, visitors to these shores were likely to be served sour milk and rancid butter. The icebox did not become a household fixture until the eighteen-sixties. The ice business itself began as early as 1805 when Tudor, scion of a prominent Boston family, began to harvest ice from the ponds of Massachusetts to sell to such faraway places as Martinique.

Vain and ruthless, Tudor became America's "ice king." Although he lost four thousand dollars on his first business attempt, he persevered. He cut ice from the ponds in chunks of uniform size by using cutters with teeth set in parallel runners, experimented with insulating materials, built more efficient ice houses, and got his "meltage" down to less than 10 per cent of his output. He built ice houses in Cuba and the West Indies, undersold his competitors, and urged his customers to eat ice cream and iced foods. In 1832 he tried the fur trade in the Northwest, but five years later was back harvesting ice from the Great Ponds of Massachusetts. In 1833 Tudor shipped 180 tons of ice all the way to Calcutta. Henry David Thoreau observed that the waters of Walden Pond were now mixed with the waters of the Ganges.

But such ventures were little noticed. There were more pressing issues at hand that had affected the world of business—the consequences of Jay's Treaty, British-French wars, Hamilton's funding operations, and the First Bank of the United States kept exercising the entrepreneurs of the new nation. The strong ties with British countinghouses had modulated somewhat the general sympathy with the French Revolution. English investors were now placing their funds in U.S. Government securities and banks. British and French quarrels were affecting the United States through depredations by both sides on commerce.

Obviously, American merchants had too much to lose by fighting the British; and so John Jay was sent to negotiate with them. As a *quid pro quo* Jay agreed that the U.S. Government would compensate British subjects for some old debts. However, most of these debts were in the South. The planters vehemently protested the treaty. That the British surrendered certain western posts, kept American claims alive by having them referred to a commission, and assured commercial privileges in the West Indies for American merchants simply proved to the southern planter that it was all a scheme to benefit northern commerce. On the other hand, the merchant and shipper looked favorably on the new Government that had been so great a boon to them. John Jacob Astor, especially, was a heavy gainer.

Astor had been one of the greatest of the fur traders. Emigrating from Germany in 1783, he began in a small store in downtown New York. He quickly learned the sharp practices of the trade, adding a few of his own on the way. Tight-fisted and penny-pinching, he sent scores of trappers across the wilderness of America to gather pelts, making the business profitable enough to enable him to enter the shipping business as well. The West was his province, and intruders were expelled, often under threat of arms. The Indians were plied with liquor, the easier to cheat them, and whatever laws existed were simply ignored with impunity. Profit was gathered from two sources: by overcharging for the items sold at the trading post and by cheating on purchases. In the meantime, Astor could stay in New York and tally up his gains.

The businessman was particularly grateful to the Secretary of the Treasury, whose funding scheme promised stability and handsome profits. Hamilton had promised not only to re-fund the national debt but to assume responsibility at face value for a state debt of some $20,000,000 as well. To accompany these measures, he also wanted a national bank and a tariff system. While speculators might profit handsomely, as indeed they did, and merchants and nascent manufacturers be assured of liquid capital, the landowners objected, for they feared that a rise in taxes would be needed to finance all of these operations. They were not convinced by Hamilton's assurances that a tariff on imports would be sufficient to liquidate the debt and pay the costs of government. To be sure, there were suggestions that the debt could be discharged at something less than face value, but in view of the political and economic forces at play, it was not surprising that the merchant and speculator had their way. Only the bills of credit issued by the Continental Congress—about $200,000,000 worth—were virtually repudiated at a penny on the dollar, and the small merchant and the farmer who had helped pay for the fighting were left holding an empty bag. A bank bill was passed in 1791 establishing a national bank for twenty years with a $10,000,000 capital stock, of which the Government took 20 per cent. And with a new mint the Government was on its way to financial respectability, according to the lights of Hamilton, the merchants, and their speculator friends.

For the fact was that debt-holdings had gravitated into the hands of a few northerners; one group and one section was ready to gain the most out of the refunding operation. Although Hamilton seemed eager to repay foreign holders in full, he would by no means accept Madison's compromise proposal that some distinction be made among all holders of securities. Hamilton was obviously kind to American speculators. They were men he deeply admired, and when the Government created wealth, he believed it should be made certain that such wealth got into the hands of those who knew how to make use of it. The funding operation was a bold imitation of the British system; it could be nothing less than a blessing to those already rich. And it seemed another way of demonstrating America's affinity for the British. After all, argued Hamilton, trade with the British had not been substantially altered by the Revolution: America was still sending three-fourths of its exports to Britain and was taking $14,000,000 worth of goods in return.

The bank proposal was a patent imitation of British practice; the Old Lady of Threadneedle Street, as the Bank of England was called, should have been flattered. Hamilton wanted to avoid the dangers of the printing press. He learned from John Law that the proper amount of money in circulation could make a nation prosperous (but Law, something of a mountebank, made France too prosperous, and the bubble burst). Hamilton wanted a controlled circulating medium and instrumentalities for siphoning credit to the entrepreneur. In contrast to English practice, under which the central bank was a private institution, Hamilton's bank was mixed: the Government was to supply three-fifths of the capital, while operation of the bank was to be in private hands. Note redemption was to be in specie to avoid overissue, and the bank was to be a kind of handmaiden to the Treasury, helping to collect taxes and making loans to the Government on occasion. The plan went through Congress quietly. One morning America discovered that it had a national bank.

Jefferson and Madison immediately challenged the whole business on grounds of constitutionality. Madison in particular thought the bank would undermine state systems. However, Hamilton persuaded Washington to sign the bill, asserting that its constitutionality was assured by the "necessary and proper" clause. It was an early case of action justified by the doctrine of implied powers. Establishment of the bank, though, merely meant more speculation, notably in its own stock. Once again the result was a concentration of important securities in the hands of northern commercial interests. Hamilton was not disturbed by such a contingency, for it meant placing economic affairs in the hands of such trading people as Thomas Willing and William Bingham, who did, in fact, become directors of the bank.

What farmers and planters might get out of the bank seemed very little indeed. Right from the start the bank refused to make loans on commodity collateral; the consequence was a sharpening of sectional differences. Hamilton hoped that at least the important state banks would tie in with the national bank. He had helped found one state bank and he was anxious that they not be hurt. Hence he opposed establishing branches of the national bank, but the directors went ahead anyway, opening offices in Boston, New York, Baltimore, and Charleston—eventually eight branches in all. The national bank quickly acquired political as well as economic significance. If the bank meant that the commercial and creditor groups would find it easier to collect what they had risked, and if the bank strengthened the sort of government that could help them collect, then, of course, they wanted a national bank.

Jefferson and Madison agreed with each other: they simply saw no need for the bank. The agrarians who distrusted the intent of the Constitution also distrusted its financial offspring. Nevertheless, the new nation acquired a kind of central bank, which regulated the activities of other banks at the same time as it competed with them. John Jacob Astor disliked it, but only because he had been refused credit. Jacob Barker, a speculator, denounced it vehemently, but he hoped to make a killing by speculating in its stock. Henry Clay had no more use for it than he had for Albert Gallatin, its director. The constitutionality argument was finally used as a way of letting its charter expire. When liquidation was finally completed in 1852, returns to the stockholders totaled well over 100 per cent of capital. In a growing economy, banking, no matter how controversial, was enormously gainful.

While banking was assuredly a deadly serious affair, it did give rise to some comic-opera performances. The directors of the Farmers Exchange Bank of Gloucester, Rhode Island, which failed in 1809, received some specie for a few days and promptly appropriated it, substituting their own IOU's. The year before, they had $380 in specie with $22,500 in notes outstanding. Andrew Dexter of Boston got control of the bank and simply took the note plates with him to run off bills whenever the spirit moved him. He kept his cashier working nights signing the notes, which he then sold at whatever price he could get. The poor cashier spent his days evading payment. Dexter then gained control of another bank and kept each alive with the other's notes. When the affair collapsed, some $800,000 in notes had been issued on a capital of $45. Such were the antics that made bankers a breed about as popular as a skunk.

Nevertheless, the economy was becoming viable enough to disprove Lord Sheffield's prophecy that America outside His Majesty's Imperial System could not succeed. Sheffield's "Observations on the Commerce of the American States," which went into six printings, proved that the future for the former Colonies was hopeless. The rebuttal was Hamilton's Report on Manufactures, which suggested that Government bounties and premiums would overcome all impediments to development. Then a moment of prosperity prevailed at the end of the century: exports were increasing and businessmen hailed Hamilton as a great man. The Report on Manufactures, which relied on the views of the ever-optimistic Philadelphian Tench Coxe, noted a strong potential for manufacturing and advocated its advancement. Of course, the middle class that was forming was willing to undertake any sure proposition, and Hamilton was simply suggesting that the Government should provide that sure proposition. He noted that British industry employed women and children for fourteen hours a day, six days a week: he believed that this was precisely the sort of labor force the country should have. Yet the report was a mercantilist document that owed more to Colbert, the French minister, than it did to Adam Smith. It contained proposals for building more roads and canals, and for bounties to "sick" industries. So optimistic was Hamilton that he failed to note the number of business failures counterbalancing business successes. More significantly, his plans were intended to benefit a minority. So far as the southern planters were concerned, the Hamiltonian system merely substituted a northern merchant for a British factor.

Jefferson clearly was at the opposite pole from Hamilton. Reserved, uncomfortable in the company of others, and given to wearing clothes that seemed to have resulted from a tailor's error, Jefferson was more of a frontiersman than a Virginia gentleman. He was described as a kind of shy philosopher who would rather employ subtlety than force as a way of scoring a point. His enemies thought he was shifty because he seldom looked a man in the eye when he spoke, though everyone granted that he was a superb conversationalist. His maternal forebears had been aristocrats, but his father had been a middle-class farmer who gave to his son a keen understanding of agrarian and frontier ways. The famous Jeffersonian sympathy for small farmers, trappers, and tobacco growers had been naturally acquired. A wide distribution of property seemed to Jefferson to be most desirable in a democracy: he was a leveler a century and a half after the term had been invented.

Although Paris was a delightful place to serve as ambassador, that did not mean that the politics of the *Ancien Régime* were acceptable to him. In actuality, he despised a system that "dedicated the sons of peasants as cannon fodder in remote wars precipitated by the whims of a prostitute." He was a humanitarian who opposed capital punishment and slavery and wanted to bring about the reform of prisons. When he wrote the Northwest Ordinance, Jefferson made special efforts to insure that slavery would be prohibited in the new lands. To him, religious freedom meant the separation of church and state, a principle embodied in the Bill of Rights, and he pressed for it with vigor. And while he accepted the Constitution, he rigorously opposed any plan for the new Government that might be based on monarchical notions.

In contrast to Hamilton, Jefferson was instinctively tactful with lesser men. He was able to get along even with those whom he opposed politically.

Yet he was an excellent organizer with a sharp insight into the minds of the mass of men. And he had no aversion to compromise, so long as he could reach his objectives. Jefferson was shrewd enough to send his opponents into disarray by refusing to take a stand whenever that seemed expedient. Philosophically, he rejected the Industrial Revolution and all that flowed from it, believing that agriculture was the proper foundation for a sane social order. He saw the American people being led down the primrose path by the promise of the Hamiltonian system, and he was alarmed. As much as Hamilton distrusted the mass of people, so much did Jefferson have faith in their innate potentialities. Although he thought that Congress ought to be a genuinely representative body, he acknowledged, when he became President, that it was possible for the executive to be *the* representative. He had been forced to modify his principles.

As leader of the Republican forces, Jefferson opposed virtually all of the Hamiltonian plans, which after all were expressions of the commercial and urban interests. But for Jefferson, the latter were simply creating channels of exploitation, chicanery, and speculation—all anathema to an agrarian. Federalists called Jefferson an atheist, and great was the consternation in Boston, New York, and Phildelphia when he was chosen President. Hamilton was so perturbed by the prospect of a Republican victory in 1800 that he urged New York's governor, John Jay, to alter the method of selecting electors to prevent "an atheist in religion and a fanatic in politics from getting possession of the helm of state." Jefferson's response was, needless to say, sharp: it was a plan, said he, "fished up from hell," but to Hamiltonians anything was fair to save the country from "the fangs of Jefferson." Fortunately, Jay did not accept Hamilton's idea and nothing came of the matter. Yet Aaron Burr seemed even worse: when the House had to decide the election after the tie vote in the Electoral College, Hamilton used his influence in Jefferson's favor.

The young republic was a noble expression of the innate democratic sentiments of the people, said Jefferson. He had led the fight to abolish primogeniture in Virginia and to disestablish the Church, and he was no doubt pleased when, with the spread of Jeffersonian sentiment, the states began to abolish property qualifications for suffrage and public office and to eliminate the old debtor laws. The Government's role, according to Jeffersonian political philosophy, was solely that of extending justice. That philosophy was essentially humanistic and in bitter conflict with the aristocratic expressions of Hamiltonian tenets. When Congress paid $24,000 for Jefferson's library, which he had offered as a replacement for the Library of Congress burned by the British in the War of 1812, the Federalists were most vehement in their protests, though the sum was, in fact, paltry even by the standards of the time.

The debates accompanying Hamilton's proposals polarized the country's political opinion. Parties gradually came into existence with all the ritual of conventions, speeches, symbols, and the division of spoils when victory had been achieved. The Jeffersonians wanted the funding of the debt to be more reasonable: they resented the speculators' requisition of windfall profits. But financial interests had seized the reins of power and were in a position to exploit farmers, planters, and artisans. John Taylor charged key congressmen with holding Government securities and therefore of being likely to gain substantially from the Hamiltonian schemes. When the Jeffersonians were about to take over the Government in 1801, and thus have access to the Treasury's files, a fortuitous fire in the Treasury building destroyed many of the records that might have revealed the truth. The records of Federal loan offices in some of the states were opened a century later to substantiate the Jeffersonian indictment. By then it was academic.

Attitudes on moral and constitutional questions were conditioned by the varying intensities of economic interest. The planters might have been critical of Hamilton and his schemes, but they made sure to defeat a proposal to abolish slavery in 1790. So powerful was the nationalist sentiment becoming that Hamilton had no difficulty in getting Washington to suppress the Whisky Rebellion in Pennsylvania with a strong show of force. Republican hostility to Federalist views grew intense enough to convince Washington that he should not seek a third term. He had not been spared political attack and he was disturbed. To be so vilified at the end of forty years of public service was a painful experience.

But the Federalists had a trump card in the personage of John Marshall, who had been placed on the Supreme Court by Adams in 1801, a month before Jefferson was inaugurated. The office of Chief Justice was not highly regarded at the time, and the appointment drew few notices in the press. But in some thirty-five years time, Marshall had converted the post into a position of stature. The Articles of Confederation had appeared to him as an exercise in futility, and he was determined to implant Federalist and nationalist views into the law of the land. As it happened, such views frequently coincided with those of Boston, New York, and Philadelphia merchants. In *Marbury v. Madison* Marshall declared that the judiciary had the power to nullify acts of Congress when they were unconstitutional. But the criteria of constitutionality were a matter for the judges to decide. In *Fletcher v. Peck* he annulled a Georgia statute that seemed in error. *Mc-*

Cullough v. Maryland asserted the superiority of Federal over state instrumentalities. A *cordon sanitaire* was drawn around the principle of contract
in the Dartmouth College case. State court decisions could be appealed to
the Federal bar in *Cohen v. Virginia*.

And so it went. In Marshall's hands the Constitution became what he
said it was, and it was clear that constitutional meaning would be shaped
only by the Supreme Court. He made the Court a powerful tribunal and set
a model for its later development that has not yet been surpassed. Marshall's decisions were clear and forceful expressions of the business views of
Boston, New York, Philadelphia, and other centers of enterprise. The
national purview was only too obvious. For example, when some states
issued bills of credit, calling them "certificates," a practice presumably
forbidden by the Constitution, Marshall insisted that it was a usurpation of
congressional powers. His decision was a dissertation on the evils of paper
money and a rejection of state interference with the prerogatives of the
Federal Government.

Yet, as early as 1812, the Federalists were heaving their last gasps. The
financiers who had supported Government loans were demanding that the
war with Britain come to a halt. They were being injured, for despite a few
minor American naval victories, the seas were still ruled by Britain. The
American Navy had little power, and it could not protect American shipping. Northern interests literally sabotaged the sale of Government bonds,
while Connecticut and Massachusetts failed to supply their quotas of
militiamen. The Federalists finally expired in Hartford in 1814 at a convention that proposed constitutional changes intended to strengthen the
commercial interests. Southerners laughed out loud at the spectacle of a
Federalist threat of nullification and a demand for states' rights. Younger
businessmen ignored the Federalists, turning toward the Republicans, who
were promising to meet their needs for expansion and growth. It seemed as
though the slate had to be cleared of the names of the older, now moribund,
aristocrats of business before a new group of money-makers could arise.

The Jeffersonians, of course, did not repudiate the national debt, but
simply paid it off as quickly as they could. The Treasury was in the able
hands of Albert Gallatin. The excise tax on whiskey, a particular bone of
contention with the agrarians, was abolished, and as many Government
posts as possible were filled by the republican partisans. John Adams'
"midnight judges," who had been appointed with the dying rattle of the old
administration, were eased out. Funds for highway improvements were
voted because these measures would help farmers. The fortunes of state
were turning full circle: Jeffersonians were soon exercising broad powers

while their opponents were now advocating a strict interpretation of the Constitution. Jeffersonians finally became the defenders of the rights of American commerce on the high seas, and by 1812 they acknowledged the virtues of a national bank and a protective tariff.

Banking as an industry flourished. Although the national bank was allowed to expire, by 1816 the number of state banks had increased to almost 250. All sorts of groups wanted banks: even artisans had to have their own institutions. Americans were becoming convinced that only faith was needed for a bank and currency; there was no need to worry about specie or reserves. On this faith many a bank was to founder. One historian has suggested that these developments implied a democratization of business. Opportunities were opened to many, not merely the old aristocrats. A new generation of entrepreneurs had lined up with the agrarians to gain access to advantage and to provide a basis for the flowering of laissez faire. Jefferson's ideology had always been favored by the agrarians; his pragmatic policies were now favored by business.

If Jefferson's Louisiana Purchase appeared rather irregular, it nevertheless opened a continent to farmers, and commerce was necessary to carry their goods overseas. In New England, though, political concerns impelled the merchant interests to oppose such expansionism, for it would only provide a base for planters and farmers. Obviously, the opportunity to acquire the vast lands of the West could not be missed: when Napoleon, pressed for money, expressed a willingness to sell, Jefferson gave him $15,000,000 for the huge tract, basing his authority on the treaty-making clause of the Constitution. The shoe was now on the other foot; eastern merchants and their Federalist supporters could only see that more roughnecks would be shouting in the political corridors of the nation. The northerners grumbled that maybe they would secede from the union, and North Carolina, of all states, jumped to the defense of Federal authority.

Gradually, in the first quarter of the nineteenth century, businessmen began to attend to their internal economy. It was becoming diversified enough to be attractive to men in a variety of pursuits. The American response to the Napoleonic Wars turned the entrepreneur's gaze inward, toward his country's resources, which he was to discover were enormous. Political tensions stemming from the Jay Treaty, the XYZ Affair in 1797, the Alien and Sedition Laws, Jefferson's Embargo, and the war itself were serious enough to threaten the union. But the growth of an internal market was balm enough: population grew from 4,000,000 in 1790 to almost 10,000,000 in 1810. There were five more states in the Union in 1812, and

Whitney's ginning device was making cotton sovereign in the South. By 1812 there were eighty-seven cotton mills and eight thousand spindles working to supply a nation with materials for cloth.

Men in the business community—which was growing at a faster rate than ever before—began to see the advantages to themselves of improved inland transportation. Nor were they averse to asking the Government for help in creating and exploiting all the potentialities that had been revealed. Robert Morris pressed Pennsylvania to develop its inland navigation, mainly to prevent trade from passing to other cities. When three navigation companies were formed, he became president of all of them. The state was badgered to spend more than it was ready to offer, but the best Morris and his friends could get was permission to run a lottery to raise funds.

However, in 1811 Federal money was provided for the start of the Cumberland Road, running from Cumberland, Maryland, over the mountains to Ohio and eventually on to Vandalia, Illinois. It was known as the National Pike and became a major thoroughfare for migrants going west. Pennsylvania spent about $40,000,000 to link Philadelphia to Pittsburgh with an ingenious canal system that cleared the Alleghenies with inclined planes up which boats were hauled by steam engines. When private attempts to build roads in the South failed, the public insisted that the states undertake the task. To be sure, private companies had undertaken construction of roads before 1812: the Lancaster Pike, built in 1794, had been fairly successful, as were other ventures of the same kind. Profits were not great, but they were adequate. When the projects became too costly, the cry was on for public participation. By 1821 Pennsylvania had provided 35 per cent of the $6,400,000 outlay on turnpikes, of which there were by that time about 150.

It was soon evident that the "capitalist" providing funds for such "social overhead" was the public official rather than the private entrepreneur. The notion that laissez faire ruled, at least in the field of internal improvements, was patently unfounded. Massachusetts, Pennsylvania, Georgia, and other states were not inhibited by the myth of free enterprise. In fact, private groups demanded Government aid, which had been indeed suggested in Hamilton's *Report on Manufactures*. Nor were state and local governments ready to contemplate the relative merits of costs and benefits. Would the improvements enhance land values? Would they increase the tax base? If so, it all seemed worthwhile.

By 1817 the public outcry for internal improvements was great. John C. Calhoun urged that public works would make America a great imperial power and advocated that the profits from the national bank be employed to finance a communications network connecting the major cities in the country. New York, however, was interested only in its Erie Canal. Madison and Monroe both vetoed bills providing Federal participation, as they saw no constitutional warrant for what Congress wanted.

But the states could and did extend grants of privilege to private groups through incorporation; nevertheless, the latter simply lacked the resources for internal improvements, and government had to do the job. Pennsylvania had all sorts of plans and ideas for investing in public works. By 1844 the Keystone State had placed public directors on the boards of over 150 corporations. Its investment in transportation was enormous, reaching at one time over $108,000,000 in canals and railroads alone. From 1826 to 1875, over three hundred New York municipalities had pledged more than $37,000,000 for railroads. Not only did such aid rescue many a company, but it reduced the cost of improvements to the private sector. The South acquired some 9,200 miles of railroad by 1860; public agencies had supplied over half the $245,000,000 capital. Clearly no private group could pay for canals, roads, and railroads; construction was undertaken by state and local governments and was eventually handed over to private interests. The transition to private ownership was facilitated by the mixed nature of the companies, whose boards included private investors as well as public representatives. But the initial stages demanded deep involvement by public authorities.

Only after public funds made improvement enterprises successful did private enterprise begin to direct its capital toward canal and road investment. Government interests diminished as the private corporations improved their abilities to acquire capital, although corporations tried to obtain government subsidies in one form or another. This mixed mode of early financing contrasted sharply with the British pattern: railroads in England were built in well-populated areas and considerable capital in private hands was available. Hence, the individual entrepreneur did not mind entrusting his surplus funds to promising but untried ventures. In America, the early railroads may have started somewhere, but they generally went nowhere, sustained only by the hope of their builders that a population would soon follow in sufficient numbers to make the effort profitable. And so the Federal Government built the National Pike, New York State dug the Erie Canal, and cities subscribed to railroad security issues. Sometimes outright gifts of public land were made to a company for its right-of-way. The provision of "social overhead" in America became a public utility.

American industry received a powerful stimulus from the War of 1812, and the protection it later obtained from the tariff of 1816 was substantial enough to satisfy the staunchest of Hamiltonians. Although New England's manufacturing interests had opposed the tariff for political reasons, they discovered that Government aid was remarkably helpful. Manufacturers then wanted protective rates to go higher and higher. A second national bank was established by the Republican politicians in power. They simply had to set it up or come to terms with eastern bankers, a most unpalatable prospect. State banks proliferated, the more powerful ones locating themselves in New York where there were many energetic and aggressive businessmen ready to borrow for new and growing enterprises. As a financial center, New York soon outdistanced both Philadelphia and Boston. Commercial banking, in which specie was paid in for bank capital and assets, consisted mainly of short term loans. Or on occasion a corporation like the Manhattan Company might be formed to build a reservoir, although its main purpose was banking.

The country was becoming too big to be confined to the constricting space between the Appalachians and the Atlantic. Even as the nation was being formed, at the end of the eighteenth century, people were pushing westward through the mountain gaps. Prior to the Revolution, the New England Colonies required that the settlement of towns be under the jurisdiction of the parent colony, while in the South persons could go where they wanted to. The New England system generated considerable squabbling among the states, but this was finally settled by the Ordinances of 1784 and 1785, about the only constructive acts of the Continental Congress. The Ordinances established a policy of carving new states out of western lands. Surveys were made, and the sale of lands began, preferably in large blocs to such companies as the Ohio Company and the Scioto Company. Hamilton wanted to raise funds quickly by huge sales, but the little buyer was forgotten until cries of protest arose. Under Jefferson the individual buyer had a better chance to purchase a tract for himself. By 1820 some 20,000,000 acres of land had been sold for a total sum of $48,000,000, much of it on credit. As of that year, over $21,000,000 was still due, and it took twelve years and eleven relief bills to settle the entire matter. Speculation in land reached extraordinary proportions, particularly in Alabama and Mississippi. The credit system had created a class of landholders hopelessly in debt to the Government.

Nine states had been carved out of the first western lands. Settlers came through the Cumberland Gap and along the Mohawk trailways in New York. The army, under General Anthony Wayne, had chased out the Indians, and John C. Symmes, a large speculator, saw a fortune in buying land from Congress and selling it to newcomers. He initially obtained forty thousand acres in Ohio and then added still more, in an attempt to build his holdings up to one million acres. One of the colonies he started was at Cincinnati. Even the little fellow speculated, taking more land than he could use. The movement westward mounted into a mass migration. Eventually the area west of the Appalachians became a land of freeholders, who were to oppose the political views of the East, where the speculators, their ostensible enemies, were centered.

In 1821 Moses Austin and his son Stephen penetrated into Texas, then a part of Mexico. He and those who followed him secured large grants of land, bringing in their families from Louisiana and Mississippi. They used the land to issue scrip, hoping that this method would yield a great profit. Stock was also issued to a public ever ready to take a few scraps from the tables of financiers. By 1835, there were twenty thousand Americans in Texas: the ground had been laid for a quarrel and for blatant imperialism. John Quincy Adams was horrified; he predicted that an imperial America would meet the fate of an imperial Rome. A Republic of Texas was formed, and it proceeded to issue at least $7,000,000 in bonds and notes that then began to depreciate. And with the demand for annexation of Texas by the United States, speculators once more had visions of profiting, for the Federal Government just might assume the debt. Despite opposition from the North to the admission of Texas, the holders of Texas paper prevailed. Jay Cooke, who was deeply involved in Government finances at the time, conceded that prospects for profit were a major force in getting Texas into the union.

In the meantime, Americans were learning about California, then still Mexican territory. As early as 1796 ships from the Northeast had gone around the Horn to reach Monterey. Skins were bought from the Indians for trinkets worth pennies and sold in the Orient at fantastic profits. The Americans also reached California overland. Jedediah Smith, Ewing Young, and John Bidwell were among those who came in the quest for skins. The drive for expansion eventually added California to the territories of the United States. Then, in 1848, the discovery of gold convulsed the continent in a feverish spasm. Newspapers blared forth the glad tidings and merchants stocked up on things that prospectors could use—tools, pans, camping outfits, and canned goods. Bands of women were dispatched from the East to find themselves husbands who might have struck rich veins in the earth.

With variations, the same skein was played out in the Northwest. The China trade took ships to the Columbia River. Explorations in the region had been conducted by Robert Gray in 1792, and Lewis and Clark cut across the area in 1803 in a scientific expedition sponsored by Jefferson at a cost of $2500. Fur traders penetrated the wilderness as Astor pushed his agents to establish a post called Astoria. Only this time it was England, not Mexico, that was the antagonist. War was barely averted in 1846 with a compromise setting the boundary at the forty-ninth parallel.

Expansion was great for the profit mills back East. A classic example of the successful businessman of the day was Stephen Girard. Born in Bordeaux, France, in 1750, in a family of fifteen children, he went to sea at the age of fourteen. In 1774 he found himself in the Colonies, and by the age of twenty-eight he had become a rising young merchant in Philadelphia. Like others, he engaged in the financing of privateers with a fair measure of success. With his brother, Jean, as residential agent, he developed a profitable trade with Santo Domingo. Both brothers were adept in evading the law. If sugar and coffee shipments were proscribed, the cargo became lumber. It was not uncommon to mix poor grades of flour into a higher grade; adulteration was not likely to be discovered until the bread was being baked. At one point brother Jean was able to extract some monies owed to him by Stephen only by threatening to expose the illegal transactions in which they had engaged.

By the time Stephen Girard was forty years of age, it was prudent to address him as "Mister," so wealthy had he become. He possessed a large fleet of ships traveling all over the world and bringing him, on the average, gains of $100,000 per voyage. He was now too rich and respectable not to obey the laws of the land, even though he might find them irritating. The Embargo of 1808 became "Dambargo," but he did not try to break it. When one of his ships had been captured by the British, he simply had Baring of London buy it back for him. Girard kept close watch on his business; he was tightfisted and extracted every last penny from a transaction. For many Americans who watched the Girard fortune grow, his wealth seemed to stem not from the opportunities of the moment, but from hard work and frugality. In his case, wealth was equated to virtue.

Work and more work was the only guiding principle in Girard's life. He was not a likable person, and though he could entertain a visiting dignitary with graciousness, he was thought to be quite miserly. But it may have been that his withdrawal from all worldly affairs except business stemmed from the emotional shock he suffered when he lost his wife and child in the plague. Only John Jacob Aster ranked with Stephen Girard as the wealthiest of the wealthy. When the Bank of the United States lost its charter in 1812, Girard bought the Philadelphia branch, lock, stock, and barrel, for a million dollars. It became the Bank of Stephen Girard. When he died in 1831 the bank's assets were $5,000,000. He was called a patriot when he subscribed $10,000,000 to a lagging Government loan, but it was at a 12 per cent discount, yielding a profit of $2,900,000.

His was a Midas touch: investments in railroads and land were virtually all profitable. People noted that Mr. Girard was a wealthy man, and since he had no heirs, they wondered how he would dispose of his fortune. Great was the public acclaim when it became known after his death that most of his wealth had been left to public purposes, including a provision for a college for "poor, white orphan boys," which was not opened to blacks until the nineteen-sixties. By willing his money as he did, Girard had done more to win approval for men of wealth than any kindness he might have extended while he was alive. Few wanted to balance his bequests against the way in which he had accumulated his wealth: it was enough that virtually all had been given to the public.

Business in the third and fourth decades of the nineteenth century was no longer what it had been in 1775. The cities were becoming more populous and provided a growing domestic market. Turnpikes, bridges, and canals had been built, and companies were operating banks and factories. Stock exchanges, dealing first in government securities, now had private paper to handle. However, the ways of farming and tending the store were quite the same as in earlier years, if perhaps a bit more complicated and involved. Most ventures were still conducted through *ad hoc* partnerships, although more and more the corporate form of business was coming onto the scene.

Some merchants preferred to operate alone, as did Girard, Astor, William Whitlock, and Moses Taylor. Astor's American Fur Company was really a partnership: generally the term "company" signified the presence of one or more silent partners. In 1833 New York required that all partners be designated by name. A limited partnership would allow a person to participate in a venture for a fixed investment and restricted liability. Ships were usually held by multiple partners, but they might be owned outright, as in the case of Cornelius Vanderbilt. During his lifetime, Vanderbilt owned thirty-four steamboats and ferries and seventeen ocean liners. He may very well have deserved the title of "Commodore." The active partner in a ship was its "husband," arranging for cargos, hiring a captain, handling port and clearances. Goods were usually sold at auction to jobbers and wholesalers.

who provided the means of distribution. Allied with shipping were, of course, men in the business of marine insurance, who soon learned that the risk had to be distributed.

Despite a long history and their important role in the discovery and exploration of the New World, joint-stock enterprises and corporations were few in number in the early nineteenth century. The single entrepreneur, incorporating ownership and control in his own person, predominated. Major concerns, such as Astor's fur company, were really partnerships in disguise. Enterprise remained, in the main, small in scale, and the supply of capital was limited. But as the economy grew, more funds became available, and a fair amount of capital could be brought together from divergent sources through the corporation. General incorporation acts for churches, eleemosynary institutions, and schools offered a precedent. By 1801 some three hundred charters of incorporation were recorded; sixteen years later the number increased to almost eighteen hundred.

The power to grant a charter was one of the issues on which the Constitution was silent: it was presumed that this power was reserved to the states. However, from *McCullough v. Maryland*, it was evident that Congress too had the right to grant a charter—at least that was what Chief Justice Marshall had indicated. In most states, however, getting a charter required a special act of the legislature. But this was not a serious handicap to the myriad canal and turnpike companies, banks, insurance firms, and manufacturers that wanted to tap an expanding capital market. Some corporations took out more than one charter, since the document usually restricted them to a single line of endeavor. Some were more clever: the incorporators of the Manhattan Company inserted a blanket clause in their charter that allowed them to start a bank, which was what they wanted to do in the first place anyway.

The corporation was becoming a familiar form. Obviously, merchants would constitute the largest class of stockholders, since they were the major source of private capital. And it paid to be a stockholder in a local bank: it helped one's credit. Moreover, support to a local bridge or highway company could bring business one's way. Overseas investors—Dutch, French, and English—invested first in canals and later in railroads. Frequently it was the large capitalist who managed to gain control of these important corporations. But all were rather riskless ventures: if the capitalist was certain of the outcome, he would invest heavily; if he was doubtful, he would hesitate or abstain entirely. Risk was something to be shifted to smaller investors or the government. The big fellow gambled only on a sure bet. The notion of entrepreneurial risk-taking was becoming a myth.

CHAPTER 4 The Roots of Industry

The simple economy of the eighteenth century had been transformed by expansion and enterprise. All too frequently, however, the latter was defined by dubious promotions, scheming, pirated inventions, speculation, and outright embezzlement. Business was more often a matter of cunning than acumen. A money economy founded on promises to pay was coming into being, and the promises were rather easy to break; for the victims business had some of the attributes of a swindle. The disappearing virtues of an agrarian society led men, rightly or wrongly, to identify business with corruption.

In the meantime, pressures were accumulating for a more democratic government. The states gradually allowed a popular vote for the Presidency, at least. In the eighteen-thirties nominating conventions displaced the congressional caucus as a way of selecting candidates for high office. And in the election of 1828 a "man of the soil," born in poverty, came into the White House. Andrew Jackson—Old Hickory—had been a speculator, horse trader, and army general. He had been ever ready to fight the Indians and had killed one man in a duel. Jackson's fame spread quickly when he defeated the veterans of Waterloo in the Battle of New Orleans. Later he took Florida from Spain and hanged two British subjects who were in the way.

He had his "Kitchen Cabinet" in the White House and made blatant use of the spoils system in handing out jobs. His distrust of eastern bankers evidently stemmed from the loss of some land he had offered as security in endorsing seven thousand dollar's worth of notes that had been protested. He had suddenly become a debtor, and he felt that he had been jobbed out of his property. Jackson's philosophy was simple enough: he believed in the common man and in equality, and he hated monopoly, privilege, and high finance. It was much too simple a credo for easterners; they were thoroughly discomfited by it.

The Second Bank of the United States was a crucial issue during Jackson's tenure in Washington. Established in 1816 under James Madison, the bank had its origins in the fiscal needs of the Government, in the disorder of an unregulated currency, and in the ambitions of businessmen. The first bank had done a creditable job of restraining the license of the state banks. An organized effort was made to obtain a widespread, popular subscription to the stock of the second bank, but the attempt was none too successful. Stephen Girard then bought $3,000,000 worth, letting Astor take a portion. This action at least insured the bank's establishment. However, its beginnings were not auspicious, and by 1819 many persons were wondering if the project had been a good idea after all. An attempt to gain control was made by a group of businessmen in Baltimore, and several states tried to tax the operation, only to be rebuffed by the Supreme Court in *McCullough v. Maryland*.

The bank's later troubles could be traced to Jackson's clash with Nicholas Biddle, its head—a clash that may have originated in Biddle's refusal to allow the bank to become part of the spoils system.

Biddle himself came of a wealthy Philadelphia family. Although he had been trained in the law, he much preferred to study literature and the classics. Entering politics, he became a member of the state legislature; he was appointed a Government director of the Bank in 1819. At the age of thirty-seven, he was named its president, and for the next sixteen years was fully absorbed in its affairs. An arrogant and politically inept man, he was no match for Jackson, although he thought he was. The President wanted a currency backed by specie, and so far as he was able to grasp the matter, the bank was not pursuing such a policy.

Yet when Jackson had achieved his triumph over the bank, he set in motion precisely the monetary problems he wanted to avoid. So far as the business community was concerned, it had little more love for Biddle than it had for the President, although there was a fair measure of popular support for the bank. Biddle was not really of the world of business, though he understood the businessmen's habits only too well. Lacking the ruthlessness and hardheadedness of businessmen, he nevertheless won their admiration when he tried to resist the Government. Jackson was a general, a hero, the President of the United States, and a man accustomed to annihilating those who opposed him. Perhaps Biddle might have achieved more if he had been content to play central banker, but he took the bank into politics, and that was his undoing. He was too naïve to mix in the company of politicians and businessmen.

Biddle placed members of Congress on his payroll: Daniel Webster once unashamedly reminded Biddle that he had not yet received his retainer. Henry Clay was also a beneficiary of the bank. At one point Biddle called in loans in the hope of provoking a depression to wear down the opposition. As a central bank, it could influence the flow of money into the economy, but farmers hated Biddle and his bank because he would lend only to businessmen in the city. He even tried to control what the press had to say about the bank. Various factors led Biddle to play directly into the hands of the President, not the least of which were a general desire for easier credit, the identification of the bank with the nation's aristocracy, and the prevailing agrarian antipathy toward a central bank. As tensions mounted, Biddle decided to apply for a charter renewal four years before the old charter was due to expire. It was an inept move. Jackson vetoed the bill; his message was a stinging rebuke to Biddle and to those who supported him. The President commented that eastern capitalists held $13,000,000 of the $28,000,000 in outstanding bank stock, and that over $1,600,000 in profit had come from western communities where very little stock was held. He ordered his Secretary of the Treasury to withdraw the Government's funds from the national bank and to place them in favored state banks.

The struggle over the bank was hardly a class struggle: it was rather a conflict between two sectors of the propertied class, one of which, seeking to attain the status of a new elite, resented the restriction of credit by the other. To be sure, opposition to Jackson came from financiers, manufacturers, and merchants, but these were precisely the groups that wanted "stable" credit and currency. Nor did they relish the notion of a new middle class shouldering them aside in both business and politics. But the new businessman was seeking to break out of any sort of restriction that might be imposed on him by others. There were opportunities in the land, and he was determined to make the most of them. Jacksonianism became a movement toward a freer capitalism, toward laissez faire in the true sense of the word. Its political voice—a demand for democracy—was that of the small capitalist who wanted to become a big one, and the chief barriers were those set up by the old Federalist, aristocratic nabobs in the East. More specifically, the demand was for a policy of easy credit, more and freer use of land, and restrictions on special privileges for corporations. To all this, Jackson could be sympathetic, for he had been a small entrepreneur himself.

Jackson's Kitchen Cabinet, which led the fight against the bank, consisted mainly of new-style businessmen. Duff Green had a prosperous but modest business in St. Louis; Samuel Ingham had been a paper manufacturer; Preston Blair was a journalist in full agreement with the new capitalist credo; Churchill Cambreling had worked as an agent for Astor. These men took the philosophy of laissez faire quite seriously; Hamiltonian centralization was not for them. But they were no more idealistic about politics or business than their opponents were. They wanted to make money and wanted to do it as fast as possible, for life was short. The Jacksonians became just as wealthy, if not wealthier, than those they had displaced. The President himself was a planter, but his agrarian origins did not prevent him from siding with the capitalists. Except that these capitalists were now a new breed, ready to exploit the resources of an untamed continent as never before. As one historian remarked, "Jackson never really championed the cause of the people; he only invited them to champion his."

Meanwhile, men were making money and lots of it. John Jacob Astor was now buying as much of Manhattan Island as he could put his hands on. He had learned to be ruthless and single-minded in the fur trade, in which he had built an effective and powerful organization, fighting his rivals to the bitter end. To move the trappers westward, keelboats were employed, propelled by long poles. These were later to be replaced by steamboats. Caravans would form at the westernmost point in Missouri and then move forward in search of pelts and of trade with the Indians. Trappers might go into the wilderness singly to rendezvous later in the year at a specified spot. Astor was the shrewdest and most successful organizer in a rough and sometimes brutal business. Born in Waldorf, Germany, in 1763, he came to America twenty years later, with a stopover in England, to learn the fur business. He opened a small store on Water Street in New York and began making trips to upstate New York and Canada seeking furs. Soon he had agents bartering for skins with the Indians in exchange for rum and trinkets. The export market to Europe for furs was quite profitable; by 1800 Astor was reputedly worth a quarter of a million dollars.

To gather more furs, Astor formed the American Fur Company in 1808. He became his own shipper and pushed his trappers farther and farther west. He dreamed of a chain of trading posts across the continent reaching to the Pacific Northwest. In fact, his men did set up a post at the Columbia River, but the War of 1812 made it indefensible, and he had to concentrate on the Great Lakes region and the Rockies. As the American Fur Company moved across the land, it merged with rivals, or it simply fought them to a standstill. The company was not above the use of force and fraud in an effort to control the supply of pelts. Beyond the frontier there was no government, and Astor's men were free to do as they pleased.

The company was essentially a partnership arrangement, with the agents sharing in the profits. But Astor was not always willing to part with a man's share, and on occasion a trapper returning home to collect his back pay was assassinated. Furs had to be obtained cheaply: this meant plying the Indians with liquor, in direct defiance of the law. One trapper observed that philanthropy was not the object of the hunt. The Indian was a pawn in the game of business, and he had little meaning except as he met the needs of the fur trade. Consequently, the Indians would at times react rather violently, slaughtering a few dozen whites. But such recalcitrance could always be corrected by Government soldiers. Troops and trappers alike considered the Indian to be lacking in principles, dishonest, a liar, and a cheat. Hence, whatever the white man did was justified.

Astor was not averse to employing bribery to get the Government on his side. At one time he gave $35,000 to Lewis Cass, then governor of the Michigan territory and later Secretary of War. The fur trade was exploitative of agent, Indian, and Government. Meanwhile, Astor lived comfortably in his home-office-warehouse-salesroom at 233 Broadway in New York City. He was deemed a patriotic and astute businessman, but rather tight-fisted. Once he wanted to demonstrate his public spirit by building a library. When he learned from a builder that it would cost $15,000, he told the man, "That will do," and filed the plans away. In his will, he did leave $400,000 for a library, but very few bequests for anything else.

In 1800 Astor entered the China trade, sending furs to Canton in exchange for Chinese goods to be sold in New York. There was profit at both ends: the furs cost little, and silk brought a handsome price. When the Jeffersonian embargo halted his ships, he let it be known that he had to take a Mandarin home. The other merchants protested when his ship left, breaking the blockade; they insisted that Astor had picked up a stray Chinaman on the docks.

When he sensed that the fur trade might decline, Astor decided that land purchases looked better than pelts. A few Canadian land parcels came to him cheaply. Thus he got into real estate, following the same rules that guided him in furs: get it for little and squeeze firmly for profits. In one instance, Astor learned that the title to the confiscated lands of an old Loyalist in Putnam County might be defective. He bought a tract of over fifty thousand acres for $100,000 and calmly advised the seven hundred residents that they were now his tenants. An uproar ensued, and the litigation was not settled until 1827, when Astor "gave" the land to New York State for $500,000. Nor did he mind selling some useless land to his own brother. Accommodating politicians in New York City gave him water grants through which he gained control of numerous parcels of land. He watched foreclosure announcements and took over heavily mortgaged farms that might pass to him upon bankruptcy. He made loans, foreclosed, and bought back the land at low prices. During the Panic of 1837, Astor appeared as complainant in at least sixty proceedings. He came to wish that he had not dabbled in Canadian real estate, but had paid closer attention to Manhattan Island.

As the population of New York increased, Astor found himself a landlord of extensive urban properties. He was now also a banker. By 1847 he was worth some $20,000,000, a fortune that towered over those of Peter Cooper, Moses Taylor, and Cornelius Vanderbilt. He always insisted on a daily accounting of rentals from his agents. He pressed the city to give him fire protection for his properties, but he paid little, if anything, in taxes. Nor was he overly quick in meeting ordinary debts. Although he had subscribed to Audubon's book on ornithology, he had not paid the one-thousand-dollar price. Audubon finally tracked Astor to his home and was told that times were hard. Turning to his son William, Astor asked if there was any money around. Taking his father's question literally, William listed bank accounts totaling over $500,000, whereupon Astor interrupted, "That will do."

"It seems," he said to Audubon, "William can give you a check for your money."

He died in 1848, aged eighty, feared by many and thoroughly disliked by most. James Gordon Bennett called him a Croesus who made his money from the industry of New York's citizenry. He left nine-tenths of his fortune to his son William, little to charities, and nothing to his servants and employees. There were some doubts that all that wealth had accrued through personal virtue.

The old Dutch stock in New York was now gone. People like Robert Lenox, Jeremiah Thompson, the Bayards, and the Pintards, of British or Huguenot origins, typified the merchants of the era. By 1840 there were over four hundred commercial houses in the city engaged in foreign trade, supplemented by some nine hundred commission merchants. New businessmen were coming from Scotland and Germany, as well as from England.

There was August Belmont, representative of the House of Rothschild, who was powerful enough to have his own company rather than operate as a branch of the European financiers. Belmont, who was born in Germany in 1816, had somehow entered the employ of the Rothschilds. In 1837 he was assigned to Cuba, but quickly took off for New York when he heard of the Panic. A recession was a good time to make a killing by buying securities in a depressed market. He helped negotiate a loan for the United States Government from Rothschild and was soon setting fashions for the upper social strata. Perhaps that was necessary, for businessmen were still crude: Astor, for example, could remove the chewing tobacco from his mouth before a visitor to draw designs with it on a window. Belmont's financial skills won an appointment for him as consul-general to Austria in 1844. His dueling scar became a mark of social distinction. Belmont's .greatest achievement was an invitation to the Union Club three weeks before his marriage. When he finally said hello to Joseph Seligman, another banker, the latter knew he had arrived.

There were other businessmen. Moses Taylor, the son of an Astor agent, started in the Cuban trade and wound up as head of the City Bank. Junius Spencer Morgan came to learn the banking business; Rowland Macy laid the groundwork for a large mercantile enterprise; Jonathan Goodhue, helped by his contacts in Massachusetts business and social circles, built up a major commission house; Seth Low moved his China-trade enterprise from Salem to New York, built fast ships, and waxed rich on the profits. Low's grandson and namesake became president of Columbia University and mayor of New York.

There were not many college graduates among these businessmen. Some attained wealth and prosperity through the proverbial school of hard knocks, but the usual road to success was through inheritance and a good marriage. Many of those who had arrived moved into New York's fashionable First Ward, which overlooked Bowling Green and the harbor. Many went into real estate, avoiding the scramble for money: they became four-per-cent-coupon clippers and consumed enough fancy wines to keep the ships from France well loaded.

Boston was trying to keep pace with New York, but once in second place it stayed there. The Hub City, however, did become a financial center for New England manufacturing: its banks successfully withstood the Panic of 1837. It might have had its Emerson, Longfellow, and Thoreau, and businessmen in publishing might issue their works, but Boston was primarily a commercial city, whose merchants were not interested in proposals for reform. While shipping was still a mainstay of business, the merchants began hesitantly to move into railroads. Textile men were interested in railroads that could service their mills; the merchants had visions of tapping the hinterlands as far away as the Great Lakes. The early railroads pushed out of Boston north to Lowell, south to Providence, and westward to Worcester. Some businessmen even screwed up their courage to the point of investing in railroads as remote as the Attica and Buffalo and the Philadelphia and Reading. But it was all done to protect existing investments in trade and manufacturing; it was not a case of supporting a bold new innovation.

Packet lines began to cross the ocean; when Samuel Cunard of England decided to dock his ships in Boston rather than in another port, the city was so overjoyed that it gave them free use of its facilities. Merchants still followed the Colonial custom of meeting at one o'clock to talk business and world affairs and then repairing to their homes at three o'clock for dinner. An exchange building was constructed in 1842 so that conversation could be carried on out of the rain. Fashionable Boston began to occupy Beacon Hill with homes that followed the designs of Charles Bullfinch, a noted architect of the time. They built country places in Nahant or Swampscott. Merchants were still at the top of the heap, although manufacturers were beginning to claw their way up.

Developments in business and economic life required an expansion of transport facilities; according to some it may have been the other way around. In any case, this was an era in which canals were built and the railroads started. The canal mania went back at least to 1792, when a company was organized to dig a canal between the Susquehanna and Schuylkill Rivers. Only a thousand shares were offered for sale, but the demand was for five times that number. General Schuyler organized a company to build a waterway from Schenectady to Lake Ontario. Yet, in the main, the canals had to be built by state and local governments, with a small admixture of private investment. Such ventures as the Delaware and Hudson Canal were exceptions: the Delaware and Hudson ran between established population centers, so its promise of profit was great.

By 1808 considerable agitation had developed in New York for connecting Lake Erie and the Hudson River. The movement was led by Gouverneur Morris, whose extensive land holdings along the route would rise sharply in value. Stockholders of the defunct Western Inland Navigation Company entered the scene in the hope that the state would compensate them for earlier losses. The vision of bringing the Atlantic Ocean and the Great Lakes together was irresistible. Moreover, such a canal would undercut Canadian business rivals in reaching to the hinterland of the West.

Advocates dug into the archives for favorable statements by Cadwallader Colden and Elknah Watson, popular writers of the previous century. Like Gouverneur Morris, anyone who owned land in the Mohawk Valley dreamed of making a fat killing. Some surveys were made, and there were many arguments for a Hudson–Lake Ontario route and many for a canal separated from natural waterways. But it was the movement of population westward through one of the few easy overland routes that brought the greatest pressure: by the first three decades of the eighteenth century, over 700,000 persons had pushed their way into the Genesee and Seneca regions.

DeWitt Clinton discovered in the canal an issue that might restore his political fortunes: he had been beaten by Tammany, and the canal was a popular idea. And so the Erie was started in 1817, with New York State a heavy financial participant. It took eight years to build: in 1825 Clinton, now governor of the state, poured a keg of Lake Erie's water into New York Bay and a thin four-foot ditch helped open the West. The flour industry shifted westward; thousands of immigrants used the canal as a passageway to virgin lands; and tons of farm produce found a cheap and relatively faster route eastward. New York City, already first among the nation's ports, became firmly entrenched in that position. The canal had cost $7,000,000, an incredible sum supplied by the state, and its very existence was a rebuke to the Federal Government, which had refused to back the project in any way at all.

Money for most canals came from state and local government sources. The British example, in which private enterprise built canals, had been an exhilarating one; but in Britain the market was compact enough to make such efforts profitable. The situation was much different here. The technical problems were more severe: where to place locks, where to obtain water, and how to prevent leakage and siltage were serious matters. Besides, America was a land of greater distances, higher mountains, rougher climates, sparser population, and scarcer labor. Under such circumstances, development depended on government. Half the investment in canals prior to the Civil War came from state governments: the private share was only about a fourth. By 1840 there were some three thousand miles of canals, but now the railroad was coming into existence, and it was to be a most formidable rival.

Pennsylvania was determined to catch up with New York, but it had no comparably level route. The Allegheny Mountains were in the way; yet they were conquered with a combined canal and rail system that cost $12,000,000, was 395 miles long (of which 118 miles were in railroads), and which at its peak rose to a height of 2,300 feet. Half the cost was paid by Philadelphia, Pittsburgh, and Allegheny County. While the canal-rail system contributed to the industrial development of the state, it could never really compete with the Erie.

Some of New Jersey's canals were built with private funds, but here canal-building was all wrapped up in devious politics. The Morris Canal in that state was really a banking company with its main offices in New York City. Within two years of its formation in 1825, four of the firm's directors were indicted for fraud in connection with manipulating the company's stock. Besides, New Jersey's concentrated population implied a greater prospect for gain. It was another case of private enterprise seeking a riskless venture.

Most persons think of Robert Fulton as the inventor of the steamboat, but he was no more responsible for it than Henry Ford was for the internal combustion engine. Fulton was not the first to build such a ship, nor did he invent the engine or paddle. He did calculate more accurately than others water resistance, the angle of the paddle wheel, and the size of the engine that would be most useful. His *Clermont* was a poorly designed affair as it chugged up the Hudson River, but it did better than most of its rivals. Having successfully combined the work of others, Fulton was astute enough to try to monopolize steam transportation on waterways.

Fulton had been a pamphleteer and promoter, traveling between America and Britain seeking to promote canals, and at one point, a submarine torpedo. He thought that canals ought to be small, handling small boats, to circumvent the need for big and costly locks. He tried to convince the French Revolutionary Government that canals such as he advocated would bring it all the revenue it needed. He promised also that his submarine torpedo would destroy the British Navy. Failing to sell these projects to the French, he then offered to organize a private company to wage war on the enemy Navy, payment to be made for each ship sunk.

He returned to the United States to tinker with his steamboat, borrowing most of his ideas from John Fitch and James Rumsey. At this point, Fulton's luck soared: he secured the interest of Robert R. Livingston, the U. S. minister to France, who had acquired Fitch's rights. But John Stevens and Nicholas Roosevelt were also working on the steamboat idea. When Fulton's *Clermont* steamed upriver, it meant monopoly rights on the Hudson River and in New York Bay for him and Livingston, and threatened to freeze out Stevens. In any case, that is what Fulton's New York charter said: the monopoly was his. Stevens did not take this idly: he fought back, and the Fulton monopoly was finally declared unconstitutional by Chief Justice Marshall in *Gibbons v. Ogden*. Interestingly, Fulton was in his early years a determined opponent of monopoly created by the state, but he did not mind having exclusive rights to ply the Hudson with his steamboat: that one surmises, must have been a just reward for industry.

Meanwhile, the use of the steamboat spread to western waters. A high-pressure engine devised by Oliver Evans, an ingenious inventor whose flour mills used no hands, was more effective for river transport than the low-pressure engine employed by Fulton. Evan's engine was lighter and easier to repair but liable to blow itself up, along with the passengers. Accidents were frequent, caused mainly by incompetence and a desire to race one's rivals down the river. It was said that owners preferred Irishmen to slaves as firemen, because this meant that there was no financial loss when the ship blew up. Needless to say, ship-repair services proliferated. James P. Allaire took over the old Fulton works around 1815 and by the eighteen-thirties was building engines and boilers out of Corlears Hook in New York. By the middle of the century his Novelty Works stretched from Twelfth Street to Fourteenth Street, with over eleven hundred employees.

The *Sirius* and the *Great Western,* which crossed the Atlantic in 1838, were not the first steamboats to do so. Twenty years earlier a combined rigger and steamer had crossed to Liverpool in twenty-seven days. Steamers were first tested on coastal runs and then sent across the ocean. Once again Government came to help out: the mail subsidies began. In the eighteen-forties the U. S. Mail Steamship Company had a subsidy of $200,000 a year to carry the mails to the Atlantic side of the Panama Isthmus, while the Pacific Mail Steamship Company received about the same to serve the far side.

Soon John Stevens, a Hoboken speculator and banker, advised the New Jersey authorities that railroads had a bright future as a mode of transportation. He appealed to Congress for support, asserting that railroads would bind the nation more tightly than canals ever could. The South hastened to create a road: the South Carolina Canal and Railroad Company. Majority opinion, however, held that the railroad could never be more than a supplement to a great canal system. The early railroads were looked upon with some skepticism: they were limited in value; they were too crude and too dangerous to both cattle and homes. The canal people sneered that the railroad would never be a match for the canals. Even railroad officials were dubious of their prospects: they thought only to carry passengers and provide a feeder service to the canals.

But by the eighteen-forties all doubts were dispelled. The railroads, assisted by Government grants, kept developing, and with better technology and some four thousand miles of track in the East, they began to cross the Appalachians. The roads pushed into virgin lands in the hope that population would follow. Technology was still as slovenly as in water transport, despite improvements. True, the edgerail was devised: the flange was placed on the wheel rather than on the rail and roadbeds were a little better. Generally, though, there was little concern for the passenger, who was apt to be impaled by a "snakehead," a section of track curling through a carriage. The curves were often too sharp to hold the train on the track, which was generally poorly graded to begin with, and roadbeds were carelessly made. When English locomotives were imported, the railroad companies were dismayed to discover that they were too heavy and too sturdy: bridges collapsed under their weight. American builders were not concerned with durability, for another track could be laid or another locomotive built to replace the one that had blown up. Fortunately, advances in construction and design were forthcoming, so that with the cowcatcher it was the cow rather than the train that was derailed.

Communities fought to attract railroads, even though they were apt to start nowhere and go nowhere. Private capital was hardly sufficient to build the roads, and subsidies and other forms of aid were solicited from Federal, state and local governments. With such assistance it was not hard to become a railroad magnate. In fact, communities were induced to compete in extending financial aid, on the theory that theirs might be the town to become the terminus. By 1836, state aid to the railroads came to almost $40,000,000. Mail contracts were made available in 1834. While John Quincy Adams was wielding a spade to start the Chesapeake and Ohio, the first rail was being laid for the Baltimore and Ohio.

The Baltimore and Ohio had at first used horse-drawn cars to get to Ellicott's Mills in nearby Baltimore. Peter Cooper then proved to the Baltimore and Ohio that a steam engine could pull a car. By 1831 the Baltimore and Ohio had reached Harper's Ferry and had gone south to Washington. Ten years later it was in Cumberland, Maryland. In 1830, the first locomotive built for sale in the United States hauled passengers from Charleston to Hamburg on the South Carolina Canal and Railroad line. The Boston and Worcester, assisted by $5,000,000 in financing from the Commonwealth of Massachusetts, moved toward the New York State border. The Mohawk and Hudson, between Albany and Schenectady, became the first link in what was to become the New York Central. In 1840, twenty-two of the twenty-six states had some trackage. By mid-century, railroading had become big business.

The career of Erastus Corning is a striking illustration of the manner in which antebellum merchants became railroaders. Born in 1794, Corning lived seventy-eight years, spanning business history up to the age of the corporations. When he was thirteen, he went to work for a hardware merchant in Troy, New York, meanwhile carrying on a side venture selling whips and other items to save up for his own store. Such ambition was not unknown in those days. In 1814 he did manage to acquire a hardware store in Albany. As he prospered, Corning began to manufacture nails (initially to supply his store), speculated in land, helped form banks, and finally got into the railroad business. Knowing the connection between business and politics, he ran for Congress as a Jacksonian and was elected.

By the eighteen-sixties Corning's Albany Iron Works consisted of three rolling mills, an axle factory, and factories for spikes and nails. There were the usual patent battles with rivals over the right to use rail and spike-making equipment, but as often as not, Corning won out in the courts. Mainly to insure a market for his spikes, he began to buy into the small railroad companies that were proliferating in upstate New York. One way of guaranteeing the necessary contracts for spikes was to gain control of the purchasing company; for this, Corning quickly discovered that proxies were necessary. The result was an intimate relationship between Corning, the railroad man, and Corning, the iron manufacturer. There was much profit, for example, when the Utica and Schenectady replaced its rails at an expenditure of over a million dollars.

Working capital was no problem for Corning since he controlled the Albany City Bank, one of the state banks that emerged under Jackson's system of "pet" banks. Land holdings provided coal supplies that went to the Utica and Schenectady Railroad and to the Albany Iron Works at a small markup over cost. Hence Corning's roads and plants could show a smaller operating expense than could rival lines. Efficiency was more a matter of market advantage than of productive skills. These activities demonstrated that the Jacksonian businessman was as hungry for profit as had been his Federalist forebears. Agrarians and artisans were left behind, as in the past.

Corning's peak achievement was the creation in 1853 of the New York Central, running from Albany to Buffalo. As the various local lines were merged, the capitalization reached $23,000,000, making the Central the largest corporation in America. Operating problems were minimized, inasmuch as most of the lines between Albany and Buffalo were already cooperating on passenger service and prorating fares. There were ten railroads in the merged organization, two of them on paper, as the lines had not yet been built. The merger seemed logical enough, for the region was suffering from keen competition for western traffic offered by the Pennsylvania and Baltimore and Ohio lines. In the exchange of securities creating Corning's merger, stockholders were given a premium, consisting of thirty-year 6-per-cent bonds of the New York Central that ranged from 17 per cent to 55 per cent of the value of the original holdings.

This "profit" on the deal represented nothing but water and in effect mortgaged the future income of the Central. Variations of this technique were to appear again and again in American business history. Corning's premium amounted to $77,500. As Central's stock rose some 70 per cent above par on the exchange, another $70,000 was added to his gain. In addition, he made certain that most of Central's iron contracts went to his works. In the next year and a half the railroad spent over $1,000,000 on new rails. Corning then sold several parcels of land to Central for $250 an acre, a rather exorbitant price at the time. To be sure, there were objections to practices of this sort within the company, but Corning ruled with an iron hand, displacing any board director who opposed him. Later on, however, his astuteness abandoned him: he allowed Cornelius Vanderbilt to pry him loose from control of the New York Central. By that time Corning was well on in years and ready to enjoy an opulent retirement.

The sea continued to attract the more adventurous entrepreneur. The whaling industry, with centers in New Bedford and Nantucket, reached its heyday in the eighteen-forties. New Bedford merchants possessed a particularly good harbor with good rail connections to the hinterland. When whaling gave out, the businessmen could shift to cotton mills. But the pursuit of whale oil was a cruel and ruthless affair. The usual mode of operation allowed a shipowner to exploit his own men. Whaling soon became a disreputable business, and few regular seamen were willing to step aboard a whaler. When the cargo finally arrived, after two or three years at sea, the owner was likely to set the price far below the going market rate so that a seaman's share might be reduced to the lowest possible amount. Deductions were made for outfitting the men, who were also charged interest and the cost of insurance, and for a mysterious item called "leakage." A whaleman might even be charged for the casks used to store the sperm or whale oil. Only an innocent farm boy looking for excitement, an immigrant, a millhand wanting to escape the factory, or a fugitive from justice would sign on for whalers, which became known as hellholes and death ships. Desertions were frequent, and many a whaler became a beachcomber on a Pacific isle, never to return to civilization. Some owners even pretended to prepare for a whaling trip when they were really planning to go slave-trading. The business became a system of peonage that fortunately ended when the ship finally came home.

A burgeoning economy needed manpower, and the supply was always limited. Attempts were made to overcome so serious a handicap through encouraging immigration. In the early days, however, the flow of immigrants was catch-as-catch-can. Agents roamed Europe to persuade people to come to the Land of Golden Avenues, and they often perpetrated outright fraud by absconding with payments for passage entrusted to them by prospective migrants. Then came the movement of tens of thousands of English, Irish, and Germans; the business of getting immigrants across the Atlantic was organized with true entrepreneurial spirit. Francis Thompson and William F. Harnden (who later set up an express service) began to contract with shipowners to fill the space below deck with human cargo. Thompson even acquired an immigrant line of his own. The expectant newcomers were crowded together, as many as the hold could take, and given bread and salt meat for the long voyage to America. As no fires were allowed, it became a choice between eating uncooked food and going hungry for the duration. The ships carried few lifeboats, so an accident became a disaster. A more prevalent danger was an epidemic of typhus, or some other disease, on board. Port facilities at the point of arrival were incredibly bad. It was not until 1890 that the Federal Government took control of ports of entry for immigrants, improving conditions somewhat.

Although most immigrants passed into the mainstream of American labor, digging ditches, building homes, living in city slums, and suffering the problems of adjustment to a new continent, some quickly learned the ways of business. Joseph Seligman came in 1837, and his brothers followed within a short time. Starting as peddlers, they acquired a small shop in Lancaster, Pennsylvania, and then went south to sell to the planters. They branched out across the country, going as far as San Francisco. When Jesse Seligman arrived in that California city in 1850, he was able to sell his stock of tin pans, blankets, and whiskey to the gold-crazed citizenry for enormous prices. Soon he had a brick building for his enterprise; when a fire broke out in 1851, devastating the city, Jesse saw to it that a fire brigade and the staff of a nearby brothel went to work to save his emporium.

Manufacturing began to be important enough to threaten the merchants' primacy of place. There is no doubt that cotton textiles were an important starting point. The need for cloth had impelled Americans to try hemp, flax, wool, silk, and cotton. Technology, however, had not yet been developed to a level that could supply a mass market. To be sure, Samuel Slater's mill, built in 1789, was adopting English techniques, but the long-staple cotton that could be used most effectively had to be imported. The cotton grown in the South was suitable only for coarse materials, as the bolls could be cleaned neither properly nor quickly. Southern planters were eager to produce cotton for the new mills up north; however, they were able to supply only the rough green-seed variety. A few cleaning gins were around, but these did not effectively separate the seed from the fiber. Cotton seemed to be a costly and unprofitable business.

A young teacher, Eli Whitney, encountered the problem of ginning cotton in 1793 while serving as a tutor for the family of a Major Dupont in Georgia. Within ten days he had constructed a model of a machine that he claimed would clean ten times as much cotton in one day as a man could. The machine fulfilled Whitney's hopes: it really worked and, in the event, made cotton king in the South and slavery a profitable endeavor. The gin contained wire teeth on a roller that tore the cotton from the seeds, which then fell into a hopper. A brush cleaned the cotton off the teeth, ready for stuffing into a bale. Whitney returned to the North to obtain a patent, but his invention was freely pirated all over the South. Whitney fought for his rights, and the users fought back. Finally, South Carolina thought to pay him fifty thousand dollars. In 1812 Congress refused to renew the patent. In 1806, when Whitney finally obtained a judgment in Georgia for two thousand dollars, cotton production had zoomed to 167,000 bales, as compared to 6,000 bales before the gin had been invented. Whitney returned to New Haven to resume toolmaking: after the Revolution he had constructed equipment for the manufacture of hatpins. By 1798 Whitney was close to bankruptcy, but the Government came to his rescue, and thereby hangs the tale of one of the great myths of American history.

The development of interchangeable parts in manufacturing, generally attributed to Whitney, was no doubt a significant contribution. Interchangeability is in effect a substitution of the machine for human skill: it breaks down the manufacture of an article into its component parts, which may then be independently mass-produced. The item—in Whitney's case, a gun—consequently could be easily assembled. In 1798, in dire need of working capital, Whitney offered to manufacture ten thousand muskets in two years for the Government for a sum of $134,000. France was threatening war, and the country was virtually unarmed. Whitney's proposal to mass-produce arms quickly seemed a godsend. But he could not deliver. He had insured his contract in 1801 by demonstrating to President Adams and his cabinet how muskets could be assembled with interchangeable parts. Yet the fact is that the French had developed the principle of interchangeability before Whitney, and it was being employed in both the Springfield and Harper's Ferry armories.

Whitney did not deliver, and the ever optimistic Tench Coxe doubted that he could. It took Whitney ten years to fulfill his first contract, which simply gave him enough credit to save his enterprise. Whitney's struggle over the cotton-gin rights had been costly, and he was at his wit's end. When he agreed to deliver the first stand of four thousand muskets to the

Government he had not even a factory! In fact, he did not know how to make guns. Perhaps that is why he remained behind schedule and was perpetually obligated to the Government. Moreover, from 1801 to 1806 he was too busy trying to secure reimbursement for his cotton gin to bother about guns.

Part of the legend of Whitney's interchangeability evidently stems from the assertion that skilled gunmakers were lacking. That too is a myth. From 1795 to 1801 the Springfield Armory produced some sixteen thousand guns with about seventy-five skilled workers, and through the years it was able to expand its work force without difficulty. The greatest likelihood is that Whitney got the idea of interchangeability from Jefferson, or simply borrowed the technique from the Springfield Armory, where it was being developed, as it was also Harper's Ferry. While output was growing at both places, Whitney produced only promises. The principle of interchangeability stemmed in all probability mainly from the work of John Hall and Elisha King Root at Harper's Ferry.

Samuel Colt was another gunmaker, but the record suggests that his was a major contribution. Colt was born in Hartford, Connecticut, in 1814. He was a strong-willed lad, with a flair for guns and chemistry, whose pyrotechnics got him expelled from Amherst College. He went to sea in 1830, and evidently the turning of the ship's wheel gave him the idea for a revolving barrel. He began to whittle models of gun cylinders out of wood and then abandoned the sea, which he disliked intensely. Later he would concoct devices to blow up ships. Work in a side show enabled him to save enough money to build a functioning model of his gun and persuade several New Jersey capitalists to form a company to manufacture it. However, no amount of salesmanship, charm, and wine could sway Congress to approve a contract for the new firearms.

Somehow Colt's guns got to Florida, where they were used against the Seminoles, and to the Texas Rangers, who really needed a repeating firearm. Just how the gun got to Texas is unknown, but the Rangers suggested that it be made strong enough to be used as a club when emptied. Colt's gun was apparently first used against the Indians in the Battle of the Pedernales, and from then on there was no question who would win the War of the Plains. This ought to have meant a fortune for Colt, but in 1842 his plant went bankrupt, the patents were sold, and Colt was a ruined man. He then experimented with a time bomb; again he could not arouse the Government's interest. There was really no market for the Colt: the main body of the frontier was still in the timber, not on the plains. When Texas began to quarrel with Mexico in the late eighteen-forties, there was a sudden demand for Colts, but none were being manufactured. The Texas Rangers offered Colt a contract for 28,000 pistols; he had them made by the Whitney shops in Connecticut, and while he lost three thousand dollars on the first order, he could consider himself a millionaire a few years later. He built special machines and opened his own shop. Hearing that Elisha King Root knew all about interchangeability, Colt hired him away from the Collins Brothers' axe factory in 1849. Seven years later the Colt factory had 400 machines in an area of 125,000 square feet. It was able to produce 25,000 pistols a year by combining various manufacturing techniques developed by Root and other master machinists.

Some of the major sources of American manufacturing could be located in the textile industry. Its main development began when Moses Brown decided to employ a young immigrant, Samuel Slater, late of England. Slater, who had worked in English textile mills, left for America in 1789 ostensibly as a farmer, in order to evade English regulations against the migration of technicians. He went to work for the New York Manufacturing Society, but, appalled by its incompetence, he wrote to Brown asserting that he could build machines to spin yarn.

His claim was well founded, as Brown discovered, for Slater was a mechanical genius who could duplicate from memory Arkwright's textile machinery. Brown offered Slater a share of the profit if he could indeed build the machines. Not that manufacturing was lacking: Christopher Tully had a Hargreaves jenny in Philadelphia as early as 1775, and there was an Arkwright frame with twenty-two spindles in Providence. But Slater was more successful than the others in copying the Arkwright design, and in all probability was a better mechanic than they. In 1790 Slater and Brown had a mill with seventy-two frames, and three years later they opened another factory in Pawtucket. Within a decade or so, Slater and Brown were training mechanics from an area thirty miles around Providence. Small streams were harnessed to turn the wheels and drive the frames. Factory towns began to crop up, dominated by a kind of extended family group in which the most experienced member was the man in charge.

But business was business. Slater's share in the first partnership had been quite small. When it prospered, his partners decided to set up another competitive mill. Slater then got some other partners to establish a third one. The number of plants increased, all serving to meet an expanding demand for cloth. Textile printing became an important activity with the growth of the Borden-Durfee interests. Most of the Bordens married cousins to keep the business inside the family. When corporate structures were adopted by such family enterprises, the transition to the broader impersonal forms of business was eased.

In 1814 Francis Cabot Lowell began to shift his interests from shipping to manufacturing. A paper mill in Waltham, Massachusetts, was one of the first of his many successful ventures. By 1822, his Boston Manufacturing Company was successful enough to pay dividends of 100 per cent on the original investment.

John Amory Lowell was not only a leading merchant and banker, but also treasurer of four cotton mills, member of the Harvard Corporation, and sole trustee of the Lowell Institute. As a scion of an important family, he was able to live in the president's house while a student at Harvard, and at twenty-four he was director of the Suffolk Bank. When a new plant was started at Chelmsford, the town was renamed Lowell, so important had the family become. A new kind of factory town evolved: instead of drawing workers from nearby farm families, the owners built dormitories and recruited workers from as far away as New Hampshire. They wanted to employ mainly young girls anxious to supplement the family income, thereby creating a work force without roots in the community and easily controlled by the factory superintendents. Capitalists set up whole new towns, complete with banks, real-estate offices, and even railroads.

After these initial developments came the Appletons and the Lawrences. Nathan Appleton and Abbott Lawrence began to build their mills in 1829, and by 1845 their efforts culminated in the town of Lawrence. By this time the character of the towns was undergoing marked change: American mill girls were being replaced by Irish and English immigrants who did not take kindly to the authoritarian ways of factory superintendents. The beginnings of industrial conflict had become evident. But the owners believed (and often still believe) that they knew best. When Humphreysville was established in 1806 near New Haven by an arch-Federalist, the founder thought that *his* plant would be free of the evils of industrialism. Most employees were unpaid apprentices and women who received wages of fifty cents to a dollar a week. This, Humphrey insisted, would rescue youth from poverty and a career of crime.

These experiences reflected a kind of halting thrust toward industrialism. Not only in industrial relations, but in techniques of manufacturing as well, the American fumbled his way forward. Capital accumulation had been no serious problem, for shipping and trade had supplied the wherewithal. But knowledge had to be smuggled in from England, and American efforts to copy the English were not always successful. The need for water power required location away from urban places, making the manpower problem a difficult one: not until immigration supplied a work force was industry able to develop the necessary basis for a take-off into full-fledged industrialism.

One development of great significance for a later era was the improvement in rubbermaking. Fascination with "India rubber" dated back to the white man's arrival in the New World. The Indians had learned to use latex, the milky fluid of the hevea tree, for various purposes, and by the early nineteenth century crude rubber shoes were being made from it. Commercial use began in 1791, when fabrics were waterproofed with a solution of rubber, and there were factories for manufacturing rubber articles in England and Scotland at the start of the nineteenth century. A rubber factory was established in Roxbury, Massachusetts, in 1833. By that time investment in the industry had grown to about $2,000,000, only to be virtually wiped out in the Panic of 1837. In any case, the industry could not produce an acceptable article made of rubber until Charles Goodyear began his experiments to obtain a strong, pliable product. His nitric acid process was a failure, as was his sulfur treatment, but one day in 1839 he accidentally dropped a piece of fabric containing rubber, sulfur, and white lead (which acted as an accelerator) onto a hot surface, and vulcanizing had been discovered. With the aid of William deForest, a woolen manufacturer who supplied the capital, Goodyear spent another five years perfecting the process.

The usual patent suits cropped up, especially in England, but Goodyear did manage to obtain a Scottish patent. He proselytized all sorts of uses for rubber; the major application, however, remained for boots and shoes. In 1840 several firms joined together as Goodyear Associates and Licensees to pool their royalties for prosecuting patent infringers. They also established prices, production quotas, and discounts. A tight control was maintained over the production of rubber footwear until the patents ran out in 1865. The case vindicated Adam Smith's suspicion that somehow free enterprise was transformed into monopoly.

Other energy sources besides water power were being made available. It is generally thought that oil refining began with E. L. Drake's oil well at Titusville, Pennsylvania, in 1859. But somewhat prior to that year a satisfactory illuminant known as kerosene had been developed by Dr. A. Gesner, and in 1853 there was a company in New York manufacturing the product. Gesner, a physician and chemist, had obtained a patent to distill gasoline and kerosene from asphalt rock. Whale oil had become too expensive, and other products were either dangerous or smelly. Kerosene gave a far better light and was much the cheapest illuminant available. It was sold by Gesner and his associates through the North American Gas Light Company for use in an Argand lamp or Vienna burner. But it was all a small effort compared to the future growth of petroleum products, and in 1875 Gesner's firm passed to the Standard Oil Company.

In the main, the basic elements of mass production were developing, especially in firearms, clocks, locks, and machine tools. Standardization and interchangeability were characterized by Europeans as the "American system." While borrowings from overseas were still quite frequent, independent improvements by Yankees were not uncommon. By the eighteen-fifties Americans were turning out agricultural equipment, firearms, and sewing machines. But they were all quite crude and lacked the finish that Europeans had come to expect in fabricated goods. Moreover, American products were not nearly as sturdy as those made by Europeans, giving rise to the habit of rapid obsolescence. Only in agricultural equipment did America lead the world. Often it became a matter of improving what had been started in Europe, a task that Americans could carry out successfully because they possessed a superior machine-tool industry. But in the main, American consumers preferred not to pay for quality when an article produced by mass production could be easily replaced. Mass production, based on large energy sources, seemed to be the American way. European visitors were quite certain that an American looked at Niagara Falls only to calculate the number of wheels it could turn.

Radical changes in business and in the economy were taking place. As population increased in the antebellum era, the problems of urbanization and sectionalism began to emerge. In 1840 about 250 immigrants a day came into the United States; a decade later the daily average was 1,000. The pursuit of happiness became a pursuit of money-making, justified by a philosophy of freedom. But the overt expressions were imperialism, greediness, and lawlessness. Under these conditions, Jefferson's ideal of an independent yeomanry could not survive. Businessmen became boosters, the forerunners of Rotary. And with boosterism came a greater ease in turning a profitable dollar. Enthusiasm, whether from products or places, became endemic. William B. Ogden was just as enthusiastic about Chicago in 1835 as he had been about New York in 1830. As the western city grew, he invested heavily in land, worked mightily to bring in railroads, and tried to entice industry. A city, said Ogden, had to attract people, and it could do that only with enthusiasm. Many a city was built that way.

The cotton gin made slavery in the South a permanent institution and cashcropping a way of life. And in the North advances in technology were changing the economy, with the capitalists as the chief beneficiaries. There were tinkerers aplenty; Fulton and Whitney were succeeded by Howe, McCormick, Goodyear, and Morse. But behind each inventor there stood a businessman with capital, ready to take a large share of the gain. Industry was burgeoning, and by the time of Lincoln's inauguration, capital in the North exceeded in total value that of all the farms in the United States.

CHAPTER 5   The Clash of Classes

With expansion came political tension. The fact that different sections of the country were growing at varying rates and in virtually opposite directions was bound to create the conditions for a civil war. The Democrats had dominated national politics for decades, appealing again and again with marked success to planters and farmers. Their planks expressed opposition to protective tariffs, to a public debt, to a national bank, to the support of internal improvements by the Federal Government, and to any interference with that peculiar institution, slavery. The Whigs might gain an occasional political victory, as in 1848; however, the party of Alexander Hamilton was not merely moribund—it was dead.

In the meantime, businessmen were redesigning the economic landscape to suit their own tastes, even while they pleaded with Government for subsidies, sound money, and the protective tariff. Moreover, they wanted friendly justices on the Supreme Court who would defend their conception of property rights. Of course, it was quite difficult to clearly demark the boundaries of economic and class interests. While cotton planters advocated a low tariff, or none at all, sugar growers, interested in insuring domestic markets, wanted a high one. Capitalists still engaged in shipping demanded subsidies, but they abhorred a tariff structure that threatened to interfere with the carrying trade. Yet tariffs had apparently not impeded the China trade that had started to flourish when the United States opened the Orient in 1840: it was soon to reach a volume of $9,000,000 a year. Some northerners had their investments below the Mason-Dixon line, and they were inclined to place their sympathies with their pocketbooks. Independent farmers wanted a liberal land policy, clashing with southern planters who looked upon free farming as a distinct threat. Southern delegations to Congress had killed a homestead bill in 1852, and eight years later were delighted to see President James Buchanan veto a similar bill that had passed both the House and the Senate. Meanwhile the union between East and West was being sustained by such slogans as "Vote Yourself a Farm— Vote Yourself a Tariff."

And so the politics of the middle period were muddied by the cross-currents of economic interests. Webster and Calhoun were clear and explicit in expressing the divergence of ideologies. When the Democrats were in power between 1830 and 1860, they were able to force tariff rates down fairly steadily, much to the chagrin of northerners. Southern writers depicted their own region as but an economic vassal of the North, and for all the evils of a wildcat banking system, both South and West stood four-square against a third national bank. By the time of the Civil War the disorderly monetary system was sustained by six hundred banks circulating over $200,000,000, in notes against an available specie of $88,000,000.

To be sure, there were careful bankers who handled their businesses conservatively, but the wildcatters cut corners with impunity, faking their reserves when inspectors appeared on the scene, and even lending one another specie in advance of an inspector's visit. Notes became "shin-plasters," selling for as low as five cents on the dollar, thus reflecting the low level of public confidence. Supreme Court decisions tended to favor the southern view, and under Roger Taney, the court moved steadily toward states' rights and state sovereignty. In banking, the court's views threatened to re-create the conditions prevailing under the Articles of Confederation. The conflict over land policy was especially troublesome: in essence, it revolved around the question of allowing slavery to penetrate the new territories of the West.

Henry Clay might come up with compromise after compromise, but these were sooner or later nullified by the pressures of economics and politics. Abolitionists, prodded by William Lloyd Garrison, might cry like Cato that slavery must be destroyed, but they were a small group, considered anathema by most proper citizens, North and South. For slavery was not the central issue of the day: abolition would have meant the destruction of millions of dollars in property, affecting all of the South and much of the North. This was unthinkable. The question was, rather, whether a new capitalist class would burst the bonds imposed on it by the planters. Such a situation was fraught with revolutionary implications.

The planters needed an adequate supply of labor—Negro labor. Some southern hotheads even flirted with the notion of annexing Cuba and Nicaragua to get more labor, as well, perhaps, as more land. In the main, the North could not forgive the South for its insistence on low tariff rates or for its opposition to a national bank. Continued Democratic domination of Congress suggested that the Constitution had been a slaveholder's document. When Wilmot proposed, in 1846, that slavery be excluded from any lands to be acquired from Mexico, he was voted down in Congress. Issues were discussed under conditions of extreme tension: the South once more began to talk of seceding.

The issues were inordinately complicated. While the tariff had driven South Carolina to the brink of rebellion long before 1860, the frequent compromises were, in the event, temporary stopgaps. Some northern merchants might side with southern planters if only to protect their lucrative shipping trade, and some manufacturers might feel safe despite low tariffs, because they had become efficient enough to compete with foreign goods. Cotton manufacturers knew that conflict would jeopardize their supplies of raw materials, and there was horrified opposition in the North to the notion of war. Yet the drift toward conflict seemed irrepressible, rooted as it was in tensions that were longstanding.

Both industry and business had grown rapidly enough to create a common interest between East and West in establishing a more favorable political climate. William Seward observed some years before the Civil War, with no little asperity, that the South had selected 30 out of 62 senators and 90 out of 233 representatives. The White House, he said, was apologizing for the slave-owners and all the important congressional committees were dominated by members from the South. Even the Supreme Court belonged to the South, and all the branches of the Federal Government were filled by southern jobholders. Compromise seemed to him fruitless, as he prophesied the coming conflagration. But in 1852 and 1856 the Democrats again swept the country. The Louisiana Territory was opened to slavery in 1854. The Dred Scott decision in 1857 affirmed the right of slaveholders to enter the new lands with their human chattel, and the tariff was once again reduced. In the decade from 1850 to 1860, it was patent that the United States was being run by the plantocracy. Even southern Whigs made a virtue of necessity and shifted to the Democrats.

When the Missouri Compromise was repealed in 1854, a group of men met in Ripon, Wisconsin, to form a new party. They included northern Whigs, Free Soilers, and those simply tired of planter domination. Calling themselves Republicans, they entered the name of John Fremont in the election of 1856. The Democrats surrendered completely to the planter faction, merely restating the views of that group in its platform. The old Whigs who cared not a whit about slavery and just wanted government aid for business, seemed trapped between the two parties. The noose was being drawn tighter and tighter. In 1860 the Democrats reaffirmed their position: the Federal Government was to do nothing about business, and the planters were to hold on to political power to prevent anything from being done. But planter intransigence was to split the Democrats, for the northern wing, led by Stephen Douglas, was not ready to surrender unconditionally to its southern cohorts. The Republicans were jubilant, and despite the formation of still another party, they felt they just might win. Abraham Lincoln became the Republican standard-bearer, and as he sat out the campaign in Springfield, Illinois, his fellow northerners depicted him as all things to all men. The subsequent events are well known. With Lincoln's election and the threatened loss of political power, the South decided to go it alone.

Slavery did not become a real issue until the war was well under way. There seems little question but that slavery flourished as an effective labor system right up to the war. At the same time it was a disaster as a social system. The Negro was outright property, lacking even the elementary personal protection that had been accorded by other slave societies to their victims. Southerners might argue that only Negroes could work under near-tropical conditions, but this was fallacious, for there was enough evidence to demonstrate that a white man could also work under the hot sun. After all, many southern farmers did not own slaves, and white indentured servants had worked the same fields before the slaves came. Slavery had become entrenched because it provided the lowest possible labor cost. But with the whole world beginning to look at slavery as a moral issue, the antebellum southerner found himself in a minority justifying his actions with a carefully concocted mythology. By 1830 slavery had become to the southerner a positive good, supported by the Bible and the subtle rationalizations of John C. Calhoun.

Most of the slaves were owned by the larger planters. The majority of the population in the South was comprised of small landowners tilling their own plots without the help of slaves. Less than 400,000 out of a total of 1,500,000 free families had slaves, and of these, 88 per cent had less than twenty. Almost 200,000 slaveholders had fewer than five slaves. The planter aristocracy was limited to about 10,000 families, each of which lived off the labor of fifty or more slaves. Despite their larger numbers, however, the small farmers took their lead from the plantocracy.

By the time of the Civil War, slaveholding was considerably more prevalent in the Deep South than in the Upper South. Plantations were operated as business enterprises. Most masters lived on the land, supervising their slaves and managing, with the help of overseers, an agricultural undertaking. If a rich planter were fortunate enough to have a capable foreman, the planter might even become an absentee owner. But wages and other rewards were generally inadequate to attract men of ability, so that masters had to remain on the plantation in most cases. Overseers usually designated one of the Negroes as a slave driver—a kind of sub-overseer. Specialization was used on the larger plantations, with specific tasks assigned to each slave. Some slaves became artisans skilled in an essential craft. Others became house servants, a notch above fieldhands. Cotton was, of course, the chief crop; of 2,500,000 slaves in the South in 1850, about 1,800,000 were engaged in cotton cultivation. But there were other crops as well: sugar, rice, tobacco, and hemp. Indigo had been abandoned shortly after the Revolution. There was some diversification, but this was to be found mainly in the smaller slave plantations.

The economics of slavery required that output be calculated according to fieldhands utilized; these numbered, of course, fewer than the total count of slaves. That is, some slaves were tallied as "half a fieldhand," or "a quarter hand": sick slaves and pregnant women were not full fieldhands. In 1860 about a million slaves worked in saw mills, quarries, fisheries, mining, and construction, and as deckhands on river boats. Some southerners dreamed of industry employing slaves, as in the Tredegar Iron Works in Richmond. The few slave-using textile mills in the South could produce only coarse grades of cloth. The hiring out of slaves by their owners did introduce a measure of flexibility into the work force, though the labor market could by no means be as mobile as that in a fully developed capitalist economy.

Throughout the plantation system, work was hard and the conditions severe, especially when the overseer's pay depended on the output of his gang. But the slaves were not always passive; there were many instances of resistance—often in the form of malingering or simply running away—and even of rebellion. As Kenneth Stampp has remarked, the slave was a troublesome property: tools were misused, and soldiering on the job was not uncommon. When something like Nat Turner's rebellion occurred, the whites in the South panicked, and repression was severe.

The planters operated on the theory that slaves had to be trained for servitude much as a dog needs training. Such conditioning was attained by inculcating a sense of inferiority and demonstrating the enormous power of the whites. By ruling every minute of a slave's life, the owner converted him into a completely dependent being. Recalcitrants were sold, or given the lash, or confined in a stock. The only restraint on a master's handling of his slaves was economic value. A maimed slave could be worthless.

As the plantation system moved deeper into the South, the older areas, such as Virginia, became exporters of slaves; there is evidence too that they also bred slaves like cattle. The fertility of Negro women could be a decided asset. John Armfield made a fortune trading slaves out of Alexandria, Virginia. The business was highly competitive and quite risky, as the demand for slaves was derived from demand for cotton, and cotton prices were set in the world market. On occasion slave traders might move into cotton planting. Although importing slaves was prohibited by a law passed in 1808, Federal enforcement was lax; in the eighteen-fifties, the illegal slave trade from Africa became brisk enough to constitute a virtual revival. The South wanted more labor, and it didn't care how it was secured. Moreover, additional slaves meant increased power in politics as five blacks were equivalent to three whites in apportioning House seats.

Was slavery profitable? Or was it so uneconomical that it would eventually have been abandoned? Granted, the plantation system was inefficient; yet if returns to planters had been low, why then a trend of rising prices on the slave market? The fact is that the slave system in the eighteen-fifties yielded enough surplus gain to show signs of growth and in 1860 slavery was still profitable. The rate of return in typical cases appears to have ranged from 4.5 to 6.5 per cent on investment, and on the better plantations the rate went as high as 12 per cent. Of course, profit depended on a variety of factors: land fertility, the availability of low-cost transportation for cotton, and the effect of the economies of large-scale production, especially on the larger plantations. To be sure, not all farms were efficiently operated, but the large slaveholders were always spearheading the adoption of improved methods of doing business. The southern entrepreneur had chosen slavery as an economic way of life; alternative opportunities which took capital out of the system would not have reduced rates of return much below 4.5 per cent. Moreover, the political underpinnings of the system had hardened, and it was unlikely that the southern planter would have wanted to shift his capital out of farming, even if he could have done so. It became evident that abolishing slavery would require armed force; this could be done only by a rising industrial class whose interests were inimical to those of the plantocracy.

Cotton production went from 167,000 bales in 1806 to 4,500,000 bales in 1859. The area of production moved from the Old South to Mississippi, Louisiana, and Texas. England became the South's best customer, with France, Germany, and the rest of Europe far behind. Prices, of course, were subject to world demand and given to periodic fluctuations. Marketing was done through factors, many of whom were located in the North, an old pattern of doing business. In time the factor came to dominate the cotton trade. He marketed the crop, acted as purchasing agent for the planter, and supplied financing. While he sold to whomever he wished, the risk was borne by the planter, who, ignorant of world market conditions, was neces-

sarily tied to the factor. But the planter was rarely unhappy with this de-
pendence; he fancied himself an aristocrat, not to be troubled by the mundane ways of business. Invested capital was relatively immobile, that is,
not apt to move easily into other endeavors, even if these were seemingly
more profitable than cotton.

Between 1815 and 1860 cotton had a marked influence on the American economy; it contributed to the growth of northern manufacturing, particularly of textiles, and by 1830 it was a major element in the export trade.
By 1849 almost two-thirds of the cotton crop went overseas, mainly to
England, which was getting 80 per cent of its supply from the South.
Clearly, the cotton economy was an important component of the capitalism
of the day.

But the South was not a bourgeois economy based on city life. There
were few cities there of any significance, aside from New Orleans, and that
city was unquestionably dependent on cotton. The South represented a
system of planter capitalism, rather, whose aristocrats and cavaliers looked
upon northerners as a gang of greedy money-grubbers lacking in charm,
grace, and culture. But the moral and political differences between the two
regions were rooted, in the last analysis, in diverging economic interests.

It might have been expected that the war would disrupt the North's
economy. At least, that is what southern rebels hoped it would do. But after
a slow start, the North became more active and more prosperous than ever
before. Keynesian conditions for growth were vindicated by war outlays long
before Keynes was born: the Government contract demonstrated its power
to create prosperity. The output from western farms and mines, and from
eastern factories, was extraordinary. In 1839 the new states of Indiana,
Illinois, Wisconsin, and Ohio had produced one-fourth of the wheat crop;
twenty years later their output was 138,000,000 bushels, or about half of
the total. The 1862 output from these states reached 177,000,000 bushels.
Efforts to produce cotton in the North failed, so wool became an acceptable
substitute. All this was accomplished despite the war's drain on manpower.
Agricultural implements, such as the reaper, were employed more and more,
and women and European immigrants replaced American men on the farm.
Land grants, which helped to subsidize the railroads, also aided colonization of the West. The major trunk lines—the Erie, the New York Central,
and the Pennsylvania—were pushing their way westward. Furthermore, the
disastrous wheat harvests in England from 1860 to 1862 generated a huge
overseas demand for American wheat. More than likely, the fact that
Britain's need for bread was more pressing than her need for cotton in-

hibited outright recognition of the Confederacy. Salt mines were discovered in Michigan, replacing lost sources in the South. Drake's oil well in Pennsylvania initiated the growth of a petroleum industry, as discovery of the Comstock Lode in the Sierra Nevadas and the Gregory Lode in Colorado helped add to the supply of gold and silver.

Even such poor investments as the Illinois Central Railroad and the Cleveland, Columbus and Cincinnati began to look more attractive as Government war contracts flowed to them. Chicago, a onetime swamp at the edge of Lake Michigan, boomed as the major point of convergence for western railroads. But the roads were still backward: gauges were not uniform, enforcing frequent changes by passengers; and many rivers could be crossed only by ferry, as bridges were lacking. Accidents were so frequent that critics charged the railroad companies with a greater concern for profits and riches than for people. The only source of heat in a passenger car was a wood stove, itself a major danger.

Meat packing moved to Chicago, and its slaughterhouses became a threat to the public health, with their boiling of bones and rendering of fat stinking up entire neighborhoods. The filth of the slaughterhouses filled the river and discomfited the populace.

Gains were made in every possible manner. Whiskey manufacturers, for example, whose product had always been a favorite target for taxation, had the tax removed from stock on hand, gaining enormous sums through the time-honored technique of corrupting legislators to achieve their aims. Woolens became a thriving business when cotton was no longer available for army uniforms. Nevertheless, during the war's first winter, the shortage of uniforms, blankets, and coats was severe. Any sort of cloth was used in any available color, causing Union soldiers to fire on each other on occasion. But profits were high: one manufacturer confided to the correspondent of the London *Economist* a few months after the start of the war that he had already made $200,000. Poor quality was endemic; the materials of the uniforms, rather than wool, was frequently "shoddy," a rag pulp pressed into a felt-like cloth that came apart in the field, leaving a soldier in his underwear. "Shoddy" became a synonym for cheating and corruption, and was applied to all Government contractors whose profits were too great to make them honest.

Munitions contractors often supplied to the Government useless or obsolescent equipment that was then junked. The average cost of a musket delivered by a private contractor ran to about $22, while Government arsenals could make the same product for half the price. A Philadelphia gun supplier made four thousand muskets, using many parts that had been previously rejected by Government inspectors. Marcellus Hartley admitted selling the Government a shipment of defective carbines. Such chicanery involved even the young J. P. Morgan, later to be known as "the Magnificent." It seems that a large number of Hall carbines declared in 1857 by the Government to be obsolete and unusable were still in an arsenal in New York when the war broke out. Arthur Eastman offered to buy them at $3.50 each, but lacking the money, he went to Simon Stevens, who then turned to Morgan.

Morgan took legal possession of the carbines as security for his loan. They were offered to General Fremont of the St. Louis department of the Army, and Fremont, in dire need of arms, accepted. The three businessmen—Eastman, Stevens and Morgan—paid the Government about $17,500 for the lot, which, after some alteration, was shipped to St. Louis at a price of $22 per carbine. A congressional committee declared the whole affair a swindle in 1862 and the Government refused to pay, whereupon Morgan and his friends sued for breach of contract. At this time Morgan's name, strangely, dropped out of the transaction, leading some historians to assert that he was really not involved. An adjudication commission appointed by the Secretary of War recommended settlement at $13.31 per carbine, but the vendors accepted the offer as partial payment only, demanding their full pound of flesh. The courts finally found for the Stevens-Morgan group, which realized a profit of over $95,000.

Some writers have suggested in exculpation, that Morgan did not know the carbines had been declared obsolete and no longer serviceable, that he only financed the transaction, and that, after all, there was nothing illegal about it. Even the most ardent defenders of the transaction have conceded that the Hall carbine would often explode the stock of the gun or shoot off a soldier's fingers. But Morgan did refuse to answer charges that he had gained from a tricky, though perfectly legal, operation. Others have called the story a legend, but to charge that the tale was resuscitated by "radical" writers for malicious reasons, as does one former Morgan partner, seems an easy escape from the pressures of history. (Further, "radical" writers such as Lewis Corey and Matthew Josephson, who tell the story in their books on Morgan, were quite fair in their recital of the facts.) The Hall carbine affair was no doubt a shrewd deal by Morgan and his associates; he was only twenty-five years old at the time.

Business was so good during the Civil War that manufacturers were declaring dividends of 30 per cent. By 1864 profits were averaging as much as 15 per cent on investments. The loss of the southern debt to the North, totaling about $300,000,000, was easily offset. Although the banking system had bordered once again on chaos, the National Banking Act, with all its deficiencies, brought about a measure of order. At least the state bank notes were driven out of circulation by the 10 per cent tax. Banks prospered as seldom before; the Chemical Bank of New York declared dividends of 24 per cent in each of the war years. Trade associations cropped up, sponsoring excursions and free railroad passes for businessmen, and incidentally suggesting price schedules to their members. Such suggestions were not binding, but price advances were always curiously uniform. Delegations of businessmen visited one another's cities with all the fanfare of reciprocal boosterism. One of the few casualties of the war was the shipping industry; Britain, quick to use steam to capture the transatlantic trade, gained a sizeable lead, and the Americans ran to Congress for subsidies. And while the war raged, those who were profiting from it enjoyed their gains at the theater and opera, and at Saratoga and Nahant and other watering places. Wartime prosperity created an orgy of extravagance—appeals for economy and plain living fell unheeded on the ears of the new rich.

In the meantime, the South was devastated. By the end of the war southern wealth had shrunk over 40 per cent. A large part of the decline stemmed from the collapse of land value in which so much capital had been tied up. The supply of livestock was seriously depleted, and the war played havoc with southern farming. Business institutions were in virtual decay. By 1865 the South had been set back to a mere subsistence level.

A major source of capital in the North stemmed from the earlier merchant and shipping activities in which entrepreneurs had operated chiefly as commission agents, placing their orders with independent producers who operated in their own cottages. Prior to the Civil War, centralized factories were a rarity; not until the eighteen-fifties when the domestic market began to burgeon, did the capitalist shift to factory methods of production. Mercantile pursuits were on the decline: the British had moved ahead in shipping, and the political domination of the country by the South meant few or no Government subsidies. Besides, better ways to earn a profit were opening up. Take-off conditions for economic growth developed just before and during the war. By 1865, there were flourishing industries in boots and shoes, textiles, clothing, and meats. In one sense, this represented increasing specialization. The general merchant was being replaced by the industrialist and the banker, the blacksmith by the manufacturer. Sometimes these were the same men, but most often it was a new generation that came forward to engage in new ways of doing business.

The industrial proletariat was not yet a significant factor; the kinship system in plants and the employment of farm girls inhibited its spread. Boots and shoes remained cottage industries right up to the time of the Civil War. Producers who owned their tools would obtain raw materials from the "manufacturer" and give him a finished product. Even meat-packing had been organized before the war on a kind of "domestic" basis. Thread was being turned by mills, but weaving was still done in the cottage. With the Civil War came more centralized production; armor plate, shells, and rails began to pour out of plants established in and around Pittsburgh.

Investors in this nascent industrialism were former merchants and shippers. Merchant families had once placed surplus funds into canals and turnpikes, so going outside their trade was not an unfamiliar pattern to them. John Murray Forbes, a foreign trader turned financier, brought Boston capital into the railroads. A new industrial class was in the making, displacing the older merchant-capitalist. The future belonged to the industrialist, and he wanted sound banking, an adequate supply of free labor, and a domestic market all to himself. To achieve these aims he had to break the power of the plantocracy, and he did so with history's first mass war.

There is no doubt that northern agricultural output was increased by such implements as Cyrus McCormick's reaper. There were many such devices available, but McCormick's machine was perhaps the most successful. Born in 1809 on a North Carolina farm, he found its chores quite distasteful, preferring to tinker with the tools that were around the barn. McCormick's father had attempted to build a reaper, but the task was completed by Cyrus. In 1832, he demonstrated the device to his neighbors. It was a technological success, but sold very slowly. McCormick decided to move to the West, where the prairie might make the machine more practicable. After trying out licensing arrangements with other manufacturers, he decided to make the machines himself, settling in Chicago in 1848. Turning for financing to Chicago's chief booster, William Ogden, he soon put up a factory. Shortly afterwards, McCormick bought out Ogden to go it alone. He could afford it; his reaper had been a major triumph.

McCormick was a merchandiser par excellence. He formed his own sales organization, guaranteed the reaper, and offered to sell it on installments. Exclusive agents were selected at key points throughout the marketing area—this was, in effect, the dealer system later employed by the automobile industry—and control of agents was just as tight under McCormick as it was to be under General Motors. He challenged builders of other reapers to field tests. It was like the automobile speed races of later years. Many of these contests offered entertainment to surrounding farmers, but sometimes they degenerated into roughhouse and violence. The inevitable patent suits occurred: when McCormick sought to obtain a renewal of his patents, he was charged with attempted bribery, which he vehemently denied. In any case, the reaper had become too valuable to be controlled by one man; his suit was denied by the courts.

There were many such machines around. No less than 167 harvesters and 62 mowing machines had been patented by 1851. McCormick's worked better than most and was marketed more aggressively. In fact, Obed Hussey's machine had the advantages of being sturdier and simpler, but it operated better as a mower than as a reaper. Hussey's major error was moving to Baltimore, while McCormick went West. We need not now concern ourselves with the conflicts McCormick had with his brothers and sisters over the business, and the story of International Harvester belongs to a later period, but we should note that while the reaper was also successful overseas, its greatest victory was on the American farm during wartime.

It was a time of innovation, not only in technology, but in ways of doing business. The sewing machine, a product really of several minds, is a case in point. Elias Howe, Isaac Singer, James Gibbs, and Allan Wilson had all contributed to the development of the sewing machine: in fact, its antecedents can be traced as far back as 1790. Howe had gained some experience in the manufacture of textile machinery and in instrument-making. When he came to building a sewing machine, he shifted the eye of the needle to the point, and moved the needle horizontally. Though this required holding the cloth vertically, the device worked. Unfortunately, most people looked upon it as but a toy. It was Isaac Singer and Edward Clark, his lawyer, who placed the sewing machine in the home. Singer, a restless, energetic machinist, made the needle move vertically, devised a "foot" to hold the cloth in place and a wheel feed to keep the cloth moving. Singer tried marketing his machine and was promptly sued by Howe for patent infringement. While Singer lost the suit, and had to pay royalties, Clark foresaw great possibilities. In contrast to Singer, Clark was quiet, yet shrewd: he did not hesitate to use installment selling. Curiously, of all the machines on the market, Howe's was by far the least efficient, but he held basic patents requiring other manuacturers to pay him royalties. His income was big enough to make him a millionaire. Soon Singer, Wilcox and Gibbs, Wheeler and Wilson, and Grover and Baker—all the leading makers— pooled their patents. By 1860 one machine was much like any other. Installment sales kept the Singer firm in the lead and enabled it to survive the panic of 1857. The company did well enough to enable Singer to indulge the pleasures that he could not afford earlier and to leave the business end to Clark.

The sewing machine was obviously important for the ready-to-wear clothing industry. That had started as far back as 1837, turning out cheap clothing for southern workers. Crisis and prosperity had always affected its growth, but it developed steadily in New York, Boston, Philadelphia, and Cincinnati. By the Civil War, it had recovered sufficiently from earlier vicissitudes to supply uniforms for the Union Army. Productivity increased sharply with the advent of the sewing machine. For example, a man's shirt, which had absorbed fourteen hours and twenty minutes of hand labor, could now be made in one hour and sixteen minutes. McKay's sewing machine, which facilitated the stitching of uppers to soles, moved the boot and shoe industry from the cottage to the factory. Several hundred pairs of shoes could be produced in a day, and a new factory industry, to be located in New England, was in formation. Leasing his machines, as well as manufacturing shoes himself, McKay was soon garnering an income of over $750,-000 a year.

The railroad, however, was perhaps the most important factor in American economic development.. Such a characterization is still valid, despite recent efforts in the scholarly literature to deprecate its contribution. One historian has suggested that America would have had substantially the same economic growth without railroads, relying only on waterways. His calculations, however, covered but a few years, revealing a "small social saving" generated by the railroads. Yet even if their direct contribution had been no more than 5 per cent of the gross national product over this period, it would have been significant. The full period of railroad growth actually covered decades, and its impact was incalculable. Railroads were responsible for some 15 per cent of capital formation from 1849 to 1858. They affected the construction, coal, and iron industries and contributed markedly to rapid geographic expansion. Transport costs were reduced, and without the kind of transportation supplied by the railroads American business and economic historians would have had a somewhat different tale to tell.

When it came to placing their investments in railroads, many of the early capitalists believed that a killing was in the offing. There were only a few who thought of long-term growth and investment. Much of the initial capital came from Boston capitalists such as Francis Cabot Lowell and Nathan Appleton, whose wealth had been acquired in overseas trade. They had been shifting their available funds into textiles. Often they thought of the railroad as a means of solving the transport problem for their mills.

Perhaps a more important source of capital was the younger group of capitalists, who had earned their spurs in the China trade. Using capital accumulated there, they were always on the lookout for new endeavors. One of them, John Murray Forbes, who had been in Canton on two occasions and returned to America to stay in 1833, became an important figure in both railroad and western-land development. In his China-trade affairs, Forbes had established close relationships with John Cushing, John Griswold, and William Appleton, among others. Financial connections had been established between these men and such financiers as Baring, Rothschild, Crommelin, and Berenberg. When the time came for Forbes to search out new capital, he already had access to important sources. As the Boston and Worcester Railroad began to show some returns, capitalists in Boston really became interested. In most instances, of course, the early railroad had to look to the state for aid. Early private investments were not reassuring, being mainly local, but such outlays did give the capitalist some experience.

The career of David A. Neal typified that of the capitalist of the time. He had been a seafaring merchant, and, once on land, he turned his interests to railroads. From Salem to Illinois, railroad development and land speculation were intertwined for Neal. Others attempted a more cautious approach—John Murray Forbes and John Bryant were good examples—but their involvement in railroad expansion inevitably carried them westward. Yet, caution aside, the attractions of the West could not be denied. The soil was rich enough to attract farmers and land speculation could bring all kinds of riches. The Lawrences, whose money was in textiles, began to invest in western lands; eventually, they acquired a considerable stake in the development of the West. The Western Land Company, organized in the eighteen-thirties by forty-three New England capitalists, developed ties with the Forbes group in Boston. Caleb Cushing and Robert Rantoul, Jr., placed some of their investments in Wisconsin timber lands. Western promoters sensed that the East could be a source of capital and were active in arousing the interest of Appleton, Cushing, Derby, and Forbes. John W. Brooks, originally from Stow, Massachusetts, did his utmost to involve capitalists in the Michigan Central Railroad, though he thought that such an investment might be risky. Forbes helped secure the Michigan Central charter and in time became quite optimistic about its prospects.

But having committed their capital, the Bostonians pressed for the sort of continuous development that would in time lead to the concept of a railroad system, rather than local, piecemeal lines. In the Illinois Central,

Federal land grants were used to advance development. There seemed to be an opportunity here to run a north-south line through Illinois, and then perhaps to New Orleans. Again, eastern capitalists who had been in the China trade were involved. Senator Stephen Douglas, who owned some land in areas through which the line would run, became interested, and fought in Washington for appropriate land grants, though later he was more circumspect. The land grants were to be used as securities for a bond issue, with management holding but a small equity. The gains were to be made from land speculation. Attempts to market the bonds overseas were unsuccessful at first: both the Barings and Rothschild were dubious. But instead of calling upon stockholders to complete their subscriptions, the railroad's management decided to borrow still more. Prospective settlers were coaxed to come; however, David Neal, delegated to sell the land parcels, used his inside information to buy up locations intended for depots, in some cases using company funds to purchase on his own account. By 1860, the Illinois Central had sold over a million acres, with many of the transactions processed by Neal through the Associates Land Company, which he used in effect as a third party to disguise a personal interest.

Of course, the major revolution in transportation came after the Civil War. Between 1865 and 1890, about seventy thousand miles of railroad were added in the West. The expansion was encouraged by the Federal Government and by local communities that were eager to have a railroad run on Main Street. There is no doubt that railroad development was haphazard. It was a situation in which stockholders and bondholders were often duped by promoters, in which the public domain was plundered for private interests, in which settlers were often defrauded. It seemed a huge economic waste, and there was some doubt that the game was worth the candle.

Monopoly power seemed to some operators the easiest way to profit. One case that backfiired involved the Camden and Amboy Railroad, which had obtained exclusive rights from the State of New Jersey to run a line from New York to Philadelphia. In fact, the charter guaranteed the railroad the absence of competition, in return for which the state was to receive ten cents for every passenger and fifteen cents for every ton of freight. The Camden and Amboy paid enough to cover the state's debt and expenses of government and still leave the railroad a surplus The arrangement clearly was of dubious legality, since it involved interstate commerce. New Jersey then allowed another line, based on a fusion of several small lines, to crop up, to which the Federal Government turned for transport needs during the war. The Camden and Amboy promptly had its new rival closed down by the state courts. It took an act of Congress to correct the situation; New Jersey protested that as a state it had its own rights and must be allowed to run its affairs in its own way.

Perhaps more significant was the impact of the railroads on the way business ran its internal affairs. The railroads represented America's first "big business." By 1860 there were thirty-one companies engaged in railroading. The problems of managing them were certainly unique at the time. First of all, relatively heavy investment was required; second, operations extended for hundreds of miles, creating enormous difficulties in supervising them. Inspection of even a short line could take several days; keeping check on freight cars to prevent jams along the line; scheduling runs back and forth on a single track; setting rates in a business with heavy fixed costs; carrying a great variety of goods; accounting for revenues—all required organizational skills that were substantially different from those needed in a textile mill. The scheduling problem disclosed itself quickly when the Western of Massachusetts suffered several catastrophic collisions in the eighteen-forties.

Overcoming these problems required a table of organization with decision-making power flowing from the president to the chief engineer or superintendent to divisional roadmaster and on down the line. Timetables were published; the Erie started to control train movements by telegraph; and finance and operational responsibilities were separated. Companies instituted regular daily reports for key officials. Modes of organization, of course, varied; the Pennsylvania and Erie utilized decentralized structures, while the New York Central insisted on centralized operations. Within thirty years the railroads began to move toward patterns that were to characterize the world of the future: the creation of private bureaucracies and a corps of professional managers.

Henry Varnum Poor became the philosopher of this movement. As editor of the *American Railroad Journal* from 1849 to 1862, and later as publisher of the *Manual of the Railroads,* he studied and wrote extensively about railroad construction, finance, operations, and administration. From 1845 to 1849 he had helped his brother build the Atlantic and St. Lawrence, connecting Portland and Montreal; he knew the business. For him the railroads were creative ventures and their growth a vindication of his faith. He popularized the mortgage bond as an instrument of financing, analyzed the conditions of the investment market, and urged bankers to participate more. A self-appointed salesman for the industry, he would also give advice on management problems, insisting that responsibility and accountability were central. In effect, he antedated the organizational theorists of modern times. Yet his call for open publicity on financing and management was not well received, either by Wall Street or by the railroad operators. They preferred the freebooting that was to prevail, especially in the postwar years. His was a voice crying in the wilderness.

And what a wilderness it was to become! The sort of men who were to seize control—Cornelius Vanderbilt, Jay Gould, Jim Fisk, James J. Hill, E. H. Harriman—could not have cared less about public reaction, so long as power and wealth were theirs. The railroad became the source of some of America's great fortunes, although some of the promoters were millionaires before they got to the nation's rail lines. Cornelius Vanderbilt fell into this category: having gathered enormous wealth in shipping, he shifted to railroads rather late in life. Using the same rough-and-tumble tactics in rails as he had used earlier, he earned for himself the label of "buccaneer."

Vanderbilt had started his business career as a ferry captain in New York. He had one passion: making money. Virtually illiterate, scarcely able to sign his own name, he cared little for books or the other accoutrements of learning. At best, he was able to scan the large print in newspaper headlines. But in business he had a native cunning suited to the times. Profane and pugnacious, he could hold his own in a brawl. Once, after quarreling with his wife over a new house, he simply put her away in an insane asylum. During the War of 1812—he was then eighteen years old—he secured a Government contract ferrying supplies to harbor forts in New York, and from this venture made enough to acquire several ships for the coastwise trade. But schooners, he reasoned, would soon be passé. He took a job with Aaron Gibbons, who was operating steamboats, in order to "larn bilers." Gibbons was fighting the Fulton-Livingston monopoly, and Vanderbilt had a great time outwitting the Fulton combine. Gibbons finally won in the Supreme Court; five years later Vanderbilt went into business for himself, plying the waters around New York. He soon bought out the first of his rivals, then cut rates on the Hudson River run and began his lifelong battle with Daniel Drew. Between 1829 and 1834, Vanderbilt's profits averaged about thirty thousand dollars a year; by the age of forty he had become a powerful shipping magnate.

Carrying passengers around Long Island Sound in competition with others meant speed and more speed, to a point that the boilers of the day could not take. The ships were driven mercilessly; often the safety valves were removed from the boilers, which then might blow up under the relentless pressure. Even "flying landings" were essayed: while the ship was edged to the wharf, it kept moving, forcing passengers to jump ashore. Unwanted baths were frequent. The business demanded cunning and chicanery, and in these Vanderbilt excelled. Although he always fought Drew, a sanctimonious hypocrite, the two men seemed to get along well outside of business. Vanderbilt evidently was contemptuous of Drew, priding himself on his ability to outwit his friend.

Vanderbilt would watch a rival build up a business and then attack him by every means he could, in order to destroy him or be bought off. It was a form of commercial blackmail, but perfectly legal. With the gold rush under way, he decided to capture a share of the Panama traffic. The Pacific Mail Steamship Company was charging six hundred dollars a round trip, with portage across the isthmus, but Vanderbilt knew he could save six hundred miles by cutting across Nicaragua. He put two small steamers on the San Juan River and a large one on the lake. He ran four ships on the Atlantic Ocean and five on the Pacific. When he sold out in 1853, he had been making a million dollars a year on the run. An attempt by the Nicaraguan Government to revoke Vanderbilt's charter only inspired him to organize an invasion to eject the Central American state's president, with the help of the United States Marines. While ostensibly competing with the E. K. Collins Company which had the mail subsidies for transatlantic runs, Vanderbilt made certain that he got a share of the Government monies. Threatening the Pacific Mail Steamship Company and the U. S. Mail Steamship Company with competition, he extracted $56,000 a month from them just to keep out.

In 1853, Vanderbilt took a trip to Europe, leaving his affairs in the hands of Charles Morgan. Upon returning he concluded that Morgan had not discharged his duties very well. Vanderbilt threatened to ruin him, and he did. As the Civil War approached—Vanderbilt was now almost seventy—he decided to sell out: after all, his ships might be endangered by Confederate privateers. He had one ship left, but it was tied up, and quite unprofitable. Vanderbilt "lent" it to the Government, and was promptly hailed as a great patriot. Much to his surprise and chagrin, Congress solemnly thanked him for the "gift" and kept the ship. He was now worth about $15,000,000.

The Federal Government in 1862 decided to send a military and naval force to New Orleans, and it turned to Vanderbilt to put together a transport fleet. He did so, but insisted that the suppliers go through one of his men and pay a 5 per cent commission. He charged exorbitant prices for ship rentals, often double what the Government had paid to charter the same ship earlier. Moreover, many of the ships were in poor condition and barely seaworthy. Ships with a capacity of three hundred passengers were crowded with nine hundred soldiers. His only punishment was a Senate resolution of censure; ultimately Vanderbilt saw to it that his name was expunged from the record. These were the methods by which he had accumulated capital that was shortly to be employed in railroads. At the age of seventy, Vanderbilt was on the verge of a new business career.

Of course, there were also some less flamboyant capitalists in those days. John P. Cushing exemplified a kind of quiet transition from mercantile capital to industrial capital. Another who had built a fortune in the China trade, he settled down in 1831 to enjoy life comfortably on his estate, with Chinese servants, a superb wine cellar, and an elegant garden. He started to invest first in banks, canals, and factories, and then in railroads. Capital had to be employed, for it was fungible and could bring returns. For this task he turned to his friend William Sturgis. Cushing became a rentier, supplying funds to a burgeoning industrial order. Although he was careful and essentially conservative in his investments, the growth of the nation was such that his wealth tripled during his retirement.

Wars require high finance, and for that the Federal Government turned to Jay Cooke. As a young man Cooke had worked for a Philadelphia private banker who dealt mainly in money exchange, lotteries, and stocks. The Mexican War took the firm into Government finance, providing Cooke with the experience he needed later. He was delighted with his cleverness in gulling the government in the Mexican War loans. When speculation in the eighteen-fifties caused difficulties for the firm, Cooke left to become a kind of consultant on his own, organizing canal companies and reorganizing railroads. When he set up a banking house in 1861, Cooke himself was the main asset. He was imaginative, optimistic and self-confident, and he was a man of principle, according to the standards of his time.

The successful sale of a $3,000,000 state loan impressed Washington favorably. Cooke helped his own cause by informing various newspapers, as well as the Secretary of the Treasury and the President of the Confederacy, of the state flotation. In the fall of 1861, the Secretary of the Treasury, who was having trouble selling Union notes and bonds, appointed Cooke, after some hesitation, as agent for a $50,000,000 loan. Cooke sold one-quarter of this first loan and deemed himself a success. Twice more the Government called on him for assistance. Each time he assured the Treasury that all efforts would be made to sell at par, but he was not always sucessful.

In order to draw money in from the capital market and from small lenders, Cooke employed as many as 2,500 agents, including banks and insurance companies. The public debt was described in advertising, posters, and handbills as a blessing; appeals were made to patriotism and purse. Not infrequently, buyers were given handsome discounts, providing them with future capital gains as well as interest. When the bonds were sold at par, payment was taken in greenbacks; the securities moved quickly after the fiat money had depreciated. Again, it was a kind of discount, for bond-holders were buying securities promising 6 per cent interest in gold, often at a 50 per cent discount, with repayments expected in gold.

In all, Cooke sold about $1,000,000,000 worth of bonds, from which his net commissions, after he paid his agents, came to about $715,000, even though the commissions were close to $3,000,000 a year. While the net earnings appeared small, Cooke benefited, as the balances owed to the Government provided him with working capital. Further, his prestige had been markedly enhanced, and he was able to establish a network of relation-ships with other banks that was quite important. The business earned enough from all sources during 1861–65 to enable it to pay out about $2,000,000 to the partners. The outcome was a system of mass distribution of securities that enabled the Government to reach large and small lenders.

Right from the start, the security business had given rise to the Stock Exchange, the inception of which could be traced to an agreement in 1792 by New York stock dealers setting rates of commission and outlawing the public auction. Securities then were mainly debt obligations and bank stocks, and the deals were local. A more formal organization was established in the years 1817–20. By this time insurance company stocks were added to the supply of securities. Speculative activity and attempted corners were fre-quent. New York State's effort to control short-selling failed. With industrials and railroads, the opportunity for manipulating the market became greater. The first real corner was evidently the one engineered by John Ward, Jacob Little, and Daniel Drew on the Morris Canal and Banking Company. The stock was quietly bought long at 30 to 40 below par and then unloaded at 150 for more than 300 per cent profit for the operators.

Little, a precursor of the Gilded Age, began to sell short in 1840 on Erie. An effort to trap him by raising the price failed, for in the meantime he had purchased Erie convertible bonds in the London market and was able to make delivery. Such practices brought the Stock Exchange into ill repute, but there was no regulatory agency to harness free unbridled enterprise, nor was one wanted. By 1848, with economic expansion and the discovery of gold, a new orgy of speculation developed. The supply of securities grew, and banks gave easy credit. Railroad stock was heavily watered; cases of phony stock were recorded. Alexander Kyle of the Harlem Railroad issued $300,000 of forged stock to line his own pockets; Edward Crane sold ten thousand shares of false Vermont Central shares, forcing the legislature to increase the rail-road's capitalization in order to save his victims; Robert Schuyler of the New

York, New Haven and Hartford sold $2,000,000 worth of unauthorized shares for his own benefit. Making money became an end in itself, and the method didn't matter. Borrowing money on call permitted speculators to buy on small margins, thus adding to the speculative frenzy. In fact, the practice precipitated the Panic of 1851 when a New York branch of a large insurance company called in loans it had extended to country banks on railroad collateral. When the collateral was sold to protect the lender, bankruptcies quickly followed. The system was not overhauled until the nineteen-thirties.

There seemed little doubt that the changes wrought by the Civil War constituted a second revolution in America. The political and economic shifts were too drastic to be characterized by any other term. New class alignments resulted; there were changes in patterns of wealth-holding; economic growth was stimulated; and the Federal Government was now controlled by the enemies of the plantocracy. If the fundamental antagonisms were sectional, that was an accident of history; the destiny of the nation was forecast by the changes revealed in the decennial census. That the North should have won the war now seems self-evident: virtually all heavy industry was in the North, as was two-thirds of the banking capital. Southerners believed that the North was dependent upon them; they were astounded by its prosperity. They fervently hoped that England would intervene on their side, but they did not count on wheat-crop failures in Europe. English observers were quick to recognize economic forces in a changing America. Said one during the early days of the conflict, "The Yankees are only fighting for the tariff and their hurt vanity." The major practical outcome of the war was the destruction of the political power of the planters. Northern capitalists emerged richer and more numerous than ever before: the war had provided a powerful fillip to economic growth. To be sure, cotton production had virtually ceased for the duration, and railroad expansion did slow down. But after the war, pig-iron production, the output of coal, and railroad trackage virtually doubled. The entire economy exploded after the Civil War, and it was a capitalist explosion.

The Emancipation Proclamation, issued by a reluctant President, "destroyed" the property of the slaveholders in the rebellious states. A few months before, in April and June 1862, slavery had been abolished in the District of Columbia and in the territories. Confederate war debts were canceled, much to the consternation of Europeans who had invested in the future of the South. Northern capitalists got their national banking system, tariff, immigration laws, and "due process" to protect corporations from arbitrary actions of government. The due process clause had been introduced into the Fourteenth Amendment by John A. Bingham, a railroad lawyer and a member of the House of Representatives, for the express purpose of making corporations, as well as former slaves, "persons." Through the decades the clause was to serve business well, though it did very little for the onetime slave.

The small core of Radical Republicans who fused manufacturing interests with abolitionist ideals momentarily became real revolutionists, but the movement soon petered out and expired in a "mire of corruption." Although they were backed by the iron and steel interests in Pittsburgh, by some railroad people, and by labor, the Radical Republicans could not gain the support of the financial community. The latter was to become perhaps the most powerful of all capitalist groups, and without its support success was not possible. For Thaddeus Stevens, leader of the Radicals, control of the Federal Government meant destroying southern power, breaking up the plantations, and treating the enemy as a conquered land. Military power was used to insure minimal property and voting rights for the Negro. But an attack on southern property was an attack on property in general, something that most northerners could not abide. The defeat of Stevens' confiscation measures in the House in 1867 sealed the doom of the Radical program. The plantation system evolved into sharecropping, a form of peonage just a few notches above chattel slavery. The large planter remained in control and the South kept its one-crop system as white men of means returned to power. When the Federal troops were removed from the South in 1877, it was Thermidor.

PART TWO

After the Civil War, the economy soared. The railroads pushed their iron fingers across the land as eastern potentates built roads to meet the barons of the West, while the Pacific Big Four—Huntington, Stanford, Hopkins, and Crocker—made the West Coast their private reserve. America was a nation rich in resources, ready to be exploited, and all made the most of it. Commodore Vanderbilt, already a millionaire many times over, went into railroading in his eighth decade to increase his fortune even more. He and the Erie gang—Jay Gould, Jim Fisk, and "Uncle" Danny Drew—played a hilarious game as they fought for control of a railroad that otherwise might have become an important piece of property.

The steel industry supplied the rails and other materials, and industrial magnates like Andrew Carnegie stood ready to sell the railroads what they needed. Carnegie made sure that his steel works would be his and his alone: his partners fell by the wayside one by one, with an occasional assist from Carnegie. And in Cleveland, a pious bookkeeper, John D. Rockefeller, cast

The Masters

a cold stare at the unruly oil refinery business and determined to bring order out of chaos. In the process he gained control over a large slice of that business, and became one of America's richest men and the target of popular obloquy. Industrialists required financial ministration, and men like J. P. Morgan, James A. Stillman, and other bankers were prepared to help them obtain funds for an appropriate fee. The bankers often insisted on providing tutelage as well, so that promotion, production, and finance were all intertwined.

The antics of the railroad men were duplicated in industry after industry, for America was a free country where a man of ambition, energy, frugality, and foresight could pick a fortune from the branches of trees. These were the Masters, who knew that millions could be made by playing with paper—the manipulation of securities. That the public might demur and sometimes question the propriety of their ways troubled them not a bit. America was theirs for the asking.

CHAPTER 6 The Coming of the Buccaneer

The western frontier was beckoning to restless Americans. Resources beyond the Mississippi seemed incalculable: gold and silver abounded in the mountains, pasture for the cattle kingdoms filled the Great Plains, and there were ample stands of timber to replace what had been depleted from the forests of the East. The pioneers discovered after the war a lenient Administration in Washington that had appeared to be more than eager to give away the Federal lands. No longer restrained by southern politicians, Congress passed the Homestead Act of 1862. It was said to be a great instrument for creating a widespread independent yeomanry that would be the mainstay of a free democratic way of life. It was nothing of the kind. Much of the land that was still available in the eighteen-sixties was simply not adaptable to homesteading: it was more suitable for timber, mining, and cattle-grazing, endeavors that were soon to be undertaken by aggregations of capital that excluded the small farmer. The good land was east of the hundredth meridian and had been long since taken up.

Yet the pioneers came, and as they moved across the West, they found the Indians in the way. Of course the Indian had to go, and so, even as the guns roared in the South, the Federal Army moved against the savage of the plains, destroying him or shunting him onto bleak reservations, away from the sight of the white man. The 175,000,000 acres held by the Indian in 1862, and sanctified by solemn treaties with Washington, were too good a prize to leave in his hands; he was forced to surrender more and more, as he continued to fight for twenty-five years to retain what had belonged to his forefathers. It was to little avail; the white man was destined to gain the continent.

Generous grants of land helped the railroads cross the continent west and south. Before the war, Asa Whitney, a New York merchant, had advocated building a railroad to the Pacific. The discovery of gold in California and silver in the Sierras had pointed up the need for transportation faster than a Conestoga wagon train. Major cities in the East pictured themselves as termini for a transcontinental line. Surveys, paid for by

Robert Morris, colonial businessman, U. S. Senator.

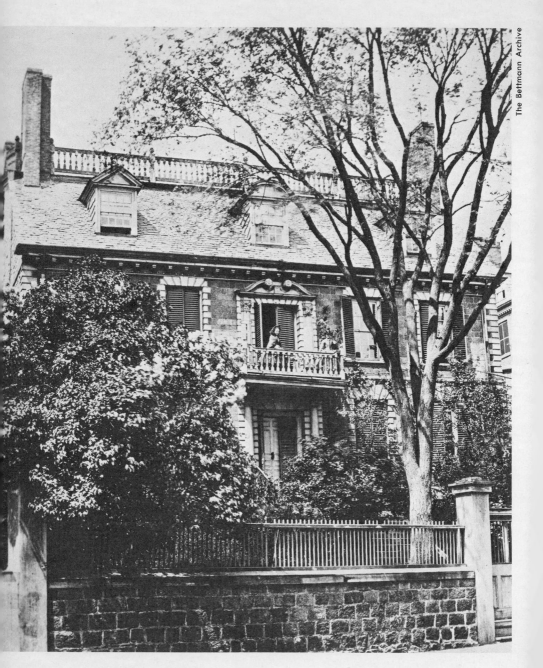

The Hancock Mansion in Boston, a particularly good example
of the style of life of a successful colonial merchant.

Eleuthère Irénée du Pont de Nemours,
founder of the Du Pont Powder Works,
in a portrait by Rembrandt Peale.

John Jacob Astor inspecting his
vast realty holdings, ca. 1842.
Drawing by Pierre Morand

General Henry Du Pont.

Cornelius Vanderbilt, about the time he entered railroading.

Daniel Drew, in a satirical contemporary cartoon.

Jay Gould, avoiding a summons server during the "Erie War."

The first Woolworth store in Lancaster, Pennsylvania, in 1879.

Congress, were undertaken as both northerners and southerners urged that projected routes should traverse their territories. The Panic of 1857 momentarily halted all the talk, but it was revived with the coming of war.

And as the West was settled, there came the usual army of speculators to buy and sell and make a quick profit. Big speculators acquired as much land as they could, and even prospective farmers bought more land than they could effectively till. National land policy, which seemed to go off in all directions at once, hindered development by letting large tracts remain unsettled too long. Often the person of small means could not afford to buy what he thought he needed. The speculators could sit around waiting for prices to rise, and when the real farmers came they could buy only from the speculators and at their price. The Homestead Act of 1862 was too late and offered too little: the 160 acres of free land for five years of occupancy was not adequate for the kind of agriculture that could be applied in the Great Plains, and anyway by that time most of the best land had been taken. And the act was no hindrance to the speculators: using dummy fronts and false papers, often in collusion with local land officers, they continued to get more land, as did timber dealers, cattlemen and miners— by the same method.

Cattlemen, who wanted open ranges, and sheepmen, who wanted enclosed land, fought bitter battles. In the end, the cattlemen lost, and the lands were fenced in. Dissension arose over the scarcity of water, causing frequent conflicts over riparian rights. Squatters who had settled on land later granted to a railroad found themselves ejected. Often such a grant would itself be vaguely defined in order to provide options for the railroad when it started construction, thus threatening whatever rights farmers believed they had. And the Pre-emption Act of 1841, the Timber Culture Act of 1873, and the Desert Land Act of 1877 all failed to prevent a growing concentration of the ownership of land. Even as early as 1844, foreign speculators held some 20,000,000 acres; at the end of the century, fifty-four companies and individuals owned over 25,000,000 acres. In short, it was doubtful that land policy had promoted an effective utilization and allocation of the nation's resources.

The drama of westward expansion—as well as the history of the interrelationships of religion and economics—is epitomized in the saga of the Church of Jesus Christ of Latter-day Saints, the Mormons. Surely nowhere else but in the America of that day could a religious sect with such bizarre origins have become a permanent element of a modern society. The Mormon religion began in the autistic dreams of a fifteen-year-old-boy,

Joseph Smith, in upstate New York. He reported in 1820 that a visitation from the Lord had led him to a set of golden plates, buried on a hill between Palmyra and Manchester, New York, on which were engraved a new history of mankind. After this revelation came others, and eventually the Mormon Church was created with Smith as Prophet and Revelator. In 1830 he published the *Book of Mormon* ("Joseph Smith, Jr., author and proprietor"), which he claimed was a divinely aided translation of the engraved tablets. To some historians, Smith was an illiterate faker, a liar, a sexual athlete; to others, a mystic, a gifted preacher, a true prophet. In all probability, the Mormon founder was more of a schizoid dreamer who had the gift and good fortune to make his fantasies come true.

Rural America at the time was a hotbed of revivalism and millenarianism, and the unfocused religious impulses of some of the people prepared them to receive the *Book of Mormon,* although to skeptics it appeared to be a concoction of contradictory pronouncements and religious fairy tales, composed in a half-literate, quasi-biblical language, a narrative distilled out of family tales and stories of pirates and Indians filtered through the parables of the Old Testament. One authority has said that it exhibited the "background of Western New York in the first decades of the 19th century as distorted by an adolescent mind and as recorded by that mind in an autistic state." And a scholar who saw of the untranslated manuscript, allegedly written in "reformed" Egyptian "caractors," declared it to be a "childish hoax." Yet its author functioned ably in his own milieu: despite the farrago the book represented, people flocked to hear Smith's preachings, were moved, and enrolled in the new church. And on that church there was eventually to be built a virtual economic empire, with features unique in America.

Disliked and distrusted by their neighbors—for whom there was but a thin line of distinction between religious fervor and debauchery—the Mormons moved their young church to Ohio. There too they were pariahs and were thought to be attracting some dubious characters. They soon got into even worse difficulties. Smith started a wildcat bank that was not even chartered, and when it failed, the Gentiles—non-Mormons—who were left holding the worthless notes joined the ranks of active anti-Mormons. And so the Mormons were driven, often with premeditated cruelty, from New York to Ohio to Missouri to Illinois, until they undertook the final trek to the Great Salt Lake in Utah after Smith and his brother had been lynched by a mob in Centralia, Illinois.

What had been a strange and turbulent sect, however, developed in Utah into a permanently established church with economic institutions fitted to the needs of development in an arid land. Economic activity had been undertaken by the Mormons in self-defense as well as to make themselves independent and distinct from the surrounding society. No doubt this activity, too, aroused hostilities, but it was effective, and it made Mormonism a business institution and an economic movement. The church was supported by tithing, and property was held by individuals as stewards for all. But having established themselves at the Great Salt Lake, the community would more than likely have foundered had it not been for the Gold Rush of 1848.

When the Mormons arrived in what is now Utah, after a carefully planned and superbly executed trek, they staked the land and prepared to build a community based on agriculture. They undertook public works and even provided a circulating medium of exchange. Under the leadership of Brigham Young, the Mormons knew what was needed for a self-sufficient state. But success was modest at best: the weather was severe, the harvests poor. And while this collective effort was taking place in the Great Basin, elsewhere there was a growing belief in the efficacy of laissez faire. Soon the Mormons had visitors—prospectors by the thousands heading for the gold fields of California. The Great Basin became an entrepôt that made the Mormons wealthy and successful.

In 1849 and 1850 about thirty thousand persons passed through Salt Lake Valley. Horses worth $25 were sold for $200 to those seeking the Golden Fleece; flour went for $10 to $15 a hundredweight. The Mormons relieved the weary travelers of their surplus wagons at about a fifth of what they had been paying. Brigham Young declared that bread could not be sold to a man who might earn $150 a day for the same price as to a poor laborer. The Mormons took full advantage of their strategic situation, behaving like an entrepreneur with a corner on the supply of a commodity. With the profits from these transactions, Young began to repatriate Saints from overseas who had been proselytized by Mormon missionaries. A carrying company and a merchandising company were started, and other localities in the West were colonized. It was a prospering economic theocracy, much to the consternation of the Gentiles. The Buchanan Administration, no doubt egged on by jealous Gentiles, took steps to keep an independent state from being created by the Mormons. Its attempt to crush the Church—the "Utah War"—failed.

Gradually the Mormons began to trade with the gentile world. They helped build the railroads that passed through their territory, and while the church elders struggled mightily to keep the Mormon community pure and independent, they could only delay its absorption into the life that surrounded it. William Godbe began to campaign for cooperation and coexistence with the Gentiles; the Mormons were as eager as any capitalist in the East to undertake the pursuit of profit. But the rest of American society could not countenance so peculiar an enclave in its midst. Polygamy, which had become a part of Mormon orthodoxy by the time the group reached Utah, was to the Gentiles a vice that had to be stamped out, and theocracy in business was an impediment to the extension of capitalism. Pressures from Washington became too strong to be withstood, and the Mormons finally gave in. The Edmunds-Tucker Act required the church to surrender its property holdings, the Mormons gave up polygamy in 1890, and in 1896 the State of Utah was admitted to the union. The empire of the Church of Jesus Christ of Latter-day Saints had become a part of capitalist society, albeit under duress.

Settling the West, however, required more than the extraordinary effort of the Mormons. Quick and regular transportation was necessary to fill the empty spaces with people. Yet southern delegations in Congress had continually blocked any attempt to build a transcontinental line unless it went across the southern frontier. With the Civil War, there was no question but that the road could go through the middle of the Great Plains or along the North. Promoters began to lobby in Washington for their pet projects. A motley crew, they included New York financiers, promoters, genuine railroad builders, and shrewd shopkeepers from California. Fulfilling their 1860 platform promises, the Republicans passed the first Pacific Railway Act, and it was signed by President Lincoln on July 1, 1862.

One of the beneficiaries was the Central Pacific Railroad of California, a company capitalized for $8,500,000, into which no one had yet paid anything, least of all the promoters. The Central Pacific was given a charter to build eastward, and the Union Pacific was to meet it at some point going westward. The two companies were granted 21,000,000 acres in public lands. The Union Pacific was to be capitalized at $100,000,000, and 162 commissioners were to solicit subscriptions to its stock. The Central Pacific and Union Pacific were also given thirty-two year loans in Government bonds, with payments ranging from $16,000 to $48,000 per mile of track, depending on the terrain. First mortgage bonds were allowed up to the amount of the loan. It was a more than generous arrangement. Within the Union Pacific, months passed while little was done. Then in 1864 Thomas Durant, the moving figure in the company, induced Congress to sweeten the original act. It all became an invitation to corruption and chicanery. General Grenville Dodge finally mounted a construction campaign, but

Durant went his merry way inflating costs. The tracks were poor, and the bridges flimsy; unnecessary curves were added to increase the trackage as a way of getting money from the Government, which paid on mileage. And shortly afterward there came five other railroads with similar arrangements.

Outstanding among the operators in these ventures were Collis Huntington, Leland Stanford, Mark Hopkins, and Charles Crocker—the Big Four from California. By 1860 Huntington had become a wealthy hardware-store owner in Sacramento, in partnership with Hopkins. They soon found themselves involved in assorted ventures with Leland Stanford, a politician and lawyer, and Charles Crocker, once a blacksmith, then a prospector, and now a dry-goods store owner. Each member of the quartet brought to their joint enterprise a special skill. Huntington was the leader—close-mouthed, bold, vindictive, and impervious to public attack. He had inherited the habit of accumulation from a miserly father. Stanford was the public relations man, the image creator. Hopkins—tall, thin, cautious, and crafty—handled the inside details. Crocker—huge, loud, boastful, and stubborn—executed the projects: on the Central Pacific, which was their creation, he charged ahead like a bull, employing thousands of Chinese coolies to complete the construction work as fast as he could. No doubt the men disliked one another personally, but, each respecting the others' talents, they worked together as coequals in storekeeping, in real estate, and in the California Street Railway Company that built cable cars for San Francisco's hills.

In 1859 they learned from Theodore Judah, a young engineer with an almost fanatical enthusiasm for railroads, of the glowing prospects of building a railroad across the mountains to the plains. The idea excited the Big Four, especially as Government aid was likely to be forthcoming. They were delighted with Judah's prediction that a railroad would enhance the businesses they already possessed. And the prospect of tapping the mining-town markets in the hills appeared most attractive. Then came the Federal charter in 1862. Judah wired back from Washington that they had trapped the elephant: the job now was to put it into harness.

But private investors were reluctant to place their funds into so dubious a venture, particularly when they could get 14 per cent for their money in San Francisco. Besides, most businessmen in the Sacramento and Bay areas questioned whether Huntington and his friends were so public-minded that they would really provide a railroad: there obviously must be a catch to the whole affair. Judah knew that solving the problems of crossing the mountains would take years, but Huntington and his friends were not about to wait very long for their profits. Quick turnover and quick gains were the rules of business in those days, and they could achieve them by organizing their own construction company so that others would not share in building the road. Judah objected strenuously to such a procedure and was eased out of the undertaking; at the age of thirty-seven he was dead of yellow fever.

Stanford swung into action. He cajoled the state and those county governments that were along the projected route into lending aid. He campaigned for a bond issue, placing money into the hands of the right politicians. When the railroad had reached the base of the Sierra Nevadas, the foursome had accumulated a half-million dollars, mainly from Federal aid, and they now commanded the respect of the doubters. They used their right-of-way to squeeze funds out of towns for terminal sites, and forced them to subscribe to Central Pacific securities. Otherwise, they threatened, the rail lines would go elsewhere.

When they planned, somewhat later, to build a line to Los Angeles, the town was bludgeoned into handing over a sum equal to 5 per cent of the assessed valuation of all the property in Los Angeles County. Their method was to begin work on a shoestring, extracting money from towns and counties to provide construction capital, after which they could get the Federal subsidy. In this manner, the Central Pacific was built without a penny of their own money, while at the same time the group was taking enormous profits out of the construction companies that did the work. To be sure, there were problems that Stanford had to solve, created by the opposition of Wells Fargo and other express companies.

But the construction itself was so hasty as to constitute a fantastic waste. It was later estimated that almost half of the outlay had been needlessly expended. Snakelike curves were added to increase the Government subsidy, and later whole sections of the line had to be rebuilt by Harriman. It became a common saying in California that while the railroad was good for Huntington, he was not good for the railroad. A shopkeeper's mentality influenced his every decision: a railroad was merchandise, and the cost of the inventory had to be kept low while turnover was to be increased, as in a retail establishment. Further, the Central Pacific meant a corner on freight and passenger business, first between Sacramento and Nevada, and then throughout the whole Pacific region. Of the $79,000,000 received from investors and the Government, at least $36,000,000 was in excess of any reasonable cost figures.

Meanwhile, the Union Pacific was pushing toward the Great Basin; the Indians watched fearfully, occasionally attacking the work crews and destroying their equipment. The Union Pacific's Thomas E. Durant, a former physician, was better at manipulating stocks than at building a railroad. The waste was just as prodigious as in the Central Pacific. Eventually the iron rails had to be replaced by steel, and a good deal of other rebuilding was required. The Union Pacific employed the device of self-owned construction companies: the contracts were let at twice the original engineering estimates. Finally, on May 10, 1869, the two lines were joined in Utah, and a nation rejoiced. It was willing to pay the price in wasted manpower and resources for the pleasure of crossing the open country on iron horses.

The promoters and politicians also rejoiced, particularly those who had benefited from the Credit Mobilier, the major construction company, which was composed of Union Pacific stockholders who made sure that fancy prices were paid for building the line. The Union Pacific had increased its capitalization from the initial $50,000,000 to $111,000,000, of which $94,000,000 was supposedly used for building the railroad. The actual cost, even with water and waste, was $44,000,000; $50,00,000 had simply disappeared through the Credit Mobilier. Some present-day historians condone the financial antics of the Credit Mobilier principals on the grounds that, after all, they *did* build a railroad. Such a view seems to adopt the crude morality of the eighteen-sixties and takes no account of what might have been the case under other standards. But businessmen gloried in their jungle-like behavior, and many of their victims gloried with them. Many legislators, and even a future President of the United States, James Garfield, were recipients of the largesse of Credit Mobilier; it handed out shares of stock in large enough quantities to create among politicians grand visions of becoming millionaires. Among the beneficiaries were Radical Republicans, whose idealism had been an expression of the coming to power of the industrialist, but they were now expiring in an orgy of corruption.

On the same day that the Union Pacific had its land grant increased and subsidies eased, the Northern Pacific was given a charter and land grants to build a line westward from Lake Superior through some of the bleakest terrain in the country. The project languished because investors were not prepared to put their funds into a railroad with such poor prospects. It was taken over in 1869 by Jay Cooke, who then pushed construction as far as Bismarck, North Dakota. When Cooke failed, it was Henry Villard's turn; construction was advanced to Helena and a connection with the Oregon Railroad. Hill's Great Northern and the Santa Fe followed in a decade or so. Within a generation after the war, five transcontinental lines had reached the Pacific Coast. But the promoters and financiers looked upon these ventures as get-rich-quick schemes, and they did not much care how they made their gains, so long as they made them. Nor did the rest of the middle class really care how it was done. By the standards of economic efficiency and the principle of effective allocation of resources, it was doubtful that the cost could be justified. However, the laws of economics did not seem to apply in a nation with such an amplitude of resources.

· The development and growth of the telegraph accompanied the railroads. In 1851 there were over fifty telegraph companies in the United States. By 1856 Western Union had swallowed eleven others in Ohio, and consolidation was on its way. Western Union undertook to extend its wires across the continent, and had done so by the time of the Civil War. American Telegraph and the U. S. Telegraph competed vigorously with Western Union, as all three expanded their lines as rapidly as possible. It was a profitable business: the line from New York to Boston paid for itself every three months, even though dividends of 20 per cent were being doled out on amply watered stock. As stock prices increased, more water was poured into capitalization. By 1866 Western Union had acquired fifty thousand miles of line and was well on its way to becoming the only telegraph company around. Later on it would have to contend with the ubiquitous Jay Gould.

The spread of capitalism in its modern form does not by any means suggest that the chief actors always agreed with one another, either on business policy or in matters of economics. The question of Government finances was a case in point. Nevertheless, there were enough similarities among businessmen to justify categorizing them as an emerging capitalist class.

At the outbreak of the Civil War Federal finances were in a deplorable state, despite prosperity and growing wealth in the North. Lincoln had selected Salmon P. Chase, a former governor and senator from Ohio, to take the Treasury post. Chase was ill-prepared for the Cabinet position, and he conceded as much. The legislators with whom he had to work on fiscal matters—Thaddeus Stevens, Justin Morrill, Elbridge Spaulding, and Senator William P. Fessenden—were of equally limited experience. The public debt was about $75,000,000, and there was only $1,700,000 in the Treasury's coffers. One could not fight a war in that condition.

Chase proposed to float a loan of $240,000,000 at once, hoping also to get some $20,000,000 more from tariff revenue. But the bond flotation was complicated by the Subtreasury System, a Jacksonian legacy: the law stipulated that only specie could be transmitted to the Government depositories. The banks knew that this would drain their reserves; they were, however, willing to transfer notes. The differences between Chase and the banking community created no little tension. Hence, although there was a general tacit agreement on the political objectives of the North, disagreements on details were liable to arise among the members of the new and now dominant class.

There were soft-money men and hard-money men. There were heated arguments in Congress, in the press, and in the pulpit over the suspension of specie payment, over the consequences of currency depreciation, over the size and impact of the public debt, and over the proposed revision of the banking system. But blanketing all the debates was a prosperity made warm by war: the country was growing while the fighting was on, and businessmen and farmers were generally well off. Soft money—unbacked paper notes—was advocated by a mixed group of businessmen interested in a rising price level, politicians, agrarians, and some labor leaders. John Sherman, Benjamin Butler, and Thaddeus Stevens fought against any Government policy that would result in contraction of the money supply, on the ground that such a consequence would impede industrial development. They were supported by the ever-optimistic Jay Cooke and virtually the entire manufacturing class. Good Keynesians long before the New Economics, they had been supplied with an ideology by Henry C. Carey, a leading economist who viewed America as an exception to the precepts of classical Anglo-Saxon economics. Some businessmen believed that a money supply expanded through the banking system would be superior to fiat money, but in any case, they too were opposed to contraction.

The hard-money point of view was expressed most forcefully by churchmen, who devised subtle theological arguments bolstering a Calvinistic attitude toward money, and by most academicians, who were constrained to justify their orthodox doctrinal purity. To be sure, strong support for adequate specie backing came from New England cotton manufacturers, especially Edward Atkinson, whose friends included John Murray Forbes and Charles Francis Adams, Jr., the grandson and great-grandson of Presidents. However, the special position of the textile industry in the Northeast allowed men like Atkinson to assume a "responsible" posture toward money issues. Textiles had matured, and the industry did not have the pressing need for capital that characterized the iron and steel industry in Pittsburgh, for example. New England had a good and effective banking system, and was, in fact, an exporter of capital to other regions that had to be protected. Moreover, rising prices induced by soft money would play hob with New England's export trade. By and large, the merchants of the region and those engaged in foreign trade followed the lead of the textile magnates.

Western businessmen functioned in a still-immature environment that needed stimulation and less orthodoxy in money matters. So it was a question of the particular capitalist who might be helped. Despite variations in the major theme, the symphonic notes were loud and clear: they sang of a burgeoning industrial capitalism. America was to become a businessman's world, with the pursuit of profit and capital accumulation striking the dominant chords. There were few who were cognizant of the anguish and pain that the search for material wealth might inflict. Although the man of wealth might live in handsome mansions and gather the art of the world to hang on his walls, his horizon was limited, and if he could garner his profit by "ripping the forests off the face of a half dozen states in a decade, he [was] content to let those who [came] later look after themselves." Having done so, he became an archdefender of what he thought was expressed in the Constitution and in the law of property.

The years after the Civil War were to become the Age of the Robber Baron. While the youth of the nation was expending its blood at Bull Run and Manassas, there were others who preferred to stay at home and engage in another sort of conflict: the business war. Ruthless and calculating, they risked not their lives—only their financial futures. They were soldiers in economic warfare, and some rose quickly to the rank of captain. They could follow their own interests and shape society for decades to come because opportunities for quick gains were open and enormous.

One of the most delightful figures among these men was Vanderbilt's bête noire, Daniel Drew. Unctuous, hypocritical, dressed like the cattle drover he had once been, Drew was one of Wall Street's major stock manipulators. In his youth, he would keep his cattle thirsty until he brought them to market, only then letting them drink their fill, thereby adding a new phrase to the speculators' lexicon—watered stock. From the cattle business he turned to tavern-keeping, steamboats, moneylending, and finally stock-broking in railroad and steamboat stocks. In 1854 he was rich enough to lend $1,500,000 to the Erie Railroad, in which he had become a director.

Although the Erie was one of the major trunk lines running from the East Coast, it was in perpetual difficulties that were to worsen under Drew's pious ministrations. Its rolling stock and rails were in exceedingly poor condition: the wrecks on the line became so frequent that newspaper headlines simply read, "Another Erie Disaster." When Drew became the Erie treasurer after the Panic of 1857, it was evident that his interest lay in manipulating its stock rather than in helping the Erie to provide service. Such manipulation might be nothing more than "accidentally" dropping a slip of paper on the floor of the Stock Exchange which, when surreptitiously picked up by another broker, was discovered to contain a "buy" order for Erie. Then everyone bought; Drew would sell short and then dump what he already held on the market, making a killing.

Drew was to get his comeuppence from Jay Gould, his longtime partner in Erie antics, who finally let the former drover go down in an attempted raid. The old man went home, climbed under his blankets, and prayed. He never returned to the market.

Gould, who came of Yankee rural stock, actually believed in his youth that honesty was the best policy. He engineered his first coup at the age of sixteen by borrowing $2,000 from his father to take from under his employer's nose a piece of land that he resold two weeks later for $4,000. Fired for his disloyalty, he went to New York and was soon speculating in leather. Zadoc Pratt, a leather dealer, was impressed enough by the young man to lend him $120,000 to open a tannery in Pennsylvania. Gould used half the money to speculate in railroad securities. Pratt soon withdrew, but Gould found another partner who, when he discovered that he was being fleeced, committed suicide.

Gould finally was ousted from the tannery in 1860. He went into the stock market, where the judicious use of the telegraph to learn of the fortunes of war enabled him to turn every defeat and every victory of the Union Army into a good profit for himself. He bought control of the Rutland and Washington Railroad, a decrepit line in northern New York, then sold out at a profit of $130,000 without adding a single mile of rail. He passed off a small Ohio line to the Pennsylvania Railroad at three times what it cost him. His favorite strategy was to gain control of several decaying but contiguous lines, combine them under a new name, advertise that the potentialities were stupendous, issue bonds for improvement, and then spin off the whole kit and caboodle for an enormous profit. Of course, he did little, if anything, to improve the physical assets. It was a great recipe for a twenty-five year-old tycoon, and he was to use it throughout his career.

In 1865 Gould met Drew and James Fisk. There is some doubt that a greater trio of rascals ever graced the business landscape. Fisk, a onetime peddler, was the showman for the group; a large man, always dressed in the loudest of clothes, he had a shrewd mind and was unafraid of the sort of infighting that prevailed at the time. Drew had taken a fancy to Fisk and had helped him establish a small brokerage firm through which orders could be filtered without letting other speculators become aware of their sources. The three men, soon dubbed "The Erie Gang," would battle the redoubtable Vanderbilt to a standstill.

It was during the Grant Administration that Gould undertook his most delicate operation, nothing less than a corner on gold. Had he not been able to manipulate railroads and the money market as he pleased? Why not gold? Although he could handle the float of gold on the exchange, a successful corner would have to neutralize the Government's supply of about $75,000,000 in gold. If this could be done, then the market price of gold could be jockeyed about as readily as Erie stock. Gould began to scheme even while fighting Vanderbilt over control of the Erie. He reached Grant's brother-in-law and several politicians to make certain that the Administration in Washington would not move.

Meanwhile he put his machinery into action to catch as many suckers as he could: the price of gold began to rise until it pushed 160. Gould was prepared to close the trap when Grant, finally goaded into action, ordered the Treasury to sell gold. The price dropped sharply, but not before Gould himself was able to squirm out of the market. The sheared sheep of Wall Street were ready to lynch him on the nearest lamppost, but he escaped through a back door of his office. Finally, Erie's English stockholders moved against Gould. He was the last of the triumvirate: Fisk had been assassinated by a rival for the affections of his mistress, and Drew had been earlier pushed overboard. Besides, Gould was ready to move on elsewhere. Forced to surrender control and to return Erie properties ostensibly worth millions, he announced his abdication. Erie stock bounded up, and Gould, who in the meantime had been buying Erie, unloaded his last batch at a profit of $1,000,000. The properties he had returned were discovered to be worth no more than $200,000. The Erie was to lie prostrate for decades to come.

The victim of the Erie Gang's most spectacular venture was none other than old man Vanderbilt—the Commodore himself. Although he was almost seventy years old when the war broke out, and assuredly America's richest man, Vanderbilt could not remain idle. Becoming interested in the New York and Harlem Railroad, which ran up to Brewster, New York, Vanderbilt knocked the price of its stock down to nine dollars a share, to acquire the line at a bargain. After Vanderbilt took it over, the New York and Harlem stock bounced back to fifty dollars. He then paid Boss Tweed and his New York gang the appropriate "fees" for a trolley franchise that would run from the Battery to the New York and Harlem at Forty-second

Street. The price of the stock moved up still further, adding millions more to Vanderbilt's coffers. When Daniel Drew, as well as others, tried a bear raid on New York and Harlem stock, Vanderbilt responded by cornering the market, taking Drew for at least half a million dollars. Drew tried again, only to be hit hard by the resolute Commodore.

Vanderbilt then moved against the New York Central upstate by refusing to allow his line from New York to cross the Albany bridge with either freight or passengers. Despite some powerful backing, the New York Central surrendered, and a new trunk line was to run from New York City to Buffalo. The legislature threatened an investigation, but the threat did not ruffle Vanderbilt's composure. "Hain't I got the power?" he retorted. The New York Central was recapitalized at twice the previous value by the issue of a stock dividend of $44,000,000. Vanderbilt's share of the profit was $6,000,000 in cash and $20,000,000 in new stock. By 1873, the railroad had $50,000 worth of water for every mile of track between New York and Buffalo. At one of their parties, Wall Streeters brought in a statue of the Commodore holding a watering pot. A participant declared, "It's the use of water, not as a beverage but as an element of public wealth, which has been the distinguishing characteristic of . . . . Commodore Vanderbilt's later years." All this was justified on the ground that the new capitalization was based on *potential* earning power rather than actual asset value. Watered stock presumably took account of values that might adhere to property as a consequence of future profit. It was to become the standard way of valuing properties under the aegis of the new capitalism. It represented, in effect, the beginnings of the paper economy.

Earnings potentials were, of course, high, because Vanderbilt now enjoyed a central position in the economy, exercising tremendous power over the life of other enterprises. He could levy whatever rates he desired on shippers, and it became the rule to charge what the traffic could bear. One prickly thorn, however, was the Erie, which competed on the other side of the Hudson. The stage was set for a comedy of heroic proportions—one that was to ruin the Erie and cost countless individuals their investments.

Vanderbilt had his rapacious eye on the Michigan Central, but suspecting that Drew also coveted the Michigan Central, he decided to make a friendly gesture by buying some Erie stock and going onto the Erie board. However, Vanderbilt was quietly buying as much Erie stock as his agents could lay their hands on, in the hopes that his major target, the Erie, would soon be his. The supply of stock, though, seemed inexhaustible. By some legerdemain Drew had been able to throw some $2,000,000 worth of stock onto the market, and Vanderbilt kept gobbling it up. Together with a group of Boston financiers, Vanderbilt proposed that Drew resign his Erie directorship. Typically, Drew came hat in hand, pleading that he not be ousted, that he would behave. Sensing a victory, the Commodore did not press his advantage, only to discover later that Drew was still flooding the market with stock. At one point Vanderbilt sought to borrow funds from a group of bankers, using his Erie stock as collateral. When they refused, contending that Erie was worthless, Vanderbilt, confident that a large part of brokerage loans had been made on the New York Central, threatened to dump its stock on the market and break half the houses on Wall Street. The bankers surrendered. Injunctions and counterinjunctions from friendly judges flowed back and forth, but in the end Vanderbilt was taken by the Erie Gang for $6,000,000.

Vanderbilt now got his judge to order the arrest of Drew, Fisk, and Gould, who promptly fled across the river to Jersey City, where they established themselves in baronial style with a private army to protect them. Gould emerged as the leader of the Erie crew; he denounced Vanderbilt as a "monopolist" and cut Erie's rates. Meanwhile, Fisk was enjoying his mistress' company in Jersey City, and Gould took off for Albany with a $500,000 bundle to urge the legislators to legalize what he had perpetrated. When Vanderbilt refused to match bribe for bribe, the legislators gave Gould what he wanted. Finally Vanderbilt sent Drew a note asking him to come and work out a truce, for he was "sick of the whole damned business." Vanderbilt got back $4,500,000, and the trio kept the Erie, from which vantage point they could generate other mischief. When Drew essayed a bear raid on Erie stock in 1868, Gould promptly made short shrift of him.

Gould then tangled with the up-and-coming thirty-two-year-old J. P. Morgan over control of the Albany and Susquehanna. When the financiers and lawyers could get nowhere, Gould tried physical possession, seizing one end of the line. Morgan's men held on to the other. One day a train started out from Gould's terminus with a small army aboard, as another train, filled with Morgan men, headed in its direction. When they met head on, with a fearful crash, the war had started. But the Erie men retreated, and Gould gave up the battle to try his wits elsewhere. Morgan was hailed for his victory; he had proved himself just as crafty as the Erie Gang and well able to beat them at their own game.

Morgan had been born with several silver spoons in his mouth. His father, Junius Spencer Morgan, had been a partner in the banking house of George Peabody and Company in London. Reserved, even morose, with no visible talent, the younger Morgan was nevertheless able to put his mathematical aptitude to good use while learning the banking business. In 1857 he came to New York to start his own firm and he soon acquired a reputation for "conservatism," which meant that he was loyal to those who would join him in engineering a deal. During the Panic he bought up essentially sound securities and resold them when recovery came. He helped transfer capital overseas when other capitalists got nervous. Some Wall Street observers were taking a rather dim view of his activities: the Union League Club suggested he be hanged for his speculation in gold during the war, when he shipped over a million dollars' worth overseas. For several years, he kept a close watch on railroad securities, just to be certain he would do the right thing whenever he decided to plunge into such a risky business.

Meanwhile, other capitalists were coming into a prominence of their own. Andrew Carnegie migrated from Scotland, imbued with ideas about the great prospects of America. He became a telegraph clerk for Thomas Scott of the Pennsylvania Railroad, and from him learned much of the nature of business intrigue. Ambitious and aggressive, Carnegie was not inclined to let rules prevent him from getting things done. To promote a sleeping-car venture, he borrowed some capital and soon had an income from it of five thousand dollars a year. Strangely enough, the Pennsylvania was soon buying more sleeping cars than ever. In time, Carnegie was to exclaim, "I'm rich, I'm rich!" On the inside of the Pennsylvania Railroad power structure, Carnegie was able to observe how business dominated communities and even whole states. In 1863 he created an iron company and a bridge company, and acquired an interest in a foundry. In 1865 he resigned from the railroad to devote himself to selling his companies' products. Carnegie was probably the greatest traveling salesman of his day; his production men were among the best, and he devoted many hours to courting philosophers, reading Robert Burns, and encouraging senators to pass high steel tariffs. In his spare time he even undertook to market bonds for others.

During his travels in England Carnegie discovered Bessemer steel, which had been produced there for a decade. Initially Carnegie had resisted using the Kelley-Bessemer process, although the railroads were replacing iron rails with steel. Finally Carnegie began to make steel rails at his Thomson works with an enthusiasm he had not displayed earlier. He now visualized replacing every mile of railroad track in the United States with steel. By this time, the Kloman brothers and all of Carnegie's early associates had been frozen out; he now controlled two-thirds of steel production.

Carnegie's vanity and self-conceit were colossal, as befitted a master salesman. He had an infinite capacity for gathering about him men cleverer than he. But Carneigie made sure that he got all the credit and substantial part of the profits. Before the war, it was Andrew Kloman who made Kloman and Phipps successful; the Thomson mill was proposed by William Coleman, father-in-law to Carnegie's brother, Thomas; Billy Jones, a master craftsman, had the skill to make the Thomson works a marvel of production; and it was Henry Clay Frick who converted the scattered Carnegie enterprises into a huge vertical operation. Carnegie's skill remained salesmanship and the manipulation of others. And it all paid well— profits rose from $2,000,000 a year in the eighteen-eighties, to $5,000,000 in 1890, to $40,000,000 by the turn of the century.

In Cleveland, Ohio, a produce bookkeeper also knew that he was going to be rich. John D. Rockefeller had been well tutored by his father, who prided himself on training his sons to be sharp by cheating them whenever he could. Rockefeller was reared in a pious household, learning habits of abstinence and parsimony. He lived to the age of ninety-five, never troubled by public opinion. As a youth he had studied bookkeeping; it was often said that he had the soul of a bookkeeper. He went to work for a produce merchant, saving the larger part of his earnings. He soon learned to lend his money at 10 per cent and was buying produce in carload lots. Rockefeller had a reputation for secretiveness and silence: he was seldom seen to laugh or smile.

Drake's discovery of oil in 1859 had converted the landscape around Titusville, Pennsylvania, into a forest of derricks and oil pumps. Drillers worked frantically and incessantly to extract the black wealth beneath the soil before someone else pumped the pools dry. Rockefeller inspected the industry on behalf of a group of Cleveland capitalists and came back with a negative report. Extracting oil was too wild a business for Rockefeller's sense of order. However, when Samuel Andrews, who knew how to extract kerosene from crude oil and how to use the by-products, proposed building a refinery, Rockefeller hesitatingly invested five thousand dollars. However he was quickly fascinated by the business; the demand for illuminants was high, and Rockefeller was agile in obtaining crude oil at the lowest possible prices. In 1867, Rockefeller brought in Henry Flagler, whose seventy thousand dollars helped build a second refinery. The Rockefeller firm became the largest in Cleveland, and he began to dream of monopolizing the entire industry, starting in his hometown. Demanding secret rebates on freight charges from the railroads, the company obtained a market advantage over its rivals. The Standard Oil Company of Ohio was formed in

1870, with Flagler the dynamo, William Rockefeller the suave front man, and John D. Rockefeller the power in the background. Within two years, Standard had absorbed twenty of the twenty-five refineries in the area.

The oil fields were occupied by so many producers that complete chaos ensued. But businessmen like Rockefeller had to have order—if not in the fields, then at the refineries. The Rockefeller firm spearheaded the formation of the South Improvement Company to create the cartel-like order it preferred. Rockefeller maintained that he had nothing to do with starting the South Improvement Company: it was all the doing of Flagler and William Rockefeller. But the Standard crowd did control South Improvement. Rival companies were bludgeoned into joining it: if one refused, a price war could easily force it out of business. Besides, the railroads were on Rockefeller's side. They supplied him with copies of the independents' way-bills revealing the latter's prices, and kicked back to South Improvement a substantial portion of the freight charges *paid by the independents* to Rockefeller and his friends. Operations were secret, in strict conformity with Rockefeller policy.

But word did leak out, and when the railroads attempted to double freight rates in February, 1872, the producers banded together, refusing to sell crude oil to any member of the combination. Rockefeller waited, biding his time in the belief that greed and hunger would break the producers' ranks. This time he was mistaken: the railroads caved in when the New York Central reduced its rates. When the independents met with the railroads, Rockefeller tried to crash the meeting, only to meet with forcible ejection. The Pennsylvania legislature revoked the South Improvement charter in 1872, causing the whole cartel scheme to collapse. But Rockefeller simply waited, licking his wounds. He knew that order could be established in the industry only through ruthless combination. Besides, he already controlled 90 per cent of the refining business, all the major pipelines, and all the oil cars on the Pennsylvania Railroad.

Playing hob with the resources of America seemed to be a way of life after the Civil War. Some of the worst examples of railroad corruption could be found in the South. North Carolina issued $17,600,000 in bonds between 1869 and 1871 to thirteen different railroads, but only ninety miles of road were actually built. Milton Littlefield used the funds he received to hand out liquor and cigars at the state house; George Swepson paid state legislators more than $133,000 for favors; Hannibal Kimball sold sleeping cars that he never delivered to Georgia railroads, depositing the money to an account held by the governor. One company auditor explained that he was able to save $30,000 in a few years on an annual salary of $2,000 only by engaging in "rigid economies."

But while southerners stole thousands, northerners took millions. The railroad magnates considered themselves a breed apart from ordinary men. William H. Vanderbilt, who had been placed in the presidency of the New York Central by his father, once exclaimed: "The public be damned!" Bankruptcy was not a serious matter, for the receivers, once freed of the burden of bond interest, could generate severe competition by cutting rates. When Commodore Vanderbilt wanted to buy a competing line that was in the hands of receivers, the sellers were quite indifferent when the old man balked at their asking price. "Do you want to compete with a receiver?" was the question put to him.

While the tycoons were fighting each other for big stakes, and often at the public expense, other entrepreneurs were building their enterprises with somewhat more patience. When Andrew Dennison left shoemaking in 1844 to try his hand at making jewelry boxes, he was unaware that he would be laying the foundations for a major paper-box company. His son, Eliphalet, a born salesman always searching for goods to market, expanded the business to include tissue paper, cards, and tags. A box factory was added later; by 1868, the business was well on its way. In retailing, A. T. Stewart, assisted by railroad rebates, moved ahead of his rivals, inaugurating the one-price system. Retailers began to woo customers with guarantees for merchandise. Dry-goods stores added new lines: Wanamaker and Lazarus offered men's clothing; Lord and Taylor introduced furniture and shoes; and thus the department store was created. The Mutual Life Insurance Company, lacking actuarial data for the United States, simply took the British tables, added arbitrary numbers to give higher mortality figures, and by 1858 had some $30,000,000 worth of policies in force.

Seeking new worlds to conquer, Jay Cooke picked up the Northern Pacific charter in 1869 for a mere fifteen cents a share. His interest in railroads had been kindled by the successful sale of $4,000,000 in bonds for a Minnesota railroad. He now wanted to build a road out to Oregon; he dreamed of turning the bleak Dakotas into golden fields of wheat. The usual brisk campaign was launched to raise $100,000,000 in bonds to build the road. Since the Northern Pacific had land grants but no other subsidies, Cooke sought a charter revision which came through in 1870. He was to receive $200 in stock for every $1,000 bond sold, plus a 12 per cent commission. Protests from questioning senators and rivals in Philadelphia were to no avail.

However, the market was beginning to back away from railroad securities. Cooke brought in Henry Villard to encourage settlers to come into the Northwest. Construction problems were even more serious than they had been farther south: one section of hastily built track simply disappeared into a lake and had to be done over. The corruption of the operating president was too great to be tolerated even then, and he was fired. Cooke tried to raise more money from the Government, only to discover a new rival in Drexel, Morgan and Company, which was seeking a hold on Government business. The conflict resulted in the failure of the Government loan of 1873.

The economy began to show signs of strain. The railroads were not showing a return, and European investors were grumbling that some of the promises ought to be redeemed. Cooke had spent over $15,000,000 on the Northern Pacific and had only five hundred miles of track to show for it. In the first eight months of 1873 some twenty-five other railroads had defaulted on their bonds. Cooke began to borrow on short-term notes, hoping to repay as he floated bonds. His financial maneuvering did not succeed. Rumors flew rapidly from New York to Washington to London. Then, on September 17, 1873, as Cooke sat down to dinner with President Ulysses S. Grant, he learned that his banking house had been forced to close. He had gone into bankruptcy, and with him thousands of others failed also. It was one of those periodic catastrophes that no one knew how to avoid. Morgan, Rockefeller, Carnegie, and Gould waited out the storm, as others—Hill, Harriman, and Henry Clay Frick—got set to sail as soon as the waters calmed down.

CHAPTER 7 The Era of the Barons

Economic changes in the last quarter of the nineteenth century irrevocably altered the shape of American society. Within a few decades, a nation of petit bourgeois, many of them independent farmers, was converted into one in which ties to the soil were broken, and men went to work for others in cities and factories. Life was no longer measured by the seasons, but by the clock, and by the whir of the machine. The city, with its belching smokestacks, began to dominate the landscape as the economy moved from extractive industries to manufacturing. The change was a haphazard one, and its ugliness was to generate problems that have persisted down to the present.

The city became an instrument of industrial development to be manipulated freely by those who controlled its resources and who could gather personal gain in the process. Everything that was engaged in was directed toward material ends only; the aesthetic was either secondary or nonexistent. City government became a source of wealth to politicians like Boss Tweed and his corrupt machine in New York. Everything seemed to reflect an overwhelming pressure to measure success by the only standard that counted—money. Industrialists dominated the cities—Carnegie in Pittsburgh, Gustavus Swift in Chicago, Ford in Detroit. A city's growth was judged by their criteria: bank clearings, population growth, car-loadings, real-estate values, and the height of skyscrapers. The very ugliness of the latter-day nineteenth-century city was intimately related to its industrial function. Farming was also altered: the family farm as a way of life diminished sharply in significance as the market penetrated the hinterlands. But what was taking place in America was not unique: it had occurred earlier in England and was beginning to reveal itself in Germany and Japan as well.

Among the major industries was the railroad, now really big business. The traditional methods for exercising social control—competition and the discipline of the market—were eroded as the railroad magnates pursued the goal of combination and monopoly power. Some succeeded in achieving their aims and were able to gather unto themselves huge fortunes. Others

136

fell by the wayside; the theme of rags to riches and riches to rags was often played out in one lifetime. Occasionally farmers and consumers would benefit: the struggle for power would sometimes mean lower rates. But in the main, they had to bear the burden of economic conflict as victory usually meant an effort by the magnates to recoup earlier losses by charging what the traffic would bear. Moreover, the frequent financial reorganizations after bankruptcy invariably wiped out armies of investors. Workers, of course, were merely units in a giant profit-making machine: the inevitable tensions exploded in the great railroad strikes of 1877, when workingmen clashed with militia in West Virginia, Maryland, and Pennsylvania, and throughout the Middle West. The strikes seemed to "threaten the chief strongholds of society and came like a thunderbolt out of a clear sky." America had for too long harbored the delusion that social disturbance belonged to Europe and would not upset their free republic. The events were a rude awakening to the coming maturity of capitalism.

But, most significantly, the groundwork for the creation of a paper economy had been laid. With the development of the corporation and large-scale business, securities themselves became wealth—the promise to pay could be converted into riches. To be sure, there was opposition to these trends, as in the Granger Acts passed in various states and in Federal legislation against the "trusts." Nevertheless, the corporation became the "master institution of civilized life." The holding company—one corporation owning the stock of others—became a central feature of railroad financing. At first the holding company required a special dispensation by the state legislature, but in 1889 New Jersey made it an element of its general incorporation law.

Despite all protests, advances toward the consolidation of property proceeded unimpeded. Investment bankers began to hover over the affairs of the companies whose securities they had sold. Perhaps they knew only too well that promoters would grasp for the sky unless checked, although at times the banker had no objection when a promoter climbed on his shoulders.

Old Cornelius Vanderbilt's empire was still a family enterprise, as indeed were a number of others. The New York Central, with a capitalization of $90,000,000, now extended from New York to Chicago, utilizing the lines of the Michigan Central and the Lake Shore in Illinois. But the Commodore was becoming even more irascible and eccentric, calling upon mediums to converse with the spirit of Jim Fisk, who very likely responded as did Achilles when Odysseus visited Hades—life on earth was more fun than existence in the Kingdom of the Dead. Vanderbilt even made some gifts to charity, and, at the urging of his young second wife, gave several million dollars to found Vanderbilt University. The rate wars continued off and on, and the old man even claimed to have improved the physical structure of his lines. Invariably, he made certain that the public paid at least part of the bill: when New York City's Board of Aldermen had been properly persuaded by the Commodore, half the cost of constructing a new roadbed for the Harlem line came out of the public coffers.

Although some thought the Commodore now senile, he remained active and alert, and still ran his business with cold efficiency. He agreed to carry John D. Rockefeller's oil for low rates—and handsome rebates under the table. It was a good arrangement for all concerned, except for the Rockefeller and Vanderbilt competitors. But his time was running out, though he fought death as vigorously as his numerous progeny "heartily sped him on his road" with hymns. Virtually the entire fortune was left to his eldest son, William. In death, Vanderbilt had his defenders in the public press, though many observed that he never cared much for others. His life, said one writer, "presents little for us to envy."

William, who for years had been relegated to a farm on Staten Island before the old man took him into the New York Central, now inherited the railroad. He was a plodding, penny-pinching watcher of detail to whom brains and money meant the same thing. When the strikes broke out in 1877, William was able to weather the storm by distributing $100,000 among his "loyal" workers. But he was no fighter and was easily blackmailed by several shrewd operators into buying useless railroads. Despite his errors of judgment, William doubled the family fortune in the short span of eight years: he had demonstrated that he could do almost as well as his father.

Meanwhile, Jay Gould kept firing away; both he and the public were appalled that 87 per cent of New York Central stock should be held by one man. The legislature began to mutter that perhaps the Vanderbilt holdings ought to be taxed more heavily. Finally, William, harassed and perplexed, decided to dispose of some Central stock, holding on to slightly more than 50 per cent to insure continued absolute control. He turned to J. P. Morgan, who helped him discreetly sell some 250,000 shares at 130, giving William $37,000,000 in Government bonds and $5,000,000 in cash. For his services, Morgan went onto the Central board, beginning his long reign of direct participation in railroad affairs. With Morgan came Cyrus Field, representing Vanderbilt's old enemy, Jay Gould. Morgan decided that it was the better part of valor to placate old Mephistopheles (as Gould was called).

Gradually Vanderbilt took his rightful place in high society, building ornate mansions, following the races, and giving grand costume balls costing as much as $75,000 each. The business was to be dominated by financiers like Morgan. When William passed from the scene, Chauncey Depew was president of the Central, and the other Vanderbilts were happy to follow the sagacious advice of Morgan. The incessant pressures from rival lines continued, and now there were occasional investment losses to be covered out of other resources. At one point, the Pennsylvania Railroad began to buy into the West Shore Line on the west bank of the Hudson River. This could make trouble for the Central; in retaliation, the Vanderbilt forces undertook to build the South Pennsylvania Railroad to parallel the Pennsylvania. Such a war promised chaos for all concerned. Morgan, who preferred order and coordination, invited everyone involved to a cruising party aboard his yacht; no one was to leave until a compromise had been reached. The Pennsylvania agreed to turn over the West Shore to the Vanderbilts, and the South Pennsylvania was returned to weeds. The Reading Railroad, with which Vanderbilt had been working on the South Pennsylvania project, was left out in the cold. The old tunnels and rights-of-way later eased the construction of the Pennsylvania Turnpike.

William Vanderbilt was now sixty-four-years old and physically exhausted; one day he keeled over in his office and died. Immediately Morgan and Depew exacted promises from other financiers to support Central stock. But nothing happened, for William had controlled virtually everything outright.

Jay Gould was still around. He had acquired, not without reason, a reputation as an unscrupulous financier who relished the destruction of others. Bold, corrupt, and amoral, with a great talent for betrayal, he was a master of speculation and a genius in looting the companies he controlled. Gould viewed the business of stock-jobbing with a cold and cynical eye. He always turned his gains into a form that would remain with him: cash, or property owned outright. Essentially indistinguishable from an Astor or a Vanderbilt, Gould was perhaps more clear-sighted about the nature of the system in which so much wealth could be gathered in one hand. Hence, he could be utterly indifferent to social climbing and its various gradations of snobbery. Indeed, he may have been bemused by the expressions of outrage hurled at him by others of the new middle class—it was a case of the pot calling the kettle black.

Gould's manipulations in railroads and the telegraph gave him a virtual stranglehold on the growing West. He had seized strategic points in the economy and by his control could extract an "infinite toll." As Thorstein Veblen was to demonstrate later, Gould's method was to make a profit by disturbing the industrial system. After the Erie affair, Daniel Drew ruefully conceded that Gould's touch was death. During a visit to Europe, Gould sought an audience with one of the Rothschilds. He was rebuffed with the comment that "Europe is not for sale." However, the man and the times were a perfect match. Business was a jungle filled with carnivores stalking their prey, and Gould was simply the craftiest of the animals. He coupled treachery with imagination, keeping the financial details of a half dozen companies in his head, a feat unmatched until the days of Ivor Kreuger and Sergei Rubinstein, financial manipulators of a later era.

After the Erie débâcle, Gould turned his attention to the West, where he thought to build a railroad. He had made two fortunes and would now start on a third. The techniques had been mastered and refined: propaganda to undermine rivals, acquisition of properties at a low price, optimistic promotion and subsequent spin-off—always using somebody else's money. One admiring biographer acclaims Gould as a builder of railroads; this is patent nonsense. Most of the railroads he acquired had already been driven to the ground; he simply pushed them into the earth a bit farther. His process of destruction became a grand highway to millions. Gould now teamed up with Russell Sage to take over the Pacific Mail Steamship Company, already debauched, and now suffering from railroad competition. By jockeying the price of its stock, Gould and Sage netted about $5,000,000. According to some, their machinations contributed to the Panic of 1873. The crash opened a golden opportunity: Union Pacific stock was now available at bargain prices. Gould soon had in his possession approximately a third of the outstanding stock, and elbowed his way onto the Union Pacific board of directors, much to the consternation of its members.

The Union Pacific seemed to be in an even worse condition than the Erie: most speculators believed that its profit possibilities had been thoroughly squeezed dry. It had a debt of $15,000,000, two-thirds of which was to come due in 1874. Gould was not troubled by the bleak prospects, however. He realized that such rivals for possession as the Pennsylvania, the New York Central, and a group of Boston capitalists who hungered for the road would cancel out each other's efforts. With the help of Sage and Sidney Dillon, Gould put his hands on 200,000 shares of Union Pacific, giving him effective control. (By this time, Gould had mellowed somewhat: with his multifarious activities, he did need to trust somebody. Sage and Dillon were excellent complements.) Gould then wheedled the Union Pacific creditors into taking long-term bonds for the obligations they were holding—the moment of truth had been forestalled. Bounteous crops in California had to be moved eastward, and Gould could dictate freight rates and indulge to his heart's content in the common practice of rate discrimination.

He now coveted the Kansas Pacific, a rival road, and he used the Union Pacific to bludgeon that road unmercifully. The Kansas Pacific paralleled the Gould line up to Denver, but it was dependent on the Union Pacific to get to the Pacific Coast, making it completely vulnerable. Like so many lines, the Kansas Pacific had been plundered somewhat earlier: it was in bankruptcy, with Henry Villard, a former journalist, acting as receiver from some St. Louis stockholders and a group of German bondholders. Gould attempted to scale down the Kansas Pacific debt, but Villard resisted. A smaller debt would have made it simpler for Gould to engage in financial maneuvering. Villard's refusal to cooperate resulted in a campaign of vilification that forced him out as the stockholders' representative; however, he held on for the German bondholders. Gould had to give in: he could not conquer an incorruptible man.

To the Kansas Pacific, Gould added the Denver Pacific, the Missouri Pacific, and the Kansas Central; put together, these could create difficulties for the Union Pacific. Meanwhile, Gould, who had purchased Kansas Pacific stock for virtually nothing, proposed to the Union Pacific board that the two lines merge, with Kansas Pacific shares to be exchanged for Union Pacific. The Union Pacific shares were selling at 60, the Kansas Pacific at 13: obviously, Gould would once again make millions on the transaction. When the other directors balked, he simply threatened to convert the Kansas Pacific into a serious competitor. Needless to say, their resistance evaporated; they decided it was the better part of discretion to assuage their anguish with purchases of Kansas Pacific stock before the merger. Gould's profit came to about $40,000,000; he was now worth about $100,000,000, much of it, of course, on paper.

In 1877 Gould decided to penetrate Western Union, a company that had Astor and Vanderbilt on its board. He may have undertaken this foray in revenge for all the snubs he had suffered from the bluebloods; at any rate, he was soon to begin his usual raid. The telegraph was not unfamiliar to Gould: during the Civil War he had, with the help of a Major Eckert, used the Military Telegraphic Bureau to secure advance information on the fortunes of the Union Army, to the benefit of his speculative activity. After the war, Eckert became superintendent of Western Union, only to shift over to the Atlantic and Pacific Telegraph, a Gould company. While doing so, Eckert gulled Thomas A. Edison out of the quadruplex sending system, the research for which had been paid for by Western Union, which then sued in the courts, but to no avail. With Atlantic and Pacific such a nuisance, Western Union bought it from Gould for $900,000 and 12,500 shares of the Western Union. Gould then decided he wanted more, so he formed the American Union Telegraph to battle Western Union in the field, while he conducted bear raids against its stock on the exchange. He employed the New York *World*, which he then owned, to scream "monopoly," and he quietly aborted an attempt by the legislature to investigate the situation. Vanderbilt finally caved in: he had no stomach for Mephistophelean infighting.

The merger of the Western Union and American Union was quite a deal: the capitalization was raised to $80,000,000, one-fourth of it consisting of water. American Union stockholders, the chief of whom was Jay Gould, received $15,000,000, and a 38.5 per cent dividend was paid out. Gould, Sage, Eckert, and Dillon went onto the Western Union board, with Gould now in firm control. Much of the profit on the merger was siphoned off through a subsidiary construction company, creating a miniature Credit Mobilier. Some years later Gould would confront the Postal Telegraph Company, organized by James Keene, an old enemy. Postal Telegraph was then taken over by James Mackey, a mining tycoon who teamed up with James Gordon Bennett to give Western Union the sort of headache it had created for others. The two companies engaged in bitter battles over domestic rates and tie-ins with overseas companies. Though they both finally agreed to a truce, Western Union eventually swallowed Postal Telegraph.

Gould's progress generated cries of monopoly: at a meeting of the Anti-Monopoly League in New York, there were demands that Gould be hanged from the nearest rafter. Congressmen were beginning to react. Said one senator of the new businessmen, "When they speak they lie; when they are silent, they are stealing." Gould remained unperturbed; he now cast his eyes on New York's elevated system. It had been built in the usual corrupt fashion and was controlled by three different companies, all of which were inefficient and buried in legal slime. No dividends were paid, and taxes were in arrears. But Gould sensed the system's genuine potentialities, for, with the growth of the city, the elevated could prosper. He directed the editor of the New York *World,* a man of doubtful character in any case, to initiate a campaign of "reform." Gould then brought in Cyrus Field, whose probity was well known and who was well regarded for his Atlantic-cable venture. Field was the unwitting front in a suit to nullify the charter of the Manhattan Elevated, the real purpose being to drive the price of its stock down. The demand for receivership, injunctions, and rumors were all part of the campaign. When a receivership was imposed on the hapless company, Gould's subseuqent bear raid enabled him to gather enough shares to exercise control.

Suddenly the Manhattan's health improved. The other companies also came under the wing of Gould, who then put Field in charge. In financial circles, Gould, formerly "Mephistopheles," was now "the skunk of Wall Street." Of course, the companies were recapitalized, and fares were increased from five cents to ten cents. But a public uproar made Field remorseful enough to cut back on the fares. Gould was furious, and some years later, when Field tried to corner the Manhattan's stock, Gould gave him a financial drubbing. Friends of Gould insisted that he really had tried to help Field in a pinch, but the fact is that he did profit from the latter's fall from grace. The New York *World* went into decline, and Gould sold it to Joseph Pulitzer for $346,000. Later Pulitzer was to remark that Gould was the only man in the world who could capitalize a 20 per cent loss.

Gould knew how to take care of his enemies. Years before, he had been manhandled one day in Wall Street by James Keene and A. A. Selover two other speculators, and he took his revenge by arranging a transaction that cost Selover $15,000, then conducted a bear raid against Keene that cost the latter $7,000,000 in a few days. After that incident, Gould went about town with several bodyguards in tow. Gould had little interest in social engagements, preferring a quiet evening with his family, but he was not as miserly as some of his contemporaries. His great pleasure lay in outwitting others and in gathering wealth. His five-hundred-acre estate on the Hudson was filled with the world's largest collection of orchids, and his yacht, a luxury that befitted the era, cost one thousand dollars a week to maintain.

It seemed that Gould was now at the top of the heap. Yet his western railroads were continually under attack by competitors. The Union Pacific debt was an awesome burden, the New York Central and Pennsylvania both sniped away from the East while Collis Huntington was blocking passage to the West. Moreover, Huntington was pushing toward El Paso and New Orleans, even as Gould maneuvered for a window on the Pacific. The struggle between the two titans was declared a draw by most observers. In 1883 the commodity and stock markets became erratic. Gould tried to still rumors that he was selling out, though in fact he was quietly doing so, for losses had to be cut. His control of the Wabash and the New York and New England slipped. Finally, in 1884 he even lost out in the Union Pacific.

When Charles Francis Adams Jr., who had succeeded Gould in the

Union Pacific, examined the books and records of the company, he discovered that the assets had been juggled and the accounts rigged. He declared the Union Pacific financial statements a fraud. The road's floating debt stood at $10,000,000. Dutch bondholders in the Kansas Pacific were wondering how $3,000,000 could disappear without a trace. The Government wanted to know why the Union Pacific's bonds had not been retired on schedule; but how could they have been, when revenues were being used to pay dividends? Pressures accumulated as an assortment of bears began to gang up on Gould. Through all the harassment, he maintained an iron nerve. His response was a threat to assign enough of his property to create bankruptcy and generate a panic severe enough to curl the hair on every stockbroker's head. "Like Samson, he stood ready to tear down the house in which they all lived." A temporary settlement with his opponents was reached; then Gould turned and promptly trapped a gang of speculators who were selling short the Missouri Pacific. But it was a close call, and Gould decided to consolidate and quit while he was still ahead. He doubtless remembered the spectacle of Daniel Drew, down to his last shirt. By now he had become somewhat conservative in his ways: he even took part in the pool to shore up the market when William Vanderbilt died. In earlier years he would have devised a scheme to make another killing.

Suffering now from tuberculosis, he became testy—fully aware of how thoroughly he was hated. Yet he did not care. From time to time he essayed another venture, trying to penetrate Hill's Great Northern and thumbing his nose at J. P. Morgan. In December, 1892, he died, much to the relief of other nabobs. At the age of fifty-six, he had left an estate of $125,000,000.

While Gould was still a young man, Russell Sage had already become an accomplished entrepreneur. By the time Sage met up with Wall Street's Mephisto, he was an old hand at taking care of the needs of legislators and in manipulating the assets of companies. Miserly, given to few extravagances, he was disliked even by the members of his own class. He owned a comfortable home on New York's Fifth Avenue, but his clothes were something of a laughingstock. Descended from upstate New York farmers, he had worked in a Troy grocery store as a young man. By 1839 he had his own business. Together with two other gentlemen of similar stripe, he carried through a complicated deal in 1851, involving the foreclosure of some property in Milwaukee. In the process, Sage executed a triple double-cross against his partners, acquiring the property for considerably less than its actual worth. All this was mere on-the-job training for what was to come.

During the eighteen-forties Troy, like many other cities that wanted to enjoy the advantages of progress, had built a railroad to connect with

Schenectady. As an alderman, Sage served as one of the directors of the publicly owned facility. Some sentiment arose favoring sale of the road to private interests. Sage was on the committee that recommended the sale. And so it was sold—to Russell Sage for $50,000 down and $150,000 to be paid in fourteen years. Sage then turned around and disposed of the line to Corning's New York Central for over $800,000, consisting of $650,000 in capital stock plus the 25 per cent bonus that Corning had so lavishly handed out. Sage was now a leading citizen and was sent to Congress by a grateful electorate, where he could observe at close range the subversion of congressmen and the subtle guile of such public-minded bankers as William Corcoran.

Sage then became involved with the La Crosse and Milwaukee Railroad, a line that was the offspring of dubious promotion verging on fraud. He adapted himself readily to the business methods of the day. A land grant in Minnesota was obtained, a number of small lines acquired—several of which existed only on paper—and bonds were sold to unwary Dutch investors. Very little trackage was constructed, but a large part of the proceeds seemed to disappear as though down a bottomless sink-hole. During this period Sage met Gould; the two made a good pair. Sage became a moneylender, placing his funds in call loans at rates that were virtually usurious, an activity that made him none too well liked in Wall Street. He left his entire fortune to his widow, who promptly began to give it away to universities, churches, and eleemosynary institutions. When she died in 1918, the bequests totaled $40,000,000, plus $5,400,000 for the Russell Sage Foundation.

Meanwhile, the California quartet of Huntington, Stanford, Crocker, and Hopkins continued on its merry way. With a monopoly hold on railroad traffic in California, they could make shippers dance to their tune. Their rates were the highest in the country. To protect their control of the West Coast, the foursome extended their control of key ports, frustrating the efforts of competitors to gain a foothold in the state. They moved into southern California, pressuring counties and towns to pay the cost of constructing railroad lines. The objective was almost self-evident: no other railroad was to be permitted entry into their preserve. While Huntington lobbied in Washington, falsifying reports whenever necessary, the Big Four pushed their lines across Arizona and New Mexico whether they were authorized or not. At one point, they simply laid a track through an Indian reservation, though clearly prohibted from doing so: the Government and rival lines were presented with a *fait accompli*.

The Pacific Mail Steamship Company had become convinced that Panama would be a better terminus than San Francisco: this would forestall competition. Politics became a way of dominating the state and insuring control of its resources. For years no governor could be elected without the Big Four's approval. They soon acquired the title of "The Octopus"; their empire included not only railroads, but steamship lines, coal, iron, land, and an army of political sycophants. A community of interest with Gould, Carnegie, and Rockefeller developed. Hopkins and Crocker were to leave behind $20,000,000 each; Stanford's estate came to $30,000,000; and when Huntington died, only the Standard Oil group was rich enough to buy the properties he left behind.

The Pacific Northwest had been Jay Cooke's province, but after the debacle of 1873 it became the realm of Henry Villard. A man of culture and imagination, Villard learned the none-too-gentle ways of high finance when he acted as representative for the German bondholders of the defunct Kansas Pacific. Enchanted by the prospects of the Columbia River basin, he raised enough money among his friends to purchase an option to buy the Oregon Steam Navigation Company for $100,000. Villard then incorporated the option, obtained a mortgage on it in the amount of $6,000,000, and took over the company. It was a brilliant stroke. Slowly Villard began to combine properties. His moves were facilitated by an issue of $18,000,000 in stock against assets in the navigation company of $3,500,000. He roamed over the countryside, searching out strategic points—confluences of rivers and mountain passes. Coal deposits were brought into the growing conglomerate to provide future traffic. Jay Gould was interested enough to offer his help, but backed off when Huntington threatened to attack.

In 1880 Villard learned that the Northern Pacific, under Frederick Billings, had placed $40,000,000 in bonds with Drexel, Morgan and Company. This was a distinct threat, for with additional funds the Northern Pacific might be extended into territory that Villard had come to look upon as his own. He promptly took off for New York, gathered together fifty friends and supporters, and talked them into contributing some $8,000,000 to a "blind pool." Villard commanded their faith, for he did not specify that the money would be used to buy into the Northern Pacific. A second pool provided $12,000,000 for a holding company that could issue $30,000,000 worth of stock. Northern Pacific officials responded by trying to throw $18,000,000 in treasury stock on the market. A court suit restrained the Northern Pacific and Villard went on its board of directors with enough votes in his pocket to control the line.

The now-victorious Villard undertook to populate the Northwest. He sent agents to Germany, Russia, and Scandinavia with picture slides and glowing tales to induce people there to come to America. The immigrants were to discover little joy either in the trip or their destination. Invariably, the railroad promoters—and not Villard alone—overstated the case. The area was a true frontier, rough and inhospitable to all but the hardiest. Travel was so unbearable as to influence some congressmen to introduce a bill for the prevention of cruelty to railroad passengers. Villard finally completed his road in 1883 and staged a triumphal ride across the continent. Investors were delighted with the high dividends that were promptly paid.

But on the sidelines there waited James Jerome Hill, who was coming into the Northwest with his Manitoba, a more efficient and better-built road. Hill suspected that Villard had overextended himself. Construction costs on the Northern Pacific had exceeded estimates by $14,000,000, raising the debt of the line to $19,000,000. Villard was being buffeted by minor-league buccaneers who were building, or threatening to build, parallel short lines. Gould and Huntington were leveling attacks on his land grants in Washington, trying to convince legislators that the grants should be canceled. Villard attempted to float another bond issue; it was not successful. The Northern Pacific hovered on the brink of bankruptcy. In 1884 Villard resigned as head of all Northern Pacific holdings to retire to his mansion in New York.

Through all this tumult, Hill, a new sort of capitalist—one who believed that a railroad should be a sound and solid property—sat waiting his chance. A one-eyed legend of the Northwest, Hill had migrated to St. Paul from Canada in 1856, when the Minnesota city was still known as "Pig's Eye." The region was a frontier, and like any frontier, it was peopled with adventurers, land-grabbers, and other assorted rogues aggressive enough to grasp opportunities on the palpitating edge of society. Hill was a man of paradox: to some he was a demigod, to others he was a prime scoundrel who corrupted the whole Northwest. His empire was to range from the Great Lakes to Puget Sound, from Canada to the Missouri River, and across the Pacific Ocean to the Orient. His willingness to let his stockholders share in his good fortune was an unheard-of gesture. Usually, he behaved otherwise: when the town of Wayzata complained about the noise of his trains, he moved the railroad station a mile down the road, forcing Wayzata residents to go out of their way to board a train. Although Hill had a fearsome temper, he was usually laconic in speech and direct in action.

When Hill arrived in St. Paul, he had been thinking of a trip to the

Orient, but he stayed on for the next sixty years to build one of America's great fortunes. His first job was as a clerk for a firm engaged in operating river packets. He was quick to note the growth of the area: during the Civil War he watched wheat move in vast quantities downriver, and he saw the immigrants coming into the region. Becoming a forwarding agent, he was increasingly involved in the transportation business. His Red River Transportation Company took him throughout the area, and he was more convinced than ever that there were riches present to be harvested.

Hill had been supplying fuel to the St. Paul and Pacific Railroad, a small line that was getting nowhere. He became interested in it, for it had both Federal and state charters and 5,000,000 acres of land. But it was burdened with a debt of $28,000,000 held by Dutch investors, and it was in the hands of a receiver. This man, who was ignorant and greedy, lent himself readily to the plans of Hill and his accociates. When the representative of the overseas bondholders appeared on the scene, Hill deplored the condition of the property, asserting dolefully that the road was a poor risk. Actually, he knew the line was worth about $20,000,000; he offered to pay $5,000,000.

After Hill gained control of the St. Paul and Pacific, the erstwhile receiver sued in the courts for his share of the loot, claiming that he had deliberately mismanaged the line to depress the price of its bonds, with Hill's connivance. It was poor grounds for a suit, and the courts gave it short shrift. In any case, the Hill crowd picked up the company at a farcical foreclosure sale in 1878 for about fifty cents on the dollar. Moreover, the property was bought on credit, as Hill was not required to pay until the company had been reorganized. The line was renamed the St. Paul, Minnesota, and Manitoba, and its stock was promptly watered to account for the promoters' conception of its true value. Out of a $32,000,000 capitalization, Hill and his partners took $5,000,000 as their "dividend."

Hill, now a tycoon, was confident that he was on his way. He visualized an increase in profit; besides, he knew that the receiver had juggled the accounts of the road and that earnings really had improved. Construction was undertaken, and then came the boom year of 1879. A bumper crop provided the necessary traffic. Hill began to dream big, and as he utterly lacked scruples, he could make his dreams come true. In fact, he eventually became so big and so important that he could talk to J. P. Morgan without losing his trousers. But, in contrast to earlier promoters, Hill was a capitalist who possessed also a producer's mentality. He believed in development, and he strove for a large volume of traffic at reasonable rates. Roadbeds and trains were markedly improved.

The Guggenheim boys in a family business conclave.

E. H. Harriman, railroad tycoon.

J. P. Morgan, Zeus in the world of business.

Completing the first transcontinental railroad, May 10, 1869. Leland Stanford is at center, surrounded by Central Pacific officials.

Thomas A. Edison at work in his laboratory.

The final assembly line at Ford's Highland Park plant in 1913. Bodies skidded ... to be placed on the chassis as it moved below.

Brown Brothers

The New York Times headline, October 29, 1929.

New York Times.

Copyright, 1929, by The New York Times Company.

YORK, TUESDAY, OCTOBER 29, 1929.

TWO CENTS

THE WEATHER

Rain today and probably tomorrow; somewhat colder tomorrow.

Temperatures Yesterday—Max. 51, Min. 49.
U. S. Weather Forecast—For details see Page 63.

THREE CENTS | In Greater | FOUR CENTS | Elsewhere
New York | Within 200 Miles | Except 7th and 8th Postal Zones

STOCK PRICES SLUMP $14,000,000,000 IN NATION-WIDE STAMPEDE TO UNLOAD; BANKERS TO SUPPORT MARKET TODAY

Sixteen Leading Issues Down $2,893,520,108; Tel. & Tel. and Steel Among Heaviest Losers

A shrinkage of $2,893,520,108 in the open market value of the shares of sixteen representative companies resulted from yesterday's sweeping decline on the New York Stock Exchange.

American Telephone and Telegraph was the heaviest loser, $448,905,162 having been lopped off of its total value. United States Steel common, traditional bellwether of the stock market, made its greatest nose-dive in recent years by falling from a high of 202½ to a low of 185. In a feeble last-minute rally it snapped back to 186, at which it closed, showing a net loss of 17½ points. This represented for the 8,131,955 shares of common stock outstanding a total loss in value of $142,002,663.45

PREMIER ISSUES HARD HIT

Unexpected Torrent of Liquidation Again Rocks Markets.

DAY'S SALES 9,212,800

EUROPE IS DISTURBED BY AMERICAN ACTION ON OCCUPATION DEBT

London Urges an Explanation of Move for Direct Payments by Germany.

BANK'S PRESTIGE INVOLVED

Britain and Continent Feel That We Do Not Have Faith in Young Plan Institution.

Memory Honored Day Fete on Ships

...a and in port offi-
...ted Navy Day yester-
...gh major land cele-
... held on Sunday, the
...of the birth of Theo-
...Similar ceremonies
... were reserved for

... was kept by ships
... public was invited
... Flags appropriate
...ere broken out on all
... ships, and even some
...raft in the harbor
...pennants in honor of

...ngeles and the new
...tigible and other
...ir craft at Lake-
...nere ordered out and
...n along the Atlantic
...g over this city and

T. G. BURTON SCHEME IS LAID TO HOOVER

Samuel Insull entering the Cook County jail in Chicago, after
being brought back from Greece, 1932.

Hill was determined that the Manitoba should reach the Pacific. Villard looked askance at this new phase, for Hill was a rough-and-tumble competitor who pressed for reduced costs and genuine railroad service. But to extend the Manitoba to the Pacific seemed to others little more than sheer folly. Nevertheless, Hill watched closely what the Northern Pacific was doing: he saw its weaknesses, and decided to let time and the sheriff take care of Villard. The Manitoba edged its way through the Dakotas and, en route, changed its name to the Great Northern. One day the company notified settlers that they would have to vacate 75,000 acres of land to which Hill laid claim. Outraged, the farmers appealed to Congress, which then offered Hill other lands. He accepted as balm valuable timber stands in Idaho, Washington, and Montana, worth considerably more than the plains of Dakota.

To insure that the freight cars would always be full, Hill went after business with the Orient. Timber for the East was also a good item. And once more agents were sent to Europe to induce immigration from the Old Country. Newcomers were offered low fares, and town sites were developed to populate a burgeoning economic empire. Steadily, Hill pushed his way toward the Pacific, recapitalizing from time to time, and gaining from each financial operation. By 1893, he had four thousand miles of road under his control.

Meanwhile, the Northern Pacific had failed, and Villard was gone. J. P. Morgan entered the picture as reorganizer of the defunct line. Hill picked up $26,000,000 worth of Northern Pacific stock for about $4,000,000. The Northern Pacific was to become a Hill property. Soon he sought to add the Chicago, Burlington and Quincy, a road that would supply a direct connection to St. Louis and Kansas City and entrée into the lumber-consuming areas of the Midwest. But E. H. Harriman also wanted the Burlington to insure his entry into Chicago. The inevitable struggle began, with the initial victory going to the Hill-Morgan forces, which had bought up Burlington stock at 100 to 175. (It was later to be transferred to the Great Northern at 200; legerdemain with paper was still profitable.) While Harriman was seeking to obtain Burlington shares, he discovered that "strange forces" were blocking his efforts. He turned to Jacob Schiff of Kuhn, Loeb and Company, a New York investment house, who then confronted Hill. Hill denied on his honor that he had been responsible for Harriman's lack of success. Schiff tried again, and then questioned Morgan. While "Jupiter," as Morgan was sometimes called, could be ruthless, he had no need to be devious; he admitted that he and Hill had acquired the Burlington. Harriman would be denied any share in its management. Then

Morgan, satisfied that everything was under control, went off to Europe for one of his periodic vacations.

But no one reckoned with Harriman's fury—he proposed to buy the Northern Pacific itself. If he could not buy the Burlington, he would buy up Hill. His plan was bold and boggled the imagination. With the Rockefeller-National City Bank forces behind him, Harriman would beard the Morgan lion in its den. The Union Pacific issued $60,000,000 in bonds to provide resources; appropriate rumors were floated to allay any suspicions in the Morgan camp; and the increase in Northern Pacific stock prices was ever so gentle. Even Morgan sold some of his holdings to take a profit; all of the stock found its way into Harriman's hands. Not that Harriman really needed the Northern Pacific—what he wanted was revenge.

One night, while he was in the Northwest, Hill had an anxiety dream. He felt that something was awry, and, hitching up his special train, he stormed across the continent to face Jacob Schiff in New York. The broker admitted he was buying Northern Pacific stock for Harriman; the market began to gyrate in reaction to the battle of the giants. Hill then agreed to place Harriman on the Burlington board. But he never intended to keep his word; he was simply buying more stock to strengthen his own position. Harriman sent Schiff an order for an additional purchase. Unfortunately, it was the Sabbath—Schiff was not in his office, and the order was never executed. By Monday morning it was evident that Hill and Morgan controlled more than half of the outstanding Northern Pacific shares. When it became clear that the stock had been cornered and none was available to cover shorts, the market snapped as brokers began their parade through the windows of their offices. When Morgan was asked whether he owed the public some statement on the panic that resulted, he growled: "I owe the public nothing." Morgan's rage was towering and magnificent. That his system of consolidating and controlling the American economy should be jeopardized was infuriating enough; to learn that it had been threatened by that "little squirt" Harriman working with Schiff and Stillman and Rockefeller was too much to be borne.

The peace that ensued was a temporary one. Battles between the Hill and Harriman forces were to continue well after both were dead. Hill was irritated by the way Harriman had elbowed his way onto the Northern Pacific board and he planned to build into Oregon. Harriman retaliated by organizing "paper" companies with rights-of-way that conflicted with Hill's plans and then followed by fomenting gang fights between work crews. Harriman knew that not Oregon, but rather California, now a Harriman preserve, was Hill's real objective. He countered with the Deschutes Railroad along the Deschutes River in Oregon; the whole country was treated to the spectacle of the last of the great railroad construction battles, with dynamite hurled by both sides and man-made landslides suddenly descending on a work camp. Again a truce was established, and the Great Northern finally reached San Francisco after Hill's death in 1916. He had left behind $53,000,000. But Hill had not wanted to create a dynasty: he advised his sons to quit the railroad business at an early age, counsel they were to follow faithfully. All the warfare, however, seemed worthwhile, for it meant control of the nation's wealth.

Such marshaling of gigantic forces required great financial skills as well as enormous resources. These were supplied on one side by Drexel, Morgan and Company and on the other by the National City Bank, whose power was James A. Stillman. Eldest son of a well-to-do cotton merchant, Stillman was born in Texas in 1850. At the end of the Civil War, the family moved to New York. When his father suffered a stroke, the lad had to assume the role of family head. Gravitating to a cotton broker's office, Stillman could watch the Wall Street peregrinations of a Vanderbilt and a Seth Low. The Street was then the training ground for "Ned" Harriman, and it looked upon J. P. Morgan as a comer. Stillman became a protegé of Moses Taylor, head of the City Bank, who helped the young man place some judicious investments. When the National Banking Act was passed, Taylor took advantage of its provisions and prospered thereby. The Panic of 1873 found Stillman sitting quietly on the sidelines, refusing to buy; he came out of the cataclysm quite whole. With a banker's innate instinct for safety, he would study investment prospects thoroughly, never purchasing equity shares, only bonds. He was a taciturn, morose man, seldom speaking even to his wife and children. Most people thought his silence an indication of a powerful analytical mind (which he did possess), but his taciturnity was due mainly to slowness of speech, though he was quite articulate in correspondence. His business prospered; he purchased securities carefully; he grew rich. By 1884 Stillman had become a director in the Hanover and City Banks.

About this time Stillman and William Rockefeller met and found that they could be agreeable partners. William was far more ebullient than his dour brother, John, and was generally regarded as more human. While both Stillman and Rockefeller loved money and power, the future banker preferred to abjure risk and, wherever possible, to create the conditions of certainty himself. "He preferred to watch from the sidelines and leap in at the psychological moment and carry off the pelf." In 1891, he was chosen to head the National City Bank, which had been the longtime base of his mentor, Moses Taylor.

Stillman, insisting on efficiency and organization, probed into all sorts of detail. Ruthless with both employees and customers, he ruled mainly by fear. One young stenographer could not bear his gaze and fainted dead away. The same gaze was turned on the bank's portfolio, which he scrutinized again and again. Like John D. Rockefeller and J. P. Morgan, Stillman knew that the age of centralization and combination had arrived, and he meant to be part of it. When the Panic of 1893 seemed to threaten the economy, he obtained gold from Europe at a premium to fill the bank's vaults and show depositors and customers how strong the institution really was. Again he bought securities at bargain-basement prices. Needless to say, he demanded a proper rake-off when he supplied finance to entrepreneurs.

Stillman was now important enough to be of occasional assistance even to J. P. Morgan. Years later he claimed that it was he who obtained the $20,000,000 in gold that Morgan had supplied to the Government during the Panic of 1893. Although Morgan tried to warn him away from E. H. Harriman, Stillman was fascinated by the manner in which the Little Wonder converted the Illinois Central into a profitable venture. Stillman courted Harriman and was soon allied with him. National City interests focused on the Middle West and the hinterlands of America; Morgan's orientation was to the Northeast and Europe. William Rockefeller was intimately involved in all of these developments. The bank became Stillman's home, and it belonged as well to Rockefeller. Big business was polarized, with the House of Morgan at one end and the Rockefeller-National City Bank interests at the other. Yet in any conflict Stillman could always play the role of mediator. The bank merged with rivals; in 1897 the National City took over the Third National. Deposits reached a height of $110,000,000; resources were $115,000,000.

When Jacob Schiff tried his hand at reorganizing the Union Pacific, he was to discover that Harriman, backed by Stillman, also coveted the road. The National City syndicate obtained control, making millions in underwriting fees. Stillman was also involved in the Chicago and Alton reorganization in which capitalization was increased from $34,000,000 to $115,000,000, giving him and his partners, Harriman, Schiff, and George Gould, a profit of $23,000,000. In the process, the Chicago and Alton books were adjusted to transfer $12,000,000 to surplus on the ground that that's where the figures belonged. The idea was to draw a 30 per cent dividend and recapitalize at $93,000,000, which, in the event, grew to $114,-

000,000 in the short span of seven years, giving Harriman, Schiff, Gould, and Stillman a profit of $23,000,000. According to Professor William Z. Ripley, a noted economist, the road had been ravished in the process. During the McKinley Administration, the National City Bank seemed to have a pipeline into the Treasury, learning in advance what re-funding operations were to be undertaken. It was a connection worth millions of dollars. When Stillman bought the Old Custom House for a building site, the McKinley Administration helpfully turned over a property worth $75,-000,000 for $3,200,000. The National City Bank had become a power.

In the Northern Pacific imbroglio, it was in fact Stillman and his lawyer who urged that the invasion of the Morgan stronghold be undertaken. Yet it was Stillman who negotiated the final stand-off. In 1906 Harriman decided to declare a 10 per cent dividend on Union Pacific; Stillman warned that it would raise the price of Union Pacific stock and generate an uproar. Harriman persisted, and though the banker had been opposed to the action, he nevertheless bought Union Pacific stock, just to be in on the ground floor. When the storm broke, he calmly took off for Europe.

During the Panic of 1907, Stillman participated in the Morgan syndicate that supported the market to counteract the hysteria generated by the bears. Some historians deem this event to have been Morgan's greatest moment; only Morgan, they say, could have saved the economy in its time of tribulation. Be that as it may, the more mundane motive was clearly a determination to protect the Morgan-National City portfolios. The question of public service was subsidiary to the rescue of immediate interests.

E. H. Harriman, the object of J. P. Morgan's special scorn, was, like Hill, another of the new breed of capitalists for whom profits could flow from both stock-jobbing and production. Harriman was clever—too clever for most of his contemporaries—brusque, and frightfully efficient. Though his public image was a poor one—Harriman was one of Teddy Roosevelt's malefactors of wealth—he was quite unperturbed. As most successful capitalists of the time knew, ruthlessness was a necessary ingredient of success. When Stuyvesant Fish, associated with him in the Illinois Central, ran into financial troubles, Harriman did not hesitate to dump him overboard.

Harriman was born in 1848, the son of an impecunious preacher. Middle-class mores dictated that he attend the Trinity School, but at the age of fourteen he insisted on leaving school to go to work on Wall Street as a "pad shover," gathering information for a brokerage house. It was excellent training for a future capitalist; his ability to provide quotations to his employer without consulting his notes helped earn him a good reputation. In 1870 Harriman borrowed $3,000 from an uncle to buy a seat on the exchange. He soon developed a blue-chip clientele and was able to include Vanderbilt, Jay Gould, and August Belmont among his customers. The sort of financial cleverness that portended future greatness was revealed when he sold short on certain railroad stocks that were being cornered by the notorious speculator "Deacon" White. When the trap snapped, White was cleaned out, and Harriman was richer by $150,000. However, when he tried the same stunt on the Delaware and Hudson, Harriman did not take into account the Astor interests, whose resources were big enough to strip him of his new-found gains.

Harriman might have remained a "two-dollar broker" had he not married into the Averell family. His father-in-law, an upstate New York banker and railroad tycoon, installed him as a director of the Ogdensburg and Lake Champlain Railroad, setting him on the road to riches. In 1881, he took over the Ontario and Southern, a small, decrepit line, improved its physical properties, and then proceeded to play off the Pennsylvania and New York Central against each other. Having decided to sell to the Pennsylvania, Harriman disappeared from his office as the Central's option reached its deadline. This shrewd transaction foretold the sort of man that the world of business would have to reckon with. He gave little quarter and expected none. He was also blessed with a cynical and somewhat sadistic notion of what passed for humor; one day he took on a camping trip a champion professional boxer disguised as a financier to chastise several braggart camp-guides.

The Illinois Central offered Harriman an opportunity to join the big parade. The Illinois Central had become an important railroad, with connections into the South, but it was entering upon sad days. With the help of Stuyvesant Fish, Harriman clobbered those selling short against the Illinois Central, and was placed on the line's board of directors. Two years later, in 1885, he decided to give full time to the railroad business: Harriman had recognized its lucrative potentialities. He pushed for physical improvements and increased trackage by about a thousand miles. Then he had his first clash with J. P. Morgan.

The Illinois Central was operating the Dubuque and Sioux City under a lease arrangement. Harriman decided to take over the shorter line outright. However, Morgan, who held a large number of proxies on the Dubuque, insisted that Harriman buy his holdings at par. When the little road's board met, Harriman, who dominated the session, declared that proxy voting was illegal in Iowa, and forced the furious Morgan to sell out. Improvements on the Illinois Central were continued; suddenly, in 1890, a sixth sense told Harriman to declare a halt. When the crash hit in 1893, the Illinois Central was in a strong position while over 150 other railroads went bankrupt. Harriman was now in absolute control of the Illinois Central and was able to force the resignation of officers who disagreed with him.

Then Harriman tangled once again with Morgan, who, at the time, was carrying through another of the interminable reorganizations of the Erie. Harriman owned some second-mortgage bonds that would have been relegated to a kind of second-class status under the Morgan plan. Harriman sued, but the courts held with Morgan. The plan failed to work, and some of Harriman's ideas had to be adopted. The incident did not endear him to the House of Morgan. But the Little Wonder was after bigger fish than Erie second-mortgage bonds. The Union Pacific was prostrate; not even Charles Francis Adams, Jr., could salvage it after Jay Gould had wrung it dry. Morgan had refused to touch it, a tactical blunder on which Harriman would capitalize. Some of the Union Pacific stockholders asked Jacob Schiff to try his hand at recapitalization, for the physical plant was becoming pure rust. With Morgan's permission, Schiff went ahead, but he encountered strange resistance in the press and among certain groups of stockholders. Schiff thought that perhaps Jupiter himself might be behind these maneuvers—perhaps the great man was jealous. But Morgan pointed the finger at Harriman, who made it clear to Schiff that he wanted the Union Pacific for himself. He insisted he could rescue the railroad: the Rockefellers' support and $100,000,000 worth of Illinois Central bonds could turn the trick, he thought.

Schiff finally had to give in; Harriman became a director of the Union Pacific and was soon chairman, turning his vast energies to making a silk purse out of a sow's ear. He traveled all over Union Pacific territory, carefully inspecting the line to see what was needed for a gigantic rebuilding job. The money was raised and spent on new ties, new rails, more freight cars, and heavier engines, and on the elimination of the unnecessary curves that had been added in earlier incarnations. Harriman wanted the Union Pacific to be able to handle the traffic and heavy freight that the West was generating. He told one banker that he would put the road in such good condition that "if I were to die and you succeeded me, not even *you* would be able to undo my work." Everyone was surprised that the "two-dollar broker" should know anything at all about practical railroading.

The Union Pacific became a prime piece of property. Crops along its lines were good, people were coming into the region, trade with the Orient brought more tonnage, and business generally revived in the last two years of the century. In 1901 the Southern Pacific and the Central Pacific were added to the empire. It took a $100,000,000 bond issue by the Union Pacific to take over the old Huntington roads. Again, Harriman hastened to rebuild and remake the lines in his own image. But he was arousing hostilities all over the land. His 10 per cent dividend in 1906 brought charges of stock manipulation. The Interstate Commerce Commission investigated, uncovering the rather unsavory Chicago and Alton affair. His biographer's defense of the Chicago and Alton manipulation on legalistic grounds does not refute the fact that the public was gulled. However, Harriman soon lost control of the Chicago and Alton to the "Rock Island crowd," who took it by the same method he had used in grasping for the Northern Pacific: an attack in the open market. This group, the Moore brothers, Daniel Reed and others, added something new to the game of business: control of huge properties through a minuscule investment of their own. They had only recently completed reorganizing the Rock Island, in which control of a capitalization of several hundred millions was vested in a small bloc of preferred stock totaling but $20,000,000.

Harriman's ambitions were unbounded. He had plans for organizing railroads in the Orient and for double-tracking the Trans-Siberian Railroad. The age of outright financial plunder was over; now stock-market machinations could be combined with genuine properties whose real earning power might offer even better ways for playing with paper. In any case, the various techniques still meant a transfer of money from hopeful domestic and foreign investors to promoters and financiers.

Whatever Harriman did was geared to his own interest, though his actions might bear the patina of public service. The development of a community around his home on the top of a mountain was intended to keep out the hoi polloi. Sponsorship of a scientific expedition to Alaska was a good investment, for it might suggest new possibilities for a railroad; besides, it cost only food and board for the scientists. He could not let San Francisco go into decline after the earthquake and fire of 1906 because the city was the western terminus of his railroads.

But, in the end, Harriman proved to have gone too far: his industrial kingdom was an affront to the antimonopoly myth of America. After he died, the Supreme Court ordered the breakup of the Harriman empire. It was more than the American conscience could bear.

CHAPTER 8 Trolley Cars, Tobacco, Meat, and Copper

The business antics of the railroad men were duplicated in other enterprises as well. While the transcontinental trunk lines were being built and plundered, at the same time transportation was developing for expanded urban areas. New York City had its first horsecar line as early as 1832; by 1870 virtually every major city had railways of this sort. Ten years later 18,000 street cars across the nation were being pulled by 100,000 horses and mules, many of them rejects from the farm. New York's elevated lines, however, were using steam locomotives, and though electricity as a source of power had become feasible, electrification developed rather slowly. Jay Gould was once invited to observe a test of electrical power and was so frightened by flying sparks that he would have nothing to do with so uncontrolled a source of energy. For a few more years, New Yorkers had to bear with the dirt, soot and noise—the "external diseconomies," in the economists' phrase—that were visited by growing industries on the public.

The organization of local transportation, however, continued to be as chaotic as it had been on intercity lines. New York had thirty different companies, each with its own franchise, each operating independently of the others. It occurred to no one that competition—the ideology of the new capitalism—could generate social diseconomies. Passengers had to pay several fares as they traveled from one end of the city to the other. And since most of the operators were interested solely in the profits to be derived from stock manipulation, the physical properties became threats to life and limb.

Obviously something better was needed if such areas as downtown Manhattan and Brooklyn were to be exploited properly; in the absence of adequate local transit facilities, it appeared more than likely that an independent city to the north would spring up. By 1890 even steam was inadequate. Some localities installed cable cars, but these could not handle the growing traffic; the few cable cars that remained in later years were relegated to the status of curiosities for tourists.

The application of electricity to the growing transit problem was

solved by Frank J. Sprague, an inventor and tinkerer in electricity. Born in
1857, Sprague attended the U. S. Naval Academy, where he received training in electrical engineering. A visit to London convinced him that steam
was a poor source of power for an urban railway. Unfortunately, the
alternative system he was to develop fell into the hands of such speculators
as Thomas Fortune Ryan, whose manipulations were to bring a fortune to
financiers but not to inventors. Urban transportation became a happy
hunting ground for as greedy an assortment of rogues as could be gathered
in the narrow alleys of Wall Street.

After his Navy service, Sprague had gone to work for Thomas A.
Edison, but in 1884 he resigned to start his own electric-motor manufactur-
ing company. He was invited to electrify the traction system in Richmond,
Virginia, and after enormous obstacles he got it into operation.

Although his solution was a crude one by later standards, Sprague
demonstrated the practicability of using electricity for a traction system.
After his firm had been bought out by Edison General Electric, Sprague
shifted his attention to elevators for skyscrapers. It then dawned on him
that an efficient traction system ought to place motors in each car: up to then
an electrified "locomotive"—a passenger car filled with motors—simply
pulled the whole train. Putting a motor in each car made the system much
more flexible. Sprague then did for Chicago what he had done for
Richmond. The traction industry was never the same thereafter. The inevitable patent-infringement suit was brought by General Electric but when it
seemed likely that Sprague's case was superior, the new giant meekly settled.

Sprague was that rare instance of a creative entrepreneur who had the
ability and good fortune to come out victorious in a struggle with big
business. By and large the traction industry was dominated by financial
syndicates of dubious reputation, who for twenty-five years behaved like
fabled vampires living on human blood. These syndicates went from city to
city, bought up the franchises of scattered companies, created corporations
and holding companies, and floated well-watered securities, by now the
traditional device for transferring someone else's wealth to one's own
pocket. It was purely incidental that the capital accumulated by these
methods might be used for economic growth.

Among these later nineteenth-century economic buccaneers were
Charles Yerkes, William Elkins, Peter Widener, and Thomas Fortune Ryan.
Their financial predations took place all over the country—New York,
Philadelphia, Chicago, and Pittsburgh—controlling the traction systems,
and in some instances electric generation, of well over seventy-five cities
and towns. Some historians are kind enough to perceive some good in all

the stench stirred up by these men: they provided a cheap transit system, it is said, and extended the cities' borders outward, enabling the masses to reach suburbia and even exurbia. The only trouble with this argument is that the masses didn't leave for suburbia until well into the twentieth century. In any case, traction became a sordid business, embedded in the slime of municipal politics and the worst of Wall Street. From 1880 to 1905 those who developed local transit and electric utilities were virtually indistinguishable from the dominant factions in city politics. The admixture was essential, as the city franchise provided the legal *raison d'être* for the whole business: to operate a company one had to have the right of eminent domain and the right to use the city streets and to tear them up at will.

How to loot the public was amiably demonstrated by Charles Yerkes, prototype of a character in several novels by Theodore Dreiser. Yerkes had once served a seven-month prison term in Philadelphia for embezzlement. Since that city was no longer fertile ground, he went off to Chicago, there to ply his merry trade as a small-time broker. He then secured control of Chicago's horsecar lines, electrified them, and built the "Loop," an elevated railway line encircling the downtown area, to this day a major eyesore. Yerkes simply bought off Chicago's aldermen to insure his use of the streets, and reorganized the companies to death, meanwhile drawing in the public with as much watered stock as he could issue. His capacity to corrupt others became notorious: he controlled mayors, governors, and legislatures. He admitted that his way of making money was to buy up "old junk," repair it a bit, and then unload. So far as he was concerned, it was the "strap-hanger that paid the dividends," refreshing candor in a financial buccaneer. When the politicians finally got around to their brand of double cross, Yerkes unloaded his holdings on Ryan and Whitney for $20,000,000 and simply went off to England, never to be heard from again.

Yerkes got his start with an assist from Peter Widener, a Philadelphia butcher whose shop in the eighteen-seventies had been a gathering place for local politicians, and from William Elkins, a former grocery clerk who had made a killing in Pennsylvania oil. Widener dominated City Hall, learning the ways of politics before he became a financier. It was obvious that experience in one field was good training for the other. Widener and Elkins were as skillful in financial skulduggery as their onetime protégé Yerkes had become. They were soon involved in various New York deals and manipulations with William Whitney and with Ryan. They knew that with electrification the potentialities for building fortunes would be greater than ever. Widener brooked no opposition: he could tell a group of recalcitrant stockholders at an annual meeting who wanted to talk over a proposal,

"Vote first and discuss afterwards." And as the traction systems and utilities were gathered under a single umbrella, there was little of their own money that Widener and Elkins would use in their financial machinations.

But Thomas Fortune Ryan was the prince of the group. One historian has called him the "hero" of traction scandals. Ryan was born in 1851 in Virginia and at the age of seventeen was a clerk in a dry-goods store in Baltimore. In 1879 he went on to New York to work for a broker. In a relatively short time he had made enough to purchase a seat on the Stock Exchange. Ryan was always close-mouthed, keeping all information to himself. At one point, he became involved with the Guggenheim brothers in a Congolese venture. The Guggenheims had obtained a concession from the Belgian king, Leopold II, who held his African territories as a private fief. Half the capital for the exploitation of the Congo's resources was contributed by the Guggenheims and Ryan. Out of this came Intercontinental Rubber, a $30,000,000 promotion that Bernard Baruch, an upcoming broker, floated on Wall Street. When Ryan was confronted with the charge that his Congo companies literally made profits from human slavery, he responded, "I sleep like a baby."

The Metropolitan Securities Company was the vehicle for Ryan's operations in New York's transit system. Ryan, Widener, Elkins, and Whitney bought a franchise from one Anthony Brady for $250,000. The franchise was then resold to Metropolitan for over $950,000, giving the traction gang a profit of some $700,000 and an almost useless franchise to Metropolitan. This was only one of several similar transactions. The manipulations became a maze of stocks, bonds, leases, operating companies, holding companies, construction companies, and reorganizations. Political maneuvering enabled Ryan and his friends to break the hold of another corrupt operator, Jacob Sharp, on the Broadway line. A cable line costing $2,500,000 was turned over to Metropolitan for $10,000,000 in stock. The Columbus Avenue line was exchanged for $6,000,000 in stock—the original cost was $500,000. The defunct Fulton Street line was transferred for $1,000,000. Of course, the gang was taking paper for a group of small and almost useless properties. But there was method in this seeming madness, for the ultimate purpose was to build up Metropolitan for slaughter in the stock market. Unable to buy several profitable north-south lines held by old families not eager to sell, they leased the better systems for exorbitant leasehold fees. Rebuilding their tracks would yield an additional profit through construction companies. For trackage that cost $150,000 a mile, the syndicate charged $500,000 to $600,000 on the books.

When the Public Service Commission decided to investigate, records were unaccountably lost or destroyed. Of course, all of these antics did not differ much from what was taking place elsewhere. Only Yerkes did not mind showing his books with a brazenness that brushed others off. Now Ryan and his pals were ready to strike. Suddenly, Metropolitan began to pay dividends: not that earnings were that good; the largesse to stockholders simply flowed out of current receipts. Eager buyers were drawn to the stock as soon as it was listed on the exchange in 1891. The syndicate helped build the price up to 279 and then simply sold out. Finally, Metropolitan, thoroughly plundered, and with thousands of stockholders, went into bankruptcy. In all, some $90,000,000 had gone to the syndicate. Nevertheless, Ryan's political connections were good enough to enable him to escape prosecution. When Whitney, who was a member of the syndicate, died in 1904, leaving an estate of some $40,000,000, there was not a single share of Metropolitan among his assets.

There was little in which Ryan was not involved, from insurance to tobacco; in each case he was concerned with finance rather than production or service. In the Equitable Life Assurance Company incident he came up against bigger financiers than he, and had to step out. The insurance company had been established in 1859 by Henry Hyde as a stock company. It did well, and by 1899, when Hyde died, its assets were over $400,000,000. But the directors had engaged in various forms of "milking," using the company's resources to purchase securities on which they could personally profit. Moreover, the company was becoming involved in strange promotions. When a struggle for control broke out, young James Hyde, who had inherited his father's controlling shares, sold out to Ryan for $2,500,000, although the stock was worth close to $7,000,000. The Equitable board included several well known and powerful buisnessmen, among them E. H. Harriman and Henry Clay Frick. Harriman didn't think Ryan was good enough for Equitable, and opposed him: the company's financial resources were too large, he thought, to be left in such hands. Besides, Harriman wanted a piece of Equitable for himself. Ryan finally sold out to J. P. Morgan in 1910, reluctantly handing over control of $504,000,000 in insurance assets for $3,000,000. By this time even the public was aware how men like Morgan had used insurance companies as a dumping place for poor securities. Five years later Morgan sold Equitable to T. Coleman du Pont.

Then there was the tobacco affair. In 1898, Ryan, Whitney, and several others organized the Union Tobacco Company after having previously bought the National Cigarette and Tobacco Company. More important perhaps than these acquisitions was their control of the ever-popular Bull Durham brand and an option to buy Liggett and Myers. This was a dire threat to James Duke's American Tobacco-Continental empire. A deal was subsequently worked out, with American Tobacco taking over Union and Continental purchasing Liggett and Myers. When the Consolidated Tobacco Company was organized as a holding company in 1901, Ryan and his friends magnanimously took common stock, then worth less than bonds, without informing anyone that the contemplated reduction in internal revenue taxes would soon reverse the relationship between the two types of securities.

And finally, there was William C. Whitney, the urban, polished scion of a New England family, whose good student record at Yale matched that of his classmate, William Graham Sumner. Through marriage, he had established a connection with Standard Oil. At first Whitney was quite civic-minded, helping the reformers in New York to bring Boss Tweed to book; in the process he won control of the Tammany machine. His political activities took him up the ladder of Democratic party politics to the post of Secretary of the Navy in the Cleveland Administration. But he had made enough money to acquire a lavish mansion on Fifth Avenue in New York, and he needed more to support it. Embarking on the road to wealth, he locked arms with Ryan, Widener, Elkins, and others to engage in a sometimes hilarious, always venal dance.

It became evident that any business that might develop a wide market for its product would wind up under a financier's umbrella. Entrepreneurs themselves would be converted into financial tycoons, as was the case with James B. Duke, for if money could be made by supplying consumers with goods and services, infinitely more could be gathered by manipulating securities. Duke and his tobacco empire are striking not so much for size or importance of product, but because they illustrate so well the methods that were employed in bringing together disparate branches of a new industry and the way in which a new technology—mechanized cigarette-making— could enforce combination. Tobacco, of course, was an ancient plant that had been smoked by the natives when Columbus stepped ashore in the New World. By the sixteenth century, tobacco was well-known in Europe. Jean Nicot, French ambassador to Portugal, had sent some leaves back home where it was supposed they could cure certain ailments. Today "nicotine" is considered something less than the perfect remedy it was thought to be three centuries ago.

Tobacco had been an important antebellum plantation crop, and after the Civil War provided the basis for a growing industry. John Ruffin Green sold tobacco under the trade name of "Bull Durham," after Durham, North Carolina, the town in which it was processed. The picture of the bull became a noted trademark that Blackwell and Carr, successors to Green, fought diligently to protect. They learned quickly that testimonials and advertising were essential in convincing the consumer that he should either smoke their tobacco or buy their chewing plug. By 1884 the Blackwell and Carr factory had become the largest in the world. Soon all sorts of brands of tobacco were being produced in Durham; their processors were determined to make the city the tobacco capital of the South.

However, the town of Winston, near the sleepy village of Salem, in North Carolina, soon began to rival Durham as a center for manufacturing tobacco products. One of the aggressive young salesmen in that area was R. J. Reynolds, who had shifted the family business to Winston in 1875. Lewis Ginter and John Allen had a thriving business in Richmond, and Liggett and Myers was a growing firm in St. Louis. There was a lust for tobacco in American jaws all over the nation, and chewing and smoking brands flowed in ever-increasing quantities to satisfy it. Concerned with the protection of their trademarks, which clearly distinguished one brand from another, manufacturers passed out premiums and coupons, gave rebates to jobbers and dealers, and distributed bribes in appropriate places to put their brands in strategic stores.

It was not long before Buck Duke would outpace all the others. Born in 1856, James Buchanan Duke was named after the Democratic President elected in that year. It was the last time a Duke was to go Democratic. Duke's father had been a small farmer before the Civil War. After Appomattox he returned to the land to grow and peddle tobacco under the trade name of "Pro Bono Publico." His little curing factory grew steadily, and by 1872 it was producing 125,000 pounds of tobacco a year. In 1874, the elder Duke and his two sons, James and Ben, moved the factory to Durham. By this time, James had become quite active in the business, with the hope of eventually going into business for himself. Instead, the elder Duke took both boys in as partners to form W. Duke & Sons. To obtain more capital several partners from outside were brought in.

Cigarettes had been popular in Europe for many years, though in America they could not yet compete with plug and smoking tobacco. But Duke felt that he was hitting his head against the stone wall of Bull Durham; Blackwell and Carr had moved far ahead of their rivals. Duke knew that he could not compete with them, and so he decided on cigarettes. But these had to be rolled by hand, and although Duke had some of the best workmen in the business, their output was still too modest for an expanding market.

With the acquisition of the Bonsack cigarette machine, however, there was little doubt that the Dukes would forge ahead of everyone else, for the machine could turn out 120,000 cigarettes a day. Aware that cigarettes were an urban indulgence, Duke set up a branch in New York, competing vigorously and successfully with the better-known firm of Ginter and Allen. He gave premiums and matched Ginter advertisement for advertisement. A favorite selling device was to insert a picture of a "sporting girl" in each package of cigarettes. He put artful drummers on the road to stimulate business; men were hired to go from store to store asking only for Duke's product; and incoming immigrants were given free cigarettes at ports of entry. By 1890, W. Duke, Sons and Company had become first in the industry.

Meanwhile, Duke was watching developments in oil, steel, cottonseed oil, whiskey, and sugar. All were being pressed into the mold of combination through trusts. Why not tobacco? But first one had to get into the good graces of financiers. Duke began to negotiate for small thirty-day or sixty-day loans with New York bankers, always repaying promptly. Soon clean-cut Wall Street representatives were dropping by to solicit loans: Duke had established a line of credit with the powers that counted. Finally, he was able to convince four other large concerns that they all ought to get together, and in 1890 there was born the American Tobacco Company, a fusion of Duke, Ginter, Kinney, Kimball, and Goodwin—90 per cent of the cigarette industry. Capitalization was set at $25,800,000, though the combined tangible assets were just slightly over $3,000,000. With a generous allowance for goodwill and other intangibles, the amount of water was at least $12,500,000. Eight years later a subsidiary was formed to handle plug tobacco. Dealers were forced to take other items through tie-in sales: if they wanted cigarettes, they had to take the combine's plug.

American Tobacco continued to expand by all means available, some fair, many foul. Virtually absolute control of cigarette-making machinery was worked out. Dealers refusing to take the combine's products were blacklisted and subjected to ruinous price wars. Through all these operations, Buck Duke ruled with an iron hand: he did not hesitate to fire his star salesman, Edward Small, when the latter refused to move his family to Cincinnati. By 1905, American Tobacco and its related Consolidated Tobacco Company, both headed by Duke, dominated three-fourths of the plug-tobacco business, three-fourths of the smoking-tobacco, and over nine-tenths of the snuff, in addition to having virtually complete control of the cigarette market.

Doerhoefer, Whilock, Marbury, and G. W. Gail were absorbed in the early eighteen-nineties; capitalization jumped another $10,000,000. But there were problems: an anticigarette campaign was mounted, and Duke's business practices were generating antimonopoly sentiment. Appropriate charitable donations, however, lessened some of the hostility. More serious was the attention Duke attracted from Wall Street.

Oliver Payne, a Standard Oil potentate, and several friends decided to buy American stock in order to gain control of so lucrative a venture. Duke told Payne that he could have the company and that he would simply go off to start another. Payne backed down, and Duke's control was never again threatened. Liggett and Myers was taken over at about that time. In 1899, it was R. J. Reynolds' turn to join the fold. The process of consolidating within the industry went on unchecked. With each step, capitalization was increased, until it reached $68,500,000 in 1899. Consolidated, which had been set up in 1898 for the plug business, became a holding company in 1901, but its common stock was closely held to insure control. Somewhat earlier, Thomas Fortune Ryan and his traction crowd decided to get into tobacco. Ryan got hold of National Cigarette and Blackwell's Bull Durham to form Union Tobacco, generously capitalized at $22,000,000. After a brief tussle, Ryan and Duke beamed at each other, gave Union to American Tobacco, Liggett and Myers to Continental, and a $20,000,000 profit to Ryan. The results were not bad for a few months of work. The board of directors of American Tobacco now included Ryan and Widener, as well as the old tobacco men.

To make up for the milking Ryan had given him, Duke went after other companies. It was at that point that Reynolds came into the fold. Once again securities were manipulated to yield a profit to insiders. Operations were always carried out in secret. During the 1901 recapitalization, stockholders were not told that the trust had learned, probably through Senator Nelson Aldrich of Rhode Island, that the 1898 tobacco tax would be cut. Had this fact been known, holders of old securities would have demanded a higher price. Of course, cigarette prices were not reduced.

Another reorganization was carried through in the hope of getting around the Supreme Court's decision in the Northern Securities case. In all of these maneuvers, there was reason to doubt that Duke and his confreres were overly considerate of the rights of the many stockholders that had been drawn in. The technique for dominating the market included price cutting, creation of bogus independent companies to create a fiction of competition, offering of the usual premiums and rebates, initiation of rival brands to confuse consumers, and the outright acquisition of rivals. Once a market had been won, retail prices were kept on an even keel, while the jobber was now squeezed with higher wholesale prices. Nor was the foreign market neglected. Duke tried to penetrate Japan, but the Government there decided to set up its own monopoly. He bought a factory in England, only to inspire the formation of the Imperial Tobacco Company, as British manufacturers thought to protect Englishmen against the onslaught of American cigarettes. After several years of conflict, the inevitable cartel agreement was reached: the United States and Cuba were given to Duke, the United Kingdom to Imperial, and the rest of the world shared through the British-American Tobacco Company.

The entire industry, with the sole exception of cigarmaking, was now controlled by the "Tobacco Trust." Inevitably, it became the object of investigation; frequent lawsuits were filed in the state courts in an attempt to break the trust's hold, but just as frequently the judges held with American Tobacco's lawyers. It was obvious that Duke had little to fear from the state courts. Then in an appeal taken by the Government from the New York Federal Circuit Court, the Supreme Court surprisingly ordered the dissolution of American Tobacco. It was evident from the facts the Government had uncovered that American Tobacco was a monopoly: not only did it control virtually the entire industry, but it had achieved its exalted position by price wars, industrial spying, phony independents, and other activities that bordered on criminal conspiracy as defined by the antitrust laws.

All this Duke blandly denied: he had conducted his business as a gentleman. His only comment on learning the Supreme Court's decision was, "In England, if a fellow had built a whale of a business . . . he'd be knighted. Here they want to put him in jail." But Dick Reynolds, who had been forced into the trust, was delighted: he was to give Duke "hell" with his fast-selling cigarette, Camel. The company's assets had to be distributed among the original members; nevertheless, Duke got the lion's share—one-third of the cigarette business. Yet so far as restoring "fair competition" was concerned, the dissolution decree of 1911 did not seem very effective. At any rate, such was the view of none other than Louis D. Brandeis, and he was supported by fuming farmers and disgusted liberals. (The Government's zealous prosecutor was James C. McReynolds, later one of the most conservative justices on the Supreme Court bench.)

Duke had thoroughly absorbed the ideology of big business through the years. Deeply resenting the Federal Government's intervention, the only kind words he had to say were directed to the Federal Reserve System. Yet there were other fields in addition to tobacco: electric power seemed a noteworthy investment also. By the time of his death in 1925, Duke's Southern Power Company was one of the largest in the South: he had paralleled Vanderbilt with a second career. Like most capitalists of his day, Duke was violently antiunion: a strike on his estate in New Jersey was broken by having seventeen workmen thrown into jail. There was ample time to enjoy the huge estate as well as three other homes. The lawn in New Jersey was reportedly tended by a crew of forty men who were instructed to use nothing but filtered water. When he gave $40,000,000 to Trinity College on condition that its name be changed to Duke University, he was charged with having bought himself a monument to perpetuate his name. Not even Rockefeller had gone that far with the University of Chicago. Learning that the institution was to be coeducational, one wag suggested that it be called "Duke's Mixture." Another asked, referring to old Washington Duke's puzzlement over the Holy Ghost, "Why don't they call it the Father, the Son, and J. B. Duke University?" Duke distributed most of his property before 1925 to avoid inheritance taxes. A third went to his wife, a third to his daughter, and a third to the Duke Endowment. It was thought that the estate's $75,000,000 comprised controlling shares of stock in a number of companies. Like Hill and Harriman, Duke embodied the characteristics of industrialist and financier, and in the age of high finance, it was the latter that predominated.

Such an admixture was evident in other fortunes as well. When Simon Guggenheim took his family from Switzerland to come to America in 1847, his primary reason was to escape religious persecution and perhaps to discover a freer life in the new country across the Atlantic. Neither he nor his son Meyer really dreamed that they would become millionaires many times over. When the Guggenheims arrived in Philadelphia, the only trade they could undertake was peddling. Meyer soon realized that it was more profitable to manufacture and sell one's own product than to act as middleman for another's. He selected stove polish, an important housewife's item, and when he accidentally discovered that adding soap made a better polish, the Guggenheims were on their way. Meyer was soon able to expand into tailoring and groceries. He produced a large family over the years, among them seven sons, several of whom were to play a central role in the building of the Guggenheim fortune. Their lye business threatened the Pennsylvania Lye Company's monopoly, and when that company offered to buy him out, Meyer made a handsome profit in the transaction.

Meyer Guggenheim moved up the economic and social ladder with perceptible achievements in the world of business. When an uncle in Europe asked him to dispose of a shipment of machine-made embroidery, Meyer turned over another handsome profit, for the product was superior to and cheaper than the domestic handmade variety. Lace embroidery became the foundation of the early Guggenheim enterprises. Soon there was a branch in Europe that was used as a training school for several of the sons. But all of this was as nothing compared to what was yet to come. Once, years later, a distant relative congratulated Meyer for having used his head. Meyer pointed out that he had built his fortune by buying good things and sitting on them. "I do not owe my prosperity to my head," said he, "but to another extremity entirely."

One day a fellow Philadelphian persuaded Meyer to join him as a partner in a Colorado silver mine. Dubious even while inspecting the property in the West, Meyer nevertheless invested $4,000, later adding more funds to put the shafts and tunnels into working order. He need not have fretted so much, for a rich strike was made, and overnight Meyer Guggenheim became a millionaire, at least on paper. But the ore had to be taken to smelters; it seemed to Meyer that these were making all the profits, while mine producers had to take whatever the market could bring. In 1887 he went into smelting and found that his suspicions had been correct. Later, when a new smelter was to go up, the town of Pueblo, Colorado, was delighted to provide the $25,000 to help out, as suggested by Guggenheim. The sons were now old enough to go into the business and most of them did. Meyer was certain that each would become a millionaire in his own right. He did not care for Wall Street machinations, insisting that all holdings should be kept under tight control by the family. When an English group of investors offered Guggenheim $4,000,000 for his mining and smelter properties, he conceded that he might accept $10,000,000, although he was not overly anxious to sell.

To be sure, much of the early Guggenheim prosperity stemmed directly from the Sherman Silver Purchase Act of 1890, which committed the Government to buy 4,500,000 ounces of silver a month, almost twice the quantity purchased previously. With the price of silver drifting up to $1.25 an ounce, it was no surprise that Meyer was determined to hold on to his mines and smelters. He negotiated a concession with the Mexican government—no small coup indeed—as a way of circumventing tariff barriers. By 1895, the Guggenheims were taking out of their properties a profit of $1,000,000 a year. The lace business was sold, and the family now devoted themselves exclusively to mining.

With their European attitude, neither Meyer nor his son Daniel, who became the driving force in the Guggenheim enterprises, would have much to do with trade associations or other price-fixing ventures. They could undercut any rival and could hold their own in business warfare. Eastern financiers began to cast interested stares at the mining and smelter business. H. H. Rogers of the Standard Oil crowd assembled several properties to create the Amalgamated Copper Company, capitalized at $75,000,000, of which at least $38,000,000 consisted of the usual water. Rogers followed up this coup by merging several smelter operations into the American Smelting and Refining Company, a $65,000,000 giant with $50,000,000 of watered stock included. There was general headshaking: it was madness and folly. But Rogers was confident that he could eventually create enough tangible value to absorb all lead and silver production. The Guggenheims watched with some apprehension. As a kind of counterploy, they formed, with William Whitney's help, the Guggenheim Exploration Company: Guggenex. American Smelting and Refining soon ran into trouble: its labor practices were antediluvian, to say the least, and the Guggenheim Mexican operation proved to be a formidable rival. In 1900 Rogers gave in, and American Smelting was reorganized, with the Guggenheims now part of the combine. Capitalization was increased to $100,000,000, with $45,000,000 going to the Guggenheims in return for some $15,000,000 in cash and credits. It was enough to control the entire empire.

Meanwhile, Rogers and his associates, the Lewisohns, had planned to make their profits as overseas selling agents for American Smelting. The Lewisohns' background was quite similar to that of the Guggenheims. Adolph Lewisohn had been a copper importer who frequently evaded custom regulations by recrating his ingots; or he would fill freight cars with low-grade ores from his Montana copper mines to take advantage of lower railroad rates. When Lewisohn and Rogers learned that the Guggenheims planned to employ their own selling channels, they were furious. Rogers wanted to dissolve the merger, and even conducted bear raids against American Smelting and Refining. He sued in the courts, forcing Guggenheim to give some business to his United Metals Company. But the Guggenheims withstood the Rogers onslaught undisturbed; they felt quite magnanimous in handing over a slice of the marketing business to Rogers and Lewisohn. Although the bears, mainly Rogers, were trying to hurt American Smelting and Refining in the stock market, the Guggenheims simply picked up more stock to bring their holdings over the 51 per cent mark. They came out of the fracas several million dollars richer.

Up in Montana, mining had also become a way of life—dominated by the Anaconda Copper Mining Company, often described as the Big Snake. The big men in the Montana fields were William Clark, Marcus Daly, and Augustus Heinze. They came into conflict with each other frequently enough to generate violent industrial warfare. Clark had come to Montana in 1863, after a stint as a schoolteacher in Missouri. Becoming a store-owner in Virginia City, Colorado, he acquired one day a supply of rare tobacco in Idaho and resold it for a small fortune. After several similar ventures, the next step was a bank. Meanwhile, Butte had become a gold-mining town. Clark had shipped some gold to the mint, and now he turned to that field in earnest: he went off to the Columbia School of Mines in New York to learn the business, literally from the ground up. His entry into mining began with the foreclosure of a small stamping mill and refinery; several larger ones were built later. It was the same successful method employed by the Guggenheims: the profits were in the refinery end.

Marcus Daly first came into the area as a mining engineer for a Salt Lake City banking house. He knew mining, discovered Montana prospects to be quite good, and put up a refinery for his Utah sponsors. When the bankers rejected his advice to take over a small mine, the Anaconda, Daly bought it for himself. He got all the capital he needed from several California friends which he used primarily to buy up the land around the original hole in the ground. At three hundred feet he found what he expected: a huge vein of pure copper, the mainstay of the Anaconda Copper Mining Company.

Daly and Clark had been good friends, but a falling-out over Clark's decision to run for territorial representative to Congress spelled trouble. Clark would have been elected had he not slighted Daly, who saw to it that Clark's opponent, a Republican, was elected. When Daly wanted Anaconda named the state capital the next year, Clark conducted a successful campaign for Helena. Clark's next political try was for the Senate. Again Daly had him defeated. In 1898, Clark tried once more, this time succeeding by spending huge sums of money and having his henchmen steal ballot boxes in Daly's stronghold. Whereupon, Daly instigated an investigation which forced Clark to resign. Two years later, Clark returned to politics, making his election stick. He now had the help of the flamboyant Heinze, who loved to pose as a Robin Hood. Meanwhile, Daly, together with H. H. Rogers, had created the Amalgamated Copper Company, a $74,000,000 giant with the Anaconda as a base.

Heinze had come to Montana in 1899 directly from the Columbia School of Mines. In 1892 he leased a mine and built a smelter for small miners to whom he posed as an antimonopolist. As a diversion, he got a paper railroad charter to annoy the Canadian Pacific, forcing the railroad to buy him out. Now he was ready to attack Daly, counting on Clark's support. When the Boston and Montana sued to halt encroachment on its veins, Heinze responded with the "apex theory," asserting that the owner of the land under which a vein came to its apex could follow that vein wherever it went, even under another's land. He almost made the theory stick, closing down several Amalgamated mines, which had inherited the lawsuit from the Boston and Montana, only because the judge was one of Clark's henchmen. When the dispossessed workers threatened to lynch the judge, the order closing the mines was rescinded.

Nevertheless, Heinze continued his legal battle with rapid-fire lawsuits, meanwhile extracting about a million dollars' worth of high-grade ore from beneath Amalgamated's holdings. Amalgamated retaliated by blasting Heinze's cross-cuts into its property. The Montana underground became a scene of physical battle that spilled over into the saloons of Butte, where flying beer bottles became a common sight. When the pliant judge finally declared Amalgamated an illegal trust, the Daly-Rogers forces simply shut down tight to starve the enemy into submission. This time the people turned on Heinze. He met the mob, 15,000 strong, crowded around the country courthouse, and like Mark Antony, soon had the crowd on his side. Finally, peace was restored between the contestants when the legislature passed a bill to remove prejudicial judges in a lawsuit. Secretly, all the Heinze properties went into an aptly named company, Butte Coalition, which paid Heinze $10,500,000. Butte Coalition itself was then swallowed up by Amalgamated. Years later Heinze was to pay dearly for his challenge to the Rockefeller interests—who had backed Rogers—when Morgan and Rockefeller allowed him to go down the drain in the Panic of 1907.

Heinze had taken his $10,500,000 to New York, buying control of the Mercantile National Bank to help peddle securities of a "paper" company he had organized, the United Copper Company. The Standard Oil crowd watched Heinze force up United Copper, and then suddenly in 1907 the oil men unloaded all the shares they had accumulated at low prices. Banks began to call in loans on United Copper; soon Mercantile National was in trouble. The New York Clearing House forced Heinze out, but the panic was on. The Knickerbocker Trust Company was next. The Standard Oil crowd, in their search for revenge, had in effect triggered one of the severest financial crises the nation had ever suffered. To be sure, they only wanted to ruin Heinze; the Knickerbocker failure had not been anticipated. Heinze was indicted, but acquitted. He returned to Montana shorn of his $10,500,000.

For the Guggenheims it was time to undertake world-wide endeavors. They employed John Hay Hammond, one of the world's leading mining engineers, at a fabulous salary to seek out new properties wherever they might be. Capitalization was increased still more, as the Guggenheims ventured into international operations on a scale hitherto unseen. American Smelters Securities was formed in conjunction with British interests; capitalization was $77,000,000. The Guggenheim mines were transferred to American Smelters Securities for $22,000,000. The complex of corporate relationships meant control of Guggenex through M. Guggenheim's Sons, an older company held by the family; control of American Smelting and Refining by Guggenex; and control of American Smelters Securities by American Smelting and Refining. The whole structure supported a heavy debt and capitalization. The Guggenheims' personal fortune had reached at least $50,000,000 based on their holdings of the mineral wealth of the Rockies and Sierra Madres. The investment of the public in Guggenheim securities now totaled about $200,000,000.

The Guggenheim empire seemed to many to have become an absolute monopoly. The prosperity of many a small community depended on its decisions. The combine controlled over ninety properties. By closing down smelters they no longer wanted, they could bring disaster to dozens of towns; by refusing to take the output of a single mine, they could bring ruin to its operators; nor would the Guggenheims bother with the little fellow. All this power, exercised at will, brought them hatred and suspicion throughout the West. After the death of old Meyer in 1905, the brothers' association with Whitney and Ryan took them into the chief financial circles of Wall Street. They were now directors in many companies, and they became great philanthropists. Brother Simon, who had always wanted a political career, bought votes at $2,500 to $5,000 a head from Colorado legislators to have himself appointed a U.S. senator. His role in the Pinchot-Ballinger affair—a dispute over conservation policies—was hardly a creditable one, although somewhat later he was accused of harboring "socialistic" ideas.

Overseas activities became central to Guggenheim operations. Together with Thomas Fortune Ryan, the brothers found themselves involved in the Congo. A Canadian venture proved a fiasco when their man, Hammond, underestimated a mine's potential. Some said that the Guggenheims had used a question over title to gull investors; eventually the mine paid nearly $30,000,000 in silver. When the Rockefeller interests started to buy into American Smelting and Refining, Bernard Baruch came to the rescue with additional funds. Then, with Morgan support, the Guggenheims decided to exploit the mineral riches of Alaska. Though it was to be an expensive and not very profitable venture, Alaska became known as a "Guggenmorgan" enterprise.

However, a burgeoning industrial society was bringing other problems.

Union organizers prowled the fields to encourage organization as the only way of protecting the rights of the workers. They noted the vast gulf between the Guggenheims and their employees. The Western Federation of Miners found that their attempts to improve conditions for the miner were to be crushed with strikebreakers and militia again and again. Labor relations became a brutal jungle as workers fought back with the only weapon they had, the strike. The Guggenheims were not averse to importing foreign labor to break the union, and while one of the brothers did leave his comfortable office in New York to investigate what was happening in Colorado, he made no effort to halt the flow of strikebreakers. Smelter workers in Mexico were paid $1.50 a day, a tribute only to their hardiness. One historian claims that stockholders received more in dividends than the workers did in wages. Accidents in the Guggenheim mines were extraordinarily frequent. It seemed—at least to the worker—to be the age-old tale of capitalism: the Moloch of capital accumulation demanded their sacrifice.

By the early twentieth century it was evident that the Guggenheims had arrived: they were now one of America's richest families. Despite occasional charges that they had used their companies for self-enrichment, giving little care to the ordinary stockholder, they had become a living embodiment of the American dream of rags to riches.

The movement toward "trustification" and merger was affecting virtually every industry in the land. Even an industry so highly decentralized and geographically ubiquitous as meat-packing was being squeezed into the mold of centralization and large-scale operations. Prior to the last half of the nineteenth century, meat-processing had been quite primitive, done either at home or by local butchers. Cincinnati had become the pork center of the nation; the industry did not shift to Chicago until after the Civil War. The creation of a major industry based on hogs and cattle was the work of men like Philip Armour, Gustavus Swift, Nelson Morris, and Michael Cudahy.

Armour was born in upstate New York in 1832, and at the age of nineteen went on to California, intending to prospect for gold. Digging, however, was not to his taste; instead he organized a business to provide laborers for others, preferring rather to supervise the work and drum up trade from hopeful gold hunters. After five years of this activity, he came back to New York with eight thousand dollars in savings, and promptly went off to Milwaukee, where a brother had gone into the grain business. After a while he persuaded his brother to move with him to Chicago, where he went into the meat business with John Plankinton. The Civil War provided a market ample enough to make the firm prosperous, but Armour's greatest coup came when he sold short on pork at thirty to forty dollars a barrel in anticipation of the defeat of the Confederacy. He was able to cover his commitments at eighteen dollars a barrel, as commodity prices took a nosedive. The profit on three months of speculation came to over a million dollars.

With fresh capital supplied in this manner, Armour and his partner began to expand, buying out small rivals and making their plant one of the largest in the Middle West. But shipping animals to local slaughterers in the East was most unsatisfactory, for the shrinkage and loss was costly. Such losses could be prevented by selling "dressed meat": by slaughtering first and shipping afterward. But this arrangement demanded refrigeration to prevent spoilage en route.

The problem was solved by Gustavus Swift, whose method for refrigeration en route was soon adopted by all the packers. Swift had been in the meat business in Massachusetts, and through the years had moved his buying activities further and further westward, coming to Chicago in 1875. Refrigerated cars with ice tanks and heatproof doors were available, but the railroads would neither supply them nor undertake the risk of keeping them iced. Besides, dressed meat meant less freight than livestock on the hoof. Swift bought his own cars, and using the route of the Grand Trunk Railroad of Canada, he was able to overcome railroad opposition.

Meanwhile, Armour was competing vigorously, especially with his closest rival, Nelson Morris. Each would arise early in the morning to beat the other to the cattle market. One midnight Armour called his buyers together, supplied them with lanterns, and told them to hunt up all the owners of stock and buy up the entire supply. Morris countered by going to the countryside to acquire animals even before shipment to Chicago. Eventually, however, Armour and Morris came to a gentlemen's understanding, living togther in peaceful coexistence. The industry began to use by-products, making a variety of goods out of the parts of the carcasses once dumped into the river. Fertilizer, glue, buttons, combs, bristles, felt, glycerine, and oleomargarine were some of the items that chemists rescued from bones and hair. Armour was particularly fond of German chemists, who were quite clever in devising new by-products. He once told a supervisor to receive cordially an expected visiting German, as he "may have something more in his head besides dandruff."

Inevitably, all the major packers began to "cooperate" with one another. Small firms were bought up by the larger ones, distributing agencies

were established in Omaha, Kansas City, and St. Louis. The Big Four—
Armour, Swift, Hammond (later merged with Armour), and Morris—fixed
prices and divided sales territories. When they bought from livestock
dealers they made certain that none would bid up prices. It was an "accidental harmony of minds," functioning through secret pooling arrangements. But these pools were often unstable. The Allerton pool of 1888
collapsed, to be succeeded by the Veeder pool of 1893. Eventually, a more
stable relationship would have to be established. In any case, by acting in
concert, the packers were able to force down freight rates on one railroad
under the threat of turning over their shipments to another.

The business demanded a highly liquid position, one that Armour was
generally able to maintain. When a banker once sought to recall a $100,000
loan before the due date, Armour berated him mercilessly, finishing his
tirade by throwing $100,000 in currency on the browbeaten banker's desk.
The packers resisted interference from all sources, including the Government. The efforts of unions to organize the workers were fought off in
campaigns akin to Grant's storming of the Confederacy. Employer violence
and blacklisting of union sympathizers won the admiration of all industrialists. Neither the tainted-beef scandals during the Spanish-American War
nor the stark publicity of Upton Sinclair's exposures halted the packers in
their march toward monopoly. Sinclair's novel, *The Jungle*, aroused the
public's reaction by turning its stomach: it revealed the unalloyed brutality
and stench of the stockyards and created an almost instantaneous demand
for meat inspection. To call the beef supplied to the Army merely bad
would have been euphemistic: at one training camp thousands of maggots
dropped from a shipment as it was unloaded. Armour insisted that he
personally knew nothing, that he would not do business in such a manner,
and that he was hurt by the Government's subsequent charges.

After Armour's death in 1901, the packers set up the National Packing Company, thus formalizing their habitual mode of cooperation. In
addition to the packers—Armour, Swift, and Morris—there were stockyards and refrigeration-car companies in the combine, eleven companies in
all. The Federal Government investigated in 1904, and finally in 1905 the
Supreme Court ordered dissolution. This was ignored on the ground that
the packers were immune because they had previously given information to
a Federal agency. The claim was upheld by the court in 1906. Some wags
thought that Washington would become a health resort for "immunity
baths." It was clear that the antitrust laws were having little effect, at least
on the meat packers. Between 1902 and 1910 no less than six antitrust
actions were undertaken against them; each time they managed to wriggle

out. When action was again threatened in 1912, National Packing was finally dissolved.

Like many businessmen, Armour indulged in his favorite philanthropies. One of his major benefactions was a grant of $4,000,000 to start the Armour Institute of Technology. Yet when his favorite preacher solicited a donation at a time when prices had fallen, Armour told him, "There's a lot of daylight between you and the ground." Many persons were quite willing to counterbalance the less savory aspects of their business careers with eleemosynary pursuits: to their minds one was a perfect offset to the other.

CHAPTER 9 The Big Three

American business was dominated in the last quarter of the nineteenth century by three men, each of whom had his own domain. Steel belonged to Carnegie, oil to Rockefeller, and Wall Street to J. P. Morgan.

While he was still working for the Pennsylvania Railroad, where he started as a telegrapher and rose to a division superintendency, ambitious young Andrew Carnegie had already become a successful investor. His early enterprises provided him with enough money to undertake the first of his many trips to Europe. Sensing in 1865 that iron was going to replace wood in bridge construction, he secured the backing of J. Edgar Thomson and Thomas Scott of the Pennsylvania to set up the Keystone Bridge Company. One month after Keystone was organized, Carnegie resigned from the Pennsylvania Railroad to give full time to his own interests. The Union Iron Mills Company, in which he was a partner, supplied raw material to the bridge firm. The railroads were expanding and there was a great market for iron. Yet the attractions of Europe were irresistible: he could very well leave the business of producing iron to his brother, Tom. Carnegie was not a practical iron man, and never became a true steel man. He cared little for the details of business, leaving those to the men he employed, who would give him the facts he needed. But there were few who could match him in the art of salesmanship.

Still, Carnegie knew enough about business to want absolute control for himself. Union Iron Mills and Keystone Bridge were organized as co-partnerships, a pattern that was to be followed in all the Carnegie enterprises later on. The first step toward personal domination was to squeeze out Tom Miller, an early associate. Carnegie wept crocodile tears over the lack of trade and offered to buy out Miller. It was a technique the little Scotsman was to use over and over again. In any case, Miller was fed up with Carnegie's machinations and backbiting, and he left. With the purchase of Miller's share, Carnegie was now the boss of Union Mills. He then had visions of making a fortune out of stockselling, and for the time that he gave to it, the security business proved to be quite profitable. He opened an office in New York, and through his frequent trips to London was able to place about $30,000,000 worth of securities with English investors.

Meanwhile, he became a culture vulture, haunting museums and concert halls and reading books that would broaden his mind. His business methods were direct and forthright: he would secure an order for a bridge, Union Mills would supply the iron, then Carnegie would sell the bond issue financing the bridge. Profit came from iron manufacturing, bridgebuilding, and commissions on the bonds. English investors were once assured that the United States Government itself had chartered a bridge company; this bit of blarney helped boost the price of the bonds. Having invested in the Pullman Company, Carnegie persuaded his former employers, the Pennsylvania Railroad, to give Pullman exclusive rights for sleeping cars. On his word Thomson and Scott lent $600,000 to the Union Pacific, taking several million dollars of Union Pacific stock in trust. The transaction forced up Union Pacific stock prices on the exchange, offering Carnegie, Pullman, and Scott an opportunity to dump their own holdings of Union Pacific. This diversion cost Carnegie his seat on the Union Pacific board and strained his friendship with the Pennsylvania Railroad executives.

The iron business kept growing—how much it grew was a secret that Carnegie and his associates kept to themselves. New furnaces went up in 1870. But the men who knew the production end—Andrew Kloman and Tom Carnegie—wanted to make steel. The Bessemer Kelly process had proved itself in England. Carnegie, however, refused to be a pioneer, until he had made another trip to England in 1873, taking enough time to inspect several mills rather than talking to bankers. Finally impressed, he returned as fast as the boat could travel to set up a steel firm— Carnegie, McCandless and Company—with a capitalization of $700,000, of which he took $250,000. The Panic of 1873 was harassing to everyone, but Carnegie was adept in holding off his creditors while dunning his debtors without letup. Kloman had gotten himself into trouble with several investments and had to turn his share of the Carnegie enterprises over to the Scotsman for safekeeping to avoid losing it. (Kloman had not the protection of limited liability in the troublesome investments.) Carnegie helped Kloman settle his debts, and when the storm blew over, refused to return his partnership. The second man was now out.

A new steel mill was to be built, but Carnegie's old boss, J. Edgar Thomson, was annoyed because its location was too close to the Baltimore and Ohio Railroad. Carnegie promptly named the mill the Thomson Works to placate him: the Pennsylvania Railroad rebates were too juicy a morsel to relinquish. The Edgar Thomson Steel Company replaced Carnegie, McCandless, and capitalization went up to one million dollars. The production genius was Captain Billy Jones, a great steelmaster whose driving energy converted Carnegie's conception into reality. In 1875 the mill was completed, and soon Jones doubled the company's output of steel.

Now it was the turn of William Coleman, Tom Carnegie's father-in-law, to be shown to the exit gate. It was Coleman, in fact, who had encouraged Andrew Carnegie to go into the iron business in the first place. Carnegie applied his technique for generating friction, and Coleman, disgusted, took $100,000 for his share, though the true value was undoubtedly considerably greater. Carnegie would hand over no more than what he considered the book value to be, pretending to pay no attention to earning power, at least for purposes of these transactions. His appetite for wealth and power became insatiable. Wanting half the Thomson stock for "sentimental reasons," he subscribed to an additional amount, paying for it on a "pay-as-you-go" plan, that is, out of profits. In industry pool arrangements, he fought strenuously for a bigger slice of the pie that the companies divided among themselves; he sidled up to the politicians to make certain that they would maintain an adequate tariff on imported steel; he cast about for ways to dump other of his associates. McCandless was next on the list, but the old man thwarted Carnegie by dying before he could be shoved out. Carnegie wrote the remaining partners a maudlin letter: "I shall never be able," he said, "to think of [McCandless] without a stinging pain at the heart . . . Let us try to be as kind and devoted to each other as he was to us. . . ." McCandless' widow got no more than the vastly understated book value of her late husband's share.

When Carnegie went after William Shinn, another partner, he discovered he had caught a tartar. Shinn went to court to avoid being ousted from the company. Carnegie retreated, contemplating his next move. It soon came, with the designation of Tom Carnegie as head of the company; Shinn resigned in anger. Again came the offer of "book value." Again, Shinn went to court. Rather than have the company's earnings records displayed there, Carnegie paid over an extra $200,000. There were now seven partners left, but only the Carnegie brothers and Henry Phipps counted. In 1881, all the properties were tied together in one package as Carnegie Brothers and Company, Ltd. Its capitalization, still far less than earnings would justify, was $5,000,000, of which Carnegie took $2,000,000 for himself. And while Billy Jones and brother Tom were laboring diligently to turn out steel in Pittsburgh, Carnegie himself cavorted through Europe, cutting capers at elegant parties.

In 1882, Carnegie latched on to Henry Clay Frick, who was becoming known as the King of Coke of Connellsville, Pennsylvania. Young Frick had come off the family farm to go to work as a bookkeeper in a distillery. With his eye steadily on the potentialities of making coke, he enlisted the financial support of Judge Thomas Mellon, founder of a bank in Pittts-burgh. Mellon liked the young man, introducing him to his own son and heir, Andrew. Frick and the younger Mellon were to become close friends in the years ahead. By the eighteen-seventies, H. C. Frick and Company controlled 80 per cent of the coke output around Connellsville. It was a prosperous business, with profits running as high as three dollars a ton. When Carnegie and Frick met, the Scotsman decided to buy a minority interest in the coke enterprise. His anaconda appetite soon revealed itself: the Frick company's capitalization was increased to $3,000,000 and Carnegie took half. He then bought up enough shares from others to become a majority stockholder. But Frick was not the patsy Carnegie's other associates had been: more than once he told his acquisitive partner that he liked neither the tone of his voice nor the tone of his letters. Carnegie, for the time being, decided to bear with his recalcitrant associate. More ovens had been installed and coke output was up to six thousand tons a day.

Then Carnegie grabbed up the Homestead Steel works, which seemed unable to get under way, plagued by labor troubles. The new acquisition began to fashion structural steel shapes for the coming age of skyscrapers. All the while Carnegie was hunting up as many celebrities as he could, hobnobbing with such British luminaries as Herbert Spencer, and announcing to everyone that he was indeed Mr. Steel himself. Yet he knew little of what went on in his plants. Once asked by a Government inspector why steel with 25,000 modulus of elasticity rather than 20,000 couldn't be supplied, Carnegie offered the assurance that the extra 5,000 modulus would be forthcoming. He then turned desperately to one of his men to ask for an explanation.

Carnegie got married in 1886, after his mother had died; she had extracted a promise from him not to take a wife while she was alive. The conflict with Frick began to intensify, though on such issues as unionization they generally agreed: neither one wanted unions around their plants. However, in 1887 Carnegie ordered Frick to settle with the union, and the latter promptly resigned. Again, Carnegie retreated, giving his stubborn partner a free hand to deal with labor in the coke fields. Frick quickly acquired the enviable reputation among business men as a "labor buster," for he would brook no interference from outsiders. When Jones was killed in a plant accident in 1889, Frick took over the steel operation too. Now in command, he showed himself to be as skilled an organizer as Carnegie was a schemer. Both were possessed of a ruthless lust for money and power, and while Carnegie was given to moralizing at the drop of a hat, Frick was contemptuous of what seemed to him little more than unctuous hypocrisy.

The Duquesne Steel Company was next to be absorbed into the expanding Carnegie empire. Carnegie circulated rumors through the trade that Duquesne's new rolling methods were defective. He kept the company out of the industry pool and generally caused enough trouble to enable Frick to acquire it without much difficulty. Carnegie began to write articles filled with words of praise for the workers. He was full of maxims and homilies that he wrote down or recited to anyone who would pay attention. He gave numerous parties at which his guests might enjoy themselves—provided they followed their host's prescriptions for gaiety. The companies were reorganized into the Carnegie Steel Company, Ltd., in which Andrew Carnegie held $14,000,000 out of the $25,000,000 capitalization. Employing some thirty thousand workers, it was the largest steel and coke combine in the world.

Of course the union—the Amalgamated Association of Iron and Steel Workers—was quite weak, but it did have an agreement, expiring in 1892, covering its members at the Homestead plant. Carnegie sent a notice that thereafter the plant would be nonunion: paraphrasing Lincoln, he declared that the company could not be half organized and half unorganized. Obviously, his choice was the second. At the same time, he advised Frick to build up inventory in anticipation of trouble. Frick ignored Carnegie, undertaking to negotiate. He then proposed a wage cut. The men were stunned: after all of "Andy's" public declarations of love for the workingman, surely this was not what the top boss really wanted—Frick must be kidding. Had not Carnegie been a pal to the men in the mills? They could not know, of course, that Frick's desk was piled high with cables from Carnegie in Europe urging a declaration of war against the union. When the workers realized that Frick meant business, they struck.

Meanwhile, Frick had arranged with the Pinkerton Agency, a strikebreaking organization, for three hundred guards, who approached the Homestead plant on barges floating up the Monongahela River. The union men greeted the Pinkertons with bricks, rocks, and catcalls. Someone fired a gun, and the war was on. The Pinkertons were driven off, but eight thousand National Guardsmen—a full division—were dispatched by the governor to restore order. From comfortable quarters overseas, Carnegie cabled Frick to be certain that no strikers were rehired. Two days later he assured a reporter that he was no longer active in the steel business and that he really had no knowledge of the events at Homestead. About a week afterward, a young anarchist, Alexander Berkman, inveigled his way into Frick's office, wounding him with a pistol. Frick recovered, and Berkman went to jail. Eventually, the strike was broken, but the world had now caught up with Carnegie's hypocrisies, which could generate such tragedy. It recognized at long last the great gap between his creed and his deeds.

A congressional investigation ensued but with indecisive results. Leading Republicans, worried about the political consequences, thought that Frick should come to terms with the union. The steel and coke magnate was adamant. The politicians then came to collect a Carnegie pledge to contribute $50,000. Frick gave them a check for $25,000. Later he found a note from Carnegie cautioning not to give the party more than $10,000. When the union finally called off the strike in November, Carnegie cabled Frick from Florence, Italy, "Life worth living again! First happy morning since July. . . ."

Homestead now had a new manager, Smiling Charlie Schwab, who had worked his way up under Jones from the lowly job of stake driver. Schwab had been a grocery clerk in Braddock, Pennsylvania, and was offered a job in the plant by Jones, who liked the lad's looks. Within six months he had been raised to assistant engineer and at the age of twenty was an assistant superintendent. When Jones discovered that Schwab had the gift of gab and could get along with Carnegie, he made him his chief messenger to the big boss. Schwab was able to match the great man story for story; he knew he could climb the company ladder by working on Carnegie's vanity and playing the role of court jester. But he also had an unquestioned talent for directing production; he introduced many a laborsaving device to increase the plant's output. Schwab was full of ideas, and he never hesitated to put them before Frick and Carnegie.

Schwab was elevated to the presidency in 1887, as Frick began to draw away to involve himself more and more in other affairs with Andrew Mellon. In 1893 the Government discovered that test armor plates made by the company had been doctored, and obviously Schwab was responsible. But, although the Government considered this to be outright fraud, Carnegie was able to reach into President Cleveland's office, and the company escaped with a penalty of $140,000 and a mild rebuke.

Frick moved ahead with his scheme for an integrated combine: he built a company railroad to connect all the plants; he acquired the Bessemer ore mine from Rockefeller, despite Carnegie's opposition; he bought a small railroad from the Great Lakes to Pittsburgh; and he built a fleet of ore-carrying steamboats. All the middlemen had been eliminated, siphoning the profits of these activities directly into the coffers of the company.

The rift between Frick and Carnegie was widening. Frick did not care for Carnegie's delusions of grandeur, and Carnegie was jealous of Frick's growing stature in the world of business. The final break stemmed from a quarrel over the price of coke to be charged to the steel works. The market was bringing $3.50 a ton, but Carnegie saw no reason why his steel plants should pay more than $1.35 a ton to Frick's coke company. Carnegie resorted to his favorite gambit of passing out slurs behind his victim's back. But Frick was no easy mark. When Carnegie once more offered to buy him out at the book price, Frick simply filed a suit in equity, calling Carnegie a fraud and a cheat; of course, he received as much venom as he gave. The public looked on with widening eyes as the company's enormous profits came to light. Moreover, Frick had incontrovertible evidence that Carnegie didn't need a protective tariff. The implication was clear: the tariff had been a means for maintaining high prices. Carnegie, unable to take the revelations and unprepared for what might come, caved in.

The reorganized company—the Carnegie Company—merged steel and coke. The capitalization was now $320,000,000, of which Frick took $31,300,000, and Carnegie $174,400,000. But Carnegie was now getting tired; it seemed time to sell out, and he did, eventually, retiring with an immense personal fortune. Needless to say, he drove a hard bargain. Every time a new prospective purchaser came along, the price went up. When Rockefeller thought he would buy the steel combine, the asking price was $250,000,000. The oil man threw up his hands, and the price promptly doubled. Yet Carnegie might not have sold at all if Wall Street promoters had not thought that they could outflank him by building their own steel operation. Carnegie responded by starting a tube plant, threatening J. P. Morgan's National Tube Company. He lent support to George Gould's plan for a new railroad from Pittsburgh to the East Coast, giving fits of prostration to the Pennsylvania. At the same time, he bought new ore ships that would rival those of the Rockefeller empire.

It was clear to the other moguls that Carnegie had to be bought out. A deal was negotiated with the House of Morgan. Carnegie's price came to almost $500,000,000 in gold bonds, giving him a mortgage on what he knew was a profitable business. Morgan had to pay, for he knew that his own companies, with their heavy load of debt and watered stock, were vulnerable. Besides, he had never liked the little Scotsman and just wanted to be rid of him. There was no room for a Carnegie in the new United States Steel Corporation.

Retiring with Carnegie were most of his associates, who suddenly discovered themselves to be millionaires. Pittsburgh went wild with their antics. One had dozens of portraits painted of his wife; another gave each of his friends one of those newfangled contraptions, an automobile; a third quoted the prices of his many possessions to anyone who would listen. It was a hilarious affair; some observers thought that all of Carnegie's philanthropies could not balance the harm done by the sudden wealth of the Pittsburgh millionaires.

Now Carnegie was ready to become a public-spirited citizen. He proceeded to give away his money, and by the end of his life his charities and gifts totaled over $350,000,000. He established relief and pension funds for steel workers; gave $5,700,000 to the New York Public Library; built over 2,800 local libraries, each one to have his name attached; set up the Carnegie Institution with a grant of $22,300,000; built the Carnegie Institute of Technology in Pittsburgh; gave $29,000,000 to the Carnegie Foundation for the Advancement of Teaching; provided Carnegie Hero Funds to eleven nations; supported the Simplified Spelling Movement; funded the Scottish Universities Trust and the United Kingdom Trust; gave new organs to churches; established the Dunfermline Trust to bring "sweetness and light" into the lives of the toiling masses of his native Scottish town; granted $10,000,000 to the Carnegie Endowment for International Peace; and topped all of these with the $125,000,000 Carnegie Corporation to act as a clearinghouse for his vast network of philanthropies. Of course, there was some grumbling: the citizens of Dunfermline growled that "Andy" was trying to get them to eat as he wanted them to. In 1919, Carnegie died in his eighty-fourth year, hailed as a great benefactor to mankind.

As these developments moved along at their steady pace, John D. Rockefeller and his friends were molding the oil business into a single cohesive unit. A favored device was the secret rebate on railroad freight charges, facilitated by the control of tank cars. To be sure, Rockefeller had not invented the rebate, a kind of quantity discount, but as the largest shipper in the industry, he could demand that it be denied to his rivals, thus converting the rebate into a formidable weapon of industrial warfare. By the eighteen-seventies the Rockefeller business in Cleveland had grown into a huge operation. Since general incorporation laws were becoming common, Rockefeller and his partners, Flagler and Andrews, formed the Standard Oil Company of Ohio with 100,000 shares of stock, of which Rockefeller took about 25 per cent. Rockefeller's associates were an interesting group. S. V. Harkness provided the financial image, easing the way for Rockefeller's numerous borrowings. However, Henry Flagler was perhaps the most important associate of all: he was a hard driver and restless, with an imagination that roamed farther afield than even Rockefeller's.

To Rockefeller's orderly bookkeeper mind monopoly appeared to be the primary objective. Plans were prepared—in secret—to dominate Cleveland's oil-refining market. The rebates extracted from the railroads gave the group an enormous advantage over the twenty-nine other refineries in the area. Output was increased, and competition intensified; the other companies in Cleveland simply had to go. These methods were extended to other cities, where there was always some operator ready to fall in with Standard's plans. The railroads were told to end their rate wars, which had been a most disorderly way of conducting business. Rebate agreements were then worked out with them, territories were parceled out to the cooperating oil companies, imports of crude oil from overseas had to be curtailed, and production plans were to be coordinated. In short, the entire industry was to be cartelized.

Small refiners and oil producers reacted sharply, of course. Rockefeller was roundly denounced, but that disturbed him not a whit. Relentlessly, he went ahead with his scheme. Monopoly was to go to those seeking it, for in an economy of free enterprise it meant precisely the sort of power that Rockefeller was determined to achieve. Flagler's South Improvement Company was duplicated in Philadelphia, Pittsburgh, and New York. Once Standard had dominated the refining business, it was obvious that it could dictate the price of crude oil, giving Rockefeller the same sort of control that the Guggenheims were to develop with their smelters. The collapse of South Improvement did not deter the Rockefeller forces. Flagler proposed another road to domination: a cooperative producers' association. Such opponents as J. J. Vandergrift were won over to become key members of the new combine. However, producers in the oil fields could not be controlled easily, for as prices fell their output of crude was increased; Rockefeller simply withdrew, blowing up the whole arrangement.

During the depression after 1873, Rockefeller managed to take over the terminal facilities of the Erie Railroad in New Jersey, adding them to his recently acquired New York Central terminals. Now every barrel of oil shipped east by his rivals passed through his hands, giving him information on what his competitors were producing at the refinery and to whom they were selling. A complicated freight-rate arrangement, which provided for the elimination of freight charges on the shipment of crude from the well to the refinery, was forced down the throats of the railroads. When the New York Central balked, Rockefeller quietly told them he would take his business elsewhere. This was a serious threat, for Rockefeller was the heaviest shipper of refined oil.

The scattered collaborators in New York, Pittsburgh, and Philadelphia, including C. H. Pratt and H. H. Rogers from New York, and John Archbold, who was operating in the oil fields, were then brought together under one umbrella. Standard was reaching out to grasp the entire industry when it suddenly found itself set against the Pennsylvania Railroad. The Empire Transportation Company, a major pipeline firm, had bought out several refineries with the help of the Pennsylvania Railroad, which was interested in business for its lines. When Rockefeller heard of this, he recognized the threat. Confronting Scott of the Pennsylvania, he complained that it was unfair for a railroad to be in the refinery business. When the railroad president stood firm, Rockefeller declared war. His first step was to cut prices in all of Empire's markets. Then he got the New York Central and Erie to start a rate war against the Pennsylvania, which, in its turn, responded vigorously as Empire went around battling for markets and refineries. It seemed that Rockefeller had met his match, but his luck held out, for soon the Pennsylvania, harassed also by labor difficulties, went into a tailspin. Scott had to sue for peace. Rockefeller's terms were unconditional surrender with Empire's pipelines and refineries to go to Standard. The pious Rockefeller might well have echoed the Psalmist: "I have pursued mine enemies and overtaken them: neither did I turn until they were consumed."

Shortly after Empire was absorbed by United Pipe Lines, associated with Standard, Rockefeller acquired the Columbia Conduit Company. By 1878 he had taken over the nation's whole pipeline business. The railroads were brought into a new freight-rate pool, as the most complete monopoly ever built in America took shape. Rockefeller was not yet forty years old. But the violence of the criticism and attacks began to mount. His only response was to remain silent, for in his own eyes he was engaged in the Lord's work. The oil business had been delivered into his hands by divine decree and was no concern of the public. Nevertheless, the number of lawsuits increased, and charges were made that Standard was gouging the independent producer and ruining countless others. Even Allan Nevins, who in his study of the Rockefeller career has been more than kind, had to conclude, "In the path which Rockefeller had left were strewn ruined men and abandoned plants: before him lay an unquestioned control over tremendous sources of wealth."

The Producers' Protective Association tried to counter Standard's continual attack on its members, but to no avail. The state of Pennsylvania moved to indict several of Standard's top men for criminal conspiracy; New York's Hepburn Committee initiated its investigations. Nevertheless, Standard stood firm, its witnesses either refusing to answer questions or telling bald-faced lies under oath. Rockefeller's belief in his mission was enormous; he was introducing order and sense into a chaotic industry whose notion of competition was really the crime to be suppressed. Rockefeller had no regard for his rivals—they were to be either absorbed or crushed. That competitors might have some rights simply never occurred to the former bookkeeper. Yet to make progress required disposition of all those annoying lawsuits. And so, raising a flag of truce, Rockefeller accepted an agreement that eliminated discriminatory rates for shipments of equal quantities. That was the rub, for Standard shipped more than anyone else.

Now Standard moved to eliminate Tidewater Pipe Lines, a seemingly unintimidated competitor. First, Rockefeller had to have a line into the East Coast. When there was some doubt about a franchise in Bayonne, New Jersey, the hesitant mayor and council were mysteriously won over and the line laid overnight, before competitors knew what was happening. The few remaining refineries were attacked with the usual price wars to deprive Tidewater of any customers it might line up. Archbold connived to throw Tidewater into bankruptcy by having one of his henchmen acquire some stock in the company and then sue for receivership on the ground of mismanagement. Roadblocks were thrown in Tidewater's way as it tried to get financing. The harassment was incessant and unremitting, until finally Rockefeller picked up enough Tidewater shares to force it into an agreement giving most of the business to Standard.

The Standard group now comprised forty companies. Rockefeller owned fourteen of them outright; he and his associates controlled a majority of stock in the remainder. Flagler was the "lawyer" and contract maker, the pipelines were under Vandergrift, Rogers supervised manufacturing, Pratt handled marketing, and William Rockefeller was moving into finance. It was quite a team. Some sneered that its captain, John D. Rockefeller, was only utilizing other men's ideas, whether about tank cars, pipelines, or by-products, but there seemed no halting the industrial conquest. In 1875, Rockefeller decided to wipe out the wholesaler and do his own marketing. The whole nation was cut up into regions, and a vast network was established to destroy the independent wholesaler and many retailers as well. Standard's delivery wagons became universal as they cut into local markets that serviced the consumer. Where price wars brought a loss, Standard simply charged it against profits elsewhere, something that the small dealer was unable to do. Even foreign markets were invaded: Standard became a byword all over the world.

When Rockefeller denied that the forty companies were all part of the Standard Oil combine, the nation's response was that he lied. In fact, every time a Standard officer denied a charge, under oath, whether true or not, he was considered a perjurer. Now, if the nation thought of the combine as one company, why not make it so? The trust form had been used in other industries, and it demonstrated how easily subsidiaries could be managed. So the various companies were reshuffled into separate state combines in which the stock of each could be held by a small group of trustees. This became the shape that the Rockefeller enterprises assumed, according to a plan devised in 1882, of which the public was unaware until six years later. The trustees controlled two-thirds of a capitalization set at $70,000,000.

Needless to say, the major figures in Standard paid obeisance to both political parties with duly appreciated campaign gifts. Rockefeller gave to the Republicans, Payne to the Democrats, thus covering both sides of the street. When Payne wanted to send his father to the U. S. Senate from Ohio, it turned out to be a not-too-difficult maneuver. Yet some producers were able to send well-placed darts into the thick Standard hide. When George Rice discovered that part of his freight payments were being siphoned off to Standard on "draw backs," he filed a suit that forced Rockefeller to return the money. Rockefeller sanctimoniously asserted that he hadn't known of the arrangement, yet the "draw back" had been used for some time as a powerful competitive device. It was simply a portion of the freight charged on another's shipment and turned over to Standard. In 1885 an oil company in Buffalo, New York, brought charges against Archbold, Rogers, and three other Standard officers for attempting to sabotage its plant by bribing the manager to overheat oil so that it might blow up the works. The penalties were mild, the judge evidently being in the pay of the trust. This was more than the public could bear.

The war on the oil trust escalated, and the New York State Senate ordered an investigation in 1888. In the witness box Rockefeller was all gentleness. He admitted to a $90,000,000 capitalization and control of three-fourths of the oil industry, but denied that this meant monopoly. After all, there were eleven other companies in the industry. He swore that he had not been involved in the South Improvement Company, that he knew nothing of rebates, and that he was always fair with competitors. Since there were no records, there was no guilt. In fact, the trustees in Standard had been quite law-abiding: it was all the fault of the subsidiaries. The

U. S. House of Representatives also ordered an investigation, and in 1890 came the Sherman Antitrust Act, a law with which Senator Sherman had little to do except lend his name.

Rockefeller was now getting tired. He was enormously wealthy, with investments in banks, railroads, and other industries, and he was concerned over the state of his health. More and more he moved into the background. Nevertheless, Standard kept on the move, going into natural gas. At one point, Toledo, Ohio, decided to give a franchise to a private company; it discovered that both applicants were owned by Standard. "Was there no end to the tentacles of this octopus?" asked people all over the nation. The attorney general of Ohio discovered that the trust structure violated state law and moved to revoke the company's charter. Then, in 1892, the United States Supreme Court declared the entire edifice an illegal monopoly. But this hardly undermined Standard's power, as it kept grinding away at real and fancied rivals. Rockefeller's gestures at compliance revealed the Sherman Act to be a hollow statute. Holders of some 973,000 shares of Standard liked their trust certificates too well to turn them over for stock in the underlying companies. Standard decided it could not force the exchange and simply forgot about the antitrust law. The combine remained under the control of 26 Broadway, Standard's home in New York. No action was taken against the continued violation.

Meanwhile Rockefeller became a philanthropist. He gave $600,000 to start the University of Chicago and was hailed throughout the land by educators and ministers. But academic critics of the industrial milieu, such as Professors E. W. Bemis and Thorstein Veblen, were to have an unhappy time under the regime of William R. Harper, first president of the university. In the midst of his good works Rockefeller had to come to terms with the brothers Merritt, who claimed they had been done out of their Mesabi-range ore holdings by Standard. Competitors kept pecking away at the monster's flanks, but Standard countered with its network of industrial spies effectively to crush the opposition.

Another attack on Standard was now mounted by literary people. Henry Demarest Lloyd published in 1894 his *Wealth Against Commonwealth,* a damaging indictment of the Standard monopoly. Some present-day historians, overanxious in rewriting the annals of American industry, have charged that Lloyd loaded his case against Rockefeller and that he was hysterical and even dishonest. Their charge is a weak, latter-day apologia for a folk hero with feet of clay. As Chester M. Destler has shown, Lloyd's devastating attack was, in fact, based on six years of painstaking research in all sorts of archives and was accurate down to its minutest details. Archbold's rebuttal to the Lloyd bill of particulars was hardly credible, for Archbold had ruled himself out of court as the prime corrupter for the Standard crowd. After the turn of the century came the muckrakers and Pulitzer and Hearst, exposing all sorts of evils embedded in the industrial system. Ida Tarbell's *History of the Standard Oil Company* recorded the company's abuses from 1872 to 1895. Thomas Lawson turned on his former friends in his *Frenzied Finance* with vivid accounts of the financial machinations of Rogers, Stillman, and William Rockefeller. The dirty linen was waving in the wind for all to see, and the public began to view Rockefeller and all his works as menaces to the social order. Even his charities were declared to be nothing but tainted money.

Rockefeller was genuinely puzzled. Had he not kept water out of his stock? Had he not always paid his bills? Had he not avoided the pitfalls of Wall Street? Did he not employ sixty thousand men in his plants? What did the mob want? So far as he could understand, God, and not the people, had given him his money. In fact, all the Standard men were God-fearing. Archbold was a deacon, William Rockefeller a regular churchgoer, Vandergrift a most pious person, and Stillman always finished a day at the bank with a prayer asking the Lord to protect its deposits.

Despite all the howls from literary folk and their readers, Standard was not weakened: its principals were not deflected from the road to power and ever more power. John D. Rockefeller might take a back seat, but there was always Rogers and Archbold. Rogers made no pretense of being anything other than an industrial pirate: he loved a fight and he loved to take his chances. Why not, when the cards were generally stacked in his favor? But Archbold's business behavior clashed sharply with his religious pretensions, at least in the eyes of outsiders, if not in his own. He used bribery, coyly refused to answer questions "on advice of counsel," and even destroyed books and records whenever they were likely to become embarrassing. The official money dispenser for Standard, he reached all the way to Washington through well-placed henchmen. Many a legislator was on Standard's payroll.

Standard had become a huge empire, and it was necessary to hold it together. No better device had been invented for such a purpose than the holding company, now available under New Jersey statute. The Standard Oil Company of New Jersey became the instrumentality for governing the numerous corporations from 26 Broadway. In addition to oil, Standard's holdings included six major banks under Stillman's control, Amalgamated Copper, the tobacco trust, Mesabi ore, the Gould as well as the St. Paul and the Western Maryland railroads, Rhode Island Securities, the Independent Rapid Transit and the Brooklyn Rapid Transit in New York, the Philadelphia Rapid Transit, United Gas Improvement, Metropolitian Securities, and the Public Service Corporation of New Jersey. Interlocking directorates became a complicated network that barely could be unraveled. And, significantly, the world of business was being polarized between two giants: the Rockefellers and the Morgans.

The creation of the Industrial Commission during McKinley's Administration signaled a bright searchlight on Standard as well as on other monopolies. The irrepressible Archbold thought that he could rig the proceedings of the Commission, but the facts were relentlessly exposed. Enough was revealed to supply a wealth of material to Thorstein Veblen for his mordant analysis of Western civilization. Through all this Rockefeller himself was becoming quietly imperious. When Tarrytown, New York, officials hesitated in allowing him to build a road to his brother's property, he just went ahead with it in defiance of local authority. His modest fifty-room mansion was reported to have cost $2,000,000 and $500,000 a year to maintain, including wages for some 350 employees who cared for it and the surrounding estate. In his later years, Rockefeller filled his home with enough equipment to outfit a small hospital, thereby enabling himself to outlive 20 personal doctors. While money was not equivalent to life, it did help. Rockefeller's charities, among them the Rockefeller Institute for Medical Research were also greatly increased. By 1910 Rockefeller had given away $150,000,000.

Still Standard's enemies were closing in, especially that wielder of big sticks, Theodore Roosevelt. While Rockefeller and Archbold continued to deny that they had engaged in any wrongdoing, Standard blithely kept up its ruthless ways whenever new oil fields might open up, as in Kansas. The use of bogus independent refineries was a common trick to seduce the oil producers, who invariably howled to the heavens when they discovered they had been gulled. The Security Oil Company in Texas was ostensibly owned by a British firm, but the firm's headquarters were located in the office of the Independent Development Company which was tied to Anglo-American Oil, a Rockefeller affiliate. Several states returned indictments against Standard men.

And then the big stick began to flail. Judge Kenesaw Mountain Landis of Chicago fined the Company $29,000,000 on over 1,400 different counts. Of course, this immense penalty was overturned on appeals, but it did measure the extent of the country's hostility. William Randolph Hearst acquired some incriminating papers from a disgruntled employee and spread them across his front pages. In 1909 the final blow came: the

Supreme Court ordered the dissolution of Standard. It was the beginning of the end of the company's monopoly.

Curiously, the shares had been undervalued; when the market reacted to Standard's profit realities, Rockefeller's personal holdings jumped $56,000,000. Yet public obloquy was not done. One of the many properties, presumably off to one side where it was not too visible, was the Colorado Fuel and Iron Company. Its many mines in the state were surrounded by company towns where the lives of the workers were ruled with the care and detail characteristic of a concentration camp. The United Mine Workers had been seeking to organize the men for years, and in 1913 they struck. Ejected from the towns, the strikers set up tent colonies, one of them near Ludlow. The company gathered over three hundred deputy sheriffs in an effort to break the strike. The inevitable clashes brought in the state militia, headed by a sadistic labor-hater. Suppression ensued, and the tent colony was put to flames, causing the deaths of several strikers, their wives and children. To history, the incident became the infamous "Ludlow massacre." It was an event for which Rockefeller responsibility could not be evaded, and the nation made haste to say so.

Rockefeller was now in virtual retirement, but his son, John D., Jr., was active in the business. The latter was genuinely shocked; reviewing the situation, he understood why the men had gone out, and he tried to rectify matters. The elder Rockefeller doubtless would have condoned the behavior of the sheriff and the militia. When Henry Clay Frick had brutally suppressed the Homestead strike, Rockefeller Senior had written him a note of congratulation. To John D., Sr., his properties were his alone, and the workers had no warrant to question how they were to be used. Rockefeller lived to the age of ninety-eight, finally passing to his reward in 1937. Up to his death, opinion on him was divided. For all his benefactions and his gifts of ten-cent pieces to little children, the liberal, radical, and labor press had nothing but harsh words and condemnation of all his works and deeds. To the business community he was a creative hero, a giant of industry.

Some historians attribute similar creativity to J. P. Morgan. Critics noted his utter lack of concern for social problems and his notorious anti-labor attitudes, but for the epigones of capitalism, Morgan had the quality of the self-made man, even if he had inherited millions from his father. In him were embodied the magnificence of the Medici and the self-assurance of the aristocrat. No doubt Morgan was confident that he would be as successful in heaven as he had been on earth: when he composed his last will and testament committing his soul to his Savior, it was as though he were striding through the Pearly Gates with cutaway, cane, and cigar.

The Civil War had been a period of training for Morgan. He had not learned, if he ever did, that some deals, though profitable, could be highly repugnant to the public. When there was a reaction, as in the Hall-Carbine affair, he simply shrugged it off and went on his way; there was too much to be gained from business and speculation. Young Morgan cut his financier's teeth on all sorts of transactions, not the least of which were gold dealings. These were a favorite of some speculators, though most of the business community frowned on gold speculation as unpatriotic. Nevertheless, Morgan joined with Edward B. Ketchum, the son of a well-known banker, in buying some $4,000,000 in gold and shipping half to England, thereby creating conditions for a corner on the market. Their profit of $160,000 invited attacks from the Union League Club. Morgan finally pulled out of the gold market, but young Ketchum remained in; when he was trapped by a decline in prices, he simply stole $2,800,000 and forged $1,500,000 in checks in an attempt to cover his long buys. Morgan himself lost $85,000 as a result of the defalcation.

The learning process was a slow one, as Morgan continued in his stolid ways. At the time, most of his peers thought little of him, but they could hardly be blamed for failing to prophesize the future. Morgan did not generate much confidence in others, but he was making profitable forays into the market, and he was acquiring a taste for power. Needless to say, the relationship with J. S. Morgan and Company in London was enormously advantageous, particularly as the British were beginning to show some avidity for investments in America. A $4,000,000 issue of Erie bonds was taken by British investors through J. S. Morgan, and J. P. Morgan himself helped market $6,500,000 in Kansas Pacific bonds. While others might try their buccaneering antics, Morgan stayed close to investment banking. In time he came to recognize that the health of his business required stability in railroads, and that the depredations of a Gould and a Fisk were bad for the roads and bad for him.

Yet when he had to contend with the likes of a Jay Gould, he demonstrated to the satisfaction of the entire business community that he possessed the guts, the guile, and the force to meet the thieves and best them in their own back alleys. Wall Street could only hail Morgan's rising star as he beat back Gould in the Albany and Susquehanna affair. He was now emerging as a major financier. The next target was Jay Cooke. Together with Anthony J. Drexel, whose distaste for the flamboyant wonder of Philadelphia was a longstanding one, Morgan maneuvered against Cooke by bringing pressure to bear on the Treasury for a slice of the Government-bond business. The pressure paid off: in 1873, the Treasury divided a loan of $300,000,000 equally between Drexel, Morgan and Company and Jay Cooke. While the flotation was hardly a notable success, the fact that Morgan had been able to extract equal treatment with Cooke raised him markedly in the esteem of other financiers. When Cooke failed in the Panic of 1873, there was no question in the mind of anyone in Wall Street who the leader now was.

In 1876, Morgan beat out the Belmont-Rothschild forces for a $5,800,000 Government bond issue; a year later he headed a syndicate to handle a government re-funding issue that brought a profit of $25,000,000, of which $5,000,000 went to him. Another Government bond issue of $50,000,000 was taken by Drexel, Morgan and Company in 1878. In all of these, Morgan participated as an equal with the most powerful bankers in the country. Clearly, he was now a power in the land, and such power was merely a prelude to development in industry. For a number of years, Morgan had been looking at railroads as possible recipients of capital, but, if he were to engage in such activity, he certainly had no wish to become a mere middleman of finance. His "clients" had to be protected; this meant direct involvement in the affairs of the railroads, the elimination of rate-cutting, stabilization, and even consolidation.

It has been said that Morgan's handling of his railroad ventures was unimaginative, but, if so, it was nevertheless massive and irresistible. It was a penetration facilitated by the rise of the corporation and the use of stock ownership and proxies as a way of separating the owner of property from his control thereof, particularly in large enterprises. The early buccaneers may have recognized the existence of such separation; in any case, it markedly facilitated their incessant attacks on the railroads and other businesses. Given Morgan's predilection for stability, however, the finance capitalism developed under his aegis seemed an advance over the Goulds' and the Drews', but at the same time it meant centralized power and control by a few. To many it seemed that Morgan was establishing a dictatorship, pure and simple. It was an achievement that demanded the arrogance and ferocity that Morgan brought to his handiwork. He would bludgeon others into doing his bidding, commanding absolute obedience and generating fear, if not respect.

Morgan's entrance into railroads on a significant scale came through his successful marketing of William Vanderbilt's New York Central holdings. The sale was handled so carefully that the market remained undisturbed. Morgan's profit came to $3,000,000. More important, he put himself on Central's board of directors and became its fiscal agent. The railroads had to be converted into good investments if Morgan and other bankers were to have a decent market, and that required surveillance of the properties. When one railroad had been reorganized, Morgan bluntly told its managers, "The road now belongs to me." Only Morgan could have engineered the famous stunt of kidnaping the warring parties in the New York Central-Pennsylvania rhubarb over the West Shore and South Pennsylvania railroads, and keeping them on his yacht, steaming up and down the Hudson, until they came to terms. That the settlement put the Reading Railroad in jeopardy did not bother him: two years later he reorganized that line.

To be sure, there were momentary setbacks in the march to dominance. Morgan's proxies were thrown out by Harriman in the fight over the Dubuque and Sioux City, and the reorganization of the Baltimore and Ohio collapsed soon after approval. It was clear, though, what the methods were that Morgan was pursuing: a scaling down of fixed obligations, consolidation to establish a community of interest, and control by the Morgan forces through voting trusts, interlocking directorates, or outright stock purchase. Control was motivated by the growing cult of efficiency, a *sine qua non* for the emergence of large-scale industry. In 1889 Morgan decided that the western roads ought to be better coordinated, and in the hope of achieving this, called the operators to a conference at his home, ostensibly to establish a stable rate structure within the framework of the new Interstate Commerce Act. Some of the magnates, notably Jay Gould, balked at Morgan's bald attempt to dictate to them. Morgan insisted that unbridled competition had to go; besides, all the railroads should have Morgan men on their boards. The conference was a failure. Yet Morgan's ideas could not be denied: by the turn of the century six great railroad systems emerged, with four of them under Morgan control.

In the eighteen-nineties gold began to flow out of the country. The Panic of 1893 worsened matters, as reserves fell below the statutory $100,000,000 mark. The Government turned to Morgan for help in obtaining $50,000,000 in gold. Frantic, he had to turn to Stillman, who obtained $20,000,000 from overseas sources. Still the drain continued, threatening the suspension of specie payment. Obviously, a bond issue was necessary, but the Government had to knuckle under and accept Morgan's terms. He organized a syndicate to float a bond issue of $65,000,000, agreeing only to control foreign-exchange prices as a way of halting the gold outflow. The interest rate was increased from 3 per cent to 3.75 per cent, a heavier burden for future government budgets; the bonds were turned over to the syndicate at 104, and it then sold them at prices ranging from 112 to 123. It was estimated that the bankers' profits came to around $10,000,000.

The episode did reveal the Government's helplessness in the absence of a central bank, a deficiency that was not to be remedied for another twenty years. In effect, Morgan was the central bank.

As the public learned more of Morgan's operations, he became the object of attack. The farmers, the unions, and the Democratic party leveled their fire at him and all his works. They were joined by small businessmen and haters of capitalism, but Morgan studiously ignored it all as simple malevolence. Meanwhile, bankruptcies in industry spread throughout the land. Between 1890 and 1895, companies controlling a third of the nation's railroad trackage went into receivership. European investors particularly were chagrined. Once more the situation called for a strong hand. The Richmond and West Point Terminal Company was reorganized. The same treatment was imposed on the Erie, but, despite Harriman's warnings, this one failed. The Little Wonder's intervention only intensified Morgan's dislike for him. When the Reading once more began to threaten the Pennsylvania, Morgan and his associates clobbered it in a stock raid, throwing it into bankruptcy. The Reading was reorganized by Morgan. The great man erred in refusing to touch the Union Pacific, which went to Kuhn, Loeb and Company. However, he did handle the Northern Pacific, with the result that the Hill interests were brought into the Morgan orbit. In all of these reorganizations, old bondholders lost out as new stock was issued, usually well watered in anticipation of better times.

Coal, too, joined the parade as railroads established close ties with mine operators in an effort to insure adequate amounts of traffic. When Morgan bought the Pennsylvania Coal Company for the Erie, his commission came to $5,000,000. Yet he was utterly uninterested in the growing labor unrest in the coal fields. George F. Baer, one of the largest of the coal operators, exemplified the attitude of the coal barons toward unionism. Said he, "The rights and interests of the laboring man will be protected and cared for by the Christian men to whom God has given control of the property rights of the country." Unfortunately, the protection and care usually consisted of the company-town and coal police. In one major conflict President Roosevelt's intervention was required to force the operators to accept arbitration. When the railroad and coal men, backed by Morgan, refused to accept a labor man as one of the arbitrators, Roosevelt laughed. "I will cheerfully appoint my labor man as an 'eminent sociologist.' "

Morgan's operations became worldwide: he participated in the Pacific Cable Company venture, in flotations for Mexico, and in bond issues for Britain during the Boer Wars. As a financier he had become gargantuan.

He collected art with the opulence that was his due; he gave his daughter a million-dollar wedding gift; and he paraded about as "Morgan the Magnificent," though an English prelate thought that "Pierpontifex Maximus" was a better title. While openhanded in his charities to churches, his gifts by no means matched the generosity of a Carnegie or Rockefeller.

After the railroads came industry. Some preliminary work for the sake of experience on General Electric and National Cordage in the early eighteen-nineties led Morgan to organize the Federal Steel Company in 1898, making the House of Morgan a major, if not yet the dominant, power in steel. On behalf of Federal, Morgan took over Illinois Steel, Minnesota Iron, and Lorain Steel. The National Tube Company and American Bridge were then founded as the next items on the agenda. Andrew Carnegie was forced to join in a pool arrangement. The profit on the Federal creation alone came to $4,400,000, and from the National Tube and American Bridge ventures Morgan secured $27,000,000 in stock. In all instances there was enough water injected to accommodate the needs of the promoters.

By this time Drexel, Morgan had become J. P. Morgan and Company, with a crew of shrewd financiers, though some of the partners secured their jobs because Morgan liked to have handsome young men around. Said a Wall Street wag, "When the angels of God took unto themselves wives among the daughters of men the result was the Morgan partners." J. P. Morgan and Company consisted of twelve partners and the boss. The company was often described as Jesus Christ and the Twelve Apostles. But there were capable men among them: Charles Coster, E. P. Fabbri, and G. S. Bowdoin could hold their own with any of Wall Street's sharpies. Each man had his specialty: banks, railroads, industrials, foreign exchange.

The Morgan influence spread throughout the business community. The National Bank of Commerce was controlled directly, but there were ties with the First National Bank, providing influence over Liberty, Chase, Astor National, and the Hanover. The New York Life Insurance Company, Equitable, and Mutual Life were reached through the Manhattan Trust Company. There were Morgan directors in twenty-one railroads, and Coster alone held fifty-nine directorates. Although there might be an occasional clash with the Rockefeller interests, harmony ruled by 1900. But Morgan's greatest performance, for good or evil, was the formation of the United States Steel Corporation. This indeed was a masterpiece of the financier's art—so huge, so stupendous that it boggled the imagination.

Originally the idea for such a combine was urged on Morgan by others, but the more he thought of it, the more attractive it became, and by that very attractiveness, more essential. Essential for what? Obviously, for control of what was rapidly becoming America's major industry. There was one barrier—Andrew Carnegie. The wily Scotsman did want to retire, but he demanded a heavy price. His latter-day activity and threats to build a rival to National Tube were simply devices to force his competitors to buy him out at his own figure.

The catalyst for the deal was Charles Schwab, who at a dinner of financiers and steel magnates in 1900 waxed eloquent over what a properly organized steel industry could achieve under a single umbrella. Morgan, who was present, was impressed by Schwab's oratory. The Schwab plan dovetailed well with his own philosophy of financier tutelage for industry. The trick was to get old Andy to sell. Schwab shrewdly accompanied Carnegie on a round of golf, and during the eighteen holes expostulated on his plans. Carnegie set his price, and a few days later Morgan said laconically, "I accept." Some months later Carnegie met Morgan aboard a liner and mischievously remarked that he should have asked for another $100,000,000. Morgan's response was frank: "If you had I should have paid it."

U. S. Steel was created as a holding company for twelve operating corporations, providing for complete integration from raw material to finished product. It included Federal Steel, National Steel, National Tube, American Steel and Wire, American Tin Plate, American Steel Hoop, and American Sheet Steel. Hundreds of plants were brought under a single control; they represented half the nation's steel output and encompassed a work force of 168,000 men. The capitalization necessary to fulfill all the obligations generated and to carry through all the exchanges of stock was enormous. The liabilities assumed were over $81,000,000; bonds issued totaled $303,000,000; preferred stock $510,000,000; common stock $508,000,000—in all $1,400,000,000! Ten years later the Government's Commissioner of Corporations estimated that half the capitalization was pure water. It was many decades before the nation's growth dehydrated the corporation. For years U. S. Steel remained heavily waterlogged; even by 1928 its shares were of dubious value. Henry Clay Frick, suspecting that all the water might lead to trouble, quietly disposed of his shares. By 1904 the price of the stock had fallen to $9 a share. Indeed, if the overcapitalization was justified by future potentialities, it meant, simply enough, that the increased values went to stockholders rather than to the worker as wages or to the consumer in the form of lower prices. Stock-watering proved to be a device for redistributing the national income of the future.

In any case, a market for U. S. Steel stock was created, and the corporation was in business. The Morgan syndicate took $62,500,000 worth of stock as the reward for its arduous labors, with J. P. Morgan and Company receiving $12,500,000. Elbert Gary provided an ethical front for the business: he was so proper that he would frown at board meetings when the directors flipped for the twenty-dollar gold pieces they were given for attending. Morgan's operations continued in other fields, but they were not nearly so successful. An attempt to replicate the steel combine in shipping was a catastrophe. Some side chicanery took place as Bethlehem Steel was spun off to U. S. Shipbuilding and then recaptured by Schwab when that company failed. Schwab emerged as Bethlehem's owner.

The public bridled as the price of U. S. Steel stock began to fall: Morgan was now regarded as little better than the pirates of a few decades earlier. The Morgan enterprises looked bleak indeed, for their liquid position was quite poor: Harriman and Rockefeller chortled at the emperor's unease. But they did not reckon with the old battler's capacity to wrestle with adversity: he roared that anyone who would not help him could never again expect consideration from the House of Morgan. Then came the Supreme Court's order dissolving the Northern Securities Company, which had been created to consolidate the Northern Pacific and Great Northern holdings. Morgan again clashed with Harriman, as the latter demanded that his majority holdings in Northern Pacific be returned to him rather than sharing distribution in both companies. Although the courts held with Morgan, Harriman may have had the last laugh: he sold out his Northern Pacific stock for a profit of $58,000,000.

With the return of prosperity in 1902, Morgan decided to rebuild his liquidity position: never again would he be caught napping. A $3,000,000 profit from the creation of International Harvester was a help, and the expansion of General Electric and the National Bank of Commerce strengthened the Morgan holdings. In 1907, Morgan had reached his seventieth year; it seemed that he might at long last retire. Then came the Panic and the crash of the Mercantile Trust and Knickerbocker Trust companies. Wall Street and the Government came running to Morgan to help stem the tide. The Treasury poured $42,000,000 into the banks, but in the absence of a central bank, only the financial moguls could exert any pressure on the market. Morgan gave orders, and on his word depended the lives of many a bank and trust company. He thought that there were too many of them around; hence, he directed, let a goodly number of them die. That the savings of ordinary people might be involved did not disturb him. When challenged, he made it clear that he would not be assuming such a heavy responsibility if he could not get what he wanted.

In all the turmoil, the Tennessee Coal, Iron, and Railroad Company wound up in the lap of U. S. Steel. Gary and Frick undertook a special trip to Washington to get Roosevelt's approval for the merger and assured the President that it was an essential measure in halting the crash. Nevertheless, the economy continued its downward course, as Wall Street suicides mounted. And out of the chaos, the House of Morgan emerged stronger than ever. A community of interest was established between Morgan and the National City crowd. By 1912 it was evident that Morgan had a stranglehold on key sectors of the national economy. He owned or dominated major banks and trust companies, several insurance companies, twenty-eight railroads, and sixteen major industrial corporations. The interlocking directorates represented a maze of penetration into a vast economic empire. Obviously, the objective was to achieve as high a profit as possible. Essentially, Morgan was not the builder that Hill and Harriman were. Consolidation and seats on boards of directors were simply ways of insuring absolute control.

And there were instances of outright failure as with the International Mercantile Marine Company and the New Haven Railroad. The attempt to make the New Haven a monopoly in New England was a flop; at the same time Morgan overlooked an opportunity to invest a mere $500,000 in W. C. Durant's projected General Motors Corporation. He never did understand the automobile, and he thought it had no future. In the New Haven caper vast sums were paid out to build the empire. No matter that stock was heavily waterlogged; the future would take care of that. One little railroad outside New York City that started nowhere and went nowhere was paid $36,000,000 for its property. Within nine years the New Haven's debt went up twenty times. By 1913 the whole affair was in a state of collapse. The heavy accumulation of debt was to take the railroad through bankruptcies like a man caught in a revolving door. Although the Government might level attacks on U. S. Steel, the Supreme Court held it to be a "good" trust. Yet throughout all the antics of high finance, no one could say that J. P. Morgan had been dishonest. He had simply exercised absolute capitalist power.

CHAPTER 10 Creating an
Ideology

By the turn of the century, the corporate form of business had become the major legal instrumentality through which captains of industry were able to build their empires. In time the corporation was to dominate the whole economic landscape. Its history was a long one, originating, according to some authorities, in the charitable guilds of the Middle Ages in Europe. Others thought the corporation's origins antedated even medieval times, going back at least to Rome. In any case, the distinct advantages of this form of organization made it a popular way of conducting business in America, where entrepreneurs seized upon its "persona," limited liability, and presumed freedom from government interference. Turnpike building offered fertile ground for its early development, and banks and insurance companies quickly sought the same advantages. To be sure, unincorporated businesses maneuvered to achieve similar ends, but the use of transferable shares of stock enabled the corporation to gather far larger sums of capital than either the old joint-stock company or partnership could. Further, the life of the corporation was in perpetuity, extending transferability far into the future.

In the seventeenth and eighteenth centuries a special act of the legislature was required to obtain a charter, but as general incorporation laws became common, the rush was on to incorporate business activities of all sorts. Some states, such as Delaware and New Jersey, began to compete with one another in liberalizing incorporation statutes, mainly as revenue devices. By the end of World War I, almost 90 per cent of the value in manufactures could be credited to corporations, and about one-eighth of the total wealth of the nation was under the control of manufacturing corporations. In all, corporations were in direct control of one-third of the country's wealth.

New Jersey, seeking more corporate business, allowed holding companies in 1889; its effort was successful. Of 318 "trusts"—really holding companies—set up in 1904, 170 decided to head for that state. New Jersey became the "Mother of Trusts," as all the major combinations decided it was a good home. The other states were not to be outdone: a decade later Delaware eased its laws and advertised its attractions as though the trusts were just so many tourists. When Nevada entered the fray, it trumpeted the fact that there were no "blue-sky laws," statutes governing security issues; no requirements for annual meetings within the state; no annual reports; no resident director and no taxes. Lawyers could do a thriving business in any number of states merely filing incorporation papers.

As the corporation was subjected to increasing criticism, lawyers leaped to its defense, insisting that it was a "person"; the defense against monopoly charges involved the claim that the stockholders or the trustees were the real culprits, not the corporation. Distasteful acts were committed by people, not fictional persons. Yet the corporation insisted that it possessed the rights of a person as guaranteed by the Constitution of the United States. It was the sort of pettifoggery that only lawyers could dream up, for it seldom occurred to the legal mind that a corporation's actions reflected the collective behavior of its members and officers who as decision-makers were ultimately responsible. But such an argument was not very persuasive.

It was not until the era of the robber barons that the corporation was put to so many uses on so large a scale. The ingenuity of the lawyers matched perfectly the ingenuity of the promoters. The corporation became the legal device by which a nation's resources could be plundered and an industrial society constructed. The shape of the economy was drastically altered, creating fundamental changes in the relationships of employer to employee. Above all, the corporation hastened the growth of a paper economy, one that dealt in intangibles and promises to pay as a major form of wealth. The public attitude toward the U. S. Steel Corporation was an example of the awe and wonder that the new corporation could inspire. Its receipts and expenditures were larger than those for most governments in the world; it regulated the lives and destinies of a population as large as could be found in some states; it was controlled by a new oligarchy, representing a new kind of capitalism. What overwhelmed so many was that the new industrialist counted his wealth in tens and hundreds of millions of dollars, not just a paltry few million.

Corporate businessmen were the symbols and the carriers of power. J. P. Morgan typified Wall Street (though the House of Morgan itself did not incorporate until the fourth decade of the twentieth century), just as Rockefeller meant oil and Carnegie, steel. When they were attacked it was because they controlled giant corporations; upon retirement they were viewed with a measure of affection and even adulation, and their benefactions made them heroes. The corporation was subjected to attack because it was relatively strange, and, by its newly acquired power, violated the individualist canon of the American faith. While the corporation made possible the great trunk railroads to the West, it also facilitated the work of a Gould or a Huntington, who could use the railroad as a way to personal wealth, without regard for the rights of either stockholders or employees. The small businessman, who was so often trampled upon whenever the giant corporation thought he was in the way, was especially noisy in voicing his complaints. Nevertheless, to Rockefeller and Carnegie the corporation was "not evil, but good." Charles Francis Adams, Jr., saw the corporation as a dubious model of the future: it represented the sort of power that he feared would ultimately lead to Caesarism. The corporation was a monster that could be neither exiled nor slain.

In a democracy, the corporate magnate deemed himself to be more equal than others, and it was inevitable that he would seek an ideology to prove his point. The philosophy of laissez faire sketched in Anglo-Saxon economic theory seemed to provide an easy justification for what he was doing. Even more apt were the notions of Herbert Spencer, an English philosopher whose antipathy for the state seemed closest to the ideals of the businessman. Spencer's views could be best described as anarchy plus the policeman. Yet there was a curious contradiction in the thinking of the businessman: protective tariffs and land grants were received with a certain graciousness, but aid to farmers or regulation of business or social welfare measures were outright violations of the law of nature implicit in laissez faire.

Spencer's brand of Social Darwinism had in fact been developed some years before Darwin's *Origin of the Species,* notably in the *Social Statics,* published in 1851. It was a compound of the Puritan ethic and Malthusianism, producing some rather strange notions of freedom, as well as the precept that only the fittest will survive. These yielded principles that were divine in origin, reflecting nothing more than elementary social justice. If there was no interference, then everyone would receive his proper due. The government could not be trusted, for by its very inefficiency it would generate violation of all the basic Spencerian principles. The state should be a negative one, argued Spencer, that is, it should do nothing to interfere with the actions of its citizens. It was a philosophy that ignored man's role as a political and social animal, concentrating only on his performance as economic man. As one scholar remarked, it was a philosophy for those who knew no other.

The only good legislature, it was suggested, was the one not in session. The state had no business educating the young, carrying the mails, minting the currency, providing charity, regulating industry, establishing a church, operating a lighthouse, improving sanitation, or being concerned with public health. If nature is allowed to function unimpeded and uninhibited, it will naturally expel the unworthy and the unhealthy, making room only for the best elements in society. It was clear that the state ought not come between man and his suffering.

Given such views, it was not surprising that Spencer should enjoy a great vogue in the years 1870–90. Though his prose was dense and many in Europe simply laughed at it, he was fortunate in finding Edward L. Youmans as his American popularizer. Andrew Carnegie thought Spencer as great a man as Newton. And a people so optimistic as Americans could quite easily digest Spencerian perorations on unceasing progress and how to achieve it. Moreover, there was just a hint that Americans would eventually march to domination over others; this was most palatable. Self-interest and self-concern became a positive good. Trade unions were advised that their efforts were otiose; workers had merely to surrender to a kind of predestination without a mutter, for there was little they could do about their fate. After all, academic economists, such as John Bates Clark, had proved that the capitalist order provided a just distribution of income.

A leading devotee of Social Darwinism, though less optimistic than Spencer, was William Graham Sumner, Yale's eminent sociologist. To Sumner, struggles in society were symmetrical with struggles in nature: the law of the fang ruled both arenas. A defeated man can no more ask for help than the jackal chased by the lion. Charity inevitably destroys the virtues that built modern society. When Sumner called capital the carrier of civilization, the businessman was delighted. No one, averred Sumner, ought to tamper with the complexities of industrial civilization. In short, leave things as they are. Such reforms as the state may wish to introduce must be geared solely to securing property rights. Even the tariff ought to be abolished, said Sumner, a view at which the businessman smiled most charitably.

By and large, the dominant elements in the business community felt quite comfortable with such a body of doctrine; Sumner's strictures against the tariff and other aids to business were ignored. The businessman could afford to allow academicians to pursue consistency; he took such portions of their philosophy as he could use, which, in the final analysis, was most of it. He enjoyed the implications that success was to be attributed to simple virtues, and that the poor were in such dire straits because they lacked his qualities of heart and mind. Poverty existed because some men were weak and stupid and others lazy and useless. The novels of Horatio Alger depicting an upward progression from rags to riches for all able youth were thought by businessmen to be the essence of social reality. Andrew

Carnegie's homilies could be published in the year of the Haymarket affair. If monopoly somehow ensued from competition in an unencumbered market, that too was a law of nature. As John D. Rockefeller remarked, such a result reflected the survival of the fittest. The notion that those who survived the economic jungle were indeed the fittest became a grand piece of self-congratulation, sustained by classical economic doctrine and the pieties of Social Darwinism. One railroad president insisted that a study of political economy was good because it would "harden men's hearts."

With such intellectual underpinnings, it was clear what posture public policy ought to adopt. When businessmen cried "hands off" on economic matters (except for tariffs and the protection of property rights), they had ample support from other sectors of the community. And, especially, there was to be no interference with prices, wages, and profits. H. O. Havemeyer of the sugar trust stated the issue plainly; "Let the buyer beware: that covers the whole business." To be sure, some businessmen, mainly small ones who felt pressured and choked by large aggregations of capital, demurred from these views. They wanted some regulation, and out of these demands came such laws as the Granger Acts passed in at least four western states to control railroad rates. In New York, small businessmen were behind the Hepburn investigation, hoping thus to bell the cat. The little man wanted relief, while the big fellows like Carnegie asked the Government to build canals from the Great Lakes to Pittsburgh to reduce transportation costs.

Support for Social Darwinist views came from the Protestant churches, which enthusiastically leaped to defend the spirit of business. Religious sanction was given to the prevalent theories of property, government, and labor. Ministers observed that social and economic inequalities were not only just, but inevitable. Failure necessarily stemmed from grave defects in the human soul. Laissez faire was a principle advanced by natural law and sanctioned by God: it sustained individual effort, personal gain, self-interest, and free competition. And as a consequence, laissez faire became a self-consistent system almost too perfect for the purposes of the middle-class rich.

Clearly, social action that might lead to alterations of the existing order were to be opposed with might and main as violations of God's law. Charity should be undertaken if at all, only from private resources. Such Spencerian views were adopted by Josephine S. Lowell, who in her eleemosynary campaigns insisted that society had its claims against the poor as well as the rich, for the poor could become a drag on progress. Hence, relief should be offered only in institutions and at levels so unattractive as to encourage indigent inmates to leave. Soup kitchens and other forms of aid during a depression should be abolished, said she. These views exuded a callousness and brutality seldom matched in earlier decades. The church and many social workers were utterly unsympathetic to the claims of workers and the poor, alienating them from institutionalized religion. The consequence was ultimate abdication to the Catholic Church, which attained a position of influence in the trade-union movement that has not yet been lost. The responsiveness of the Catholic hierachy to the needs of the workingman proved to be one of the more salutary developments of the time.

Given the ethos and intellectual climate, it was not surprising that the law and indeed the Constitution itself were deemed to be fountainheads of doctrine protecting property rights. Social Darwinism was eagerly adopted by conservative judges charged with interpreting the law. In earlier decades the government might have undertaken to sponsor certain activities or to regulate enterprises for the public good with the acquiescence of the courts, but at the turn of the century the law displayed quite another perspective. Businessmen eventually gained virtually complete license through legal interpretations that were obviously at variance with initial intentions. The "due process" clause of the Fourteenth Amendment could be interpreted in different ways: in the Gilded Age, it was the conservative interpretation that prevailed, creating a legal environment in which big businessmen could flourish. Although the Supreme Court might on occasion view "due process" more narrowly, allowing the states to regulate business, as in the grain-elevator case, their arguments at that time were based on moral considerations rather than on the meaning of due process. But conservative judges kept pressing, and within a few years a broad definition of due process gave the green light to business.

The lawyers even embraced the Declaration of Independence, which hitherto had been much too radical a document. Embarrassment was put aside, as the judges discovered that the "pursuit of happiness" meant the right to enjoy property as one saw fit. The Declaration and the Constitution became holy documents that really had embedded in them the precepts of Social Darwinism, even if the Founding Fathers had not been aware that they had incorporated such divine law into their deliberations. In essence, the law said that men were fools to challenge the rule of businessmen, questioning their decisions. Again and again, the courts held against those states that wanted to help individuals through the regulation of hours of work or other controls. Due process became the chief weapon employed by the courts to ensure that the government would be truly a negative one, keeping its hands off private business. The ability of the states to deal with issues of public concern was virtually nullified. Whereas due process might have been thought but a simple procedural guarantee, it was now broadened into a guarantee against "arbitrary legislation."

The legal writings of Thomas Cooley and Christopher Tiedeman provided intellectual rationalizations for the decisions of the courts. They supplied arguments that Supreme Court justices such as Stephen Field could utilize in forceful dissents from the more liberal views of the majority. Field kept pressing for his broad definition of due process until it became basic court doctrine. The counterpart of the conservative victory was a narrowly restricted meaning for police powers; it took the Great Depression of the nineteen-thirties to loosen the court's reins on state action. But throughout the first quarter of the century state labor acts were time and again declared unconstitutional because they deprived employers and workers alike of liberty and property without due process of law. The court insisted that labor was also property and that the worker possessed an inalienable right to sell his labor on any terms. It never occurred to the justices that as between employer and employee the power to negotiate was heavily weighted on the former's side. The ideology of the businessman had not only become *justification,* but was now a barrier to any effort to establish a more even balance. Laissez faire became an open season for the exploitation of both men and resources.

In fact, the philosophy of Social Darwinism, merged with the thrust toward large-scale enterprise, suggested that monopoly was inevitable. A complex industrial civilization could not tolerate competition, for it was too destructive. Competition, said one industrialist, meant death for some and injury to everyone. On the other hand, monopoly and concentration represented a creative march toward progress. Parallel with this march was an increase in efficiency which in the event became a cult to be fostered at all costs. Curiously, then, the businessman could advocate free enterprise out of one side of his mouth and hail the advent of monopoly out of the other. So far as he could see, monopoly was ordained by the very structure of business.

One consequence of such a system of thought was the myth of the self-made man. The chief glory of America was the poor farmer boy who was to migrate as a youngster to the city, there to fight his way to fame and fortune. There was no other meaning given to the word "success": it was the old stirring tale of rags to riches. Nowhere in the little fables that were retailed far and wide was there any emphasis on the peculiar concatenation of social and economic forces that made possible great wealth for a few; everything was reduced to middle-class pluck. According to Andrew

Carnegie, only a man of character would respond to the goad of poverty. A rural background always helped, and in a man's climb up the ladder he could always count on a true and good wife. Few would acknowledge that there might be some advantage to marrying an heiress. All one needed was a finely honed "organ of acquisitiveness" supported by the instinct of perseverance. Sobriety, punctuality, and frugality were also useful traits. Yet these were virtues often lacking in the captains of industry whose antics filled the annals of America at the turn of the century. While businessmen might believe their own propaganda, a few realists knew what the facts of life were and they were apt to scoff at such mythmaking. Francis Lieber, a sociologist, exclaimed, "Self-made men, indeed! Why don't you tell me of a self-laid egg?" Lester Ward observed that it was just possible that wealth and success might be attributed to social factors rather than individual capabilities. Reformers wondered where the limitless opportunities were when ten men applied for every job opening. The documentation of the critics was beginning to cast some doubt on the self-congratulations of an Andrew Carnegie. Doubt was growing that wealthy citizens had modeled themselves on the heroes of Horatio Alger.

Subsequent studies by scholars were to demonstrate that the story of rags to riches had indeed been a myth. The successful man was likely to be neither an immigrant, nor of poor parents, nor from the farm, nor a stripling when he started, nor a graduate of the school of hard knocks. A sample of three hundred executives from textiles, steel, and railroads who were working in the eighteen-seventies showed that they stemmed mainly from New England and were descendants of native families. The immigrant had few chances: he was apt to be dumped into the burgeoning working class, and a life of desperation could make him quite indifferent to official tales of success.

Most of the fathers of these executives had themselves been in business. Rockefeller was the son of a small entrepreneur, Heinze had been born into a comfortable middle-class family, Cooke's father was a lawyer, Harriman's father was a minister, and Harriman himself married a banker's daughter. The ancestry of these businessmen was mainly Anglo-Saxon, and almost two-thirds were affiliated with Episcopalian, Presbyterian, or Congregational churches (Catholic or Jewish representation among businessmen had always been small). The myth of farm origins collapsed when it was discovered that half the businessmen originated in towns with 2,500 or more persons, places that were classified by the Census Bureau as urban. It took growing up in a city to make a successful businessman; it helped to have a businessman for a father; it was useful to have an education (three-fourths of the group had at least a high-school diploma); the majority did not go to work until the age of sixteen; and one could get ahead more rapidly through selling, bookkeeping, or office work, than by taking the route through the plant. Kinship ties remained important enough to substantiate the argument that inheritance could still transfer business power. The victory of the professional and the growth of bureaucracy in the corporation was not to come for several decades. Sons, sons-in-law, and nephews found that blood was still thicker than water. Among the credentials of a William Vanderbilt, J. P. Morgan, Daniel Guggenheim, George Gould, or Louis Hill, kinship was an important element. Even today a measure of family capitalism persists in such major corporations as Ford, the Great Atlantic and Pacific Tea Company, Gulf Oil, Sun Oil, du Pont, Cudahy, R. H. Macy, Gimbels, and Safeway. To be sure, being a relative became less important through the years, as men like Schwab demonstrated how the corporate structure might be used to get ahead.

Such were the men who dominated economy and society in the Gilded Age. In 1861 there had been only a handful of millionaires; by the turn of the century one could tally some four thousand. It was said that one-tenth of the people owned nine-tenths of the wealth. They possessed the mines, factories, railroads, and city land; they were the new bourgeoisie and had long since eliminated the old plantocracy, which now counted for little. It was a plutocracy, but a cultureless one that could not rely on an aristocratic tradition of taste. Hence it had to create its own culture, which became a vulgar compound of glitter and pomp.

Most of the new rich gravitated to New York and other eastern cities, although their properties might be in Pennsylvania, Ohio, or the Far West. There was much more excitement in the big city to which these *nouveau riche* came as quickly as they could. There they built imitations of European mansions along the main avenues, wildly baroque or Oriental in style, filling their many rooms with the art and bric-a-brac of the Old World and spending small fortunes on costume balls and other social gatherings. They were intent on living a life of ease and meant to enjoy to the utmost the luxury and refinement that befitted their newly acquired status. Members of old families might titter behind their fans, though no invidious comparisons were made between slavetrading and stockjobbing. The elegance of country homes matched town houses; the formal gardens and the stables often required huge retinues of men to care for them. Status was often measured by one's command over armies of commissaries. It was no longer enough to be a millionaire: entrance into the charmed circle required that one be a multimillionaire.

Nevertheless, conversation reflected a pervasive boredom: the talk was mainly about money, with such highlights as the cost of Mrs. Belmont's jewelry. To assuage that boredom they all belonged to a number of clubs: Morgan to nineteen, Vanderbilt to fifteen, Harriman to fourteen. And, of course, a box at the opera was essential even if one used it only on opening night. The quality of mind displayed by the newly rich was described with some bitterness by Charles Francis Adams, Jr., himself a Boston Brahmin who had decided to make money in business. For his pains, he complained, he had to bear with people of "low instinct."

When one potentate received a bill for $450,000 for the interior decorations he had ordered, he could not help looking askance at the work "which constituted a study of the fine arts at high rates of tuition." During one visit to New York, Henry Clay Frick stared at a Fifth Avenue mansion and wondered if he would ever be able to afford one like it. He was looking at the home of George Vanderbilt, which, years later, he was to acquire for his own. Travel to Europe was essential; "culture" was absorbed in great gulps, remaining, however, largely undigested. Artists were imported to paint portraits of all the members of the family. And with the artists came whatever remained of Europe's nobility, which through marriage, could buttress its declining fortunes.

Europe's art galleries and attics disgorged their accumulations of centuries "to decorate the buildings of men absorbed in making soap." Fine jewels graced the necks of the wives and daughters of the soapmakers, and home libraries were filled with leather-bound sets of books tailored to fit neatly on shelves wrought of the rarest wood. The new class had to have proper antecedents, and so official-looking documents and coats of arms were obtained, tracing their ancestry back to King Arthur and his knights. Others might laugh that "we are all descended from grandfathers" but to the plutocracy it was a way of changing the color of one's blood to blue.

Mrs. William Astor set all the social standards. According to her guide, Ward McAllister, she possessed enough "social talent" to rise above the competition as society's queen. Not to have dined at Mrs. Astor's or to have been invited to one of her balls was to be condemned to a plebeian existence. Since her ballroom held only four hundred persons, that number became the outside limit for high society.

The peak of achievement was to marry into English royalty, as did Jenny Jerome, daughter of a Wall Street broker, who was wedded to Lord Randolph Churchill. By 1907 some five hundred wealthy women had found their princes and dukes. William Waldorf Astor actually migrated to England, bought himself a peerage, and entered the House of Lords. Mrs. Vanderbilt's fancy-dress ball in 1883 required weeks of meticulous research to guarantee authenticity. Dogs were outfitted with diamond-studded collars. At feasts, guests would gorge themselves after the fashion of Roman patricians, as captains of industry became "connoisseurs of manly beverages." At one famous dinner the cigarettes were wrapped in hundred-dollar bills, to the delight of the assembled throng. Diversions included chorus girls jumping out of gigantic pies. Magnates, in their roles as patrons of the arts, would command whole symphony orchestras to entertain their friends, though they might not know Bach from Beethoven. A ball in 1897 at the Waldorf-Astoria replicated the Palace of Versailles: it was a year of depression, and one in which the poverty of the masses was more visible than ever.

To build an art collection, the businessman called on the counsel of art dealers like Joseph Duveen, who ransacked the castles of England and France to ship to Americans thousands of Louis XV chairs, antique chests, and Renaissance tapestries. Each business leader had to own a private collection, and the bidding for paintings and sculpture among William Vanderbilt, Morgan, Frick, Stillman, and others became quite lively. These artifacts were the trophies of civilization; they now took on a monumental importance. Yet the tastes of the businessman were as vulgar as his attempts to fill his mansions. Vanderbilt "liked pictures which told a story": he would buy no paintings other than scenes of battle or rustic vistas. Much of what he acquired was outright garbage. For him paintings were the railroads of artistic merchandise: he knew they would increase in price.

So anxious were businessmen to grasp all that Europe had to offer that dealers in fakes did a thriving business. Morgan was once offered a Vermeer. "Who is he?" asked the financier. When told the painting was rare and would enhance the value of the collection he had already gathered, much of it junk, he happily paid $100,000. One writer compared the water in Morgan's collection to that he had poured into his industrial conglomerates. In time, Morgan's library, next to his home in New York, came to house old Bibles, Mesopotamian seals, ancient papyri, medieval illuminated books, Blake drawings, and the manuscripts of novelists. It took specialists like Bernard Berenson years to teach the industrialists what to buy. Gradually they learned that Holbein, Velasquez, and El Greco were somewhat superior to the Barbizon School. Yet one wonders how much such ragpicking among the world's cultures affected their characters. One is beguiled by the picture of Henry Clay Frick, seated on a Renaissance chair with a quattrocento painting overhead, reading the *Saturday Evening Post*.

PART THREE

While the Masters, some of the most flamboyant characters in American business history, were interested only in making money by stockjobbing and playing with the financial structures of enterprise, there were others eager to offer goods and services. They were inventors whose tinkering often resulted in unheard-of devices that turned the American economy topsy-turvy. They were innovators who created new ways of distributing an increasing flow of goods to the American public. They were Makers who moved toward mass production to build a society that Jefferson and Jackson could not have imagined.

To be sure, the beginnings of these developments may be discovered in earlier periods, but the process was accelerated in the fifty-year stretch from 1870 to 1920. Most significant was the growth of the automobile industry. It gave Americans a flexible means of transportation, but at the same time the balance between rural and urban was reversed, concrete roads began to reshape the landscape, the health of the economy came to depend on a single industry and its satellites, and the air that men breathed became in-

The Makers

creasingly noxious. Americans learned to speak to one another without seeing their listeners, electrical energy provided motive power for a burgeoning
industry, and the motion picture and radio offered them mass culture to
match mass production.

Throughout this period, the Masters hovered on the horizon seeking
opportunities for wealth by juggling securities, but the striking phenomenon
was the creation of a new economic environment through technology. One
great Master was A. W. Mellon, who from his central position as a banker
was able to control a vast empire in shipping, aluminum, coke, oil, and railroads. One great Maker was Thomas A. Edison, who preferred to devise
dozens of new and useful inventions. In many ways these men illustrated
the dichotomy between business and industry that had been detected by
Thorstein Veblen: one was concerned with pecuniary values, the other with
functional values. It was a contrast of great import for America, one of the
many divisions that was to characterize American civilization.

CHAPTER 11 Government Takes a Hand

The changing American economy was bound to wrench time-honored habits of earning a livelihood. Farming as a way of life was being abandoned with the commercialization of society. Yeomanry became a myth as men looked upon pastoral existence with pathos and nostalgia. Yet periodically Americans would express a vehemence against the new forms of business, a vehemence that only demonstrated their impotence before the roaring waves of the future. For farmers knew that the better things in life were more easily secured in the city: gazing at the good earth could only be a backward glance.

Commercial farming, which had its roots in the cultivation of tobacco and rice, was now dominant throughout most of the Middle West. Cash cropping, whether in wheat or in the corn-hog sequence, made the farmer a businessman. And as a businessman he had frequently to deal with corporations whose search for profit were often interpreted as a visitation of injury upon himself. He had to mechanize his farming, for which he went into debt. Land values increased as settlements moved westward, bringing more and more persons ever-hopeful of reaching paradise behind a plow. And as land prices drifted upward, it seemed that a never-ending boom had been generated.

However, the farmer failed to grasp one essential fact: his economic fate was driven by an impersonal market in which prices were affected by what happened outside the borders of the United States. The agricultural market was international, and when prices declined in the long stretch from 1870 to 1890, the farmer could only gasp with a sense of constriction generated by unknown forces. These were the circumstances that motivated the radicalism of the Great Plains.

There was little new in the Government intervention brought about by the farmers' revolt. Americans had always been unable to reconcile their deeds and their creed. They might talk laissez faire, but there had always been a strong measure of government participation in economic affairs. At

214

the end of the nineteenth century about a third of the approximately thirteen thousand statutes in effect placed restraints on economic "freedom." As in the eighteen-forties and eighteen-fifties, a real or imagined abuse by business interests resulted in a law designed to rectify matters. And why not? Had not municipalities and states extended themselves throughout the decades to help business enterprise with subsidies and internal improvements? To the average citizen it was merely *quid pro quo*.

As industry and the railroads grew and expanded, various states insisted on regulating their activities. By the turn of the century, twenty-six states supervised their banks, and twenty-one kept watch over the insurance business. Attempts to control monopolistic practices were common: railroad rates were subject to state approval; factories were inspected; and, in one way or another, the states legislated standards for education, health, and welfare. It seemed that businessmen had to be forced to behave for their own good. Yet historians are only now beginning to inquire whether all the regulation was really for the public benefit or to protect certain businessmen against the depredations of others. Often it was a significant part of the business community that, in effect, urged regulation.

The thrust of much of the statutory regulation was against "big" business and a large part stemmed from the complaints of farmers. The low point in farm prices had come in 1896; agrarians found that the prices from their products were too low to pay for the implements and goods purchased from industry. Creditors were enjoying a marked advantage as prices plummeted. Moreover, the farmer felt oppressed by railroads, which often held local monopolies and imposed discriminatory rates depending on what the traffic would bear. The farmer was "damned without the railroad and damned with it."

Inevitably, economic problems led to political activity. The Patrons of Husbandry, known as the Grange, had started in 1867 as a social organization for farmers, but it soon became a political body seeking redress against economic complaints. By the eighteen-seventies the Grange had obtained control of the legislatures of four states: Wisconsin, Illinois, Minnesota, and Iowa. Laws were quickly passed to regulate the railroads, the Grange's bête noire. The railroads, of course, fought back in the courts, and while they lost in *Illinois v. Munn*, they were victorious in the Wabash case.

Farmers also tried to reverse the long-run deflation that had beset the nation. In 1878 they succeeded in halting the retirement of Civil War greenbacks, and they then joined western miners in demanding the free monetization of silver. The Bland-Allison Act of 1878 required the Government in Washington to mint between $2,000,000 and $4,000,000 a month in silver. Unhappy with this statutory directive, the Federal Government monetized as little as it could get away with.

By 1880 the Granger movement had disappeared, but resentment continued to find expression through regional Farmers' Alliances. Initially a kind of cooperative venture, the Alliances acquired the balance of political power in Kansas, Nebraska, South Dakota, Minnesota, Georgia, and the Carolinas. Their activity led to the formation of the Peoples' Party or the Populists, in 1892. The political turmoil was intense: the demands of the Populists covered a wide range of issues—monetary reform, Government ownership of railroads, the income tax, direct election of senators, the secret ballot, and postal savings banks. Eventually, the Populists merged with the Democrats, only to go down to defeat before the superior political forces of McKinley and the Republican party in 1896.

Economic conditions after McKinley's election improved somewhat; now the carriers of reform could be located in the cities, giving rise to the Progressive movement, one founded on urban middle-class sentiment. The pressures for change had moved out of the countryside to the urban middle class, focusing on trusts, labor, welfare, and corruption in the cities. The corporations were a menace to society, alleged the Progressives, and corporate oligarchs were devoid of refinement, unfit to be leaders of men. Such were the sentiments that fired the flames of Progressive rebellion. Many complaints stemmed from the grievances of workingmen subjected to inhuman conditions imposed by the exigencies of a burgeoning industry. The fires were stoked by a hardy band of journalists whose revelations of the seamy side of life provoked Theodore Roosevelt to declare that they were wallowing in muck.

The impact of the Progressive movement was significant; yet much of the spirit of reform was appropriated by Roosevelt, who was eloquent when he waved his big stick, doing little else. As Peter Finley Dunne had his Mr. Dooley remark, " 'Th' trusts,' says Roosevelt, 'are heejous monsthers built up be th' enlightened intherprise iv th' men that have done so much to advance progress in our beloved country,' he says. 'On wan hand I would stamp thim undher fut: on th' other hand not so fast.' " Roosevelt may have moved against the Northern Securities combine and the Beef Trust, but he always complained that the Sherman Act had provided little power to the Government to deal with monopoly. On that point he was eminently correct.

The Sherman Antitrust Act, passed in 1890, was clearly a reaction to the spread of big business, which, it was contended, had been suppressing competition. There were some persons who thought that the law could be used as a weapon against labor unions, though this was evidently not the intention of the sponsors. The act was vaguely worded, a circumstance that required numerous court actions to extract some meaning that might be comprehensible. Yet the decisions were so conflicting that in the end little could be done to halt the march of monopoly. It seemed that Congress had simply legislated against sin, which nevertheless remained a substantial part of human nature. Some Republican legislators supported the act because they were troubled by charges that monopoly could be traced to high tariffs: they tried to demonstrate to the public that their hearts were in the right place, though they did not move to reduce tariffs.

The Sherman Act failed to halt the movement toward industrial combination and merger. Indeed, many of the major mergers occurred only after the passage of antitrust legislation. The Standard Oil Trust simply transformed itself into a "community of interests" cemented by a holding company, sustained by a complaisant New Jersey legislature ready to accommodate itself to the needs of corporations. The 1895 Knight case, in which a corporate purchase of stock of another firm was validated, seemed to keep the Sherman Act at arm's length. While quick action was taken under the Act against certain cartels that clearly affected interstate commerce, as in the Addyston Pipe Case, little was done about unfair trade practices. Criminal actions were rare; from time to time the Government sallied forth in a rash of antitrust activity, but it was all quite futile, for the shape of the economy remained unaltered. Dissolution decrees were ineffective: the separate units of a disbanded combine continued to function together anyway. In fact, after the Government lost its case against U. S. Steel, which was declared a "good trust," the "rule of reason" enunciated by the Supreme Court inhibited trustbusting for fifteen years. The "rule of reason" had only introduced even more confusion in the attempt to unravel what the Sherman Act might mean.

Even prior to the Sherman Act, efforts had been made to control certain business activities through Federal legislation. As state laws could not constitutionally regulate interstate railroads, Federal action seemed essential; and so in 1887, three years before the Sherman Antitrust Law was placed on the statute books, the Interstate Commerce Commission was established to deal with the railroads. The ICC was hailed by agrarian and reform groups as a protector of individual rights against the monsters of the rails. A twenty-year battle had raged in Washington to secure some sort of railroad regulation, and over 150 bills had been introduced into Congress during that time, all to little avail. A forward thrust to the reform movement came when the Supreme Court held in the Wabash case in 1886 that the states could not regulate interstate commerce. Originally in the Interior Department, the ICC was made an independent agency in 1889, and over the years it acquired certain discretionary powers that lent to it a quasi-legislative character.

There were arguments pro and con regarding the effectiveness of the ICC. Protagonists viewed its independence as the best way for providing a flexible administration of railroad rate-setting. Such a commission, composed of experts, they believed, would become the defender of the public interest. Opponents envisaged a softening of the force of law: the commission, they contended, would become a political football, buffeted by reformers and the very interests it was directed to control. Consequently action would be slow and cumbersome.

As events turned out, the opponents were closer to the truth. The ICC became in fact a tool of the railroads, granting rate increases indiscriminately, and in our own time, aiding and abetting the railroads' deliberate destruction of passenger service. From time to time the ICC would awaken from self-induced torpor long enough to authorize a railroad to abandon another blue-ribbon train. This seemed to be its notion of regulation. The first commissioners viewed themselves as quasi-jurists presiding over a tribunal and listening to adversary proceedings, as in a court of law. The idea of helping the industry to plan, or to alter its way of doing business, did not occur to them. This view in time affected other regulatory agencies: the judges and lawyers who were appointed to the commissions hastened to build a body of "law" and precedence that made their agencies safe and conservative. The expectation of some Progressives that regulation by experts would restore ethical standards of business behavior and do away with privilege was bootless. If Mr. Justice Brandeis welcomed the commission approach, Mr. Justice Holmes considered them all "humbug based on economic ignorance and incompetence."

The ICC frequently had to be shored up with additional statutory power, as with the Compulsory Testimony Act of 1893. Then it obtained the right to regulate carriers other than railroads when the Hepburn Act was passed in 1906. Despite these laws, and added support derived from the Mann-Elkins Act of 1910, the ICC still could not prod the railroads into meeting head on the growing complexities of rail transportation. It became the sleepiest and least effective of all independent commissions and did little to protect the public from the manipulations of railroad companies. When the United States entered World War I it discovered that Government operation of the railroads was absolutely essential for efficiency.

The ICC never set minimum standards for passenger service; in fact, it feared to do so lest the railroads be offended. It did not occur to the commissioners that the roads had become quasi-public corporations enjoying enormous land grants and the power of eminent domain, and providing essential services for goods and persons. Although passenger traffic continued to be high at the level of almost 100,000,000 passengers, the ICC, for want of anything better to do, helped the railroads to destroy themselves. For the fact was that the railroads had been unwilling to respond effectively to competing forms of transportation.

Those who preferred public ownership of the railroads, or of any public utility, could be counted among the opponents of the independent commissions. They found that the companies "sought to write the laws and have done so in some cases, and [have] modified the laws in others." Herbert Croly, a leading intellectual, thought that the commissions "may well work more harm than good." It seemed that these regulatory bodies were invitations for politicians and businessmen to become more intimately associated than was useful for the public benefit. Peter Finley Dunne's Mr. Dooley commented, "Whiniver I see an alderherman an' a banker walkin' down the sthreet together I know th' Recordin' Angel will have to ordher another bottle iv ink."

Hovering over these developments in the first part of the century was Theodore Roosevelt, a wellborn aristocrat, given to the vigorous life, and firm in his belief that he could attain self-fulfillment in politics. Public service was the instrumentality by which the wealthy could serve society: indeed, it was an expression of the heroic life that Roosevelt had long pursued and admired. That his friends were appalled when he announced his entrance into politics did not disturb him. He was even willing to start at the bottom, serving as an assemblyman in Albany. In 1889 he became a Civil Service Commissioner, then police commissioner in New York City, and in 1898 he was elected governor of the state. The machine politicians thought they had rid themselves of Roosevelt by kicking him upstairs into the Vice-Presidency of the United States, but with McKinley's assassination, they discovered that their erstwhile protégé was now in the White House.

While Roosevelt had sponsored some social legislation in his early political career, he could by no means be described as a reformer. At first totally intransigent in his attitude toward labor, he learned in time to be more flexible, though he would never surrender the principle that private property was sacrosanct. Still he seldom disguised his contempt for the corporate oligarch: he was a man of the middle passage. Nevertheless, his advisers were men like Charles E. Perkins, Nelson Aldrich, Alexander I. Cassatt, and James A. Stillman, all representatives of corporate official-dom. In his later years he paraded as a reformer, a posture that contrasted sharply with his conservative views and actions. T. R. knew no more of economics than his distinguished cousin who was to follow him into the White House in the nineteen-thirties. The complexities of banking and the machinations of financiers were beyond his understanding. When the Morgan interests sought to absorb the Tennessee Coal, Iron and Railroad Company in 1907, he allowed himself to be gulled by Henry Clay Frick into approving the take-over. And while he might borrow ideas from the "radical" La Follette, he would never acknowledge that he had done so.

Whatever reforms took place under Roosevelt's aegis did not change power relationships. Indeed, some historians have argued that businessmen wanted these reforms as a stabilizer for a capitalism that threatened to list from side to side. Moreover, in the event, the sort of regulation that evolved merely continued the time-honored intimacies of government and business. Roosevelt did not really have strong views on antitrust. The record of his Administration was one of moderation: the mechanism of business, he said, was too delicate to be disturbed. Much care had to be exercised in order not to deal with business in a spirit of rashness. Under the Roosevelt regime there were but twenty-five antitrust proceedings; his hand-picked successor, William Howard Taft, brought forty-five cases into court.

Roosevelt habitually distinguished "good trusts" from "bad trusts," including among the latter the "malefactors of wealth." On assuming the Presidency he declared that he would be cautious in the interest of both the nation and the corporations. When he had secured the dissolution of the Northern Securities Company, some businessmen became worried lest he wave the big stick at them. However, Elihu Root convinced the Union League Club that the President was the "greatest conservative force for the protection of property." It was a judgment that most businessmen came to accept.

The Bureau of Corporations, established in Roosevelt's Administra-tion, represented no threat to businessmen. Its director, James R. Garfield, exempted antitrust from the Bureau's purview, and conducting an investiga-tion became an an agonizing affair. Much was made of meat inspection, but it was hardly noticed that the inspection bills were demanded by the large packers because they wanted to reenter foreign markets from which they had been excluded for shipping rotten meat. Moreover, the small firms had to be kept in line. La Follette, who had little love for Roosevelt, once remarked: "This cannonading, first in one direction and then in another, filled the air with noise and smoke, which confused and obscured the line of action, but when the battle cloud drifted by and quiet was restored, it was always a matter of surprise that so little had really been accomplished."

While some historians look upon Woodrow Wilson as more effective in the reform arena, there are others who are as dubious about him as they are about Roosevelt. Wilson was a southerner who had practiced law before entering upon an academic career, rising eventually to the presidency of Princeton University. He had always been a political conservative, preferring Edmund Burke to Thomas Jefferson, for whom he seldom found anything good to say, at least not until he had been caught up in the Progressive movement. Nevertheless, when Wilson was elected governor of New Jersey, a surprising number of reform bills were hammered through the state legislature—bills regulating railroads and utilities, establishing workmen's compensation and a direct primary system. By 1912 he had come to the notice of the Democratic party politicians, and in a three-cornered election, Wilson wrested control of the White House away from the Republicans. Changes were promptly made in the tariff, reducing a fair number of rates, a corporation income tax was passed, and the Federal Reserve System was established. Yet the reform began to grind to a halt: Wilson hesitated to advance his New Freedom. With the Clayton Act and the Federal Trade Commission, which came in 1914, he felt that his program was complete. He was now anxious to have businessmen learn how to accommodate themselves to the new order of things.

Yet these were halfway measures. The Clayton Act represented an effort to strengthen antitrust, but it was just as vague, just as amorphous, as the Sherman Act. The antimerger provision of the Clayton Act became a dead letter as soon as the courts held that it applied only to the purchase of securities; corporations then simply bought out their rivals lock, stock, and barrel. It was not until 1950 that the loophole was plastered over. Equally meaningless were the restraints on interlocking directorates and holding companies. Senator James Reed of Missouri, who thought the original bill "a raging lion," discovered that the law as passed was a "tabby cat with soft gums."

The Federal Trade Commission was empowered to investigate erosions of competition and to go to the courts to enforce its cease-and-desist orders. These were little more than wrist slaps, but Wilson wanted no stronger action, and this is about as far as the FTC has ever gone to insure competition. He hoped it would be a minor agency, and such it became. It was never intended that the commission be a successful watchdog, and it has been as toothless as an aging hound, adding to the collection of senile animals parading as regulatory commissions.

Money, too, was a subject for government regulation. Though the National Banking Act, passed during the Civil War, had ended the chaos of the wildcat state systems, it suffered from a serious defect: the elasticity of supply in currency was reversed. As note issuance was based on Government securities, a slump would contract the supply of money, thereby worsening matters. Bank runs would reduce cash reserves, making it virtually impossible for the banks to provide loans to meet a crisis. The slump would be exacerbated in that there was no central bank to which commercial houses might go to replenish their reserves. All this the new Federal Reserve System was intended to correct: theoretically, there would now be available a currency that could respond to economic circumstance more readily than the currency issued under the Civil War act.

Indeed, the Panic of 1907 had disclosed how quickly the flow of money could dwindle to a trickle. Although the Aldrich-Vreeland Act of 1908 had broadened the base for note issue somewhat, it did not promise to be of much help. A money commission headed by Aldrich suggested that a private reserve association be created to provide a greater measure of flexibility. There were other proposals to reform the currency, but all of them—from Aldrich to Carter Glass—involved private control, and to some historians it was a matter of counteracting the growing competition from smaller banks.

Yet the need for some change had been revealed by the Pujo monetary investigation. It exposed to full view the corporate interlocks of the Morgan and Rockefeller groups, which now dominated financial institutions with assets of over $4,500,000,000 and other corporations with assets totaling over $22,000,000,000. The "Money Trust" seemed to be no figment of a journalist's overheated imagination. It appeared incredible that Morgan's testimony could be accepted at its face value: America's financial emperor had maintained that he held no power in Wall Street and that the decisive factor in all the decisions he had ever made was "character." Yet he conceded that when he called, other banks came running. He knew that his was the voice of authority, but he could not explain why.

The investigation sparked public demand for an overhaul of the nation's monetary system. Various schemes were proposed. At President Wilson's behest, Senator Glass worked up a bill that included a Federal supervisory board. But farm communities rose up in wrath to demand decentralization; the compromise provided a Federal Reserve System with twelve central banks to be coordinated by Washington. Yet it was a privately owned and privately operated affair. In New York and Chicago the large bankers gained dominant positions in their districts right from the start. Benjamin Strong, governor of the New York Federal Reserve Board, made it the leader for the whole system. New York handled overseas operations, purchased government securities for the other districts, dealt in acceptances, and controlled open-market operations. It was not until the New Deal that the money power was transferred from New York to Washington.

After the ICC and the FTC came the Federal Power Commission, Civil Aeronautics Board, Federal Communications Commission, Securities and Exchange Commission, and the National Labor Relations Board. Yet none of these agencies was independent in the sense that they functioned with the kind of neutrality and objective criteria that could be said to protect the public interest. All too often the various commissions were under the influence of the very groups they were supposed to regulate. And politics provided the broad parameter of action. In the nineteen-fifties, a new Republican Administration brought to the National Labor Relations Board a general counsel whose function it was to clean out the Democrats of earlier regimes. He did so thorough a job that a Chamber of Commerce representative could declare to an inquiring reporter that "the shoe was now on the other foot."

Neither Congress nor the executive was consistently serious about the commissions: they were given low budgets, inadequate salary scales, and commissioners whose short-term appointments made it impossible to establish continuity in policy. At best, the commissions sought to save capitalism for the capitalists: they were uninterested in change or reform, were quite timid and legalistic, and hence quite conservative. A Band-Aid here and an antiseptic there seemed sufficient for the health of the industry being regulated, and if all the firms, as in railroads, would be intent on committing hara-kiri, the commissioners would offer to hold the knife. One commissioner resigned from an agency saying that the system of independent agencies actually invited "improper influence"; another declared as he walked out the door that the commissions had become "frauds on the public." And so, as the ICC bestowed its affection on the railroads, and the FPC refused to regulate the rates of the independent natural gas companies, and the CAB protected the scheduled airlines against competition from the "nonskeds," and the FCC made itself completely servile to television and radio interests, the public discovered it had no place to turn. Discretion was the better part of government service when it was so easy to get a job in industry upon completing a Federal assignment. Meanwhile, the public waited for their *ombudsman,* or public defender, who might voice their puzzlement and concern.

How regulation could be shaped to suit the demands of business has been illustrated by the way in which the FCC has reviewed the affairs of Western Electric and American Telephone and Telegraph, the telephone monopoly. Western Electric, a wholly-owned subsidiary of American Telephone and Telegraph, makes all the phones and related equipment for the Bell System. Western Electric's principal customer, Bell, supplies it with 80 per cent of its sales, close to the $4,000,000,000 mark; the rest consists of military contracts. Western Electric, which dates back to 1856, had been absorbed into the Bell system in the eighteen-eighties to supply telephone equipment exclusively to Bell, which reserved the right to establish designs and prices. It was only in 1908 that Western Electric was allowed to sell equipment outside the Bell System, but even then only because the latter became nervous about antitrust. It was a small enough concession, since the uniformity of equipment made a take-over of independents that much simpler.

The FCC did not look into the American Telephone and Telegraph-Western Electric marriage until the nineteen-thirties. Then it discovered, among other things, that Western Electric's cost records were nonexistent, with high charges made to the parent company which would then include its greater costs in the rate base. In essence, the public was made to supply excess profits to the system estimated at more than $50,000,000 a year. When several state utility commissions pressed for antitrust action, American Telephone and Telegraph was able to induce other government agencies—notably the Department of Defense—to come to its aid. A Republican Attorney General sympathetic to the pleas of the telephone company was also helpful: he simply worked out a consent decree that left the situation pretty much as it had been. Written by Bell attorneys and accepted by the Government and the courts, the decree did nothing about separating Western Electric from American Telephone and Telegraph, constituting little more than a slap on the wrist.

The Bell System continued its conservative policy of suppressing innovations and frightening off independent inventors. The call diverter, a device for shunting incoming calls to other locations; the handset, which placed the earpiece and circuitry in one unit; side-tone controls to eliminate echoes; decorative telephones; the cartephone, a radio-telephone connector; the Ericophon, a Swedish telephone unit that was easier to handle than Bell's ugly black box; and the Hush-a-phone, a noise suppressor, were among the devices that Bell not merely resisted but fought bitterly. When finally forced to give in, the company would charge exorbitant fees to have the new equipment hooked in.

There was seemingly little that regulatory agencies could do to force the Bell System to serve the public as the public wished to be served. Regulation came first among individual states, such as Wisconsin, which found as early as 1907 that Bell's franchising system was replete with abuse of the customer's pocketbook. When the ICC was given the right to regulate interstate telephone rates in 1913, Bell averred that such regulation was a good thing. The company seemed to know that the ICC could be easily directed, and that commissions could be reduced to the role of clerks for the industry. And while Bell might magnanimously reduce its long-distance rates, it did so knowing that the ICC would not study too closely its 20 per cent return on investment.

The situation was not substantially altered when the FCC was given telephone jurisdiction in the nineteen-thirties. AT&T could, through its monumental lobbying efforts, insure that the FCC's investigating bureau would be kept small and on a survival budget. And it could also mollify state regulatory bodies by offering free service to commission members. When it reduced long-distance rates voluntarily, it raised intrastate tolls just as voluntarily, without indicating that the bulk of its business fell into the latter category. The Bell System has refused to take advantage of depreciation methods that would have reduced its rate base sufficiently to have saved subscribers more than $4,000,000,000 over a thirteen-year period. Indeed, it has tried to inflate its rate base by such bookkeeping devices as including subscribers' deposits, tax funds, and plants under construction. And throughout the years there has never been a thorough examination of its rate-setting methods by any regulatory agency. The consequence has been an overcharge to the public of hundreds of millions of dollars. While Washington watchdogs slept, "Ma Bell" continued to wax fat.

CHAPTER 12 Marketing a Nation's Goods

Retailing has always been a ubiquitous industry: wherever there have been human settlements of any consequence there have been stores. The antecedents of modern retailing can be traced as far back as the medieval fair, although many of the transactions then were wholesale in character. Generally, retailing, or direct sales to the consumer, was carried on by itinerant peddlers who packed their wares on horses or on their own backs as they trudged from hut to hut. The inventory consisted mainly of small household items such as ribbons, needles, lace, and gloves. It was a form of selling that was to survive through the nineteenth century.

Some peddlers might settle down in one spot to operate a store and provided there was enough traffic, became specialists, such as haberdashers or drapers. Oftentimes wholesale and retail functions were combined, but, in either case, the business, though it was subject to the rules of town and guild, was looked upon by many as disreputable. The growth of trade was bemoaned as a harbinger of social degeneration. Selling was as low in esteem as the occupation of the "man milliner": it was an "education in self-seeking" at the expense of the customer, and prevented its practitioners from achieving the heights of culture.

Decade after decade, the public viewed retailing and its handmaiden, advertising, as exercises in debasement, suitable only for the congenitally dishonest. During the nineteenth century, when odd-prices—such as 2 for $1.89—were devised to check on sales clerks, it was believed to be a clever way of extracting more money from the public. When one merchant asked his copywriter what new gimmick they might try in the advertising, the latter's sage response was: "Let's try honesty."

But as population grew, so did retailing. No one could anticipate that the economy would eventually turn toward trade and services. In 1870 there were 850,000 persons in trade and related fields in the United States. By 1900 the number reached 2,900,000, and by the middle of the twentieth century there were more people working in stores and offices than in factories. So prosperous a business did retailing become that merchant princes could match their stately mansions with those of railroad tycoons.

During the nineteenth century one could discover in all the major cities congeries of small shops specializing in tobacco, hats, clocks, dresses, and coats. Often the retailer had his own workshop located behind the selling floor; other retailers preferred to buy what they sold from jobbers and wholesalers. "Warehousemen" had large shops that were separated into departments, and dry-goods stores were handling non-dry-goods items, much to the consternation of specialty shops, precursors of the modern supermarket. No single pattern in merchandising had emerged, even by the middle of the nineteenth century. Some merchants imported their goods directly and engaged in both wholesaling and retailing. Some started with a single item, as did Thomas Hancock with his line of books, and then branched into dry goods, rum, and fancy hats. Layers of middlemen came between the producer and the consumer. Functions overlapped one another, as factors provided financing, and manufacturers absorbed wholesalers (as did Standard Oil), taking the profits of merchandising for themselves.

Even today there is little uniformity in retailing. Highly specialized outlets selling phonographs or ties exist side by side with discount stores offering a conglomeration of items. As today, specialty shop owners would become infuriated and advocate legislation to limit retailers to only one line of goods, as in France in the eighteen-forties. Such reactions were common in America as well, though less intense, for here the predominant trend was toward general merchandising. It could not be otherwise in a land where the population was so widely dispersed. Only with increased store traffic stemming from the growth of population was the rule of nonspecialization broken. In the main, the industry in the early eighteen-hundreds consisted of small-scale operations, conducive to general merchandising.

Yet by the eighteen-sixties, at least, four distinct lines could be discerned—groceries, dry goods, house furnishings, and hardware—with secondary specialization in books, shoes, china, haberdashery, lace, and silks. More and more, wholesaling was distinguished from retailing. The rise of manufacturing supplied an ever-increasing amount of goods to be sold across counters, and consumer demand became brisk as the home was no longer the place where one made soap and similar articles. Of course, large retailers were quick to integrate their operations, installing workshops and engaging in importing for their own account. Pursuing such methods, A. T. Stewart was able to build a kind of department store by the eighteen-fifties His adoption of a one-price policy that eliminated haggling was unique. Some stores even offered customers the privilege of returning merchandise with which they were unhappy. And the "cash only" policy simplified bookkeeping.

By 1907, when Marshall Field was ready to build his store on State Street in Chicago, bigness had become the prime goal in retailing. Field advertised his emporium as the largest in the world: he had the biggest shoe department, biggest china department, biggest book department. For years the store was a major point of attraction. The roots of the business went back to the days of Potter Palmer, who had come to Chicago in 1852 to open a dry-goods store that catered only to the ladies. Palmer's shop had no whiskey barrel; it exhibited only refinement, with the shawls and lace properly displayed with price tags. In 1856 Marshall Field showed up in Chicago to go to work for another merchant and eventually rose to a partnership. When Palmer retired in 1865, he sold his place to Field and Levi Leiter, who, within three years, were able to house the business in a palatial building.

But the Field fortune did not come solely from retailing. Profits were good enough to enable Field and Leiter to buy large parcels of land and engage in a variety of enterprises. Field's personal holdings consisted of investments in over a hundred corporations, all so successful that when he died in 1906, his estate was estimated at $100,000,000. Harsh critics have charged that the Field fortune was rooted originally in the business of Civil War shoddy. In the main, though, the Field story paralleled the rise of the Astors, depending in large part on a strategic acquisition of land that was held until the spread of the city had doubled, tripled, and quadrupled its value. To a landowner, wealth came naturally. Retailing, of course, continued to be important. Field insisted on "cash only," and his employees, like those in retailing to this day, were poorly paid. Cash boys, lads who carried sales slips to change-making booths, received two dollars a week. Employees in the workshops were paid at retail rates, that is, at the lowest possible level.

Meanwhile, the groundwork for retail chain operations was being prepared by merchants like Frank W. Woolworth, of five-and-dime fame. The low-price trinket shop had long been considered a shabby business, but with rising income, consumers demanded as many goods and trinkets as they could acquire. It remained for Woolworth to show retailers how to take advantage of their opportunities.

Born in 1852, Woolworth spent his early years on a farm in upstate New York. Such an existence did not suit him, and as soon as he could, he left to work in a dry-goods store in Watertown, New York. Curiously, Woolworth was a poor salesman, but he could dress a window well enough to attract customers. A five-cent-store venture in Watertown failed; later a five-and-dime store in Lancaster, Pennsylvania went well. Stores in Utica and Harrisburg were failures, but one in Scranton was successful, followed by one in Easton, Pennsylvania. Without planning to, Woolworth was building a chain. Each new unit meant a new partner. To keep costs down, Woolworth hit upon the idea of displaying goods on open counters, with young and not-very-bright young ladies to make change and wrap the articles. It was a policy that held turnover cost at more than 40 per cent. Only with the twentieth century's checkout counter was the typical Woolworth girl replaced by somewhat brainier clerks.

In the eighteen-eighties, when one of Woolworth's partners developed an insatiable taste for sweets (he was later to be killed by diabetes), Woolworth experimented with candy: it was to become a major sales item. By this time, New York had become the headquarters of the chain. Store expansion was undertaken in earnest; by the eighteen-nineties sales had reached over a million dollars a year. A wide market brought advantages of scale: Woolworth could buy in bulk and squeeze his suppliers for price concessions. But always labor costs were rigidly controlled. Said Woolworth, "We must have cheap help or we cannot sell cheap goods. When a clerk gets so good she can get better wages elsewhere, let her go. . . . [We] can get good, honest girls at from $2 to $3 per week."

Panics and depressions hardly affected the business; low prices made Woolworth's merchandise available to the poorest wage-earner. Store executives were carefully briefed in the art of parsimony: they had to be careful with postage stamps, wrapping paper, and twine. The last man leaving the store had to turn off the lights. A wage scale for clerks was set at $2.50 a week: it was both maximum and minimum. By 1910, the seventy-odd-unit chain was enjoying $5,000,000 a year in sales, and the penny-pinching insured more than adequate profit margins.

In the meantime, Woolworth became a wealthy man, wealthy enough to acquire a thirty-room mansion on Fifth Avenue in New York. He had now joined the company of assorted industrialists who had flocked to that city as the best place to display their wealth. In his huge home, Woolworth could indulge his passion for music by playing on an automatic organ whose mechanical gadgetry threw colored lights on the ceiling and gave off lightning and thunder. It was said that Woolworth was a master interpreter of the world's great music on rolls.

In 1904, the business, hitherto a syndicate of partners, was incorporated at $10,000,000, with the controlling common stock closely held by Woolworth and his associates. A more formal organizational structure was introduced, with the country divided into marketing districts, each headed by a superintendent. Rivals cropped up—McCrory, Kresge, Kress—who began to drop hints that they might form an anti-Woolworth combine. Woolworth countered vigorously as competition for the best store locations became intense. The panic of 1907 brought the projected combination to naught, and by 1911 Woolworth was ready to absorb some of his competition. Details were carefully worked out to bring several rivals into a $65,000,000 merger, of which $50,000,000 represented "good will and future earning possibilities," that is, pure water. Woolworth had half the stock in a corporation that controlled 611 stores in three countries.

Woolworth was now ready to fulfill one of his more cherished ambitions: to own the world's tallest building. He had always felt challenged by the heights of the Singer Building and the Metropolitan Tower. When Goldman, Sachs, the investment banking house, refused to finance Woolworth's building venture, he paid for it out of his own resources. In 1913, a handsome Gothic structure, far more handsome than today's glass boxes on stilts, opened in downtown New York, celebrated by an enormous repast of caviar and turtle soup. Woolworth's own office, opulently appointed, was graced by an enormous four-by-eight foot desk. He was now the Napoleon of retailing. In 1916 he replaced his Long Island home, which had burned down, with a marble palace in Renaissance style, and filled it with Marie Antoinette, Louis XIV, Louis XV, Italian, and Chinese bedrooms. It was an opulence that befitted the age.

Rowland H. Macy and Richard Sears also belonged in the category of merchant princes. Macy was born in 1822 in Massachusetts. At the age of fifteen he shipped out of Nantucket on a whaler. On his return four years later he tried his hand at clerking in a Boston store. With the California Gold Rush, he tried retailing on the frontier, returning east again several years later with three thousand dollars, which he then invested in a dry-goods shop in Haverhill, Massachusetts. His policy of selling for cash only did not keep him out of bankruptcy, but three years later, he appeared in New York for another go at retailing. He seemed incompetent and a drifter; only this time he succeeded. And why not? He had hit the right market: a rapidly growing city with a developing public transportation system that would bring him all the traffic he needed.

Once more Macy adopted cash-only and added to it a one-price policy: the customer did not have to engage in haggling. He advertised aggressively and gave special discounts to certain classes of customers, such as the clergy. As more items were introduced, business became successful enough to enable Macy to leave the store in charge of others as he went to Europe on buying trips. After a few years, he drew from the business forty thousand dollars a year, on which he lived comfortably. The various lines were handled by buyers, who were responsible only to the owner. The table of organization grew as floorwalkers and department superintendents were added to the hierarchy. Clearance sales were regular features to hasten turnover. Yet wages remained low, a standard retailing practice, and staff discipline was harsh. Macy was known for his outbursts of temper and for his profanity, a hangover from his sailing days. When a customer once complained that the umbrella handles were weak, Macy stomped into the department and broke every umbrella, leaving behind a pile of debris.

His first partner was A. T. La Forge, who took a job at Macy's on leaving the Army after the Civil War and promptly married Margaret Getchell, the store's superintendent. In time, other partners were admitted. By the eighteen-seventies, Macy's had become one of the few retail establishments that could properly be described as a department store. Once more such growth was not merely a matter of individual business acumen: urbanization, the spread of inner-city transportation, the development of newspaper advertising, and the use of delivery systems were all powerful elements in explaining the Macy success.

The department store became a place for one-stop shopping, providing the housewife with all her needs under one roof. Central heating kept the building comfortably warm during the cold winters, and elevators carried the ladies to the upper floors. From Paris came the idea of the *grand magasin*: elaborate architecture, fancy decorations and fittings, and elegance for milady became important features of store rivalry. As the lines of merchandise were diversified, integrated operations were introduced: workshops, repair services, delivery, and wholesaling were brought under single ownership.

When Macy died in 1877, ownership passed to La Forge and Robert M. Valentine. A year later La Forge died, and Valentine admitted L. B. Webster into the firm. When Valentine died, Webster, as yet quite inexperienced, called in his brother-in-law, J. B. Wheeler. The business continued to grow, but stress was now placed on convenience and comfort. Leased departments, providing selling space to an outside dealer in return for a share of the profits, were introduced. Impressive surroundings were provided for the edification of customers; it was a period of complacency and self-satisfaction. Macy's had lost its momentum.

One of the better leased departments had been let to L. Straus and Company, dealers in chinaware. The Strauses had come from Bavaria in the eighteen-forties, and at first operated a small retail business in Georgia. During the Civil War one member of the family, Isidor, had been relieved of his cash by several sharp confidence men while on a trip to London. It was an experience that taught him to say no to any sure thing. After the war, the family headed north to enter the crockery business. Nathan, who did most of the selling and disliked it intensely, conceived the idea of setting up china departments in leased store units. The first venture was at Macy's, and a notable success it was. The stock was supplied by the Strauses, the space by Macy's and the profits were shared. Soon Wanamaker's and Woodward and Lothrop in Washington accepted similar arrangements.

Now Webster needed more partners, and it was natural that he should turn to the Strauses. In 1896, Webster retired, and R. H. Macy & Company was acquired by the Strauses, who were to make it one of America's major department stores. By 1902 sales reached almost $11,000,000. The Strauses became vigorous competitors determined to undersell all their rivals. Retail-price cutting horrified their suppliers, who would refuse to sell to Macy's. The Strauses simply acquired the same merchandise through intermediaries and department stores in other cities. Private brands were introduced, trademarked by a red five-pointed star (long before the Kremlin appropriated the symbol). Paternalism became a feature of personnel policy, with bonuses, full lunches and other fringes supplied to employees. Wages, however, were still quite low, enough to cause the cigar makers and upholstery workers to go out on strike. In 1901, the store moved from New York's Fourteenth Street uptown to Herald Square, where it has been ever since.

Stores could not reach the entire national market, however. America was as yet dominated by a rural economy, and, even after the advent of the automobile, it was still a chore for the farmer to go to the city. Given the opportunity, someone was bound to discover a way to meet the farmers' needs for "store goods"; the mail-order house quickly filled the vacuum. Aaron Montgomery Ward initiated such a firm in 1871, selling a general line of goods through the mail. Starting with handbills that carefully described each item, Ward developed the idea of the catalogue, the pages of which were eventually nailed to the walls of outhouses. Richard W. Sears, who in 1886 had been earning six dollars a week working as a railroad agent, began to sell watches along the line, and when he discovered that the watch sideline was more profitable than handling railroad waybills, he teamed up with A. C. Roebuck to start a mail-order jewelry business.

When Julius Rosenwald was brought in as a partner by Sears and Roebuck, the business began to grow markedly. Of course, it helped to have rural free delivery, which was established in 1896, and parcel post, set up in 1913. Local stores could not possibly carry the great variety of items listed in a mail-order catalogue that offered farmers not only tools and farm supplies, but electric belts to relieve backaches, picture projectors, and bicycles. The buyer was always informed that he could operate any such instrument or piece of gadgetry without personal instructions from a manufacturer's agent. Advertising and goodwill promotions served to overcome resistance and the hostility of local merchants, who referred to mail-order houses as "Monkey Ward" and "Rears and Soreback."

When Sears left the firm in 1913, Rosenwald became the dominant personality in the company. It expanded rapidly, becoming less flamboyant than in Sears's heyday. Attention was paid more and more to sources of supply. Through the decades, growth was phenomenal; today Sears is by far the largest retail concern in the country, with hundreds of outlets that have displaced in large part the direct mail-order business. Today its sales, including such nonretail items as automobile insurance and finance, run to more than $8,000,000,000 a year. In many lines, such as appliances, it dominates a number of local markets.

By virtue of its deliberate effort to integrate, Sears has come to control numerous suppliers. Considering the fragmentation of retail markets, it is extraordinary that perhaps 5 per cent of the total general merchandise sales may be attributed to this one firm. One business journal estimated that five out of every hundred dollars spent on general merchandise in the United States passes through Sears.

An aggressive merchandising policy was motivated by a desire to achieve maximum domination of the market: Sears has sold between 19 and 33 per cent of all automatic washers and 12 to 17 per cent of all automatic dryers in the country. These were signs that retailing, the last stronghold of the individual entrepreneur, was surrendering to concentration. Creating captive suppliers became a key to underselling rivals. At first an individual supplier might be assisted in solving his production problems; soon he was selling more of his output to Sears; and before he was aware of it, he had become completely beholden to the giant retailer. Thus firms selling stoves, plumbing, paints, farm equipment, and sewing machines to Sears were to become so enmeshed in Sears's buying practices that they could not escape. Financial assistance was often Sears's mode of entry, but after the supplier had become dependent upon Sears, he was offered a price that covered only direct costs, a small portion of overhead, and a profit markup quite favorable to Sears; invariably it was the price that might have been paid by a marginal buyer. And it was not surprising that Sears always preferred to purchase from small vendors without any defenses. It was a case of the elephant dancing among the chickens.

Sears has always argued that the system reduces selling costs for

suppliers, ignoring the fact that its practices represented a clear-cut case of
what economists call "monopsonistic exploitation"—buyer's monopoly.
Though the firm has claimed that it never wanted to penetrate the vendor's
market unless forced to do so, it has been easily forced. When one lawn-
mower supplier was dropped by Sears, his sales fell precipitously from
$12,000,000 a year to $6,000,000, almost pushing him into bankruptcy.
When a lamp manufacturer balked at Sears's price offer after the company
had taken up his entire output, he was dropped, and the retail giant began
to manufacture similar lamps. (Of course, the lamp maker sued.) The
company's claim that it "protects" the small manufacturer has been often
questioned, particularly when mergers and reorganizations are imposed on
vendors. Yet through the decades, only one suit, involving discriminatory
tire prices, has been brought by the Government against Sears; otherwise it
has been able to build with impunity a privileged position in retailing.

A self-perpetuating corporate oligarchy maintains control of Sears
through its Profit Sharing and Pension Plan. Established in 1916, the Plan
has grown to enormous proportions, almost $2,000,000,000, with three-
fourths invested in Sears stock. The Plan has been the largest stockholder in
the company, holding 22 per cent of the outstanding shares. As the pension
fund is controlled by three trustees, two of whom are chosen by the company's directors, the arrangement has maintained the incumbent management in a position of "impregnable control." At one time, even the third
trustee, supposedly representing employees, was chosen by the directors.
When a Senate Banking Committee some years ago raised its eyebrows at
this relationship, the company agreed to have the third trustee "elected."
However, the voting has all the attributes of a Russian election: proxies are
solicited for a single nominee.

Clearly, any kind of selling would be hampered without advertising;
retailers have always advertised to some degree. Merchants in the Middle
Ages had their signboards, and Thomas Hancock was always quick to
distribute handbills whenever a new boatload of goods arrived from
England or the Indies. Newspapers, of course, became the chief medium:
by 1860 there were over five thousand newspapers in the country carrying
ads, some of them even informative. By the eighteen-eighties newspapers
were a major source of advertising, and publishers of slick magazines were
beginning to discover that advertisements could be an important device to
increase revenues. By 1910 about 4 per cent of the national income was
going into advertising.

The idea of the advertising agency originated in the eighteen-forties, when V. B. Palmer began to solicit ads for a New Jersey newspaper. Palmer's practices became common: he obtained a commission not only on ads that he placed, but also on any ads placed by someone who had once been his customer; he sought to be recognized as the publisher's sole agent; and he took no risks. Moreover, he was not responsible for an advertiser's failure to pay his bill. G. P. Powell then conceived the notion of buying space "wholesale" and reselling small parcels of it "retail."

In 1869, at the age of twenty-one, F. W. Ayer started what was to become one of the more famous advertising agencies. A member of the Baptist Church, Ayer could have served as a model for a colonial Puritan: work and money were the foundations of his ethics. By the eighteen-seventies he was placing ads in 325 newspapers. Advertising was a cut-throat business, filled with chicanery, and advertisers did not hesitate to play off one agent against the other, one publisher against another. Ayer gradually shifted his relationships so that he served his client rather than the newspaper. He wrote copy for advertisers, just to be certain that a campaign would turn out successfully. In time, the agency became central in the business of getting a message across to the public. In the more refined versions of economic theory, advertising hides under the rubric of selling costs. The intention, of course, is to influence the shape and direction of the demand curve: the general objective is to make demand as inelastic as possible, that is, to create in the mind of the consumer a sense of the exclusive nature of a product and to wed the consumer to it. One can discern an awareness of the purpose of advertising even in the elegant models of the economist. Information as such is hardly a significant element; much more important is the creation of a subliminal attachment to a product. It has ever been thus. The management of demand, to employ John Kenneth Galbraith's term, requires a carefully devised strategy stressing the placement of ads, packaging, and model changes to foster "dynamic obsolescence." Presumably, he who advertises best will enjoy a greater sales revenue. The consumer's power to exercise a choice of commodities is thereby weakened, and it is the producers who gain in decision-making. Again, as Galbraith has pointed out, advertising does serve an economic function in that it keeps the economy moving, for in the absence of advertising at least half the products would disappear from the market.

The other side of the coin is the patent fact that advertising usually generates wants in excess of disposable income, creating sociological problems of no small import. In any case, advertising acquired a moral urge inseparable from the business ethos it has always served. Thus half-truths and a contempt that reduces the intelligence of readers to that of a nine-year-old are part of its arsenal. A "truth," in fact, was that which sold the product, so that a successful campaign became a kind of self-fulfilling prophecy. Truth became a collection of daydreams. Jules Henry has said; "How many points the GNP has risen on the feminine buttock is an interesting question." One advertiser admitted that his output was vulgar, brash, aggressive, empty, loud, commercial, and concerned with turning a dollar, but these were the qualities, he insisted, "that have built the nation."

Joseph Bensman, a sociologist who for many years worked in advertising, once described it as a labor-intensive industry with a minimal capital investment, hence a low capital/output ratio. The major cost is labor, running as much as 70 per cent of operating costs. About 15 per cent of billings, (the value of ads placed), represents the agency's gross income, of which perhaps three-fourths is spent on wages and salaries. But since most of the staff comprises low-paid clerical workers, what is left over for professional workers—account men, copywriters, art directors, research men, and other officials—makes advertising a well-paid field. The promise of harvesting a small fortune draws young men of charm and poise who can entice clients away from other agencies. The perquisites of an expense-account existence—lunch at the best restaurants—exert their own attractions. It becomes a way of sharing in the affluent society. When an account is lost, a game of musical chairs takes place, with advertising men moving about in search of another agency job. And in the process, there are many who disappear from advertising altogether.

The origins of supermarketing—in itself a relatively new merchandising method—may be traced to the "combination" stores that cropped up in California during the nineteen-twenties, when grocery and meat departments were brought together under one roof. Such combination stores, called "cheapies," were usually opened in abandoned warehouses or garages in the slums of big cities. The King Kullen markets of Long Island, an early "super," went to the outskirts of New York City in the nineteen-thirties and called on new suburbanites to come with their cars to buy cheaply in large quantities. Food was displayed in open crates, there was little overhead, and the entrepreneurs' objective was a low-margin, high-turnover business. True, all this was started by enterprising independents who were determined to outdo chains like A & P, which had secured an initial advantage by volume buying and excellent urban locations. But between the chain and the supermarket stood the ordinary neighborhood grocer, and in the era of self-service and parking lots, he could not survive in very large numbers.

One of the more spectacular characters in the grocery business was Clarence Saunders of "Kedoozle" fame. The Kedoozle system for selling groceries, prototype of an automated store, displayed its merchandise behind glass panels beneath which there were slots in which to insert the key that the customer had been handed at the door. When the key was inserted, a record of the item was recorded on tape as the merchandise moved onto a belt toward the front of the store. Upon completing her shopping tour, the housewife was then presented with her parcels and a fully itemized bill. Unfortunately, the system, which Saunders worked on from 1933 until his death two decades later, was far too cumbersome to succeed.

But Saunders' claim to fame stemmed mainly from a battle royal he staged in the nineteen-twenties with the giants of Wall Street. Well known in his home town of Memphis for the marble palace and private golf course that he was perpetually building, he dared to outsmart the bears of the Stock Exchange, only to be frustrated by a rare suspension of rules engineered by the exchange's governors.

Saunders was born in 1881 in Virginia and as a young man had worked in the local grocery store. After some years he entered the wholesale grocery business, and in 1919 began to build his own chain of retail food stores with headquarters in Memphis. By 1922 he owned more than 600 outlets, all called Piggly Wiggly, with another 550 franchised under the same curious name. So successful was the firm considered that the New York Stock Exchange was happy to list its shares on the board. However, when a group of franchised outlets in New York failed, speculators on the exchange sensed a brilliant moment for a classic bear raid. Saunders responded with a public announcement that he would protect his company's fair name by supporting the price of the stock. With a loan of some $10,000,000 from a number of southern bankers, plus a bit of his own money, he began to contest the bears. Newspaper ads flamboyantly declared his intent to joust with the dragons of Wall Street. The price of the stock was driven to a high of 60. A shrewd offer to sell to the public on the installment plan "quarantined" a fair number of shares by keeping them out of the stock market's float. By March, 1923, Saunders had in effect obtained a corner on Piggly Wiggly stock. He then called for delivery of the shares that the bears had sold short, whereupon the governors of the exchange decided to suspend trading in Piggly Wiggly: too many bears had been actual members of the exchange. Though Saunders insisted on making call for delivery, the stock was removed from the board, and the short sellers were given five days to make delivery. The exchange was not about to abandon its boys.

Needless to say, Saunders was left holding the bag and heavily in debt to his bankers. He was forced to settle at a price of 24 points below the market high, but still good enough to make about a half-million dollars. Nevertheless, he still owed the banks $5,000,000. An attempt to raise the money by public subscription in Memphis failed, and by August, 1924, he was bankrupt. Yet in 1928 he was back in the grocery business with another chain and with his Kedoozle operation. But never again did he try to best the beasts of Wall Street.

Suburbia grew and created a mass market; the automobile provided mass transportation to shopping centers; home refrigeration made possible a weekly rather than a daily trip to market. And so the grocery business underwent a quiet yet gigantic upheavel, analogous in many ways to that experienced by the manufacturing industries in the eighteenth and nine-teenth centuries. Marketers scurried about buying or leasing new locations in freshly built towns as the small neighborhood outlet of 5,000 square feet, which could hardly accommodate a dozen checkout counters, became inadequate to handle the ever-growing traffic. The new supermarket, operated by chains, franchised licensees, or cooperatives, has expanded to an average size of 22,000 square feet in recent years, and today it is not uncommon to do one's purchasing in a mammoth 55,000-square-foot "giant" super.

The complicated network of distribution channels needed to supply these retailers can only be dimly perceived by the housewife. Behind the retailer, there are wholesalers, brokers, processers, and producers, each of whom plays a role in making prices what they are. Brokers, who are akin in many ways to the *tolkachi* of the Soviet Union, never take physical possession of goods; they merely handle orders and purchases—pieces of paper —and see to it that a retailer gets what he needs on time. There are about 2,000 brokers in the food business; they employ 17,000 salesmen who handle 30,000 different items, and who bring in $13,500,000,000 annually in sales. Food processers, from sugar refineries to huge dairy plants to small automated meat-packing installations located in southern towns, number about 14,000. Yet even with all these middlemen, the price of food might still have remained within bounds if there were a significant degree of competition in the industry. The reality of the food business, however, is concentration.

The "chain-store movement," initiated in 1859 by the Hartfords of the

Great Atlantic and Pacific Tea Company laid the groundwork by which small retailers were forced together under one management. The chains merged retailing and wholesaling functions, moved backward into processing to cut costs, and did not hesitate to use "loss-leaders," or low priced items, and spectacular specials to draw customers away from rivals and independents alike. By 1930, some eighty thousand units had been brought together into one or another form of chain store—and the grocery business had been brought into the twentieth century.

Initially, of course, resistance to the movement was strong. Some states, such as Louisiana, even tried to tax the chains out of existence. But in the long run the pressures toward integration and consolidation could not be overcome. By 1948, the chains had secured about 35 per cent of the retail market in foods; those independent retailers who had been cajoled by wholesalers into joining "voluntary" cooperatives (based on group merchandising, uniform store layout, joint advertising, and private labels) retained another 35 per cent; about 30 per cent was left for all the others. By 1963, the chains had swallowed up 47 per cent of the market, while the "affiliates" or "voluntaries" had 44 percent of what was now a substantially larger industry.

Some of the competitive practices indulged in by the chains have been attacked under antitrust legislation. Between 1950 and 1965 the Justice Department prosecuted fifty-three antitrust cases affecting retail food companies and got convictions or consent decrees in thirty-one of them. Only eleven cases were dismissed and only seven defendants were found not guilty. Some of the more spectacular suits involved Safeway, The National Tea Company, Borden Company, General Mills, Kroger, Morton Salt, Wards, and even the Teamsters' Union and the Kosher Butchers' Association of Los Angeles. Many were charged with conspiracy to fix prices and establish monopolies, others with predatory competition, some with price discrimination. That such suits had to be instigated shows clearly that old-time price competition in the grocery business no longer exists.

To be sure, it generally has been difficult to speak of market domination on a national scale. The product market—the area in which marketing takes place—has widened; once the neighborhood or town, it is now the entire region or metropolitan area. From a national standpoint, the twenty largest food retailers increased their share of the market from 1948 to 1958 by only 7 per cent. Since 1958, the situation for the so-called national chains has been fairly stable, reflecting an increased growth on the part of regional or statewide chains which, merger for merger, have been matching the pace of A & P, Safeway, and Winn-Dixie.

Nevertheless, the strength of the large national chains is such that in the nineteen-sixties the four top grocery companies obtained, on the average, half the sales in 218 metropolitan areas, while the top eight secured 62 per cent of the sales in these areas. (In the nineteen-fifties, by contrast, the ratios were 45 per cent and 54 per cent respectively.) Thus, despite rivalry with local outfits—not necessarily on the level of price competition—the nationwide chains have continued to bite off larger pieces of the market, which itself has been burgeoning. Even though their investments are high, these chains are quite mobile. Able to finance themselves from internal resources, they can close down old stores with alacrity, open new ones, spin off acquisitions no longer profitable, search out new locations, and buy out rival companies. In any one year a national chain like Safeway may shut down fifty stores and open sixty new ones; its flexibility is much greater than the balance sheet would suggest. It is this that enables such chains to hold on to, and even expand, their markets.

The chains use their strength in buying as well as in selling. They have so thoroughly invaded the suppliers' field that they are hardly convincing when they blame high prices on vendors. For, while independent food wholesalers may still occupy a position of importance, the decline in their number since World War II has been dramatic—a drop of about 20 per cent. More significant, perhaps, is the rather close relationship these middlemen are apt to have with the so-called "voluntary" chains, such as IGA, Red Owl, and Red and White.

These tendencies, moreover, have been strengthend by vertical integration, which, through ownership or by contract, links the disparate operations of production, processing, merchandising, advertising, wholesaling, and retailing. The Temporary National Economic Committee, a congressional group investigating monopoly, observed in the nineteen-thirties that grocery chains were reaching back to "bridge the entire span between producer and consumer."

A most spectacular device used by grocers, and the most pernicious so far as prices are concerned, is the trading stamp. In one form or another, this come-on has been around for years: the Raleigh cigarette coupon and the United Cigar Store ticket are familiar early examples. Trading stamps themselves—gummed stickers accumulated by housewives to be exchanged for blenders, towels, electric can openers, hair dryers, and the like—go back to the eighteen-fifties, when the B. T. Babbitt Company sold soap with coupons. In the eighteen-nineties Shuster's Department Store in Milwaukee thought of gummed stamps and books. Finally, in 1896, Thomas Sperry had the happy thought of establishing a trading-stamp company, and so

Sperry and Hutchinson—S & H Green Stamps—was founded. A group of New England retailers was the first to dispense trading stamps as a roundabout way of giving the housewife a "discount." The trading stamp is now big business, and there are many companies engaged exclusively in it. S & H, the largest of them all, gives away more catalogues than Sears, Roebuck.

The economics of trading stamps is deceptively simple. A ten-cent purchase entitles the housewife to one stamp, so that a completely filled S & H book, for example, represents a total retail expenditure by the customer of $120. Now, the average retail value of a book when turned in for redemption is $3. Since the cost to the retailer, who buys the stamps from the redemption company, runs between $2.00 and $3.00, the most the customer receives by way of a "discount" amounts to eight-tenths of 1 per cent, and in many cases it is exactly zero. The only party that gains is the redemption company, for its profit comes not only from the difference between what it charges the retailer and what it pays out in redemptions (usually at 75 per cent of retailer costs), but from unredeemed stamps as well. An additional source of profit is the margin between the cost of premium goods and the redemption value of the stamps. It is quite a business.

In the days before 1930, the basic strategy in the grocery business was to give the customer a break. As the chains expanded and added more outlets, it was discovered that savings in bulk buying gave a competitive edge and could lead to lower prices. Efficiencies were introduced into marketing, and the housewife really had a lark. Today, however, the rules of the game have been altered: competition is now focused on such matters as store location, "image," the size of the parking lot, number of square feet, types of gondolas, lighting—anything but price. The strategy now is to fit a particular mix of goods to a particular geographic location.

Aside from the area of private brands, where some price competition still exists, most retailers concentrate on competing not by lowering prices but by increasing the number of items stocked, improving carry-out services, instituting convenient store hours, or dispensing trading stamps. All these devices are geared toward increasing the cost of the market basket. As a consequence, gross margins, which measure the cost of retailing to society, have been drifting upward and will in all probability continue to do so.

Retail operators, of course, are likely to argue that wages are at fault and that payments to employees have outpaced food prices by about 10 per cent. They usually fail to add that the wage base was rather low to begin with. Costs in retailing are affected by numerous other factors—managerial skill, equipment, size of store, layout, the flow of goods from storage to selling areas, the arrangement of checkout counters, and the like—and calculated on some unit basis, they drop with more effective use of store facilities at a rate more than sufficient to offset wage increases. The retail worker, moreover, has become increasingly productive over the years, as is evidenced by the startling rise in sales per worker in grocery stores: from $14,000 in 1929 to $36,000 in 1968 (in *real* dollars). Studies of supermarket productivity suggest an average annual gain per employee of at least 5 per cent.

The significant economic element in food marketing seems to have been the continuous upward movement of gross margins. It is sometimes argued that gross margins have gone up because modern supermarket methods shift the burden of services to the housewife. No longer is a human clerk available to advise her as to which product represents the superior buy; the clerk has been transformed into a "materials handler," stamping prices on canned goods, and the only information he is able to impart concerns the location of the canned beans. In effect, the housewife herself performs services that at one time were paid for by the retailer. The housewife performs more and more tasks—searching the shelves, selecting the items, grinding the coffee, filling the basket—and contributes to the upward drift of margins because she is not reimbursed for her services. Of course, she ought to be paid in the form of lower prices, but in the context of events, that seems unlikely. In the present situation the housewife is no longer confronted by a white-aproned neighborhood grocer ready to serve her, but rather by a huge impersonal aggregation of capital whose sole objective is to separate her from the household budget. In this confrontation the housewife cannot win; she may walk the sidewalk on occasion with picket signs, protesting high prices, but when it comes time to feed the family she will go through the door of the supermarket to do her shopping, for she simply has no other place to go.

CHAPTER 13   Flivvers, Phones, and Flickers

As America moved into the twentieth century, a proliferation of inventions obliterated time, distance, and cultural differences. East Coast and West Coast, farm and city were brought closer and closer. The automobile was to weave a tight web around American society, destroying the sense of personal isolation. The telegraph made it possible to communicate quickly from one coast to the other by wire, and over the telephone a man in Maine could talk to one in New Mexico. Finally, motion pictures, aiming at anyone who could pay the price of admission wherever a box office was set up, induced a mutuality of tastes.

Although the automobile is regarded as characteristically American, its main elements were developed in Europe about a decade before it began its first forays through American streets. Steam carriages had been exhibited in Europe as far back as 1856, and by 1860 the first usable gasoline engine was available in France. In the eighteen-eighties, Gottlieb Daimler in Germany built his internal combustion engine, using gas, based on an earlier one devised by Nicholas Otto. Daimler's engine had a single horizontal cylinder with slide-valve ignition; it was to be the progenitor of all gasoline engines. The principle of carburetion had been worked out by Siegfried Marcus.

Few technological innovations have had such a traumatic impact on civilization as the automobile. Modes of transportation were drastically altered, new techniques of production were created, highway patterns dominated the landscape, people moved from the inner city to suburbs as the heart of the metropolis decayed, and air pollution and traffic strangulation became the sort of external diseconomies that signaled the price of progress.

Few of these by-products were anticipated as the twentieth century opened. As Europeans worked away improving the new motor, George Selden in this country secured a patent for a model of an internal-combustion engine that was to play a significant role in the evolution of the automobile industry. In Europe, Daimler, who had severed connections with Nicholas Otto's firm, moved to Stuttgart and there produced a 900-rpm,

80-horsepower engine which was air-cooled and used oil for lubrication. Karl Benz, working closely with Daimler, began to lay the foundations for a major European company, Mercedes Benz. Using the Daimler patents, the French firm of Panhard and Levassor built an automobile that became the prototype for the entire industry: the engine was placed up front (because the horse had been in front), and the major elements of the clutch, gearbox, and transmission were developed. France became the center of the industry in its early days, giving the English language the words "automobile," "garage," and "chauffeur."

As the basic principles of the motor vehicle became better known, Americans began to experiment and tinker with it. The Otto engine became quite familiar to American mechanics. In 1893, the Duryea brothers built their "buggyaut" and were followed by Elwood Haynes, whose automobile antedated Ford's by three years. Charles King ran an automobile on the streets of Detroit at least three months before Henry Ford had completed his model. Even Alexander Winton preceded Ford. It was evident that Ford, who became the first to mass-produce a car, had not been the first to build one.

Tinkering with motors, however, had a purpose: production for sale. Americans began to manufacture cars in some quantity. Ransom E. Olds started to build and sell his in 1893. Roy Chapin and Howard Coffin obtained financing from J. L. Hudson, the Detroit department-store magnate, and in gratitude named their automobile the Hudson. Hundreds of pioneer firms started to make and sell automobiles, and hundreds failed. Willys, Studebaker, and Packard were among the more successful and would hand their names down to posterity. Auto makers strove to convince Americans that the "horseless carriage" was the way to travel, but the industry seemed like just another marginal one that would founder because only the rich could afford to ride around in cars. Failures were strewn all over the business landscape for lack of a mass market. There were no less than three thousand different makes produced by some fifteen hundred firms, most of them expiring before World War I. Yet despite these difficulties, which seemed so insuperable in *fin-de-siècle* America, Henry Ford and William C. Durant were able to break through all barriers to stand American society on its head.

By 1903, the United States was displacing France as the leading automobile producer. This country, in retrospect, had an ideal environment for the rapid development of the industry. Oil resources were well developed, the rubber industry had matured, and steel was in plentiful supply. Both the self-measuring pump, essential for delivering fuel to motorists, and the pneumatic valve for tires were available. And, in factories, such essentials as the drill and the turret lathe, as well as other machine tools, were already in use. Bicycle and carriage shops would supply a work force of mechanics and artisans whose skills could be easily adapted in an automobile plant. With these elements in readiness, it was necessary only to take over what had long been known in meat-packing and munitions—assembly-line work —to create the auto factory of the future. Yet the public was at first hostile to the new contrivance: town ordinances were passed to restrict its speed to five or ten miles an hour, and many a farmer would derisively shout to a hapless motorist tinkering beneath the hood on a lonely road, "Get a horse!"

Yet by 1900, motor-vehicle registration reached a total of 8,000 units. By 1905 bus routes and stage lines were being established. By 1913 registration had gone over the 1,000,000 mark, and growth was steady and irresistible. In 1947 there were 30,000,000 vehicles on the road; ten years later the number was to reach 56,000,000. With the automobile, the American could travel as he pleased. Some 18,000,000 horses and mules disappeared from the farm as Old Dobbin's chores were taken over by the internal-combustion engine, and farm production grew to enormous proportions, easing the shift of people out of agriculture to other pursuits.

The steel industry found its greatest customer in the automobile industry; Pittsburgh soon became an appendage to Detroit, its fortunes largely dependent on the vicissitudes of car sales. And in time New York, Los Angeles, Detroit, and all the major towns became gigantic parking lots, as automobiles tried to crawl through their clogged streets like so many frightened ants seeking to escape an overcrowded hill. Highways cut through the hearts of cities and bounded their edges, filling the air with noxious gases and the stench of exhausts. American society gave up an annual sacrifice of fifty thousand lives: the cars kept piling into each other or careening off the road. As the automobile companies sought to create more powerful engines and faster cars, they resisted the efforts of communities and the Federal Government to establish standards of safety. Such were the costs of one of the great technological advances of the time.

Henry Ford is accorded the major credit for creating cheap automobile transportation, for in the absence of his fanatical determination to build a low-cost car, the vehicle would have remained a rich man's plaything. Detroit had become the center of the infant industry only by accident: the majority of bicycle and carriage manufacturers had located in Michigan and Ohio, and a fair number of them—Studebaker, Nash, Durant—were able to shift their operations readily to auto making. When the bicycle boom at the end of the nineteenth century collapsed, Winton, Willys, the Duryeas, and the

Dodges moved over to the new industry. In the hectic atmosphere of experiment, failure—and a few successes—Ford and several associates formed the Ford Motor Company. The year was 1903.

Ford was born in 1863 in Dearborn, Michigan, the son of a farmer. He hated farming and loved to tinker with machinery. In later life he would defend his manufacture of farm equipment, though by this time it was only a sideline with him, on the ground that farm burdens had to be lightened. At the age of sixteen, Ford left Dearborn to work in Detroit as a machinist, a trade he preferred to farming. After some years of apprenticeship and wandering about, he once again tried the family farm, only to rediscover how much he despised it.

In 1888 he was back in Detroit working for the Edison Illuminating Company and experimenting with a car in a shed behind his home. By 1894 he had completed a running model; two years later the car was officially unveiled. A crude machine, it had two cylinders; lacking a reverse gear, it could only move forward; but it worked, and it encouraged Ford to continue with his tinkering. When Ford described what he was doing to Thomas A. Edison at a meeting of electric-company officials, Edison pronounced the doom of the horse. Ford and a group of local Detroit capitalists formed the Detroit Automobile Company in 1899, but it failed as the car that was produced was too expensive. The next venture, the Ford Automobile Company, also failed, and for the same reason. It was patent that Ford and his friends had not found a market.

Ford then took to automobile racing to demonstrate the virtues of his car, and when his famous 999, driven by Barney Oldfield, proved a winner, Ford was able to return to manufacturing. Supported by A. Y. Malcolmson, a wealthy coal dealer, Ford set up a third venture, the Ford Motor Company. Arrangements were made with the Dodge Brothers to supply parts, and a small factory location was obtained, but, in the event, his most fortunate acquisition was James Couzens as business manager. Ford contributed his name, a model for a car, and some patents. It was agreed that the price of the car had to be low enough to attract as many buyers as possible. With the price set at $850, the first model produced was an instant success. Couzens, a hard-driving manager, was delighted as orders came in well in advance of production, and by making the suppliers wait a full thirty or sixty days, Couzens felt he could finance the flow of cars. Albert Strelow and Malcolmson let success go to their heads: they sold out to Ford and Couzens, with Ford becoming the majority stockholder, having 58.5 per cent of the shares.

By 1906 Ford had expanded into a three-story building on Piquette Street, and within four years the company's stock returned more than 300 per cent in dividends. Over the next few years, Ford experimented with at least eight different models, seeking the magic key to low-cost transportation.. When business slackened in 1906, the company cut its prices and still made a profit of $1,250,000; it had retreated from the luxury market in the nick of time. It became clear to Ford and Couzens that the pathway to success was to be traveled by a low-cost car, and this indeed became the keystone of the company's policy. Such a policy was not only shrewd merchandising, but in Ford's case, it reflected the attitude of a mechanic who wanted a car easy to service and a farmer who needed a good automobile that was cheap.

The outcome was the Model T, put together in 1908, a tough, rugged looking $850 black box mounted on wheels. It was an extraordinary car, even by present-day standards: given the condition of the roads at that time, Ford and his associates gave America a vehicle that could traverse the muddiest backwoods path. It could even go into reverse while traveling forwards. The details were worked out by a staff of skilled craftsmen. The ignition was provided by a magneto built into the motor, it had splash lubrication, the motor was constructed of a light alloy metal, and the planetary transmission system made it behave like a colt. The car sold itself on its ability to conquer the back roads of the prairie. Within a few years, Ford had left his rivals far behind. Yet at one point he and Couzens almost sold out to William C. Durant, who was assembling his General Motors empire. Durant offered an exchange of stock, which was the only thing he had to offer, but Ford held out for cash. Clearly, the willingness to sell was an indication that neither Ford nor Couzens was really aware of the full potential of the automobile.

Be that as it may, Ford and Couzens decided to make a real go of the business. They fought the Selden patent pool—the Association of Licensed Auto Manufacturers—to a standstill, and when the Supreme Court held that Selden's patents, while valid, did not apply to American cars, the Association of Licensed Auto Manufacturers collapsed. Ford's advance was now unimpeded. Couzens called in Walter Flanders, a genius at mechanizing a factory, to turn the Piquette Street plant topsy-turvy and put it on the way to mass production. Demand for the Model T was so high that a new plant had to be built at Highland Park. Methods of work and the organization of materials flow were altered again and again in the attempt to achieve a mass output. The techniques for line production of automobiles were being worked out painfully, and without much regard for the cost that frequent changes in methods might incur. Besides, demand was so high that any losses could be recouped quite easily.

Ford built his plant system and his car as he went along. Feeder lines were installed as men moved from chassis to chassis, repeating their operations; the plant was in a constant hubbub, but it still took twelve hours and twenty-eight minutes to assemble a single car. This was far too much time. C. W. Avery and William Klann, a pair of ingenious technicians, devised a moving assembly line that kept the men rooted in one spot as the cars passed along the belt. But still the line kept clogging until that problem was solved by Carl Emde, a German master mechanic, with a battery of simple-purpose machine tools that coordinated the work of sub-assembly and assembly.

And in the front office, under Couzens, there was more than enough drive to make marketing the Ford car a success. Everyone in the industry conceded that Ford had the best staff. The men were enthusiastic and even fanatical in their urge to make the most of their opportunities, and over the whole business there hovered Ford and Couzens, who made certain that no bench-warmers would survive the furious pace. Ford, now in his fifties, drove his crew harder and harder to achieve the goal of the largest production in the industry. James Couzens became the company's chief publicist and salesman. By 1912 he had built a network of seven thousand dealers. Often he would force cars on his dealers for cash on the barrel-head, and he built a backlog of orders that was far ahead of production. He drove a hard bargain with suppliers to keep costs down. The cheapest means of shipment was employed, and cars were sent knocked down in order to reduce freight charges.

But in the plant the worker was reduced to an automaton whose life was not his own. There was constant supervision and observation, extending even to after hours. The mechanic became a machine tender who worked in an atmosphere of continuous noise and clatter. For many workers the Ford plant was the closest thing to a raucous jail. When the incentive-pay system was abolished in 1913, those who could no longer abide the assembly line went elsewhere to work. It was now clear to Ford that the worker had to be induced to surrender his soul to the mechanized factory. Besides, the Industrial Workers of the World, a union organization, was beginning to discover some favorable response among the workers who felt that they had to turn to someone for relief.

Ford's solution was the five-dollar day, conceived in 1914 and announced in an atmosphere of great ballyhoo as a humanitarian step. Other manufacturers were outraged: they called Ford a "Socialist" and a radical, but they need not have been so disturbed, for in its application the five-dollar day was a puffed-up fraud. There is some disagreement as to whose idea it was: some say Couzens, others Ford, while Charles Sorenson, one of Ford's right-hand men, took credit for the substantive details, though conceding that Ford had the initial conception. In any case, many workers could not immediately qualify for the five-dollar minimum rate, and it was not extended to women workers, those twenty-two years of age, family men not living at home, new employees, or any worker who proved himself "unworthy" of Ford's beneficence. In July, 1916, almost a third of the Ford work force was still receiving less than the five-dollar daily minimum rate. On the average, Ford's wages did not exceed the industry's prevailing scale. Ford called the plan a scheme for "profit sharing".

If the announcement of the five-dollar day was supposed to signify a new attitude toward labor, the manner of its introduction belied its intention. A virtual war broke out at the plant gates as workers fought to be taken on the job. But the company was utterly unprepared to hire so many men. A vast migration from other parts of the country ensued as everyone sought to gain from Ford's benevolence. The chaos outside the plant was as bad as that inside. Critics began to wonder what Ford was up to, but he thumbed his nose at them, as profits rose steadily. Urged on by the promise of a higher wage, the workers produced more than ever before and at a lower unit cost. Besides, with so high a wage rate the company could skim the cream of the labor market. The speed of the assembly line was accelerated as the workers submitted to its increasing intensity.

Accompanying this magnificent inducement was the "Department of Sociology," a kind of social-work attempt to standardize lives of the workers outside the plant in accordance with Ford's conception of what they ought to be like. But it really meant a massive purge of the work force: foremen were fired, then rehired as benchhands, making the turnover frightful. Ford's self-esteem grew to unbounded proportions, as he saw no limits to the prospects of growth. However, Couzens began to chafe: he was opposed to any rapid expansion and was too domineering a personality to bear for long with Ford's habits. It was inevitable that the two would clash sooner or later. In 1915 Couzens resigned. The next to join the Ford "alumni association" were the Dodge brothers, who had objected to the ploughing back of profits to finance expansion. When Ford announced that he was fixing dividends at $1,200,000 a year, they went to court. In 1919 Ford was ordered to pay $19,000,000 in back dividends plus interest to stockholders. At that point, he announced that he would withdraw from the business to start another company. His agents discreetly offered to relieve the Dodge brothers and other minority interests of their holdings. Couzens, seeing through the scheme, held out for his price.

Much as he disliked the bankers, Ford had to borrow some $70,000-000 on short term. When $58,000,000 of that loan came due in 1921, he simply squeezed it out of his dealers by dumping 125,000 cars on them for cash. Inventories were exhausted as production was stepped up. In this manner about $87,000,000 was raised in quick order, $29,000,000 more than he needed to meet obligations. But the dealers had to take what they were fed or go under. A six-dollar day was introduced under pretty much the same conditions as with the earlier minimum-wage rate, the ratchets were turned to make the assembly line move even faster, and the factory purge was started once more. Frank Klingensmith, Couzens' successor, was the next to go. Executives, office workers, and plant men were discharged left and right. The front-office staff was reduced by half in one fell swoop. William Knudsen left in disgust to join General Motors.

Ford, of course, never did the dirty work himself; he would simply hint to Sorenson, who would then lead his wrecking crews through the plant tossing men aside with abandon. Later Sorenson would deny that he had anything to do with these purges, but it is doubtful that he would have survived for forty years without carrying out every one of Ford's whims. Such repeated reigns of terror turned the Ford Motor Company into a model for the sort of totalitarianism that was later to grace the political landscape in Europe.

Ford was now wealthy enough to indulge in such idiosyncrasies as his Peace Ship of 1916, with which he promised to "get the boys out of the trenches by Christmas." Although Ford proclaimed that he was a pacifist, and once announced that he would raze his factory to the ground rather than produce for war, his company contracted to build boats and tanks for the Government and supplied thousands of trucks, ambulances, motors, parts, and helmets. Later he tried to foster a tale that $29,000,000 in war profits had been returned to the Government, a story that was called a fable by Secretary of the Treasury Andrew Mellon in the nineteen-twenties.

Despite his wealth and enormous economic power, Ford was really an illiterate and bigoted specimen of backwoods America, as was revealed in a 1919 libel suit. The Chicago *Tribune* had repeated a story that Ford would discharge any man who joined the National Guard. He promptly sued for a million dollars. In his examination, the attorney for the defense demonstrated that the great auto man did not know what the American

Revolution had been about, had not heard of Benedict Arnold, thought the word "commenced" was a technical term, and that "ballyhoo" was synonymous with "blackguard." It was evident that Ford's mind could not venture beyond an automobile motor.

This was the man who in 1918 had wanted to be a senator. The campaign that year was a nasty one: Ford's son, Edsel, was called a slacker, and Ford himslf was described by Truman Newberry, his political opponent, as a "lover of Huns." After his defeat, Ford's vindictiveness knew no bounds. He turned loose an army of detectives to gather evidence that Newberry had exceeded the limits on campaign expenditures set by the state. Newberry was convicted, but then exonerated by the Supreme Court. However, he resigned from the Senate, to be succeeded by James Couzens.

Perhaps the most vicious, and as it turned out, the most harmful aspect of Ford's career was his anti-Semitism. As with most such bigots, Jews and international bankers were said to be the same. The effects of Ford's anti-Semitism were so damaging because he gave it wide circulation in his Dearborn *Independent,* a paper which he sponsored and force-fed to the public through his dealers. The *Independent*'s circulation at one point reached 700,000; in it one could find duplicated the notorious Czarist forgery, the Protocols of the Elders of Zion. Ford's crude poison was couched in the oily prose of W. J. Cameron, his editor, who knew how to brew a potent cup of venom. The harm that was being generated was enormous. When Aaron Sapiro, an organizer of farm cooperatives, was attacked by the *Independent,* Ford was sued for one million dollars. Fearful that he would have to face the courts again, Ford evaded process servers, finally suffering a mysterious accident that prevented his appearance. He eventually settled out of court, but was forced to retract his statements and to apologize publicly. His claim to innocence, that he had not known what Cameron was doing, was most touching. One of the high points of his career was the acceptance of the Iron Cross from Hitler in 1938. To the Nazi legions that tore through Europe in the nineteen-thirties and nineteen-forties, Ford was a hero.

After World War I, the Ford Motor Company had begun to slip. American motorists were demanding something better than the Model T. General Motors was producing cars in many hues, while Ford was willing to give the customer "any color so long as it was black." Walter Chrysler had brought out the Plymouth; Knudsen at General Motors was producing the Chevrolet; slowly but surely, Henry Ford was being left behind. Meanwhile he absorbed the Lincoln Motor Company, owned by the Leland brothers, in order to add a prestige car to his line. He promptly fired all the old Leland employees and then got rid of the Lelands themselves, despite the promise that they would be retained in the merger. Once more Sorenson was delegated to do the dirty work, a task he carried out with alacrity. At last Ford gave in to the pressures to withdraw the familiar Model T. He simply shut down until he could make up his mind what to substitute for it, idling some 100,000 workers for almost a year. Finally, in 1928, the Model A was offered to a curious public, and it was sucessful enough to enable the company to regain some lost ground. The V8 engine was also developed, creating a reputation for the company as a good builder of motors. The V8 lasted over twenty years, taking Ford through the Great Depression without too many problems.

But costs had to be cut, and this meant driving the work force with totalitarian ruthlessness. Dealers had to take parts and tools with their shipments. And, of course, unions were utterly verboten at the plants. However, in the nineteen-thirties the Committee for Industrial Organization under John L. Lewis, began to move into the plants to organize the workers; it was the only way to gain relief from industrial oppression. By 1937 both General Motors and Chrysler had surrendered and had to negotiate with unions. Ford continued to hold out, employing Harry Bennett and his gang of assorted hoodlums and ex-convicts to terrorize workers and even administer physical beatings to them. Totalitarianism needs its secret police; this was the service that Bennett provided. When demonstrating unemployed workers tried to march to the Dearborn plant, the local police and Bennett's men fired at the crowd, killing four and wounding twenty.

During the Depression Ford did little to help the community, making no gift to any relief agency. So far as he was concerned the unemployed were a lazy mob. As one historian has said, Ford was asking for it. His response to the United Auto Workers was to have Bennett's men assault the union organizers who distributed leaflets around the plant gates. When the nation cried out in horror, he answered that his "loyal" employees had resisted the union, though one photograph showed a company attacker with handcuffs hanging out of his back pocket. Finally, in 1941, the United Auto Workers Union struck. Eventually Ford had to give in to an NLRB representation election in which the union received 70 per cent of the vote. By this time Ford was patently senile and was rapidly running the company into the ground. In 1945 his grandson, Henry Ford II, was called in to revive the empire. When Henry Ford I died in 1947 he was lauded as a great citizen. The legend that had grown up around him was believed by many Americans. In many ways, it was an incredible tale:

despite his backwoods callousness and his ignorance of anything but cars, Ford had become part of the folklore of America. But as Mark Twain once remarked in another context, it was a verdict, not a fact.

Ford had not been the only automobile pioneer who visualized a mass market for cars. When he brought out the Model T in 1908, William C. Durant was already the largest manufacturer in the industry. Durant had been a successful carriage maker and was to employ the techniques he learned in the trade in expanding his General Motors empire.

In 1885 Durant was a twenty-four-year-old insurance salesman in Flint, Michigan. With J. D. Dort, another salesman, he bought out a patent for two wheeled carts and had them made under a subcontracting arrangement, while concentrating on merchandising. Farm-implement houses throughout the farming areas were used as distribution outlets. So successful did the business become that the Durant-Dort Carriage Company decided to take over the manufacturing of carts directly. Others supplied the bodies, wheels, paint, axles, and springs. By the time he was forty, Durant had become a millionaire. A sojourn in New York enabled him to see how others were building industrial empires, and he decided that he wanted one of his own. Back to Flint he went to purchase the Buick Manufacturing Company, a small concern that was in trouble. It was the start.

Within four years, during which he brought in Charles Mott, a master axle-maker, and Albert Champion, a maker of spark plugs, Durant had built Buick into one of the leading auto manufacturers. In 1908 he was selling more cars than Ford. Unable to bring together the four major auto manufacturers—Buick, Maxwell, Reo, and Ford—Durant set up General Motors with Buick, Cadillac, Oldsmobile, Oakland (later Pontiac), five other auto firms, three truck companies, and ten parts makers. It was all done by an exchange of stock, since the kind of cash that Ford and Olds (who was making the Reo) wanted was lacking. Within two years the corporation was in trouble: its creation by paper had set up a large debt, and the rapid expansion exhausted its credit. When Durant went to the bankers in New York and Boston for the $15,000,000 he needed to survive the recession of 1910, the bankers, headed by Lee Higginson and Company, insisted that Durant must go. The bankers took $2,500,000 plus $6,000,000 worth of General Motors stock, as their commission. Under their regime, subsidiaries were consolidated, and whatever was deemed business avoirdupois was cut away: they wanted profit, not expansion. This was the period when Charles Nash and Walter P. Chrysler moved in to the top layers of General Motors management.

But Durant was not idle. He teamed up in 1911 with Louis Chevrolet, a Swiss mechanic, to produce a popular-priced car that began to rival Ford. So successful was this auto that Durant was encouraged to recapture General Motors. He offered to exchange Chevrolet stock for General Motors at five to one. Pierre du Pont and John J. Raskob then helped buy up General Motors stock quietly. Soon Chevrolet owned General Motors. Du Pont became chairman of the board, a post he held for thirteen years. Nevertheless, Durant was left to operate the company as he saw fit. Expansion proceeded rapidly, with some concentration on the middle-priced range. In 1918 the whole setup was reorganized so that the Chevrolet tail would no longer wag the corporate dog. A new General Motors Corporation absorbed the General Motors Company, Chevrolet, United Motors, Delco (bringing in Charles F. Kettering), and the Hyatt Roller Bearing Company, which had been headed by Alfred P. Sloan. Expansion after World War I became massive, with an additional investment of $50,000,000 by the du Ponts. Fisher Body was bought for $30,-000,000; Frigidaire was picked up for a mere $56,000; Warner Gears and a brake company were also acquired. When the directors asked Durant why an electric refrigerator, he replied that it was like an auto: it was a box with a motor inside. The General Motors Acceptance Corporation was established to finance dealers and customers.

But General Motors under Durant had become an uncoordinated sprawling giant. Du Pont tried to introduce some organizational sense, but Durant couldn't care less; he was far more interested in manipulating his empire of paper. At one time Durant had no less than seventy accounts with stock-market brokers. Sloan offered a reorganization plan, but before anything could be done the depression of 1920–21 was on them. The money spent for plant acquisition and inventories totaled over $80,000,000. Raskob informed du Pont that another $64,000,000 was needed to save the company. The Nobel interests in Sweden supplied $15,000,000, and $21,000,000 came from other overseas investors. It was not enough, and the rest was floated through the House of Morgan.

Meanwhile Durant had been buying General Motors stock in an effort to hold up its price in the face of the auto market's collapse. The effort took his entire personal fortune, and he emerged with a debt of $30,000,000. In desperation he turned to du Pont, who cautioned against dumping on the market the 2,500,000 shares held by Durant. Instead, du Pont and Morgan took over the stock and bailed Durant out, but he had to leave the corporation. He then put together Durant Motors, which fell by the wayside just before the Great Depression. At the age of seventy-seven he was operating a supermarket in New Jersey. Durant died in 1947, aged eighty-seven, a colorful pioneer whose flamboyant ways had been long out of date.

Du Pont took over as General Motors president after Durant. The corporate structure was again reorganized. Sloan's plan suited the new corporate image quite well. Advisory groups and committees of specialists were created. Durant's loose organization was replaced by staff-line formality. Division managers were "autonomous," but the work was coordinated by the top echelon of officials. The executive committee planned policy for the corporation as a whole: authority flowed down, as responsibility and accountability moved up. The entire plan was made coherent under Sloan, who became president in 1923. The sales organization was strengthened, and an effective corporate "team" was developed. Knudsen rebuilt the Chevrolet division. Soon General Motors began to displace Ford as the industry's leader. The age of the executive, soft-spoken and dressed in gray flannel, had been inaugurated.

When the telephone was first introduced, in the eighteen-seventies. Englishmen thought it far inferior to the "well-established system of speaking tubes." Dom Pedro, the emperor of Brazil, who listened to it at the Philadelphia Exposition in 1876, exclaimed, "My God! It talks!" Even to Americans it was at first little more than a toy.

Alexander Graham Bell, usually credited with the telephone's invention, had been a teacher for the deaf, and he was more interested in doing something for his pupils than in enabling normal persons to speak over long distances. After some experimentation, he succeeded in sending the spoken voice through the wires instead. As usual, there were predecessors: Philipp Reis had sent sounds, though not voice, through wire in 1860, and in the same decade Elisha Gray worked out the essentials for a telephone but was beaten to the patent office by Bell.

Bell's magnetized wire worked fairly well, and the telephone industry was soon on its way. The early "centrals" at first employed boys who in their frantic effort to plug into the boards would allow their oaths to filter through to the customers' ears. The profanity led to their displacement by politer "telephone girls." Wires were strung on poles, and soon the cities were decorated by necklaces of cables that ran for miles through the streets; it was a public nuisance that was not eliminated until the wires were put underground. There were many who contributed to the telephone's development: John Carty devised a way to eliminate noise in transmission; Charles Scribner worked out the multiple switchboard;

Michael E. Pupin, a Columbia University professor, developed the principle of loading to permit an economical extension of long-distance wires.

Nevertheless, the industry's growth was slow at first. Bell and his assistant, Thomas Watson, would travel around the country giving exhibitions transmitting music and speech from one part of a town to another. And attempts to introduce the telephone into daily use came up against the opposition of Western Union. Two wealthy Bostonians whose daughters had been pupils of Bell gave support to the telephone, but such help soon ceased. Bell desperately offered the invention to Western Union for $100,000, but it turned him down, much to its later regret, no doubt. In 1878 capital was found to form the Bell Telephone Company, but Bell had to surrender control of his patents to a group of Boston financiers. The first general manager was Theodore Vail, whose concept of a national phone service and insistence on standardized equipment were to play an important part in the industry's growth. The Bostonians had demanded that their shares should have twice the voting power of Bell's shares. It was not long before Bell returned to his students. The National Bell Telephone Company was formed to increase capitalization. Bell was offered the job of chief inventor, but he made it clear that he could not invent to order.

William Vanderbilt realized that he had erred in turning Bell away when the inventor approached Western Union, and his quick acquisition of the Gray patents made it evident that National Bell now had a formidable rival. The situation worsened when Jay Gould announced his intention of wresting control of Western Union from Vanderbilt. The Bostonians held firm against the mounting attacks. Suddenly, Gould made peace with National Bell—since Western Union was his chief target—and to conserve his strength against Gould, Vanderbilt turned over his telephone interests to Bell. This maneuvering gave the Boston Brahmins virtually complete control of the nascent telephone industry; for the next twenty years they exercised a stranglehold on the company that was not loosened until 1902, when capitalists and financiers in New York began to cast their eyes on the now profitable business. In 1880, National Bell became the American Bell Telephone Company, licensing local exchanges in return for a controlling share. At the time, the directors literally owned the company, holding 55 per cent of the outstanding stock. By 1899 shareholding had become widely dispersed, but this in no way weakened the control of the directors, as they simply dominated affairs by use of the proxy device.

For Vail the telephone was a "natural" monopoly. The American Bell Telephone Company solidified its hold on the infant industry by Vail's determined and successful effort to impose uniformity on equipment. Vail had been a mail superintendent, and on that job he had done much to correct the chaos of mail distribution. Now Vail vigorously fostered the telephone. Local promoters were sought out to set up companies, with Bell receiving a share of the stock. The Bell people asked for board seats in all strategic cases. Since non-Bell franchises could not interconnect to complete long-distance calls, their services were limited. But in 1885 Vail quit, disheartened by the conservatism of the Boston financiers. After that, and until 1906, when he was prevailed upon to return, the American Bell Telephone Company was stagnant, adding few exchanges and allowing the independents to introduce most of the major advances in telephony. Indeed, the service of the independents was superior to that of Bell's; besides, their charges were less.

The company was known as a New England firm; New York financiers were not as yet interested in its progress. But the company's growth was steady if slow: there were 56,000 stations in fifty-five communities in the system, and the Western Electric Company had been acquired as a manufacturing subsidiary. The control of the Bostonians might have continued had not the Rockefellers, Wideners, MacKays, and Morgans awakened to the fact that here was a gold mine. The company was following a policy of limited installations with high rentals, yielding a high rate of profit. When the basic patents expired, a large number of independents sprang up, but they could not provide interconnections between the major cities; those were controlled by Bell. The Rockefeller-Widener forces set up a duplicate service in the Telephone, Telegraph, and Cable Company of America, but when J. P. Morgan decided that Bell was to be his objective, Widener withdrew. Meanwhile, the American Telephone and Telegraph Company, which had been the long-distance subsidiary of the Bell System, was converted into a holding company, to become in time the parent organization of one of the world's largest aggregations of capital, controlling virtually all of the telephone service in the United States and, through related companies, much of it elsewhere. Slowly, the New York financial tycoons, headed by Morgan, moved in on AT&T; by 1907 control was theirs.

In the process there was a first-class rhubarb with Clarence MacKay of Postal Telegraph. MacKay wanted his own merger with Bell and had been led to believe by several Bell officers that such a merger was feasible. It turned out that MacKay had been merely strung along as the Bell men were already working with Morgan. When the latter had acquired enough strength, they placed Theodore Vail on the board. This proved to be the opening wedge. The board split between the conservative Bostonians and

the aggressive New Yorkers who wanted expansion and security flotations to be handled by Morgan. By 1907 the Morgan interests succeeded
in wresting control away from the old guard and electing Vail as president.
Meanwhile MacKay tried to get his foot in the door by buying AT&T in
the market. Yet even when his holdings had reached 5 per cent of the
outstanding shares, he was not given a seat on the board. Ultimately, he
was to sell his stock in disgust.

Vail became Morgan's man completely. When the financier asked him
to lend $20,000,000 to the British Government, he did so unhesitatingly,
even though there was some doubt as to the loan's legality. Under the
charter such a loan could be made only if surplus funds were available;
Morgan created the surplus by peddling a special bond issue, a procedure
many considered to be illegal. The close ties that were developed between
AT&T and Western Union worked to MacKay's disadvantage. When telegraph messages were placed over the phone, operators would route them
to Western Union unless the customers specified Postal Telegraph.

AT&T began to move toward an organizational structure in which professional administrators were to become the decision-makers. Walter Gifford, who started with the company in 1904, climbed the ladder steadily
until he was elected president in 1925. Strong financial ties were maintained with Morgan and the First National Bank. Between 1906 and 1935
over $1,000,000,000 worth of securities were placed with the House of
Morgan, of which at least $40,000,000 went to the bankers in commissions.
Certain banks, such as the First National, the National Shawmut of Boston,
and Chase, were favored with deposits, as with Jackson's pet banks. Some
patronage stemmed from trusteeships in bond indentures and from regis-
tries for stock certificates. Morgan's community of interest was well
established.

Control was centered in a self-perpetuating oligarchy, with most of
the privileges going to the archons. It all operated like a well-oiled political
machine. Monopoly was justified on "natural" grounds, as competition in
the supporting industries was badgered and fought off with patent suits.
By the first quarter of the twentieth century the Bell System had grown
into a gigantic operation, with twenty-five associated companies in control
of almost 16,000,000 of the 20,000,000 million telephones then in service.
The total operating revenue was well over a billion dollars a year. Manufacturing was handled through Western Electric as Bell Telephone Laboratories became the research arm, mainly to seek out patents that would
insure control. "Ma" Bell was an intricate and labyrinthine corporation

whose interrelationships with other companies—General Electric, for example—were wonders to behold.

Economic strength was buttressed with political muscle, even including bribery, as in San Francisco in 1906. Independents were choked off by surrounding them with Bell subsidiaries that would not cooperate. Wherever possible independents were purchased lock, stock, and telephone. In providing interconnections to cooperative companies, Bell exacted exorbitant fees. Rural service was suppressed so effectively that even by the nineteen-forties only 37 per cent of farms had telephones. The monopoly had become a gigantic pachyderm just tolerating the approximately two thousand independent companies, who behaved like chickens that had long since learned to skip away from its lumbering legs.

A parallel to the Bell organization was built in international telephony by the Behn brothers, who had operated the phone system in Cuba and Puerto Rico. Their International Telephone and Telegraph was to function overseas just as AT&T functioned domestically. With Wall Street assistance, IT&T soon controlled the telephone systems of Cuba, Puerto Rico, Spain, Mexico, Chile, Peru, and Brazil, as well as assorted cable companies. The MacKay system went over to IT&T. As the largest telephone operator outside the United States, the complex became an expression of American business dominating its field in foreign nations. By 1930 its assets had exceeded $500,000,000.

The pattern of industrial control exemplified in telephones was to be repeated in the motion picture industry as well. There innovators sought their fortunes in a marginal industry, only to be displaced when high profits brought respectability. The motion picture's beginnings date back to 1896, but in the three-quarters of a century since then it has passed through all the major phases of capitalistic growth. Adventurous men with ideas seized the industry from unimaginative inventors, promoted it into a fantastic money-maker, and once firmly established, found to their dismay that the financiers were ready to capture another bastion for high finance.

The first inventors and promoters failed to recognize the potentialities of the movie camera. They were anxious to protect patent rights and did not seek a mass market. The task of development was undertaken by hard-driving, aggressive nickelodeon operators willing to shoulder the risks of an infant industry. They did their own financing; they wrote their own scripts; they built their own scenery; they developed the films and exhibited the pictures in their own primitive theaters. They had a capacity for work that only those on the periphery of the business world possess. These entrepreneurs had been glove salesmen, pharmacists, furriers, clothiers, and jewelers. They were innovators, arrogant and often vulgar, but they knew what the people wanted, and they created a form of entertainment within the reach of all. Responsive to the demands of a movie-hungry public, they created the feature picture and the star system.

In the beginning, the movie industry was shunned by respectable businessmen. They considered it a low form of amusement that would only ruin reputations. The public, however, felt no such qualms and demanded more films. Studios mushroomed all over the country, and anyone who could rent or steal a movie camera became a producer. By 1909 competition had become so intense that the larger manufacturers formed the Motion Pictures Patents Company as a measure of self-protection. Independent producers, however, refused to be intimidated by the patent combine's legal tactics, and economic warfare raged unabated.

The bitter struggle between the patent combine and the independents continued until, in 1914, the Motion Pictures Patents Company ceased to be a dominant factor. Carl Laemmle had formed a powerful protective association; William Fox, faced with a shortage of films for his theaters, began to produce his own pictures; the Lasky organization became too important to be suppressed. Men of that caliber did not accept easily the restrictive dictates of the early movie monopolists. Leading a shoestring existence, they did not mind an occasional hasty trip to Mexico to avoid an injunction suit.

The need for quick escapes from the patent combine's process servers compelled the independents to seek movie locations close to the Mexican border. Southern California became the ideal place, for here one found superb replicas of the deserts of Africa and the wilds of India. Continuous sunshine permitted all-day shooting, and cheap labor made filming mob scenes an inexpensive undertaking.

The experience of the patent combine proved to alert movie entrepreneurs that distribution and exhibition were the keys to absolute control. Adolph Zukor, William Fox, and Marcus Loew began to dispose of their nickelodeons and to acquire more dignified theaters. The extremes to which the early magnates went in their search for dignity were illustrated by one of Loew's theater purchases. He bought a closed burlesque house in Brooklyn that had been often raided by the police. At the time, the building was being used as a storage place by the Salvation Army. The decrepit theater was fumigated physically and morally; for several months it was used by a troupe of Italian Shakespearean actors. Loew then opened it as a respectable family movie house.

Marcus Loew was a conservative businessman in an industry marked by flamboyant extravagance. He had started life as a newspaper boy on New York's East Side and by the turn of the century had become a fairly successful furrier. Peep shows, the latest rage in low-cost, high-profit entertainment, offered a more attractive field, however, and, together with Adolph Zukor, Loew began to build a chain of penny arcades. Zukor and Loew were very unfriendly partners; each wanted to run the business in his own way. When the firm rented new office space, Loew conveniently forgot to provide his colleague with a desk and chair. Zukor could not overlook the insult to his dignity; he left to become an independent producer of films.

Throughout this early period of growth Loew sought to exhibit a better kind of picture. But he soon found it difficult to get good films, for Zukor, his erstwhile partner, who was now an important producer, stubbornly refused to exhibit in the Loew chain. In 1920 Loew decided to make his own pictures. He bought out a moribund producing company called Metro Pictures, and in 1924 added the Goldwyn Pictures Corporation and the L. B. Mayer Company. Thus was formed the alliterative Metro-Goldwyn-Mayer, Loew's producing subsidiary.

L. B. Mayer, born in Poland, came to the United States in the late eighteen-nineties. A member of the original group of furriers, jewelers, and nickelodeon operators who built the movie industry, he became MGM's chief. When Loew wanted to buy his firm, Mayer inserted a profit-sharing clause in the contract—a clause that often brought his yearly earnings close to the half-million mark.

After Marcus Loew's death in 1927, the enterprise was directed by Nicholas Schenck, a hard-headed businessman who followed the conservative practices of his predecessor. Schenck had come to America in 1892 with his brother Joseph, and together they had operated an amusement park at Fort George, New York. One day Marcus Loew came there to show movies, and the Schenck boys were imaginative enough to forget the amusement-park game. Nicholas joined the Loew organization, and Joseph became a movie producer. Nicholas Schenck soon won the reputation of knowing best where to build theaters.

It was Adolph Zukor, however, who established the pattern for expansion in the new industry. Emigrating to America with $40 sewed into the lining of his coat, he sought his fortune in the novelty-fur business. Penny arcades were more exciting, though, and in 1905 Zukor transferred his energies and his $200,000 profit from furs to that outcast branch of the entertainment world. When motion pictures became an important addition to the line of arcade gadgets, Zukor immediately realized the potentialities of the new entertainment form, and movies soon became the sole attraction.

Exhibitors in those days had very poor fare to show. Skirt dances, a daredevil ride in a barrel over the falls, or the pounding surf on the coast of Maine made up the twenty-minute or thirty-minute program. Zukor wanted pictures that told a coherent story; the unprecedented success of Sarah Bernhardt's *Queen Elizabeth* strengthened this desire. After his split with Loew in 1912, Zukor went into picture production and formed the Famous Players Company.

Within four years he was at the top of a brawling infant industry. Motion pictures in those days were distributed by so-called exchanges. Zukor did business with the Paramount Pictures exchange, headed by W.W. Hodkinson. Dissatisfied with the financial terms imposed by Hodkinson, Zukor suggested a merger. The former indignantly refused, but he failed to reckon with Zukor's pertinacity. Zukor quietly bought up most of Paramount's stock and within a year was able to oust Hodkinson.

Zukor reasoned that control of the market rested on control at the source; if the best actors belonged to Paramount, he thought, the exhibitors would be at his mercy. Within a few years Zukor assembled a great collection of talent. Film-rental fees increased sharply and block-booking—the requirement that bad pictures be exhibited along with the good—was forced upon the reluctant independent exhibitor.

To evade block-booking, several theater circuits formed First National Pictures, a producing company, in 1917. With their own supply of films, they could exclude competitors' pictures from their theaters. Soon First National had five thousand members, and Zukor began to worry about theaters rather than talent. For two years he watched First National's tactics and then decided that it was time to set up his own distribution and exhibition outlets. Convinced that theaters were a good investment, he sold $10,000,000 worth of securities through Kuhn, Loeb and Company and began to build the Paramount movie chain.

The technique by which a theater circuit was welded together was not a soft one. An independent exhibitor was approached and bluntly told either to sell his property or suffer the competition of a newly constructed theater. Independents screamed that the industry was being raped, but Zukor went his way, disposing of First National's individual members one by one. By 1921 he controlled over three hundred movie houses and in 1926 his acquistion of the Chicago Katz-Balaban circuit completely nullified First National's importance in the motion picture industry.

With more than sixteen hundred theaters exhibiting the Paramount product, Zukor felt safe in the face of the Depression. But the quiet ex-furrier discovered that even so Depression-proof an industry as motion pictures could not carry the heavy fixed charges imposed by Wall Street financing. Paramount began to hit the financial reefs, and for two years fifty-three assorted law firms, banks, investors' committees, and experts scowled and quarreled over the ailing corporation. Involved in all this high legal bickering were the Chase National Bank, the Royal Insurance Company, American Telephone and Telegraph, and the Atlas Corporation. Paramount was finally reorganized in 1935. Of the old officers, only Zukor and George Schaefer remained; the new board of directors was composed of bankers and real estate men. John Otterson, head of AT&T's Electrical Reseach Products, Inc. (ERPI), became president.

The early movie pioneers never forgot their humble origins, and their thirst for industrial power was perhaps motivated by an unconscious wish to be treated as equals. But not all of them had the urge to create financial monstrosities; some preferred to be known as artistic picture makers. Such a man was Samuel Goldfish.

Goldfish left his native Warsaw at the age of ten and arrived in Gloversville, New York, one year later. At fifteen he began a successful road salesman's career in the toughest territory in the glove business. One day he walked into a Herald Square nickelodeon and was inspired with the notion of owning a theater. He soon discovered that it was cheaper to produce and sell films. Together with his brother-in-law Jesse Lasky, a vaudeville producer, and on a capital of $26,500, he organized the Jesse Lasky Feature Play Company. Goldfish soon acquired the reputation of a man who did things his own way or not at all. When Lasky merged with Zukor in 1916, Goldfish stepped out to create a new production unit. His partners in this venture were the Selwyn brothers.

The new business was called after the founders, Goldwyn Pictures. Goldfish thought so well of the title that for the first time in the history of corporate enterprise a man named himself for a corporation: Goldfish became Goldwyn. And despite Zukor's hope that it would fail, the new company became a factor to be reckoned with.

Goldwyn's great contribution to movie making came from his emphasis on quality. In 1919 he conceived the notion that the key person in production was the writer. Before that a scenario had been nothing more than a rough outline to guide the director. Of course, the elevation of the writer to an important position may have been a shrewd competitive device turned against Zukor, who had cornered the market in acting talent. Goldwyn hired such writers as Rex Beach, Gertrude Atherton, and Maurice Maeterlinck. When Maeterlinck turned in his script, Goldwyn, came dashing out of his office screaming, "My God, he's writing about bees!" Though he failed to obtain many usable scripts, Goldwyn did get a good deal of valuable publicity.

When MGM was formed in 1924, Goldwyn tried to establish himself as production chief. Here, however, he suffered one of his rare defeats and was forced to withdraw. Not at all disturbed by this unfavorable turn of events, he organized another movie company, Samuel Goldwyn, Inc., Ltd. Here he was absolute boss, and the responsibility was all his own. He continued to emphasize quality in pictures; in no other way could they have been exhibited. Then, when sound film made dialogue an important feature of the movie, Goldwyn's emphasis on writing was vindicated.

Most producers tried to duplicate Zukor's tactics. They realized that their pictures possessed value solely in proportion to the number of theaters they controlled. Movie making could be enlarged only by tapping an extensive market, and the need for a continuous outlet soon overshadowed the processes of production. Distribution and exhibition became the major means of eliminating rivals and of acquiring control of as large a segment of a highly competitive market as one could grasp.

The struggle for the movie market produced gigantic interlocking corporations whose complexity paralleled the complicated corporate structures in utilities, finance, and automobiles. Independents were ruthlessly eliminated; production, distribution, and exhibition became the functions of a few large corporations.

With the battle for theaters increasing in intensity, eastern bankers began to recognize motion pictures as a legitimate enterprise. As Leo Rosten says, Hollywood shifted from the Arabian Nights to Dun and Bradstreet. The bankers, however, could think only of box-office receipts, and this markedly influenced movie-making policy. In the early days producers exercised their ingenuity without any financial inhibitions, but with the advent of big business in their field, the Wall Street supervisor replaced the Hollywood genius. The supervisor's job was to protect his employer's investment; players and directors were selected with both eyes on the box office. A motion picture had to have "production value," "picture sense," and "box-office appeal." And, of course, the best way of assuring these was to imitate the smash-hit formula of another company. Forced into this mold, the motion picture as an art form began a steady decline.

Wall Street men, as well as Wall Street money, entered the movie industry. Industrialists such as William C. Durant of General Motors and

Harvey Gibson of the Liberty National Bank became members of the board of directors of Loew's. The du Ponts and the Chase National Bank sponsored the formation of Goldwyn Pictures. The financiers reorganized the larger movie companies and effected mergers. Soon the public began to recognize the signatures of these new movie-makers.

Into the midst of all this, the sound film broke with an impact that further shook the hold of the old-timers and strengthened that of the financiers. While most industries were prostrated by the Depression, the motion-picture industry remained financially healthy. Wall Street gazed at this astounding example of economic health and resolved more than ever to secure absolute control.

During the nineteen-twenties Warner Brothers found itself on the downgrade; with no controlled exhibition outlets of its own, even a superior producing company could not live. At that time the Western Electric Company had just developed its first motion picture sound equipment, and, of all the leading movie companies, only Warners was willing to try it. Sound had an amazingly restorative effect. Warner Brothers became the only movie company, with the exception of Loew's, able to survive the Depression without financial reorganization.

Harry, the oldest Warner brother, started his career as a shoemaker. His brothers Abe and Sam had other ideas, however; they toured the country exhibiting their single print of *The Great Train Robbery*. Barnstorming was profitable enough to enable them to buy a nickelodeon in Newcastle, Pennsylvania, where Harry joined them. By 1917 the Warners had developed a successful movie exchange.

That year, James Gerard, a former American ambassador, published his *My Four Years in Germany*. With characteristic enterprise Harry Warner secured the screen rights and the sensational film of Gerard's experiences, grossing nearly a million dollars, made the Warners topflight producers. The picture also established the Warner Brothers pattern: their products, based on the events of the day, became "topic-snatchers."

Hollywood's financial terrain was quite rough, and it was not until Waddill Catchings, the ever-optimistic partner in Goldman, Sachs, took the Warners in hand that they learned how to become important movie magnates. Yet had it not been for the advent of sound, Warners would never have reached the top of the brawling competitive industry. It was Sam Warner who insisted that the company gamble on Western Electric's sound device. Most of the movie companies had refused to have anything to do with the new gadget. Warners obtained an exclusive license, in return for which they agreed to sell 2,400 complete theater sound-equipment systems for Electrical Research Products, Inc., the telephone company's subsidiary. Then came the remarkable *The Jazz Singer*, and all the film companies and theaters clamored for equipment. ERPI promptly cancelled its exclusive contract with Warners and sold equipment to all comers. For years, one of Harry Warner's pet antipathies was the telephone.

The Warner boys quickly realized that they would have to control their own outlets if they were to stay in business. From 1928 to 1930 they bought as many theaters as they could, and with the acquisition of the powerful Stanley circuit, they reached their goal. Selling debentures and common stock, they built up a chain of over five hundred theaters. Music-publishing firms, a radio factory, and a lithographing plant were among some of their more curious purchases.

Becoming adept in high finance, the Warners' stock manipulations were brilliant enough to dazzle the most jaded of Wall Street operators. During the nineteen-twenties, they sold stock to an investment-mad public through Renraw, their personal holding company. Renraw (the family name written backwards) then lent the proceeds, interest-free, to Warner Brothers, thus circumventing the bankers. But the Warners always held on to the voting stock—no one was going to tell them how to run their own business.

Radio Corporation of America also tried to market sound equipment for movies, but the field had already been seized by Western Electric. Within a year after Warners proved the practicability of sound pictures, Western Electric had exclusive contracts with 90 per cent of the movie firms. The only alternative for RCA was to create its own movie empire. A holding company, the RKO Corporation, was formed, with control divided between RCA, the Atlas Corporation, and Rockefeller Center, Inc. RKO Pictures was organized as the producing subsidiary and the Keith-Orpheum theater chain became the exhibiting outlet. Here was a motion-picture giant built exclusively by financiers whose sole motive was to exploit a new technological device.

Between 1927 and 1935 the industry was rocked by a struggle over control of the patents for sound equipment. ERPI signed long-term contracts with Loew's, Paramount, United Artists, and Universal. Only 95 theaters in the country had other than Western Electric reproducing apparatus, while 1,946 theaters had Western Electric equipment. RCA seemed to have been virtually eliminated from the field; only the large RKO chain used its sound devices.

RCA finally filed an antitrust suit against the telephone-company interests, and in 1935 a peaceful agreement was signed to give RCA new rights in the sound-equipment business. This legal battle was in the last analysis fought by the two financial giants of American industry: the Morgan and the Rockefeller empires.

The famous case of William Fox well illustrates the power of finance in the motion-picture industry. Fox started work in a cleaning and dyeing establishment at $17 a week. One day in 1904 he took the $1,600 he had saved and bought a movie house in Brooklyn. From then on he went ahead steadily in the budding industry, becoming one of the first to defy the old patent pool. He launched into production, and gradually expanded his theater holdings. He held also the American rights to Tri-Ergon, a European sound system; this was dangerous competition for Western Electric. Patent-infringement suits and antitrust charges, however, did not trouble the Fox Corporation. Fox continued to expand, and at one time virtually dominated the motion-picture industry in America. But even he could not withstand the unrelenting onslaughts of the telephone interests.

In 1927 Fox began to round up theater chains; in 1929 he secured control of Loew's and Baumont British. But these operations required financing, and Halsey, Stuart and Company, an investment banking firm with Western Electric connections, extended the necessary assistance in the form of short-term loans. Then came the 1929 crash. When Fox tried to renew his loans, the bankers stipulated that he relinquish control of his company. Fox sought aid from other sources, but no banker seemed willing to oppose the House of Morgan. In the end Fox was forced to sell his holdings to H. L. Clarke, an associate of Samuel Insull, the utilities magnate, for $18,000,000, never quite realizing what had happened.

CHAPTER 14 Electric Lights and Airwaves

Thomas A. Edison was by no means the first man to experiment with electricity. As early as the sixteenth century there had been research into the properties of magnetism, a phenomenon closely related to electricity. William Gilbert, physician to Queen Elizabeth I, had been able to distinguish between electrical and magnetic attraction and there were pathbreaking experiments by Robert Boyle, Otto von Guericke, Stephen Gray, and Francis Hauksbee. The Leyden jar, devised in 1746, was really a condenser for static electricity, a kind of primitive storage battery. In America, Benjamin Franklin had been so fascinated by electrical phenomena that he gave up his business to pursue studies in science; his lightning rod was an important device for protecting barns and other vulnerable structures. Galvani's experiments with electrical action led to Volta's discovery of current flow and the creation of the wet battery, a method for storing electricity that was superior to earlier techniques. Finally, Humphrey Davy drew an arc from electric current, the first form of practical electric illumination.

Other discoveries followed: Hans Oersted demonstrated that an electric current in a conductor created a magnetic field, André Ampère revealed the relation between electricity and magnetism, and Michael Faraday generated electrical voltages with mechanical power by using an electromagnetic device. Hence, when Edison began his practical work there had been two hundred years of accumulated scientific and technical experience on which he could draw. But there were serious limitations on electrical developments after the Civil War. Gas was widely used for artificial illumination, and the lack of a suitable source of power was a serious handicap for electricity. Batteries were fine for the telegraph but not for much more. Between 1860 and 1870, workers in the field of electricity were so discouraged that not one patent was filed.

But technology could not be denied for long, and soon Paul Jablock Koff, a Russian, devised a high-current arc light useful for outdoor lighting.

An arc-light system for city streets was developed by Charles Brush in 1878. Soon Elihu Thompson and Edwin Houston, important pioneers in electricity, had constructed an alternative method that competed with the Brush system. By 1886 many of the nation's streets were brightened by one or the other. Artificial lighting seemed a necessity: in addition to arc lights there were also some four hundred gas companies providing illumination to both streets and homes. An incandescent lamp with a long life appeared to be in the distant future; the stumbling block was the lack of a glass bulb with enough of a vacuum to prevent the filament from burning itself out. Thus fame and fortune awaited the man who could solve that problem: it was to be Thomas Alva Edison, one of America's most gifted inventors. He was to make the first practical incandescent lamp and to devise, as well, the system for marketing electricity so that it could compete with, and eventually displace, gas. In short, Edison showed how to build a mass market for artifical light.

Edison was born in 1847 in Milan, Ohio, of forebears who were part Dutch and part English. A mischievous lad, he was always at the center of scrapes and difficulties—growing-up problems that stemmed from an unquenchable curiosity. With one of the periodic depressions of antebellum days, the family moved on to Michigan. Edison's inquisitiveness led him to chemistry, and he continually experimented with a variety of pharmacists' compounds. Telegraphy and electricity also fascinated him and he learned what he could of the new phenomena not only by reading but also by trying out things on his own. As a newsboy on the railroad, he turned one end of the baggage car into a small laboratory. As a result of a childhood ailment he began to lose his hearing; his deafness remained with him throughout his life. Yet, curiously, the affliction did not prevent him from hearing the clickety-clack of the telegraph; if it had, the future would have been different.

Able to hear that much, Edison began to study the dispatcher's craft. In a short while he became a self-taught expert telegrapher. Meanwhile he read James Watts in preference to Isaac Newton, a choice that reflected the brilliant tinkerer to come. There followed a period of itinerant job-holding, interspersed with studying and work on mechanical devices. A repeating telegraph did not turn out too well, but Edison was still in his teens. In 1867 he headed for Boston to go to work for Western Union. His rustic ways brought him a mild sort of notoriety, but he commanded the respect of his coworkers when he kept the cockroaches out of his lunch by electrocuting them with a simple tinfoil device.

Bored by the job, he left after two years to give full time to the business of invention. He worked on a duplex system for the telegraph, and at the age of twenty-two, patented a vote-recording machine, the first of many inventions that he would patent throughout a long and fruitful life. Edison hoped to sell the instrument to legislatures, but a Massachusetts solon advised him that the machine would infringe on the "right of filibuster," and a congressman remarked that a vote-recording machine was just the thing politicians did not want because it would destroy any hope a minority had of influencing legislation. There followed improvements on a stock-ticker, the rights to which were sold to a telegraph company.

The New York area beckoned, and Edison went to that city to try his fortune. A fortuitous repair job on a gold-market indicator prevented a panic and as a consequence, he was hired as an electrician at the handsome salary of three hundred dollars a month. In 1869 he formed a company with his benefactor to work on inventions and related problems; the firm was soon bought up by Western Union, with Edison receiving five thousand dollars, more money than he had ever seen before. Not long afterward, Edison was back working as a free-lance inventor for Western Union. At one point he was paid forty thousand dollars for his efforts. When a bank teller refused to cash the check for lack of identification, Edison thought he had been cheated. The check was finally cashed, and he sat up all night with his hoard before redepositing it in the bank. But Edison had become a captive inventor for Western Union: while the company encouraged him, paying well for his contributions, it also took all the rights to his inventions. Nevertheless, he was now a success at the age of twenty-four, and though he might manufacture stock-tickers exclusively for one company, so far as he was concerned he was his own master.

Edison's endeavors during this period consisted of improvements on the inventions of others, but when he got through with the various gadgets they really functioned. Telegraph receiving, which had always caused trouble, was markedly improved, and a number of other devices operated as they never had before. In 1872 he took out thirty-eight patents; in 1873, twenty-five more. Edison's passion for work became legendary. He produced a messenger call-box, a stencil pen, the mimeograph, and, in 1874, invented quadruplex transmission for the telegraph, a system for sending four messages at once through a single wire. The economy of operation that this system afforded did not escape the attention of the telegraph magnates.

Meanwhile patent-infringement suits became weapons in the unceasing war between these magnates. The gigantic battles—among them Jay Gould's attempt to seize Western Union—raged about Edison's head. He was no match for the captains of industry, and it was an easy matter for Gould to perpetrate a swindle on him, as he had on others. By 1875 Edison was finished with Gould; the lawsuits against the prince of robber barons dragged on for thirty years.

In 1876, Edison made another move, this time to Menlo Park, New Jersey; there he would invent and manufacture his products in what was without doubt the first industrial laboratory in the United States. He gathered a highly skilled work force, an assortment of instruments and machines, and he drove his men and himself to new heights of achievement in the technical field. He employed trained scientists and he loved to tease them, if only to show that the boss had more horse sense than they. He once asked one of his mathematicians to calculate the volume of a glass bulb. The following morning the man had not yet completed his calculations: Edison took a tumbler of water, filled the bulb, and then poured the contents into a graduated beaker. He made a business out of invention; in this he was preeminent. Though Alexander Graham Bell had been first with the telephone, Edison did improve its voice transmission with a variable carbon device that to all intents and purposes was a microphone. His induction coil made it possible for telephone lines to be extended for hundreds of miles. The inevitable corporate fight between the Bell System and Western Union ensued; however, in Britain the Edison and Bell interests were soon merged, for there big business avoided the smoke of battle. After a while, Edison collected the fees for his telephone work and left the field entirely. There were other things at hand.

The central problem now was the mechanical reproduction of sound, research on which led to the phonograph, an invention that Edison thought but a toy. By now he was known as "the Wizard of Menlo Park." Yet he failed to realize the potentialities of the talking machine and laid it aside for ten years, a costly blunder. Edison became concerned with developing an efficient lighting system—to provide a long-burning artificial lamp and to distribute the power for it. If only electricity could be distributed to individual homes, much as gas was, the world would come aglow—and soon it did. Edison experimented with parallel circuitry which would take current in small amounts. When the technical problem seemed on the verge of solution, a group of New York financiers, including the redoubtable J. P. Morgan, invested fifty thousand dollars to form the Edison Electric Light Company. Egisto Fabbri, a Morgan partner, was named treasurer, thus insuring an inside track for the House of Morgan.

Achieving a nearly complete vacuum and a filament with high resistance to create a glow with a small amount of electricity were the major lamp problems. By the eighteen-eighties a half-million dollars had been invested in research and development, and it all paid off handsomely. The distribution of power was by central station and individual power plants. By 1884 the first central station, on Pearl Street in New York, was sending power into more than 11,000 lamps in five hundred homes, and 59,000 lamps were being lit by individual power-generating plants. Distribution was the key to the growth of the electrical industry. While in 1880 American industry was still based on the steam engine, by 1900 electricity as a power source could be measured by 300,000 h.p.; in 1914 the figure had gone up to 9,000,000 h.p.

Edison had employed the direct-current system, in which the electrical impulses flowed through the wire like water through a pipe. The alternating-current system was not unknown; indeed, the rivalry between advocates of the two types of current dated back to the eighteen-thirties. An AC generator produced a current that surged back and forth along the conductor like a wave, but at low voltages it gave a poor light. For this reason, Edison preferred direct current. When European improvements, notably the Gaulard-Gibbs transformer, made AC superior for short transmission, Edison was still adamant. George Westinghouse had obtained the European patents and was able to supply generators for the first hydroelectric plant at Niagara Falls, a job to which Edison's direct-current system was ill adapted. The war of the currents was on; Edison argued that AC was a "killing" current and would harm the homeowner if anything went wrong. To prove his point he electrocuted stray cats and dogs with AC and encouraged New York to use AC when it installed the electric chair; it was a forceful demonstration. But DC's low voltage limited it to a few miles in transmission, and in time AC won out. Besides, AC motors were simpler and lighter in weight. Moreover, AC was steadier in supply, and its capability of being stepped up or down made transmission possible over long distances. Only in recent years has it become feasible to send direct current through long-distance wires at high voltage.

As his manufacturing enterprises were doing well, Edison turned his attention once again to other matters. Occasionally he fumbled an opportunity: there was the peculiar emission he noted in an electric bulb which came to be known as the "Edison effect." Had he followed the lead the strange sparks suggested, it would have led to electronics and the radio.

Now Henry Villard returned to the financial scene, and with his optimism undiminished, helped consolidate the various Edison enterprises into the Edison General Electric Company. Morgan, recalling the railroad debacles, distrusted Villard; in 1892 he dictated the formation of a new firm, General Electric, bringing in Charles Coffin to replace Villard.

Annoyed at the disappearance of his name from the company's title, Edison had little to do with the new corporation—the promoter and financier had taken over. Utility stocks, which had been acquired in payment for installations, were given to the tender mercies of another corporation, Electric Bond and Share. Edison himself, however, went on to other technological achievements: the storage battery and motion pictures were still on the horizon.

Coffin, General Electric's first head, had been a shoe manufacturer. Electricity to him was simply another way of making money. He vigorously pursued the policy of establishing power plants to supply electricity to industry. He was succeeded by Owen D. Young, who had begun as a lawyer in Boston. Young had become involved in public utility matters in 1908, when a number of power companies in upper New York State failed, and he was called in to straighten out the subsequent financial and legal mess. More utility cases came his way, increasing his knowledge and expertness enough to attract the attention of Coffin, who then invited Young to join General Electic as a vice-president. General Electric was now the dominant firm in the field, manufacturing one-fourth of the electrical equipment used in the nation. It began to make consumer appliances, popularizing its research laboratory as a "House of Magic." Now conscious of the public eye, General Electric advertised itself widely as a benevolent corporation.

Playing second fiddle to General Electric was the Westinghouse Company, initiated in 1886 with profits that George Westinghouse had earned from his air-brake invention. Westingthouse was certain that AC was a superior system for distributing electricity, and indeed, with the Gaulard-Gibbs transformer, he made it commercially successful. The Tesla induction motor, which used AC, could now turn the wheels of the factory. While Westinghouse was resorting to heavy borrowing, getting through the Panic of 1907 by the skin of his teeth, General Electric employed its Electric Bond and Share subsidiary to provide capital for utilities that bought their equipment. The fact that the companies might be rivals did not prevent cooperation with cross-licensing agreements during the early days. Nor did Westinghouse mind paying General Electric a royalty for the right to manufacture electric bulbs. Westinghouse's early efforts were directed toward producing equipment for public utilities. In 1906 the company started in railroad electrification. When the railroads began to decline in later years, Westinghouse had to cultivate other pastures. By 1930 it was making consumer appliances. Like General Electric, it manufactured a great number of goods—electric irons, generators, motors, electric razors, washing machines, dishwashers, switchgear, and propelling equipment for ships—perhaps as many as 10,000 different items. It now competes with General Electric in computers, motors, transformers, circuit breakers, and nuclear reactors.

The utility industry, suppliers of electric power to homes and industry, became an impenetrable jungle that only the New Deal could straighten out. Electric Bond and Share's assortment of securities formed the basis for a huge utility empire. Created for General Electric by Sidney Z. Mitchell, it became the largest holding company in the country, with properties in thirty-three states, doing 14 per cent of the utility business. Mitichell wrote up the values of the properties to their "potential earning power," a backhanded way of pouring in water. In 1931 some $400,000,000 worth of such water had to be squeezed out. The losers were all the widows and orphans and other coupon clippers. Subsidiaries of the holding companies were milked with heavy management fees like so many fruitful cows. In fact, the antics of Electric Bond and Share, as well as those of other holding companies, provided the impetus for the passage of the New Deal's Public Utility Holding Company Act, a belated effort to regulate their activities.

The case of Samuel Insull provided a striking object lesson in the follies of public utility behavior. In the nineteen-twenties Insull was Chicago's most powerful man, with a utility complex that spanned the nation from Texas to Maine. But he was soon to fall from grace. As a young man Insull had migrated from England to take a post as Edison's secretary. By the age of thirty he was heading Edison's Chicago outlet, which he managed well enough to attain a monopoly position in that market. Like others in the business, he insisted it was a "natural" monopoly that by its very efficiency and broad consuming area could reduce rates. He became a financier by forming the Middle West Utilities Company, ostensibly for the purpose of raising capital. Some properties were sold to Middle West for $330,000; Insull then took 100,000 shares of stock, for which he paid $3,600,000. These he resold for the same sum, but kept the controlling shares of common stock for himself, so that he not only recouped his outlay but also had control of the company. The transactions were more roundabout than usual, but it was still a stock-watering job of no small proportions.

Insull had become important enough in Chicago to be called upon to rescue the local gas company and the traction system. While his support of cultural activities made him a leading citizen, politics did not trouble Insull: he contributed to both parties. Watching Electric Bond and Share and Associated Gas and Electric, another holding company, move around the country gobbling up utility properties and pyramiding their holdings, he determined to outdo them all and build the biggest empire of the lot. The holding company had become a superb device for skimming the cream off the top of operating companies, and the more layers there were to a holding-company system the richer the cream. There were more management fees, the operating companies could buy from each other, funds could be transferred, and much more. That all this added to cost was most desirable, for it inflated the rate base and meant more profit. If the operating companies were doing well, publication of their prosperity improved the financial prospects of the holding company, for now another layer could be added and more stocks and bonds could be sold. The pyramiding went higher and higher, sometimes to seven or eight stories of paper assets. Such was the technique of the utility promoters, with Insull at the head of the pack.

But trouble was brewing. Control rested on minority holdings of minority holdings, and that could be a most tenuous arrangement in a declining market. Doomsday arrived in 1929. Cyrus Eaton attempted a raid on Insull empire; the effort to forestall the raid could not be financed. The house of cards fell apart as Morgan men helped them to topple by speculating in Insull securities, selling short on all exchanges across the country. Besides, it was a splendid opportunity for the New York financial chieftains to chastise the upstart in Chicago. Insull, the major holding-company operator in America, fled to Greece—which had no extradition treaty with the United States—clutching a bag filled with thousand-dollar notes.

Such were the electrical and utility businesses, industries of dubious chastity. Questionable financial practices were paralleled by nose-thumbing at the antitrust laws of the nation. Indeed, General Electric's violations dated back to 1911, when it was accused of fixing the prices of light bulbs, and it had been a defendant in more than sixty government suits. It had been accused of deliberately reducing the life of electric light bulbs, increasing its business on this item by 60 per cent. When caught, company officials would admit that while collusion was illegal, "it wasn't unethical": corporate ethics was defined as anything that improved the health of the enterprise.

The most famous antitrust action in the electrical industry was the 1961 case in which General Electric, Westinghouse, and twenty-seven other firms were charged with price-rigging on no less than $1,750,000,000 worth of equipment each year. The violations had gone on for as long as eight years. Officially, the guilty ones came from middle management, directors of such divisions as switchgear and condensers. Amazingly enough, jail sentences and heavy fines were levied against them by the court, but they were in a true sense stand-ins for the archons—the men at the top. Fines totaled almost $2,000,000, and seven jail sentences and twenty-four suspended sentences comprised the toll of justice.

Hovering over the case, like smog in a big city, was the outraged hypocrisy of the corporate oligarchy pillorying their subordinates for having been caught in activities from which they, the top executives, pretended to have turned aside. Simply enough, these unfortunate divisional directors should not have allowed themselves to be trapped. Ralph Cordiner, General Electric's president, could hide behind the screen of decentralization; nevertheless, it was incredible that he should have been unaware of all the antitrust violations when nine out of ten of his executives either knew about them or were themselves involved.

The business conspirators had indeed behaved like Adam Smith's entrepreneurs: conviviality led to restraint of trade or monopoly. The present-day businessman, like his predecessors, wanted nothing to do with price competition; that was anathema. Meetings in the electrical industry, in fact, could be traced back to the days of World War II. Sales of circuit breakers, for example, were rotated among the firms on a fixed percentage basis with General Electric obtaining 40 per cent of the business, Westinghouse 35 per cent, Allis Chalmers 10 per cent, and Federal Pacific 10 per cent. Each fortnight the group decided who was to get the next order, since sealed bids submitted to prospective customers—governmental agencies as well as private utilities—were rigged in advance to maintain the quoted price.

The conspirators knew they were violating the law: hence, the use of Aesopian conversation. Meeting-attendance lists were known as Christmas lists, and a meeting was referred to as choir practice. Each firm was assigned a number that was used in all memoranda and phone calls. Meetings were held in winter lodges, or messages were conveyed in whispers on golf courses. It was all like a television spy thriller. Even though official company policy obligated the men to abide by the antitrust laws, the pressure was on from the top to deliver the goods, and the only way they knew how was to engage in collusion with rivals.

Whenever someone tried to step out of the cartel—which is what it amounted to—price cutting by the others would whip him back into line. Company lawyers, disturbed by the Government's investigation, initially questioned the executives involved, and they denied the existence of the arrangement. But when the case was tried and the verdicts rendered, General Electric responded with firings and demotions, thus preserving the virtue of the upper echelons. It was a case of comic hypocrisy, for the corporate executives had long pretended that their activity was in the public interest, professing an ideology in which they fundamentally disbelieved. The whole affair could not but pass the sins of the conspirators to the corporation itself. It was "an unusually vivid picture . . . of ordinary business operations in a major industry." Yet the case did little to restore price competition. The Tennessee Valley Authority, which had first complained about the uniformity of bids, kept receiving identical price offers after the verdicts were in, as did other Government agencies. Thus, while one might become disillusioned about General Electric's business morals, assuming that anyone really had any illusions, it continued to do business in what it deemed to be the normal course of events.

Closely related to the electrical industry in its technology was radio. While the inception of radio may be traced to Guglielmo Marconi's wireless, the magnetizing of metallic objects at a distance by the leakage of current in telegraph wires had been a well-known phenomenon. In 1843 Joseph Henry, an American physicist, had magnetized needles 220 feet away from charged wires, and both telephone and telegraph lines could pick up sounds by induction from other wires. Somehow noise was traveling through the air. Edison's induction telegraph for moving trains had demonstrated the phenomenon, though he was unable to solve the problem of noise interference. The key to the secret began to be revealed when the noted German physicist and electrical expert Heinrich Hertz showed in 1887 that electric waves could be emitted by an oscillating circuit. In brief, Hertz made an electric spark jump a gap from one metal hoop to another. Sir William Crookes then suggested that the leaping sparks might be employed for telegraphy.

At this point Marconi came upon the scene. Privately educated, he was attracted to the field upon reading a story about Hertz. Experimenting with the leaping spark in his father's garden, Marconi tried to add a Morse telegraph in order to regulate the spark. He also employed a tube of metallic powder, known as a coherer, through which an electromagnetic wave could pass, thus making the crude device a receiver. A grounded aerial, replacing Hertz's dipole, allowed transmission and reception at longer distances. This was the wireless, patented in England in 1896. The following year distances were increased to twenty-five miles. The British Admiralty, immediately recognizing the usefulness of the wireless for ship communication, lent its support to development of the invention. The Wireless Telegraph and Signal Company, Ltd., was organized in 1897 with Marconi as chief engineer. An American company was set up two years later, and in 1901 Marconi sent signals across the Atlantic from Newfoundland. The

Anglo-American Cable Company, with prior rights in Newfoundland, then responded as most firms do when confronted with a potentially dangerous rival: it ordered Marconi to leave.

Others began to work on further improvements in the wireless. Reginald Fessenden and his assistant Lee DeForest thought they could transmit the human voice itself: a wireless telephone. An electrolytic device seemed to make such transmission a reality. Improvements now came in such profusion and were offered by so many individuals that it became difficult to decide who invented what. A variety of detectors or receivers were worked up, among them crystal detectors. Edison just missed out on the vacuum tube. John Fleming produced a diode tube, and then DeForest offered his tri-electrode tube that became the basic invention for all radio development.

The inventors went about organizing companies to market their brain-children: DeForest had his American Wireless Telegraph Company and Fessenden his National Electric Signaling Company. Throughout the chaos, the United States Navy kept its eye on what was going on. The Marconi system had been a commercial success; the Weather Bureau adopted the Fessenden technique; and the armed services experimented with an assortment of transmission and receiving methods. The new mode of communication even created dissension among governments, as countries argued with one another over the division of tolls and the interchange of messages. Lawsuits over patent infringements became common in the young industry.

The technical problem required sending continuous signals at a high frequency. Fessenden believed that a human voice could be transmitted with such a carrier. Experiments with a high-speed alternator, built at the General Electric works, continued. Then, in 1906, operators on ships in the Atlantic were startled to hear voices on their wireless apparatuses: it was the first radio broadcast in history. There soon followed the heterodyne system of transmission, a technique for increasing frequencies. Radio was on its way and would achieve a major position in modern technology.

Early in the century DeForest demonstrated broadcasting from the Eiffel Tower in Paris, and in 1910 Enrico Caruso sang over the airwaves for the benefit of some fifty listeners. The number of enthusiasts began to multiply. The great hopes for a burgeoning new industry were momentarily deflated by renewed wrangling among the various inventors and their backers. Fessenden withdrew from his firm, which then promptly expired. Stock manipulators fixed on the Marconi company, amidst charges of corruption. The airwaves became a disembodied and sometimes grisly playground as pranksters repeatedly sent out false distress signals. Finally, in 1912, Congress directed the Department of Commerce to introduce a semblance of order and regulation.

Financially strapped, DeForest tried to sell his patent rights to AT&T, only to discover that the company was strangely cool. A mysterious intermediary appeared, offering fifty thousand dollars. Pressed by his board of directors, DeForest had to accept the offer, only to discover that the buyer really spoke for AT&T. When he learned that the latter would have gone ten times as high, DeForest knew that he had been swindled.

A subsequent technical development was the amplification tube devised by E. H. Armstrong, who had been working on radio phenomena since boyhood. The principle in this important advance was an electrical feedback that amplified the signal considerably. DeForest claimed that the idea had first been his; the litigation that resulted lasted until 1934, when the Supreme Court acknowledged DeForest's priority. This was typical of the tangled web of rights in radio. In 1917 AT&T finally took over other DeForest patents; this time the inventor had the satisfaction of receiving a munificent price.

After the war General Electric decided to acquire the Marconi patents, with Owen Young designated to carry out the merger. The Radio Corporation of America was established in 1919, in anticipation of the expected purchase. Within a few days the marriage was consummated; RCA turned over to General Electric 135,000 shares of preferred and 2,000,000 shares of common stock in appreciation of General Electric's "munificent sponsorship." The common stock was then exchanged for the Marconi assets, valued at $9,500,000. Cross-licensing agreements insured the happiness of everyone concerned.

Meanwhile, Westinghouse also decided to enter the radio field. It was simply trying to muscle in to protect a market position it saw threatened. It approached the International Radio Telegraph Company, a small firm with a high-sounding name, offering International Radio Telegraph a profit of a million dollars, so anxious was it to join the fray. However, International Radio Telegraph had few technological devices in its coffers, and Westinghouse reneged. RCA moved ahead, tying in with AT&T through cross-licensing agreements that gave it access to certain valuable DeForest patents. Western Electric, General Electric, and even United Fruit became part of the combine, with RCA given the exclusive rights to sell radio receiving sets. Relationships with European companies were firm enough to keep Westinghouse at bay.

The latter was finally able to obtain rights to certain United States

Navy patents, giving it at least one victory, of which it made the most by entering radio broadcasting. In 1920 Westinghouse's station KDKA in Pittsburgh created history when it broadcast the Presidential election returns. Unwilling to be isolated, International Radio Telegraph joined the RCA group in 1921, a cross-licensing agreement with Westinghouse was signed, General Electric entered broadcasting, and a new industry was launched with everyone behaving like members of a happy family.

Within three years of its founding, RCA was attacked as a monopoly. Cries demanding a congressional investigation were heard, particularly when the company sued smaller concerns for patent infringement. It was all reminiscent of the days of Teddy Roosevelt, when the hunt was on for monopoly. In 1923 the Federal Trade Commission published a 347-page report on RCA that fully documented the corporation's monopoly position. Once again, however, the "natural" character of its hold on the industry, providing as it did for economy and social efficiency, offered the necessary exculpation. Little was done.

RCA's leading figure became David Sarnoff, who had migrated to the United States at the age of nine. He had been an office boy for Marconi, then graduated to telegraphy. His most famous exploit was a seventy-two-hour stay at the telegraph providing the world's only "view" of the sinking of the *Titanic*. In 1913 he started a steady rise in the industry to become RCA's general manager and eventually president. When it came to radio's future, Sarnoff was more prescient than most: he knew it would become an important medium of home entertainment.

And so radio had its victories, its defeats, and even its tragic stories, as in the case of Edwin H. Armstrong, whose heroic efforts were a refreshing contrast to the domination of the large corporations. The sale and licensing of his early patents had made him quite independent of others. In 1933, while litigating the rights to the feedback amplifier, he received his patents for frequency modulation, a form of broadcasting that finally eliminated static and noise, the bane of radio. A bitter battle with the giants ensued, as Armstrong sought to demonstrate the superiority of FM by broadcasting concert music from a single station in New York. The corporations were reluctant to adopt Armstrong's FM, for they had invested too much in the older AM method. Yet, gradually and perceptibly, FM stations spread— Armstrong had been vindicated. In 1954, after a last exhausting battle with RCA over his patents, he killed himself. David had fallen before Goliath.

Most observers have agreed that radio never did fulfill its promises, and the reasons may be traced to the business ethos that dominated it. At best radio filled the living rooms of America with new pieces of furniture; at worst, it assaulted the ear of man with more noise and banalities than he had ever heard before. Radio was a business: profit-making took precedence over service. The injury to the public was not inconsiderable. Revenue was supplied by sponsors whose major objective lay in convincing the listener of the superiority of their beer, cigarettes, or soap. Programs of genuine cultural interest were rare and then apt to be dismembered by advertising spots.

While broadcasting stations abounded in populated areas (the market was there), rural places were given short shrift or left to small independents. It was a repetition of the experience of the public utilities. The medium was converted into a middleman, peddling time to advertisers; it became completely dependent on their largesse and hence subject to their pressure and influence. The network system, which brought common programs to a group of broadcasting stations, was patterned after the consolidation habits of industry. In the conflict between business and public service, the latter could not win.

CHAPTER 15 Two Dynasties: The du Ponts and the Mellons

At hundreds and tens of millions, the du Pont fortune is truly an aristocratic one. It dates from 1802 when Eleuthère Irénée du Pont de Nemours, scion of a French family that had fled the Directorate after the Revolution, established a small gunpowder plant near the Brandywine River in Delaware. Before migrating to the United States, the family had been conspicuously active in French political affairs. Irénée's brother, Victor, had been an emissary for Talleyrand, wily foreign minister for the Directorate. Before the Revolution broke out, Pierre Samuel du Pont, the family founder, had, with charm and intelligence, climbed from the condition of a petit bourgeois into French society's upper ranks. Pierre Samuel was a close friend of Quesnay and his circle of economists, and had even supplied their title, Physiocrats, a label that remained with them over the years. He wrote essays on the natural order, elevating agriculture to the queen of occupations.

When the Revolution broke out, Pierre Samuel was elected a delegate to the Constituent Assembly. He hailed the fall of the Bastille but committed an unforgivable political act by joining the Club of '89, marking himself a moderate; to the Jacobins this was giving aid and comfort to the enemy. Forced out of political life in 1791, he opened a printing shop. A year later his name was entered on the proscribed list by the revolutionists, and when he joined the Swiss Guards in defense of the King, he became a man destined for liquidation. Arrested in June 1794, he doubtless would have lost his head to the guillotine had not Thermidor released him from prison.

But the political harassment did not cease, and the du Ponts, all thirteen of them, decided to leave for America, arriving in Newport, Rhode Island, in 1799. There du Pont *père*, always fired with grandiose schemes, tried to carry through his plans for a land and colonization company. The attempt to sell shares in the project was a miserable failure. Moreover, foreigners could not own land in many of the states. Despite excellent connections with such luminaries as Jefferson, the du Ponts' future appeared bleak indeed. But fortune began to smile on the family. On a hunting trip, Irénée conceived the idea that there was room for a proper gunpowder factory. In France he had worked as a gunpowder chemist with none other than Lavoisier, and he was appalled by the poor quality of the American product. A visit to a local gunpowder plant convinced him that American powdermakers were incompetent and that he could easily outstrip them. He reasoned that with a thirty-thousand-dollar investment he could produce 160,000 pounds of gunpowder a year, clearing a profit of at least ten thousand dollers. Du Pont *père* was at first less than completely enthusiastic, but when it seemed that the project could not fail, he gave his blessings, and Irénée and Victor went off to France to get machinery and technicians.

By this time Napoleon had come to power; he was not opposed to letting the du Ponts have what they needed, if only to provide some embarrassing competition to the British, who were the main suppliers of quality gunpowder to the United States. A family company was promptly organized, with a capital of $36,000 to cover eighteen founder's shares of $2,000 each. The du Ponts kept twelve of the shares, letting in a few American and foreign investors. Only the du Ponts had the right to name the works manager; Irénée was quickly nominated at a salary of $1,800 a year. A farm in Delaware was selected for the plant site; processing was handled in a series of brick buildings with specially built walls to reduce the risk of accidental explosions. Jefferson was soon to grant the new company its first Government contract: the du Ponts were on their way to affluence.

In 1802 the enterprise was reorganized. The properties in Alexandria, Virginia, and in New Jersey were held by a New York branch; there was a Paris office; but the main asset, gunpowder, was held by the Wilmington Powder Company. The New York and Paris ventures soon went bankrupt, and Victor came down to Delaware to join his brother in powdermaking. A partner was brought in to enlarge capital, but the family could not abide strangers; he was soon out. Business kept improving: from 1804 to 1805 sales advanced from $15,000 to $97,000. Pierre Samuel watched his sons prosper and waxed enthusiastic. In 1811 they opened a woolen mill, using the fleece of specially bred Merino sheep. With the War of 1812, soldiers not only had to have gunpowder to fire their rifles, but they had to be clothed. Although the woolen mill was closed after a few years, gunpowder remained a du Pont staple. Their brand of powder could fire a ball farther than any other; the high-quality du Pont product was in great demand. With a fortunate stockpile of saltpeter gathered just before war broke out, the company was in an excellent position to fill the Government's orders for 200,000 pounds of powder in 1812; a year later Government orders reached 500,000 pounds. Expansion could now begin with the purchase of the farm next door.

Du Ponts had now doubled their productive capacity: they had become the leading gunpowder makers in America, even if the enterprise did suffer occasional unprofitable periods. The du Ponts were now well adjusted to the American scene; Victor was elected to the Delaware state legislature. But despite high demand, working capital was frequently short. Nevertheless, there was still a great need for gunpowder as westward expansion replaced war as a source of business. An explosion in 1815, which killed nine workers, caused $20,000 in damage. Fortunately, the family was able to raise the $30,000 it needed to survive as a going concern. Another and more serious explosion in 1818, killing forty persons and causing damage of $120,000, created less of a financial strain; it was evident that the company would overcome its initial tribulations.

Victor died in 1827, Irénée seven years later. Control now passed to the latter's son, Alfred. The family lived and worked together in a kind of compound around the works organized on communal lines. The company owned all the land, homes, and worldly goods, supplying members of the family with all they needed. No one received a salary: cash was made available to anyone who wanted it. The war with Mexico in 1848 added to the company's profits; for that adventure the Government purchased a million pounds of gunpowder. Command then passed from Alfred to his brother Henry, who was a West Point graduate and had served in the Army. Known as the General, he ruled the company's affairs as only a military man would, with emphasis on obedience to detail.

Aware that his competitors were making cheap powder for mine-blasting and industrial purposes, the General went about quietly ferreting out the formula, then called his rivals together to advise them that he was ready for a price war—unless, of course, they all reached an economic understanding. An agreement was signed to set prices and to make other cartel-like arrangements, and the du Ponts went about happily selling gunpowder for the Crimean and other wars. Although the General knew how to use economic power, he was less successful with technology. Were it not for his nephew Lammot, who insisted that innovations in explosives be exploited, the company would have been left behind in the technological race. Lammot devised a sodium-nitrate mixture that was more powerful than traditional recipes for black powder, and he convinced the General that it could be used, at least, for industrial purposes.

Once more war lent a fillip to the business: during the Civil War, du Pont sold some 4,000,000 pounds of gunpowder to the Federal Government. But the war effort, profitable as it was, had reduced du Pont's civilian trade, now taken over by its rivals. Meanwhile, nitroglycerin had been invented, and Alfred Nobel was able to stabilize the dangerous compound with diatomaceous earth and to utilize mercuric fulminate as a detonator. By 1866,· dynamite had been invented, the most powerful explosive yet devised by the cunning of man. But the General paid little attention to these advances: he preferred rather to create a steady market, employing appropriate business threats. In April, 1872, the General, employing his inimitable manner, persuaded all the major firms to join in the Gunpowder Trade Association of the United States, with the three largest firms, du Pont among them, having ten votes each, while fourteen votes were distributed among three smaller firms. The Powder Trust, as it was soon dubbed, survived longer than any other such combine, except for the Rockefeller empire. The Trust was dominated by the big three, and that troika was dominated by du Pont. They all sold gunpowder at the same price and divided the country into mutually exclusive territories. Du Pont then bought into the California Powder Works to give it a foothold on the West Coast; this purchase was soon followed by the secret acquisition of stock in the Hazard Company, one of the Trust's big three. The Powder combine was not not merely dominated by, but virtually under the absolute control of du Pont. The California acquisition also gave du Pont entrée into the dynamite market.

By 1880 eleven other companies were absorbed by the General, with Laflin and Rand, one of the original big three, as the only apparent competitor around. The three chief Powder Trust members then set up Repauno Chemicals to manufacture dynamite, but with du Pont's secret holdings in Hazard, that company too had to follow the General's directives. In all of this business legerdemain, Nobel received no royalties because of a patent suit that went against him. Then several of California's eastern plants were merged with Repauno to create the Hercules Powder Company. The purchase of another powder firm that had been licensed by Nobel to make his fulminate detonator finally brought to du Pont all the latest innovations.

At about this time, the family had a close brush with the Rockefeller interests. The latter had gained control of about two-thirds the supply of nitric acid and other materials used in the cracking of gasoline as well as in the manufacture of dynamite. It occurred to the Standard Oil people that they might just as well include the explosives industry in their domain, and one day a delegation from 26 Broadway appeared at the du Pont headquarters in Delaware demanding that a substantial part of the dynamite market be turned over to them. Needless to say, the family resisted; virtual industrial warfare ensued as Standard went on to build several dynamite plants in New Jersey. Independent chemical producers came to du Pont's rescue, but the struggle ended only when Standard found itself snarled in the Government's antitrust suit and had to back away from du Pont. The family heaved a sigh of relief.

The gruff old General, who had ruled the whole empire with an iron hand, died in 1889, bringing his nephew Eugene, who had been a career chemist with the company, to the helm. As soon as he had been elevated to chief steward of du Pont, Eugene set about constructing a new building, with electricity and even a telephone. A cousin, Alfred I. du Pont, demanded more voice in the company's affairs, though the rest of the family was somewhat dubious about Alfred's capabilities because he had once failed to ferret out French secrets for smokeless powder. Such failure was not readily forgotten in the family: in 1897 they had to buy Hudson Maxim's patent for smokeless powder at a cost of $81,600. In any case, the decision was made to abandon the family partnership and form a corporation, E. I. du Pont de Nemours and Company, with Eugene as president and other members of the family accorded various official posts. Alfred was a mere director.

The crisis came with Eugene's passing in 1902. The family, feeling that it could no longer carry on, decided to sell out to Laflin and Rand for $12,000,000. However, Alfred objected vehemently, insisting that the firm had to stay in the family. Indeed, at that price he would buy it himself, demanding a week in which to raise the money. Two other cousins, Coleman and Pierre, hitherto not connected with the company, were brought in. The transaction turned out to be the greatest bargain of the century. The triumvirate offered to pay the $12,000,000 plus interest out of earnings over a long period of time; the down payment was $2,100. A new du Pont firm was created with Coleman as president, Alfred vice-president, and Pierre treasurer. When the threesome had caught their breath and reviewed the powder company's holdings, they discovered them to be worth at least $24,000,000. The new owners magnanimously increased the selling price to $15,360,000, with $12,000,00 in bonds, the rest in stocks. The cash deposit of $2,100 was not increased. The happy trio gave themselves 85,800 shares of preferred stock as their reward for business sagacity.

Alfred was the only one of the three cousins with any direct experience in the company. Coleman had been active in mining and was a man of strong purpose that even the old owners knew they could trust. Coleman discovered that du Pont assets constituted only 40 per cent of total holdings. In fact, du Pont, as well as several of its subsidiaries, was in large part a holding company, controlling firms that were supposedly rivals. Of twenty-two explosives firms in the United States, fifteen were subsidiary to either du Pont or Laflin and Rand, and the interests of these two giants were so commingled that it was virtually impossible to tell who was who. Now, if Laflin and Rand, which was still ostensibly an independent concern, decided to buy du Pont that would be intolerable: the solution was for du Pont to buy Laflin and Rand. Coleman did so at a price of $4,000,000. The same arrangement that was employed in the takeover of du Pont was used here: a mere pittance—$2,000—was paid down, the rest in bonds. Delaware Securities was set up to market the bonds; in effect, someone other than du Pont paid for Laflin and Rand. With all the firms in the explosives industry so closely tied, it was no longer necessary to keep up the Powder Trust. Coleman promptly dissolved it, for there was no need to maintain a structure that might attract an inquisitive government. As skillful a financial prestidigitator as Jay Gould or J. P. Morgan, though operating on a somewhat smaller scale, Coleman had within six months achieved control of 60 per cent of the American explosives industry.

The Young Turks at du Pont realized that gunpowder could be an entrée into the world of chemistry. They established several research laboratories and acquired their first varnish and lacquer plant. The organization was streamlined, with an executive committee headed by Coleman. No longer would the General's singlehanded, tightfisted administrative methods prevail. It was necessary to know how each product was handled and how much it actually cost. Purchasing and marketing were to be made as scientific as possible. The loose confederation of many small units was to be transformed into a centralized operation. In essence, what had been done in Carnegie and in General Electric was to be done in du Pont. Another reorganization was effected in 1905, increasing capitalization to $59,500,000. Sales were good enough to retire outstanding bonds periodically and to pay handsome dividends to the stock-holders: the chief beneficiaries, of course, were famliy members.

In the company itself, manufacturing was consolidated; administrative departments were set up; and a sales group was organized. Du Pont was being reshaped—mainly by Pierre, a quiet man with a bookkeeper's mentality—in the image of corporate hierarchy. Departments evolved with chains of command: production, sales, purchasing, engineering, and research and development. In form, the company was to become virtually indistinguishable from any other large corporation.

Yet all was not well: tensions in the triumvirate forecast another crisis. Alfred's personal quirks did not meet with favor in the family: his divorce and immediate remarriage were frowned upon. Alfred was too erratic, they thought, and his antics were reported too often in the newspapers. A good part of the family simply ostracized him and his new wife. Besides, the company was embroiled in another antitrust action started by the Government in 1907, and Alfred's attitude did not seem serious enough. He was a poor risk to have around; gradually his duties in the company were taken from him. Wounded by the machinations of his cousins—he felt he had been fired—Alfred went off to Paris in 1911 to live on his annual income of $400,000.

The antitrust suit was going badly for du Pont: the arguments and evidence were all in favor of the Government. After all, du Pont had absorbed sixty-four firms and had gained control of sixty-nine others since 1902, when Coleman entered the picture. Curiously enough, and fortunately for du Pont, the Army and Navy stepped in to urge that the monopoly be continued in the interest of national security. The upshot was that du Pont held on to twelve plants, eleven smaller ones went to a new firm—again with the name of Hercules Powder—and ten others became the Atlas Powder Company. Du Pont remained the giant, of course.

Despite poor health, Coleman maintained his interest in the company, though Pierre had by now become the dominant officer. Business continued to show good results: dividends had gone up almost 12 per cent between 1904 and 1910. Besides, Coleman had other projects that occupied most of his attention: the Hotel McAlpin and the Equitable Building in New York were favored ventures. War was once more on the horizon and du Pont was again ready to deliver gunpowder and guncotton and TNT in prodigious quantities. But Coleman's health continued to deteriorate, and he was at odds with Pierre over certain policies. Pierre, moreover, was recruiting personnel that were not from the family. Needing cash for his personal speculations, Coleman offered to sell out. To avoid more intrafamily squabbling, he offered 20,000 shares at $160, ostensibly to "certain employees" of the company. Still a board member, Alfred failed to recognize the ploy: he objected that employees should not have to pay more than $125. The Allied Powers in Europe were also concerned; they feared that German interests might buy into du Pont. However, it was clear that the customer for the shares had already been chosen, and it was to be Pierre.

Indeed, a syndicate that included both family members and close associates had already been formed to purchase the shares. Financing was handled by the ubiquitous J. P. Morgan, who received a commission of $500,000 for floating a loan of $8,500,000. Alfred argued that it was the company's prestige, not Pierre's personal status, that permitted the loan. Therefore, said he, the stock should go to the company. Pierre and his associates not only closed the door on Alfred, but turned the key. A holding company with a $240,000,000 capitalization was set up to control the du Pont enterprises, while the Christiana Securities Corporation was formed to finance the acquisition of Coleman's stock holdings. Alfred's rage was prodigious. To avenge himself, he established a bank to rival the du Pont financial house in Wilmington and constructed a building higher than the du Pont edifice.

These were flanking movements: the major attack centered on a lawsuit that relatives sympathizing with Alfred instituted against Pierre and his associates to compel them to return Coleman's stock to the company. A member of the family who said that he would testify for the plantiffs was peremptorily fired. Alfred bought a newspaper through which he pilloried his hated relatives. Interestingly, when the case came before the Federal court in 1916, the value of the disputed stock had risen to $60,000,000. Testimony disclosed that the Morgan syndicate bank members had all been depositories for du Pont. Eleven of the banks had suddenly enjoyed a trebling of du Pont deposits the day after the loan was negotiated.

Pierre proclaimed that this had all been a coincidence: he testified that he did not know which banks had joined the Morgan syndicate. The bankers perspiringly swore in the courtroom that the loan had been made on Pierre's personal recognizance, while Pierre charged that Alfred's attitude had been an unhealthy one for the company. The judge was evidently convinced by all the charges and counterclaims that Alfred had been victimized, but instead of rendering a clear-cut decision, he called for an election by the stockholders, excluding Coleman's shares. In the ensuing proxy fight, Pierre frightened all the stockholders, largely family members, with threats of "serious business consequences," succeeding thereby in obtaining a three-to-one victory. In his fury, Alfred took the case to the Supreme Court, where it was dismissed in 1919.

Alfred was hardly poverty-stricken. A decade later he had correctly anticipated the stock-market collapse, selling $2,000,000 worth of securities in the nick of time. His profit was ample. Real-estate and banking speculations in Florida added to his wealth. When he died in 1935, his estate was as handsome as that of any du Pont. His was a splendid comeback, albeit not within the bosom of the family. By 1962 the trusts that Alfred left behind had reached almost $300,000,000. The income from the trusts was more than $8,000,000, the bulk of it going to Alfred's widow. The assets included sizable holdings in some thirty banks, direct ownership of a large paper company, vast timber tracts, several railroads, a telephone independent, more than 700,000 shares of E. I. du Pont de Nemours, 400,000 shares of General Motors, and substantial real-estate holdings in Florida and Delaware.

The company also thrived, especially on war orders. During World War I the Allied Powers were told that their needs could be met provided 50 per cent down payments were made and prices set at levels that would quickly amortize du Pont's expanded installations. One dollar a pound seemed a suitable price to meet these requirements. By the end of 1916 du Pont was producing 100,000 tons of TNT a month for the Allied armies. Forty per cent of Allied firepower could be traced to the company. When the United States went into the war, the price of smokeless powder was reduced to 47.5 cents a pound; Congress would not pay more. It can hardly be said that du Pont suffered in consequence, even though it could not always obtain what it wanted. The Government had been adamant: to some officials du Pont was little more than a "species of outlaws." In any case, the European Allies were grateful, for they too now paid the lower price.

New du Pont plants, such as Old Hickory in Tennessee, were built at government expense. That plant cost $85,000,000. When the war came to an end, Washington naturally canceled contracts. Old Hickory was sold to the Nashville Industrial Corporation, which then promptly disposed of much of the installation to du Pont for $800,000. All told, the Government got back for its $85,000,000 investment a mere $3,500,000. From 1914 to 1919 du Pont's profit had been close to $60,000,000 a year, as contrasted with the $5,000,000 gain in 1913. The first to benefit were the stock-holders, that is, the family. More lacquer and paint factories were acquired. Surplus war stockpiles were bought up at bargain-basement prices. But there was still some $90,000,000 left in the surplus account, and it seemed sinful to let all that money remain idle. As one writer remarked, the nest egg had to be made to hatch.

Wily John Raskob, a close associate of Pierre du Pont, came up with the notion that more General Motors stock should be purchased. Back in 1915 a du Pont in-law had been a board member of Durant's new Chevrolet company, and du Pont had taken a flyer in General Motors with three thousand shares. Shortly afterward, Durant was locked in a titanic struggle with the bankers for control of General Motors, and in the ensuing compromise four du Pont men were placed on the automobile firm's board of directors. In fact, Pierre himself became chairman, and the investment in General Motors was increased. Raskob was quick to note that the auto company would be a good customer for paints and varnishes, and so in 1918 du Pont invested $25,000,000 and a year later another $24,000,000.

When the postwar Depression ended Durant's connection with the auto company, du Pont held a one-third interest in it, and with the help of Alfred Sloan, reorganized the free-wheeling General Motors in its own image. Sloan cut, pruned, and reshaped the corporate structure of the automobile maker; it may have been dull work, but it did make General Motors a leader in its field.

The Government did not view the General Motors-du Pont marriage with kindness: in 1927 it finally acted to divorce the two giants, but little came of Washington's antitrust efforts. Then senators attacked the du Pont company in 1934 as a "merchant of death" and charged that it had supported Fascist and anti-Semitic groups while fostering a heinous international munitions cartel. Another antitrust suit was filed in 1949, but the Federal court judge held that the Government had failed to prove that du Pont controlled General Motors, even though at times it was voting 51 per cent of the auto company's stock. Finally, the Supreme Court found in 1957 that while du Pont had in fact held enough General Motors shares to create the *possibility* of monopoly, there really had been no desire to violate the law: du Pont was given a ten-year period in which to dispose of its General Motors stock. The 63,000,000 shares were now worth more than a billion dollars: divestiture would create a stock-market panic, a thought too horrible to contemplate. Distribution to du Pont's stockholders, on the other hand, would mean a capital-gains tax, an equally disturbing consequence. And so a kindly senator from Delaware introduced a special bill amending the tax laws to allow an "orderly" disposition of the stock, thus assuring that no one would be harmed. What the Internal Revenue Service did not receive would not injure it.

By this time du Pont was no longer just a gunpowder maker. The company had experimented with chemicals as far back as 1915, and a year later it began to investigate dyestuff prospects. When alien properties were seized by the Government in 1918, du Pont obtained its rightful share, mainly German patents for dyestuffs. Cellophane, invented in 1868, came under du Pont control in the nineteen-twenties. Simulated leather had been acquired in 1910 when the Fabrikoid Company was purchased. Viscaloid, a manufacturer of a celluloid-like synthetic, was next to be absorbed. The purchase of Grascelli Chemicals for $60,000,000 in 1928 heralded du Pont's entry into plastics. By 1958 the company could claim that it produced 1,200 different items.

Perhaps the most exciting development was the discovery of nylon by du Pont's chief chemist, Wallace Carothers, in 1934. Nylon was a synthetic thread that looked like silk and had the same properties. Originally the threads were long-lasting, but with their refinement came quick obsolescence for the ladies of the land who wanted sheer hose. From time to time, antitrust reared its irritating head: in 1952 du Pont was ordered to make polyethylene, another synthetic, available to all comers. The company spread itself over the globe, to England, Belgium, France, Switzerland, the Netherlands, and Canada. At the last reckoning, du Pont was listed by a business magazine as the fifteenth largest industrial corporation in the United States, with annual sales of almost $3,500,000,000 and a respectable 13 per cent return on invested capital.

The family is still dominant in the corporation and given to a style of living appropriate to such high levels of affluence. Like the patrons of old, one du Pont even maintained a concert artist on his private payroll to give organ recitals. Care was taken to insure that the fortune would not be eroded by taxes. Over the years, about eighteen foundations have been established, a few for genuine philanthropy. The two largest ones, Longwood and Wintertur, have assets of $122,000,000 devoted to maintaining the baronial du Pont estates as public museums and botanical gardens. It has been estimated that total du Pont wealth now exceeds $7,000,000,000, though the figure may be a bit overstated.

The Mellon fortune, perhaps not as large as the du Ponts'—its visible portion approximates $3,000,000,000—is rooted in a number of disparate enterprises, with control exercised through banking houses, the chief of which is the Mellon National Bank of Pittsburgh. The Mellon holdings represent the first of the great American conglomerates—combinations that cut across a variety of industries. Put together by Andrew Mellon, his brother Richard, and the latter's son William Larimer, this early conglomerate now dominates the Aluminum Corporation of America, Koppers Company, Carborundum Company, First Boston Corporation, and General Reinsurance, and holds powerful minority positions in Westinghouse, Bethlehem Steel, Pittsburgh Coal, Pittsburgh Plate Glass, and several public utilities. Residents of western Pennsylvania and other regions also pay homage to Mellon coal, coke, gas, and aluminum ware. The empire also includes oil, railroad cars, and tar products.

Andrew W. Mellon, the man mainly responsible for this successful industrial barony, was once hailed as a Secretary of the Treasury second only to Alexander Hamilton. Such high praise, of course, depended on which sector of the community was expressing its views. As a member of the Cabinet—he served in three Republican administrations in the nineteen-twenties—he was slightly more loquacious than Calvin Coolidge. A Washington commentator remarked that when Coolidge and Mellon met to discuss Treasury affairs, their conversation was filled with unpregnant pauses. The Mellon family did not have the aristocratic stature of the du Ponts: they were more like the Rockefellers and Harrimans, who had achieved the status of industrial chieftains during the turbulence of the post-Civil War period. Andrew himself was quite taciturn, even somthing of a recluse, preferring to collect works of art rather than hobnobbing with his peers at social affairs.

The Mellons were descendants of Scotch-Irish immigrants who had first settled in Pennsylvania in 1808. Ten years later Thomas Mellon, Andrew's father, arrived. Bright and ambitious, he became a lawyer and moneylender, and in later years a judge and banker. Long after he had left the bench he continued to wear a frock coat with high starched collar and white shirt. Gathering money was his passion, and he did it with perfect legality, if not with humanity. By the time he was thirty he had saved twelve thousand dollars and was ready to take advantage of the opportunities offered by Pittsburgh's growth. A strategic marriage to the daughter of a land-wealthy, cash-poor family did help somewhat. As a young lawyer, Thomas Mellon realized that dealing in mortgages and real estate was a fast way to wealth. He always sought properties in distress; his high regard for the law generally meant foreclosure in default of payment. He insisted that borrowers abide by their contracts. Quick action was facilitated by judgment bonds that accompanied every mortgage; foreclosure was swift and automatic. The mortgage books in the county seat were filled with entries of the Thomas Mellon name.

In 1859 Mellon was elected a judge in Allegheny County, serving his ten-year term with due regard to the niceties of law. Upon completing his duty on the bench, he reentered business by opening a private bank on Smithfield Street in Pittsburgh. It was a time when the demand for loans ran high, with interest reaching levels of 12 per cent. It was not difficult to climb the road to riches, provided one began with a modest capital.

Andrew Mellon was so anxious to follow in his father's footsteps that at the age of fifteen he carried through a land deal on his own, as if to demonstrate his capabilities. Several years later the judge advanced Andrew and his brother forty thousand dollars to enter the lumber business. The venture lasted but eighteen months, yet Andrew did reveal business sagacity, for he had sensed that depression clouds were descending on the country and sold out just before the collapse. A year later he entered his father's bank.

As with so many others, the Panic of 1873 caught Thomas Mellon unprepared. His deposits totaled $600,000, against which there was but $60,000 in cash. Moreover, the bank runs were severe. Somehow Mellon weathered the storm, and never again would he be trapped by unforeseen circumstances. Yet there was some virtue in a business decline, for Mellon could now buy up all sorts of properties at knockdown prices. Foreclosures were carried through according to the letter of the law—business was business. Mellon's fundamental principle was "Honesty is the best policy," and the aphorism was applied without regard to kith, kin, or other relationship. The Ligonier Valley Railroad came under Mellon control; it was to stay in the family for years as a sentimental piece of property. The judge lived to the venerable age of ninety-five; before passing on to his reward in 1908 he had the satisfaction of seeing his sons, Richard and Andrew, take over with firm hands.

By the last quarter of the nineteenth century, the economy had reached its take-off stage; many entrepreneurs were reaping a rich harvest, but for some it was only a whirlwind. One of the more aggressive businessmen was Henry Clay Frick who, needing cash to expand his coke enterprise, had visited the judge one day to borrow ten thousand dollars. The judge knew coal—he had thousands of acres of coal fields in western Pennsylvania —and he sensed a good customer in the ambitious Frick. With Mellon's backing, Frick quickly became Coke King of Pennsylvania: by the age of thirty he was a millionaire, outstripping the judge's own performance at the same age. A useful consequence was the ensuing friendship of Andrew Mellon and Henry Clay Frick; indeed, they were soon partners, dealing first in real estate and later in more promising ventures.

In 1882 Andrew assumed direction of the bank and soon of all the Mellon enterprises as well—realty, traction, and coal. He and Frick acquired the Pittsburgh National Bank of Commerce; in 1883 he formed the Union Insurance Company; in 1886, he joined with Frick and several others to establish the Fidelity Title Company to manage estates; and then came the Union Transfer and Trust Company, later converted into the Union Trust Company. Meanwhile Frick showed Andrew how an industrialist should handle recalcitrant labor by crushing the unions in the coke fields. It did not trouble the rising young magnate that the laborers he was importing from Europe had to live in foul shacks along the Monongahela, lacking sanitation and other amenities of a civilized existence. It was enough that they had dared to question his labor policies. The response was the coal police.

Mellon decided that lending money was insufficient. He should demand a slice of each new enterprise, as financiers in New York were doing. When he was visited in 1889 by Alfred Hunt and George Clapp, who had come to vouch for the Hall electrolytic process for reducing aluminum, Mellon, recognizing a desirable prospect, offered $25,000 in return for shares of stock. It was no doubt one of the many important business decisions he was to make: the result was the Aluminum Corporation of America. In 1901, Colonel James M. Guffey called for financial help to exploit an oil strike in Texas: this led to the Gulf Oil Company. In 1905 E. G. Acheson, a flamboyant inventor, appeared with an abrasive stone fused from salt, sand, and coke, all combined in an electric furnace. A. W., as he was now known, lent Acheson $50,000 to start the Carborundum Company, a significant share of which went to the bank. Sales of abrasives to industries became a rough economic indicator most useful in the banking business. The Mellon conglomerate grew: Pittsburgh trolley cars, coal mines, steel mills, railroad cars, shipbuilding, and steel works all entered the combine. The principle of consolidation was a simple one: lend money to a potentially profitable enterprise and take shares of stock in return, preferably the majority. When the loan was repaid, the stock could be kept and the money used over again to acquire another business. To be really successful it was important to dominate and control the market.

The principle of absolute control was illustrated by Mellon's coal ventures. Capitalizing the Monongahela River Consolidated Coal and Coke Company—River Coal, as it was called—at $30,000,000, Mellon sent his agents into the fields to tie up the mines. Most of the operators were not upset, for Mellon was offering good prices. Besides, he owned most of the coal barges on the river, in effect serving notice that the operators sell out to him or they could not ship. In the well-watered capitalization, engineered by Mellon's Union Trust, stock was sold to the public, but Mellon kept the bonds. A second combine, Pittsburgh Coal, with a tight grip on the area around the steel city, was also financed by A. W. When difficulties developed for both companies, they were simply merged: the monopoly was complete. The merger seemed reasonable enough, for boards of directors of both were virtually the same anyway. A $25,000,000 bond issue paid off Pittsburgh Coal's debt to Mellon, and though the whole city was angry because the banker had taken his pound of flesh first, he remained impervious to criticism. Revenues came from a coal profit of almost $6,000,000 a year, rents from the miners' homes, and a profit from company stores. Meanwhile the United States Industrial Commission charged that half the new capitalization had been pure water.

One problem in the coke industry was its failure to utilize by-products. Had American methods of producing coke been less wasteful, the industry could have gained in the eighteen-eighties at least another $20,000,000 a year. The Germans, for example, were thriftier, turning out as sidelines tar, benzol, dyestuffs, and explosives. It was a matter of the kind of oven used: American beehive ovens simply sent the volatile gases into the atmosphere, while German ovens recovered the gas and chemicals.

A Dr. Heinrich Koppers came to the United States in the first decade of the century to set up the new ovens in Illinois. Recognizing another good enterprise, Mellon bought out Koppers for $300,000 in 1914, paying him with shares in the new firm that had been formed. Poor Koppers! When the United States entered the war his stock in the new company was seized by A. Mitchell Palmer, the Alien Property Custodian, who had been informed by an emissary from Mellon that a large bloc of stock in the Koppers Company was held by a German. His shares were sold at public auction, the sole bidder being the Koppers Company, which paid just a bit over $300,000 for them, although they were then worth $15,000,000. The transaction would have delighted old Thomas Mellon.

Under Mellon's tutelage, the Koppers Company grew, expanding into utilities, behaving like a holding company. All of the stock and bond flotations were handled by Union Trust. Occasionally, working arrangements were set up with Morgan-backed utilities. Subsidiaries penetrated the New York market and played with some corporate baubles in Boston, evading the strict Massachusetts utilities laws. The operation was simple enough: gas plants were constructed for utilities and shares taken as payment. Such shares could then be pyramided several layers in a holding-company structure.

The steel industry was also an area for Mellon activity. The Pittsburgh banker joined with Henry Clay Frick to take an option on the Carnegie enterprises, but when the deal fell through, the wily Scotsman kept the option deposit of more than a million dollars. (He had insisted on cash and bonds, a demand that only Morgan could have met.) As a way of annoying Carnegie, Frick and Mellon then established the Union Steel Company, a wire and nail plant. The New York Shipbuilding Company was added, for the steel-ship market appeared strong. They took 60 per cent interest in the McClintic Marshall Construction Company, a firm that supplied structural steel for buildings. Next, the Standard Steel Car Company was tossed into the industrial basket. Then the process was reversed. Union Steel integrated its operations, becoming enough of a menace to induce United States Steel to buy it out for $75,000,000. In 1916 New York Shipbuilding was spun off to Robert Dollar, the shipping magnate, for $11,500,000. Standard Steel Car was turned over to Pullman for $38,700,000 in 1930, and

McClintic Marshall Construction was sold to Bethlehem Steel a year later for $70,000,000. The latter transactions were consummated in the worst depression the country had ever experienced.

But the Aluminum Corporation was Mellon's peak performance. An absolute monoploy, it had come under his wing by chance. When the sponsors of the electrolytic process sought a loan, he seized his greatest opportunity, employing patent control and protective tariffs to insure a tightly closed market for what had been a rare metal. C. M. Hall, the inventor of the electrolytic method of reduction, knew that he had to have a large supply of electric power; his first attempt, an approach to Cowles Brothers, had failed. In any case, the latter was interested in another process. When Mellon invited himself into Hall's company, Pittsburgh Reduction, he immediately enlarged the capitalization, keeping 40 per cent for himself. A vigorous patent-infringement lawsuit against Cowles Brothers disposed of that competition; the decision was rendered by Judge William Howard Taft. Whereas the price of aluminum had originally dropped sharply with Hall's invention, it now began to climb. A tariff helped considerably. While the cost of production was around fifty cents a pound, customers paid eighty cents. Power from the new hydroelectric plant at Niagara Falls enabled output of the Mellon metal to increase to four tons a day. Agreements with foreign firms were reached, and the monopoly was well established.

In 1907 Pittsburgh Reduction was transferred into the Aluminum Corporation of America, and new plants were built. It was now a major industry. Just before World War I broke out in 1914, a French firm tried to build a power plant for aluminum reduction in North Carolina. After the Frenchmen had invested their resources, they suddenly discovered that it was impossible to secure further financing in the United States; they were told by New York bankers that they might catch a sympathetic ear at Union Trust in Pittsburgh. That bank was happy to take over the Carolina properties: the price meant a loss to the French of not more than a million dollars.

When the Government enjoined the Aluminum Corporation from engaging in monopolistic practices in violation of the antitrust laws in 1912, the proscription was blithely ignored. If patent rights expired, there was always the tariff wall. Bauxite, the basic raw material, was brought under control by simply acquiring as many suppliers as possible; by 1906 the Aluminum Corporation was clutching to its bosom most of the better bauxite deposits. It also cornered the scrap market: indeed, old metal seemed more valuable than newly processed aluminum. Possible competitors were hampered by delaying raw-materials shipments, sending them defective material, charging excessive prices, or refusing to ship at all. Wartime demand for aluminum alloys provided a tremendous boost to the company's coffers. By then a $2,000,000 property had become worth at least $80,000,000.

Finally, the Federal Trade Commission charged in 1924 that the injunction of 1912 had been violated and recommended prosecution. No change in the leopard's spots had been visible for a dozen years. Another attack came from the Bausch Machine Tool Company, an early rival in aluminum production. It charged the Aluminum Corporation with fraud; the evidence was persuasive enough to give Bausch an award of $8,000,000. It so happened that George Haskell of the Bausch firm had turned to James Duke's Canadian holdings for power to operate his aluminum process. A tentative agreement was reached, but one of Duke's men had been working closely with Arthur Davis of the Aluminum Corporation, and Haskell soon found all doors closed to him. Davis had discouraged Duke from getting into aluminum altogether. Haskell's case seemed clear-cut. When called upon to supply a deposition in the legal proceedings, Mellon's memory suddenly failed. He was saved by the Court of Appeals, which conveniently overturned the original verdict in favor of Haskell.

The Aluminum Corporation seemed to lead a charmed life. When Attorney General Harlan Fiske Stone thought he might undertake to prosecute an antitrust case against the company, he was quickly elevated to the Supreme Court. Nine months later the Justice Department announced that the company was as innocent as a lamb, asserting that Mellon's one-third interest in the corporation by no means implied control. The department's investigation had been conducted by an examiner who was neither a lawyer nor an accountant nor an economist! Before coming to the department he had been a mere clerk. After a cursory examination that lasted ten days, he declared absolution for the corporation. After questioning the examiner, one senator exploded: "I wouldn't hire him to investigate a bootleg case." It was not until World War II that major rivals finally obtained a foothold in the industry.

The Mellons had dabbled in oil long before the creation of Gulf Oil. William Larimer, A. W.'s nephew, had wildcatted around Pennsylvania and West Virginia in search of wells, and in time the Mellons had become one of the larger independents in the oil industry, with pipelines, tank cars, and a refinery. They had fought off the Rockefeller interests for a number of years, finally selling out in 1895. They were soon to reenter the business in a way that would present real rivalry to Rockefeller. It all grew out of a lucky strike by Anthony Luchich at Spindletop near Galveston, Texas, in

1901. Luchich was a Yugoslav prospector financed by the Pittsburgh firm of Guffey and Galey. The Spindletop hit produced the biggest gusher in history; the immense effort needed to cap the enormous flow broke the prospector and his backers. The inevitable appointment with Mellon followed. A man of experience, A. W. knew a good thing when it was presented to him; the Guffey Petroleum Company was formed with a $15,000,000 capitalization, 40 per cent staying with Mellon. Petroleum output leaped ahead, leases on nearby land were snatched up, and the Mellons were back in oil. Spindletop had been the first of the oil strikes that took the industry into Texas and Texas into the twentieth century. The already-rich Mellons became super-rich. Guffey Petroleum became Gulf Oil in 1906; it is today third among the world's oil producers, and with sales of $3,800,000,000 a year, it ranks tenth among the top five hundred industrial corporations in the country. The Mellons today hold about a one-fourth interest in the Gulf Oil Company. Years later Colonel Guffey, who had been removed from the company, sued and won a $350,000 judgment, but again the verdict was set aside by the presiding judge.

Within a few years, an understanding was reached with Standard Oil providing that the Rockefellers would remain the leaders in the industry. The big fellows began to dance among the little ones. The major companies would refuse to extend their pipelines to the small independent fields unless output was increased to justify the cost of extension. When the small companies agreed, the majors would then refuse to buy unless the price was cut. It was all a jolly game.

With his domestic empire virtually complete, A. W. was ready for broader horizons. Like other companies, Gulf went outside the United States, showing a special affinity for Mexico. However, the new egalitarian principles in countries like Mexico made both the oil companies and Washington unhappy. But there was no cause for concern, for if not Mexico, then there was Venezuela, dominated by a dictator who would be more cooperative. Dollar diplomacy facilitated American penetration of the backward areas of the globe. Appropriate pressure gave the Mellon interests, for example, a fifty-year concession in Colombia. The nations below the Rio Grande could always improve their credit ratings in New York banks if their domestic petroleum problems were handled "rationally": the meaning of that word depended on Washington.

The empire was coordinated from Pittsburgh, mainly through the Union Trust Company, though the Mellons also controlled the Mellon National Bank, Pittsburgh National Bank of Commerce, Citizen's National, City Deposit, and the Union Savings Bank—institutions that together had one-third of all the bank deposits in the city. In 1902, Union Trust's surplus and profits had been $15,500,000, with 80 per cent of the bank's shares held by Mellon and Frick. A merger of the old T. Mellon and Sons and Union Trust resulted in a redistribution of shares that gave Mellon and his brother 42 per cent. Though there was an occasional business storm, there were now enough resources to keep the Mellon powder dry.

A. W. always tried to avoid public scrutiny; his private life, he felt, was his own. When he sued his wife for divorce, nothing appeared in the Pittsburgh newspapers for seven months. To protect Mellon's privacy, the Pennsylvania legislature was kind enough to provide a law allowing the court to appoint a master to hear evidence in private chambers. While the court records show A. W.'s charges, his wife's reply was removed "for inspection" and never returned. Such was the Mellon power.

In philanthropy, A. W. did not emulate such fellow-millionaires as Carnegie, at least not in his own lifetime. But Mellon was charitable to both political parties. To be sure, there were gifts on occasion to churches and the University of Pittsburgh, and Mellon did support the Mellon Institute for Industrial Research. (It was at this institution that it was discovered how to cut yeast and sugar in bread, saving millions for the baking industry, but giving America a tasteless white glob as a substitute for the staff of life.) When the Depression halted construction of the fifty-two-story University of Pittsburgh, A. W. did little about it, and the whole city wondered why he allowed a steel skeleton to grace the skyline. The university itself, too close to A. W.'s home, made certain that dissenting speakers or liberal ideas would not corrupt the minds of its young charges.

Now A. W. craved activity outside the world of business; the opportunity came with Harding's election to the Presidency in 1920. Mellon was appointed Secretary of the Treasury, and America became aware of one of its richest men. A reporter described Mellon when he arrived in Washington as looking like a "tired bookkeeper afraid of losing his job." Mellon found himself in a cabinet filled with such luminaries as Harry Daugherty, Will Hays, Edwin Denby, and Albert Fall, gentlemen ready to distribute whatever natural wealth the nation still possessed among those who already owned virtually all its industrial and financial wealth. And Mellon was ready to supply the business community with still more accommodating tax laws.

The new chief of Government finance called for economy and for reductions in the excess-profits tax and income taxes. Considering that the nation was now at peace, the proposal seemed fairly reasonable; but the income-tax cut was to affect only incomes above $66,000. Anyone in a lower bracket would continue to pay the old rates. Critics of the Mellon purview, such as Senator Robert La Follette, were simply ignorant, opined the Secretary, and were stifling business incentive; prosperity could come only if the wealthy wished it. The appeal to the conventional wisdom of the day was most attractive, and the Secretary's bill had no difficulty in passing Congress. It was signed into law in November, 1921. An incidental benefit was a saving to the Mellon family of almost $1,000,000 in taxes.

The next "reform," attempted under Coolidge, conceded reductions of 1 to 2 percentage tax points to lower-income groups. As Mellon's new plan signaled a further victory for free enterprise, stock prices on Wall Street began to mount. A few academic economists observed that tax cuts at that time would generate an unhealthy expansion and a ruinous speculative frenzy. No one paid much attention to these premature Keynesians. Oddly, the bill was defeated, upsetting Mellon considerably. A congressional coalition of Progressives and Democrats, moreover, had audaciously jacked up the surtax minimum and even increased inheritance-tax rates. When Coolidge was returned to the Presidency in 1924, A. W. was delighted, for he felt vindicated. The new Congress went on a rampage, lightening the tax burden for the wealthy by $700,000,000. The inheritance rate went back to 20 per cent; the credit for state inheritance taxes was lifted to 80 per cent; and the capital stock tax was repealed. The Mellon family saved another $2,000,000 in taxes.

The Bureau of Internal Revenue, charged with enforcing the nation's tax laws, suddenly became liberal with rebates to large corporations and the wealthy. With the frequent discoveries of past errors in tax administration, some senators wondered aloud whether Teapot Dome was not being replicated in another guise. It took but five days to audit the tax return of Gulf Oil; its refunds totaled almost $4,000,000. An effort to investigate the bureau was aborted by the Administration. Legislators were troubled by the generosity of the bureau in allowing large depletion allowances, thus obliterating profits and reducing tax liabilities. Discovery of depletion allowances and discounts on deferred receipts meant further tax losses. An 8 per cent investment credit seemed unconscionable to the Democrats, who cried that Uncle Sam had become Santa Claus. And leading the parade of those making claims for refunds was U. S. Steel: one check it received from the Treasury's disbursing officer totaled $27,000,000. The benefits for Mellon's firms came to $7,000,000. The Secretary's efforts were staunchly supported by the business community as the cornucopia poured its blessings on them all.

Nor was Mellon averse to employing the services of government in learning how to exploit the opportunities provided by tax law and tax regulation. At his request, the Commissioner of Internal Revenue prepared a memorandum explaining ten possible ways an individual could legally avoid paying taxes, at least five of which Mellon quickly adopted. The Commissioner also supplied one of the bureau's experts to prepare the Secretary's income-tax returns; the expert was soon on Mellon's payroll, setting up family corporations for Mellon and showing him how to generate tax losses by having his family corporations sell stock to one another. At the same time, the Secretary of the Treasury was urging the nation's taxpayers to pay their just obligations to the Government.

When Herbert Hoover replaced Calvin Coolidge as President, Mellon remained in the Cabinet, but his days seemed numbered. Speculative fever was gripping the nation, yet Mellon saw no reason to be disturbed. Then came the crash, and his only observation was that a little bloodletting would be good for the body politic. To Mellon, it seemed as though the world had gone mad; if only he were heeded, all would be aright again. But his kind of orthodoxy began to be questioned; he was now being called "the man who stayed too long"; he was a target for attacks on Administration policy. Some congressmen wanted to impeach him, but they were cheated of their vengeance when Hoover moved Mellon out of the Cabinet to the Court of St. James's as American Ambassador.

Yet there was a sense of resiliency in the Mellon family. When most banks shut down in the banking crisis of 1933, the Mellons stayed open. They had enough cash in their vaults to meet public demands, and besides it was a great opportunity to draw depositors away from other banks. The Depression descended on the country like the foul smog that hovered over Pittsburgh. When a community fund was set up there to help the destitute, Mellon's sense of what was proper charity did not desert him. The family gift was somewhat in excess of $300,000, though community leaders had hoped for a $1,000,000 donation. The grant was subsequently followed by a gift of $750,000. In the winter of 1931, Pennsylvania's governor visited Mellon to negotiate a $1,000,000 loan for the state's welfare needs. The loan did not eventuate, but the governor was proudly shown A. W.'s latest art purchase—one that had cost $1,700,000.

In 1935 the new Administration controlled by the Democrats charged that Mellon had defrauded the Government of $1,300,000 in income taxes for the year 1931 by transferring stock holdings at depressed prices among himself, his bank, and a family holding company. The Government asserted that these sales, which had established capital losses, were not bona fide as they had not effected any real change in ownership. In 1937 the Tax Board of Appeals held in favor of Mellon, deeming the transactions to have been quite proper.

When Mellon died he left but $37,000,000 in his personal estate; most of his wealth had already been passed on to his children. His son, Paul, who had aspired to becoming a publisher, had been induced to enter the bank after graduation from college, though he had little taste for the business. Paul has preferred to spend his inherited wealth rather than attempt to increase it; yet, despite his varied public activities and his expensive art collection, the family fortune has multiplied. The properties were managed by his cousin Richard, who presided over the vast business empire still financed through the Mellon banking system. Paul prefers to manage the National Gallery of Art in Washington, which the noted art dealer Joseph Duveen induced the elder Mellon to give to the nation. Not only did such a magnificent gift mean tax savings, but it also prevented the dispersion of a superb collection of fine art.

In the younger generation the sense of civic responsibility seems more substantial than that of their forebears. Among their useful endeavors was the campaign to make Pittsburgh a clean city, a project in which only the Mellons could have been successful. They also made sizable gifts, much larger than A. W. would have countenanced, to a number of universities and other institutions. To some observers it seemed to be partial recompense for the social pain engendered by the building of a huge family fortune.

PART FOUR

*A significant development in American business was the rise of the corpora-
tion, which eventually made it possible to sever ownership from the control
of property. Stockholders became interested mainly in the market price of
securities, and, with the proxy, simply turned over their entrepreneurial
responsibilities to a corps of managers that ran business affairs much as they
wished. To all intents and purposes, representatives—corporate procurators—took over in company after company. The behavior of corporate
leaders was sometimes questionable, as in drugs and electrical equipment.
But more important, the larger corporations came to dominate their industries and became weighty factors in the balance of economic forces.*

*In earlier days, corporations sought to integrate vertically, to control
a product from raw material to finished goods, but in recent years the
conglomerate and the multinational corporation have added new dimensions
to business. In the former case, hodgepodge combines were set up with
little economic logic other than acquiring power for its own sake; in
the latter, corporate leapfrogging of national boundaries has threatened to cast up urgent political problems. The world of business has*

The Procurators

come a long way since the days of Thomas Hancock.

Only once did businessmen seriously stub their toes: in the nineteen-thirties. They had been long accustomed to their roles as lords of creation, and they blinded themselves to the growing difficulties into which the economy was heading. The payoff came with the stock market collapse of 1929. Yet when the polity and the society insisted on establishing new rules of the game, businessmen howled in anguish, even though they could do as well, or better, under these new rules. It was a curious way of expressing gratitude for having been rescued from the gallows.

That business can do better under the new rules has been demonstrated by recent events, especially as businessmen lock feet under the table with the military and the politicos in this Age of Space. America has now to confront a situation in which business relies on dubious adventures in other parts of the globe and on the dusty wastes of the moon. Meanwhile, little attention is paid to the by-products of a business civilization: the decay of the cities, the spoliation of the environment, and the needs of those unfortunate enough to have missed the express train of history.

CHAPTER 16 Depression and the New Deal

By the mid-nineteen-twenties it seemed that peace and prosperity ever-lasting had descended on America. Editorial writers agreed that all was well with the nation. And bankers had a simple arrangement for keeping the ship of state afloat: the people would save the reward of their toil, putting it in the care of a prudent banker who would then lend the money to industrious entrepreneurs to use in building plants that made goods and supplied jobs. It was a wondrous circle that permitted the country to move to higher and higher achievements.

All were agreed that the nation was in good hands. The rich were not taxed too burdensomely by the Administration in Washington: the geese that laid the golden eggs should not be killed. Any state that sought to redress what might have been an imbalance through such devices as wages-and-hours laws was chastized by an ever-vigilant Supreme Court. Such stalwarts as William Howard Taft, Pierce Butler, George Sutherland, Clark McReynolds, and Willis van Devanter could always call on their conservative comradeship to outvote the dissents of Holmes, Brandeis, and Stone.

Adding to the general state of euphoria was the stock market, a presumably effective indicator of economic health. Prices on the market began to nose upward in the nineteen-twenties; it seemed that the rise would be unending, culminating somewhere out in space. Investment companies employed busy staffs of salesmen who peddled all sorts of securities to hungry souls panting for uncountable paper profits to come. Holding companies built layer upon layer of corporate enterprises like huge wedding cakes, creating "values" that gave a semblance of wealth. Numerous varieties of common and preferred stock as well as bonds, were floated, as promoters always made certain that controlling shares were closely held. In Frederick Allen's apt phrase, the Lords of Creation walked haughtily in the land, confident in their virtue and leadership.

Events of the decade such as the Teapot Dome Scandal did not disturb their equanimity. Albert Fall, Secretary of the Interior under Harding, had leased important oil reserves to two oil men, Harry Sinclair and E. L. Doherty, at terms that brought the two a huge profit. The public stench was unbearable, yet Fall and Sinclair were acquitted when the matter came to court. (Fall ultimately did go to jail.) Senator George W. Norris of Nebraska opined that it would be useless to try anyone worth over $100,000,000 for a crime. Sinclair's rectitude may have been preserved by heavy contributions to the Republican party. Events moved along in an even tenor, and in due course, Coolidge, who had chosen not to run in 1928, was replaced by Herbert Hoover.

Hoover, born in Iowa in 1874 into a Quaker family, became a successful mining engineer, an occupation that took him all over the world. Yet all he saw in an adventurous life was business; organizing and promoting numerous ventures brought him a modest fortune. Caught in England by the outbreak of World War I, he became involved in Belgian relief and other such projects, and discharged his duties with an efficiency not alien to an engineer. In 1919, acclaimed nationally for his public achievements, he began to be viewed as Presidential timber. Clearly, he was a logical choice for Secretary of Commerce. In that post he was perhaps the only dignified personality among the cronies and poker players that made up Harding's Cabinet.

Hoover's views snugly fitted the temper of the times: he was an advocate of "people's capitalism," the theory that corporations had acquired a sense of trusteeship and responsibility. The department under Hoover became a master sales force for American business as well as for its Secretary, who was hailed as a man who knew how to build the nation's enterprise. Hoover's reputation for probity, prudence, and energy was assiduously cultivated among both businessmen and the public. His speeches assailing Federal regulation of power were widely distributed by the National Electric Light Association, the electrical industry's propaganda arm. Hoover encouraged foreign investments, many of which later proved to be disastrous. But he could not have known; he was merely acting according to the wisdom of the time.

Humanitarianism and efficiency were the qualities that were to take Hoover to the White House. Moreover, he had been a "liberal" member of the Harding-Coolidge entourage. But when the Depression arrived, and then deepened, these qualities failed him. His cherished beliefs—enterprise, efficiency, success, and laissez faire—all collapsed like a balloon from which the air had suddenly escaped. He continued to intone nineteenth-century rhetoric, making him incomprehensible to the millions of Americans frozen by the cold blasts of the nation's worst depression. Unable to adapt his views to the needs of the unwashed masses, Hoover became a failure as a politician. His rigidity, self-righteousness, and material success made learning from the adversities of others impossible.

Not that Hoover was totally insensitive to some of the problems: his bent for the philanthropic led him to sponsor a conference on unemployment in the early nineteen-twenties. But as President, he stood solidly behind laissez faire, though he considered high tariffs for American producers reasonable enough. Had it not been for the vigilance of Senator George Norris, Government properties in the Tennessee Valley, later the heart of TVA, would have been turned over to private utilities. In fact, the utilities had long conducted a *sub rosa* propaganda campaign to bring public opinion to their side, and occasional congressional investigation revealed the sometimes comic and often expensive attempts of utilities lobbyists to twist congressmen their way.

Although businessmen in the nineteen-twenties proclaimed the virtues of laissez faire, they were ever ready for the Government to intervene in economic and political affairs on their behalf. Mellon's tax bounties to business were supplemented by such antics as those of W. B. Shearer, who had been hired by American shipbuilders to insure that the Geneva Naval Conference would be frustrated. Anyone who supported the cause of peace was vilified by Shearer in a jingoistic campaign that exceeded all bounds of decency. When asked by a congressional committee about their relationships with Shearer, Charles Schwab and E. G. Grace, steel and shipping potentates, suffered convenient lapses of memory.

The expansion in industrial productivity, which increased some 40 per cent in the nineteen-twenties, appeared as one of the beneficences of business. The statistics were most reassuring: manufactured goods rose in value by $8,000,000,000 between 1925 and 1929, and the auto industry sold more than 5,000,000 cars in 1929. Such gains might have occasioned price reductions for goods or increases in wages, but these were unlikely under the regime of business. Most of the cream was siphoned off in the form of higher profits; indeed, the latter rose twice as fast as the rate of output, underpinning higher prices for corporate securities in the stock market. As the decade came to a close, real industrial support for stocks evaporated, so that prices for securities were supported by nothing more substantial than ordinary inflation. The maldistribution of income was quite marked, widening the gap between the rich and the poor and providing virtually no sustenance for higher levels of aggregate demand. In short, purchasing power was not bestowed in equitable proportions among the populace.

Yet the economic signs suggested prosperity, and having achieved a sense of accomplishment, businessmen began to think in high-minded terms. The jungle of Social Darwinism was passé, for business had now acquired a "soul"; there was need for a morality consonant with the newly developed sense of priesthood. In the view of Bruce Barton, a leading advertising executive of the time, Jesus would have been welcomed on Madison Avenue as a great salesman of religion. Meanwhile, businessmen continued to court favor with promoters, jockeying for a favored position on somebody's preferred stock list, or inveigling invitations to become part of a stock-market pool. That public idealism expounded in popular journals clashed jarringly with private avarice did not seem incongruous.

Such land booms as that in Florida in the mid-twenties were harbingers of what was to come. The buying and selling of land, and what may have been land, generated a world of pure fantasy in which one became rich by trading in swamps. Subdivisions were marked out on flatlands shading into the Everglades: the rage to speculate and deal in "binders"—rights to buy land—forced prices up to as much as $75,000 a plot. Fed by purchases requiring a mere 10 per cent down, the dream was bound to end; it was cut short by a fearful hurricane in 1926.

Yet there was still opportunity to build substantial fortunes in industry, as the Van Sweringen railroad complex illustrated. Believers in the legends of Horatio Alger could always point to the Van Sweringen bachelor brothers from Cleveland who had expanded from real estate into transportation. Having developed the exclusive suburb of Shaker Heights near Cleveland, the brothers sought to supply their realty customers with a high-speed electric line into the city. To provide a terminal, they purchased the old Nickel Plate Railroad from the New York Central for one million dollars down, the balance to be raised through a newly formed holding company. They now had a "property" on their hands and wisely turned it into a successful venture. Slowly, they added more railroad lines; in 1925 they bought into the Chesapeake and Ohio and the Père Marquette. The Van Sweringens had done so well with their railroads that the House of Morgan voiced no serious objections when they expressed a desire to share in the Erie. Working closely with the Morgan firm, the brothers next brought the Missouri Pacific into their burgeoning empire.

But it was all accomplished through an intricate network of holding companies, difficult to unravel. The Vaness Company represented the top layer; then came General Securities and the Allegheny Corporation. The latter controlled the Chesapeake Corporation and the Nickel Plate. In turn the Nickel Plate, the original property, controlled the Wheeling and Lake

Erie, while Chesapeake kept the Chesapeake and Ohio under its wing. At the sixth layer below were the Hocking Valley, the Père Marquette, and the Erie. The lower one went through the strata, the smaller became the Van Sweringens' controlling interest. Hocking Valley control, for example, represented a less than one per cent interest, but the coordination effected by the holding company structure made that quite sufficient.

All was placid so long as the underlying properties earned enough on their common stock to provide the parents and grandparents in the upper reaches of the pyramid with enough dividends. But with the stock-market crash and the Depression, the piper's tune turned sour. Moreover, the Van Sweringen brothers had always borrowed heavily to finance their multifarious transactions: their own interest in the empire, worth about $3,000,000,000, was estimated at 17 per cent, most of it borrowed from bankers. By 1935, the system was in default. When the Van Sweringen holdings were auctioned off that year to satisfy their creditors, the losses came to $40,000,000. However, "friendly interests" bought in the properties to give the now aging brothers continued control.

A man like Charles E. Mitchell was perhaps more typical of the Roaring Twenties. A flamboyant refugee from Boston middle-class gentility, he firmly believed that the purchase of bonds—any kind of bonds—was the key to perpetual prosperity. In 1907 he was credit manager for Western Electric in Chicago, but such a post could not contain his indubitable talents. In 1911 he had his own investment house, and five years later he joined the National City Company, the investment affiliate of the National City Bank. Having demonstrated his powers of persuasion, he was made president of the bank in 1921. These powers were channeled through a corps of salesmen that was trained to find investors in the lowliest of persons and to pursue them with enthusiastic aggressiveness until the sale was closed.

They peddled all kinds of securities, including foreign issues of dubious worth, such as Peruvian bonds. It seemed that American buoyancy could absorb the most indigestible of securities. From all this frenetic salesmanship, Mitchell claimed a most modest salary. But the National City Company had a "management fund" which Mitchell parceled out, cutting the largest slice for himself: in 1928, his share was a mere $750,000. Selling securities was indeed a profitable venture; not only did an investment house enjoy a handsome commission, but, in addition, "management fees" could augment the take. In 1929, the house of Kuhn, Loeb received in commissions and fees almost $6,000,000 from one corporation alone.

DEPRESSION AND THE NEW DEAL

The first issue of a security usually went to "insiders," allegedly for services rendered. Then the securities were sold off by all the favorite sons to a public seeking immediate riches. In order to form large herds of "sheep," as picturesque Wall Street language described its gullible flock, investment trusts began to proliferate. Predecessors of present-day mutual funds, they sold their own shares to the public as they merrily speculated with the customers' money.

As the prices of securities climbed, money from overseas was attracted to American markets feeding the speculative frenzy. In the early years of the twenties, the average number of shares changing hands per annum totalled 300,000,000; in 1926 it increased to 500,000,000; in 1928 trading volume was more than 900,000,000 shares; and the following year the stratosphere was reached with 1,100,000,000 shares. The value of listed stocks, mostly on paper, increased by billions of dollars. Virtually all the trading was done on margin, that is, with borrowed money. Recourse was had to the call-money market, which assured lenders of immediate recall of their investment should prices drop below the margin. The call market became the depository for funds from banks and corporations; interest rates at 10 and 12 per cent were too attractive to be overlooked. Corporations put their working capital into the market, and with the Federal Reserve rediscount rate set at 5 per cent, it was the essence of business prudence to borrow from the bank and invest in the call-money market. At one time Standard Oil placed $69,000,000 into the market, while Electric Bond and Share "invested" $100,000,000, and Cities Service $49,000,000.

Yet at no time were there more than 2,000,000 people involved in all the frantic activity. Millions of shares were traded by Stock Exchange members for their own account; the fever had affected the professionals, those who had presumably known how to tally the sheep as they ambled their way to slaughter, while themselves staying out of danger. In 1927 prices began to recover from the shock of the Florida debacle. A cut in the rediscount rate made money easier to obtain. Speculators formed pools to force prices up still more in a churning market that threatened to become a vortex. One such pool, which included Harry Sinclair and Albert Wiggins, manipulated the stock of Consolidated Oil well enough to bring its operators a profit of $13,000,000. Another pool that worked on RCA generated a $5,000,000 profit for Percy Rockefeller (John D.'s nephew), Walter Chrysler, John J. Raskob, and Mrs. David Sarnoff. The Stock Exchange became a scene of high-level gambling, or, as Frederick Allen called it, "the Association for Improving the Condition of the Rich."

Even professors hailed the march of progress. Edwin Kemmerer, a noted money expert, Rufus Tucker, Irving Fisher, Joseph Davis, and other members of the academic fraternity could not express sufficient enthusiasm and admiration for the New Era. Only Roger Babson, looked upon by most economists as not a fully qualified member of the profession, voiced doubts that all was well. To Fisher, a Yale economist and a man of many quirks, stock prices had reached a permanently high plateau. The professors lent their authority to the formation of new investment trusts, many of which were dishonest or stupidly managed. The professors, of course, were not responsible for their incompetence, but the investment trusts did have "impressive disadvantages."

The forward movement of the market seemed like a perpetual-motion machine. Few realized that the latter existed only in science fiction; most thought that, with the proper exercise of solemn ritual, prices could be kept everlastingly high. RCA went from 85 to 420; du Pont from 310 to 425; Montgomery Ward from 117 to 440. By the end of 1928 call loans totaled $6,000,000,000. On any day the floor of the exchange looked like a dozen teams of Keystone Kops scurrying from trading post to trading post. No one scented the incipient danger; everyone believed with a truculent faith that nothing could possibly initiate the recall of loans. When Paul Warburg described the call-money market as a menace, he was thought to be not only obsolete, but a wrecker of American prosperity.

Washington remained imperturable. Interference with the ways of the market went against the grain of the Coolidge-Hoover-Mellon philosophy. And the Federal Reserve System was unlikely to administer a strong dose of corrective measures so long as it counted persons like Mitchell in its governing ranks. In fact, the Fed continued to buy acceptances in 1929, thus pouring more money into the banks, akin to spilling gasoline over a fire. With all the corporate funds that entered the market, it seemed futile to try to stem the tide. The Fed finally adopted a doleful attitude. The insanity of the market was beyond its control, it hinted, thus absolving itself of any responsibility for what might come.

In March, 1929, a market slide of 20 to 30 points presaged trouble, but Mitchell, whose National City Bank call-money rate was now 16 per cent, announced that he intended to support the boom. Within a few days the market recovered, as if to demonstrate that Wall Street still ruled the roost. But other danger signs were visible for those to see who would but look. Building contracts had dropped sharply in 1928, and the construction trades were in the doldrums. No one noticed that aggregate demand had as many holes as a sieve, that purchasing power was beginning to lag.

Business inventories began to accumulate, reflecting a slackening of retail sales, for gains in consumer spending had leveled off. Industrial output had started to fall in July, and within a short while unemployment inched upward perceptibly. These were the "real" economic indicators, but in the frenzy to make a million, no one really cared.

In early September the market broke once more. Roger Babson predicted the ultimate—a crash to curl one's hair. Wall Street promptly denounced him as a quack. The drop had been but a temporary one to allow for a "technical readjustment," a favorite market phrase when the Street had nothing else to say. The crevices in the economy were widening, and, when the chasm appeared, the market simply fell in. A few events presumably pushed Wall Street over the brink: the collapse of the Hatry enterprises in England and the exposure of the Kreuger and Toll swindle were supposed to have helped push the market from its high perch. Any blame he could assign to others might assuage the businessman's growing sense of unease.

More slippage began to show on October 19. Two days later over 6,000,000 shares changed hands, forcing a further decline. Professor Irving Fisher declared that it was all to the good, for the drop would "shake out the lunatic fringe." It did not occur to the good professor that in an asylum all the inmates are presumed to be insane. Babson advised a shift from securities to gold, a fairly sound proposal at the time. The roof caved in on October 23. Sales reached 13,000,000 shares; those unable to provide more margin were sold out by brokers to protect call loans; rumors wafted around the trading posts like ghosts in a haunted cottage; a terrifying panic descended on the stock market; sellers couldn't even give away their holdings, watching helplessly as their values evaporated with each clickety-clack of the ticker tape; it was said that speculators were jumping out of their skyscraper windows. What was happening suggested that they might have good cause to leap: U. S. Steel dropped from 205½ to 193½, Montgomery Ward from 83 to 50, and RCA from 68¾ to 44½. As for the loss of value, the country had spent less in fighting World War I.

But it appeared that help might be forthcoming from the captains of American finance: there had been a meeting at the offices of J. P. Morgan. The news brought a glimmer of hope, for had not the House of Morgan stopped the Panic of 1907? The financiers formed a pool committing $20,000,000 to $30,000,000 to support the market. Richard Whitney, Stock Exchange president, appeared on the floor early after the noon break, confidently offering to purchase U. S. Steel. As he placed other orders, fear subsided and prices recovered. But it was rumored that the bankers had

held up the market only to give themselves time to get out. Monday, with
the roof already gone, the floor caved in. The bankers announced that
it was not their intention to protect anyone. Mitchell was seen going into
the House of Morgan, and the Street was certain that he was in difficulty.
The volume of selling began to match the wild purchasing of the previous
months. Short selling by the big banks added to the toboggan slide. Loans
were called back, and by the end of the month, the call-money market had
shrunk by more than $2,000,000,000. Mayor James J. Walker of New
York urged motion-picture distributors to show movies stressing courage
and hope. A headline in *Variety,* the entertainment-industry trade journal,
proclaimed, "WALL ST. LAYS AN EGG."

And what did the Lords of Creation and their minions have to say?
Henry Ford offered a bit of characteristic wisdom: "Things are better
today than they were yesterday." In December, Charles Schwab announced that American industry was firmly entrenched for prosperity. The
Guaranty Trust Company opined that the price collapse was a favorable
development, and the president of the National Association of Manufacturers could see nothing on the horizon to cause concern. Meanwhile the
chilling winds of the Depression began to howl across the land. Hoover,
though uneasy, was not inclined to be pessimistic in public. The official line
stressed the fundamental soundness of business. When Rockefeller announced that he was buying common stock, a wag quipped, "Who else has
any money left?" Professor Fisher blamed the débâcle on mob psychology.
A large bank advertised that conditions remained unimpaired; the stock
market promptly took another dip. There seemed to be no end to the steady
decline of prices. The commodity markets began to imitate the securities
exchange. Clerks in hotels asked whether guests wanted rooms for sleeping
or jumping. Hoover announced a cut in taxes that affected very few
citizens. He then called meetings of leading industrialists to discuss and
review the situation, but nothing was done to mitigate the crisis. Though
the market started to recover in early 1930, the virus of depression had
already taken hold. America was becoming a sick nation.

It was difficult to pinpoint the culprits, for to do so, it was said,
would be to condemn an entire class, if not a whole society. No one group
was really more to blame than another for the débâcle, save perhaps the
speculators. But the search was on for a scapegoat. Hoover, by his reluc-
tance to do anything to stem the enormous tidal wave of adversity, made
himself as good a candidate as the bankers. Though the latter had suffered
like everyone else, they had become prime targets of public ire. Albert
Wiggins, head of the Chase National Bank, was a particular object of re-

proach. One of the big speculators, he had received high fees from numerous corporations for serving as a director and had participated in any number of stock pools. At one time Wiggins had even sold short Chase stock. The profits Wiggins "earned" totaled in the millions of dollars. The Rockefellers finally decided that Wiggins was a liability; he was retired on a pension of $100,000 a year, which he later magnanimously surrendered.

Mitchell's deals were less fortunate; when the Government established that his wash sales had been undertaken to evade tax payment, he was hauled into court. Richard Whitney, who had advocated Government economy by cutting soldiers' pensions, was later indicted for grand larceny: he had posted worthless stock as collateral for loans and had used other people's securities left in his custody as collateral. All of the financial potentates had dabbled in short selling, wash sales, circulation of false rumors, rigging the market, and pool operations. The stench generated by the unfettered speculation was so overwhelming that it could not help resulting in the prohibitions established by the Securities and Exchange Act of 1934.

As the Depression spread through industry after industry, gloom settled onto all corners of the nation. An immediate consequence was the increase in the numbers of unemployed. Millions of men in worn shoes and threadbare coats pounded their way wearily from plant gate to plant gate in search of jobs. Nameless terror and despair were reflected in the eyes of those gathered at street corners or queueing up on a bread line. Many resigned themselves to a life on public relief. What had gone wrong? Aggregate demand, or purchasing power, all but disappeared as corporations met the crisis by slashing payrolls. Business had become so large and so rigid that it was far easier to "adjust" wage costs and production than to cut prices. A business civilization in which promoters and speculators had had a rousing time was prostrate, slowly expiring in the agonies of economic decline. Soon the banking system too, backbone of the economy, would also enter a state of torpidity. The sins of the fathers were being visited upon the generation of the thirties.

True to his economic philosophy, Hoover did not act. The Emergency Committee for Employment, set up in 1931, proposed a plan for public works. Hoover refused to consider it, and Colonel Arthur Woods, who headed the committee, immediately resigned. Evictions from homes became common, as landlords piled household goods at the sidewalk's edge. Bread lines grew four abreast, extending for blocks, as the unemployed silently hoped for a bowl of soup and a slice of bread. The wealthiest nation in the world began to suffer starvation within its own borders. The cheerless winters dragged by, and soon local communities exhausted themselves trying to maintain a modicum of relief. Walter Gifford, AT&T head, replaced Wood on the Emergency Committee, but he was unable to tell Congress how many unemployed there were, though almost everyone knew that the number of jobless had reached at least 8,000,000. One thing Gifford did know: it would be "bad" for the Federal Government to intervene. There was one note of optimism: recovery must follow a depression, although neither businessmen nor anyone else for that matter could say how soon. One businessman offered the suggestion that restaurants might collect their leftover scraps and distribute the garbage to the unemployed in return for woodchopping. Despair had turned into tragedy.

Fortune magazine struck a happy note by observing that the servant problem had been solved for everyone: maids could be hired for $4.00 a week. Wages in the textile industry were at a level of $11.50 a week. Calvin Coolidge offered a choice bit of Massachusetts wisdom by observing, "When people are thrown out of work, unemployment results." Henry Ford felt certain that there was plenty of work and intimated that the unemployed were just lazy. Five months later he closed his Detroit plants, leaving 75,000 men jobless.

A few businessmen were somewhat more constructive with their suggestions. Walter Teagle of Standard Oil urged that the antitrust laws be suspended. Gerard Swope of General Electric advocated organizing industry into trade associations to coordinate production and stabilize prices— in short, the formation of a massive cartel for industry with a bone tossed to labor in the form of unemployment insurance. A few economists—more of the premature Keynesians—sought to focus attention on the lack of purchasing power, advocating such measures as unemployment insurance and health protection. It even occurred to certain academics and other intellectuals that basic reforms were necessary if the people were to be restrained from mounting the barricades. Their fear was exaggerated, for most Americans were immobilized by a sense of stupefaction. The warp of their stunned silence was crossed by the woof of bygone conventional wisdom. No one knew what to do, least of all the President.

The only measure Hoover would approve was the formation of the Reconstruction Finance Corporation as an instrumentality for lending money to banks, railroads, and insurance companies. Established in 1932, the RFC became the administration's major tool to combat the Depression. But to Hoover the agency was only a psychological gimmick; he was convinced that a few well-placed emergency loans would get the country around the corner of the Depression. Anticipating a limited use for RFC, it was given a short life and restricted as to the amount of aid it could

DEPRESSION AND THE NEW DEAL

provide. Loans to industry or for public works or relief were proscribed. A congressional plan to have the RFC lend to state and municipalities was vetoed by Hoover as a dangerous threat to sound public finance. Dominated by Republicans, RFC's transactions were held secret until Congress demanded reports. During its first year, the agency distributed about 75 per cent of its authorization of $2,000,000,000 mainly to banks: Congress discovered that half of the first $126,000,000 had gone to three banks. Three weeks after Charles Dawes, the RFC president, resigned, his Chicago bank received a loan of $90,000,000, though its deposits were only $95,000,000. Dawe's successor authorized a $12,000,000 loan to a bank of which he was a director. The business community was behaving like the French Bourbons: they had learned nothing and forgotten nothing.

It was inevitable that Congress would want to inquire into the causes of the Depression. In 1932 the Senate Banking Committee decided to study just how the Lords of Creation had discharged their stewardship. The committee's general counsel, Ferdinand Pecora, spread across the record a sorry tale of business venality and mismanagement. The confessions he wrung out of the men who had ruled America gave off an "odor [that] simply could not be contained." The stock-market manipulations, the pools, the price-rigging, the favored lists had involved Cabinet members, ambassadors, generals, college presidents, professors, and a former President of the United States. The élite of America had feasted together at a lavish banquet with their legs wondrously intertwined beneath the table. The nation had been a province for the rich, and they were now pilloried as traducers of the common weal.

Although H. L. Mencken, the Baltimore sage, rated Franklin Delano Roosevelt as the weakest man the Democrats might have nominated in 1932, Election Day gave the candidate 22,800,000 votes to Hoover's 15,700,000. Despite his earlier dour predictions, Roger Babson thought that there was still gold in the American cellar. Unfortunately, it was not to be discovered for another decade, and then only after the cellar had been blasted by the bombs of war. Roosevelt's inauguration was not to come until March, 1933. Meanwhile, the Republican Administration stood pat. The veterans who had marched on Washington in the summer of 1932 to demand bonus payments were ejected from their shacks along the Anacostia flats by General Douglas MacArthur, assisted by General George Patton and Major Dwight D. Eisenhower. Hoover thanked God that the Government knew how to deal with a mob. Farmers were pouring milk into the roads because prices were less than costs. Conservatives muttered that what the country needed was a dictator. Crisis followed on crisis in

Austria, Germany, and Britain: the Depression became worldwide. Millionaires panicked, shifting their money to safe places in Switzerland. In America, bank resources dwindled in one year from $70,000,000,000 to $57,000,000,000.

In October, 1932, Nevada proclaimed a bank holiday. This was followed by bank holidays in Iowa and Louisiana. When banks in Detroit shut down for a week in February, 1933, depositors throughout the nation were gripped by terror. Truly, the end had come. By Inauguration Day, forty-seven of the forty-eight states had declared bank holidays. The confusion and the fear of a total national collapse were indescribable. State authorities tried to save as many banks as they could, but this generally meant succor for the large banks. Yet often the urge to let a rival go under could not be resisted, as was illustrated in the failure of the Bank of the United States, a large commercial bank in New York City. The state's superintendent of banking had sought to effect a merger that would save the bank, which primarily served immigrant groups in the city. It had been a formidable rival to the traditional old-line banks which refused to take part in a reorganization, despite the state official's contention that failure of the bank would generate other failures. As a cheerful footnote, despite the enforced bankruptcy, 84 per cent of the bank's liabilities were paid, and the loss to depositors was much less than expected.

Immediately after his inauguration, FDR took steps to deal with the banking crisis. Utilizing a wartime statute, he closed the banks on March 6 to halt the runs until Congress could act. Constitutional questions were ignored. Congress in special session reacted as though firecrackers were going off under its chairs. A bill to deal with the perilous situation was rushed through the legislative mill as debate was brushed aside with cries of "Vote, vote!" The Treasury was given the power to call in gold, "conservators" were provided to assist national banks, and arrangements were made for RFC loans. Indeed, FDR could have nationalized the banks then and there without protest from bankers, editorial writers, or the public, but he was confident that he could lead the bankers out of the desert. Later, a senator remarked that the failure to nationalize the banks had been a great mistake, for now the moneylenders who had fled the temple were ready to reenter through the back door. By the end of May, thirteen thousand banks had been reopened, and the ground was prepared for the abandonment of that nineteenth-century fetish, the gold standard. Nevertheless, the legislation had been essentially conservative: all FDR wanted was stabilization, not nationalization.

Early New Deal legislation sought to modulate all the old abuses. Laws dealing with security flotation and speculation announced the principle of *caveat venditor,* let the seller beware, in the belief that such a declaration was all the protection the buyer needed. Bills in rapid succession provided public works, relief, and aid to agriculture. Labor hailed Section 7A of the National Recovery Act as a Magna Carta for collective bargaining, though it had been grudgingly inserted to forestall a specific statute on bargaining. A housing act, the Tennessee Valley Authority, loans for the homeowners, and railway pensions all seemed to have ended the law of the jungle. But these laws produced no revolution, nor were they intended to do so. They were, rather, emergency measures to save the system of business in spite of the potentates who had almost destroyed it.

New Deal aid to business was illustrated by the broadened activity of the RFC, now headed by Jesse Jones, a wealthy Texan. Jones believed that the only worthy things in life were religion, family, and money. His $200,000 gift in 1928 had assured the Democratic convention for Houston; shortly afterward, Jones conducted a fundraising campaign to reimburse himself. Jones invested RFC money rather than passing it out as loans, thus supplying capital to banks, but at the same time making the Federal Government a partner. In the beginning the bankers refused such assistance: their pre-Depression obtuseness had not abated, despite Jones's advice that they "ought to get smart." They finally came running to Jones when the bank-insurance law required certificates of solvency. By 1935, RFC held over a billion dollars in stock in half the banks of the country. But its program of aid was also extended to the Commodity Credit Corporation, Electric Home and Farm Authority, Federal National Mortgage Association, Export-Import Bank, railroads, and public works. Operating outside the Federal budget through revolving funds, RFC became a venture in state capitalism.

Many argued that some sort of economic planning was the only way to stimulate the economy. Industry was prostrate: production had dropped 48 per cent between 1929 and 1932, and its value had fallen 55 per cent. Construction had dropped by 80 per cent, grinding to a virtual halt. New Dealers spoke of the need for a partnership between government and business to help the latter regain its feet. There had been a precedent for planning in World War I, when industrial coordination had been attempted. Then there was Gerard Swope's 1931 plan for cartelizing the economy. And so task forces were created to write a bill providing for a general recovery program. What came out was the National Recovery Act, establishing codes of fair competition for each industry, exemption from the antitrust laws, and as an afterthought, a pledge permitting collective bargaining and the establishment of maximum hours of work and minimum wages. Both the National Association of Manufacturers and the Chamber of Commerce attacked the latter and tried to prevent passage of the clauses on labor, Section 7A. Some businessmen viewed the Recovery Act as a labor measure and would have nothing to do with it. But, in fact, the main thrust of the bill was the formation of a riskless, cartelized economy that would allow price fixing, output limitation, and the protection of investment. It was a strange way to climb out of a depression. Codes were established, even though Hugh Johnson, NRA administrator, had to ram them down the throats of some industrialists. The hoopla and fanfare sold the NRA to the public, which at least enjoyed the parades and the Blue Eagle posters.

Nevertheless, it was not long before the general enthusiasm began to wane. Most of the codes were written by businessmen, and most of the code authorities were dominated by them. Leftist groups labeled the NRA a Fascist instrument. More moderately, it was called an instrument of monopoly. When Johnson launched a "Buy Now" campaign, farmers wanted to know "with what?" By May, 1934, the NRA had become an object of scorn, if not a complete political liability to FDR. Yet, despite the fact that the NRA was breaking apart, the Administration asked for its extension in 1935. Then in May the Supreme Court administered the *coup de grâce* in the Schecter "sick chicken" case, declaring unanimously that the National Recovery Act represented an unconstitutional delegation of legislative powers, the extraordinary circumstances notwithstanding.

The New Deal had other problems at hand, but each time it sought to deal with one of them, the business community rose up in arms. Business hostility had started in 1933, when an attempt was made to introduce a more effective food and drug act. The Food and Drug Administration had revealed case after case of adulterated food, poison patent medicines, corrosive hair dyes, rat poison to remove superfluous hair, and dangerous drugs to cure obesity. The pharmaceutical industry asserted that the New Deal's legislation was grotesque, evil, and vicious. So vociferous was the industry in protecting its right to gull and poison the public that it was not until 1938 that protective legislation was passed, and then in a watered-down version.

A Senate investigation committee, headed by Hugo Black of Alabama, exposed a scandalous relationship between Government officials and the airlines. Hoover's Postmaster General had, in fact, utilized Government subsidies to favor the larger companies, freezing out independent operators.

Black's committee revealed rigged bidding, the destruction of records, and blatant favoritism. The situation was so bad that FDR canceled all mail contracts in order to allow a realignment of mail subsidies.

Again and again, business intransigence against reform was displayed as the Administration attempted to rebuild the economic order. The New Deal's efforts to apply new rules to the stock market were labeled "a road to Communism." Richard Whitney declared that the Stock Exchange was a perfect institution requiring "no reform or legislation." In fact, said he, the country had been built by speculators. He did not detail the enormous losses they had occasioned. Eugene Thompson of the Associated Stock Exchanges predicted industrial chaos if New Deal proposals were enacted. It occurred to humorist Will Rogers that what the speculators did not want was "a cop on the beat." However, support for reform came from more moderate elements. The Securities Exchange Act was passed in 1934 and, somehow, grass did not grow in Wall Street.

Equally loud cries of outrage were heard when banking legislation and public-utility holding-company reforms were introduced. In 1935 Marriner Eccles, an Administration adviser, proposed changes in the Federal Reserve System that would move control of open-market operations from the New York bank to the Board in Washington. Cries of anguish arose once more. In the battle that followed, no holds were barred. As might have been expected, certain respected academics sided with the bankers. But it was one fight that the Administration was to win. The most powerful device for pumping money into the economy or withdrawing it—what open-market operations really implied—was at long last placed where it ought to have been, with the Federal Reserve in Washington.

Even louder were the screams of pain when FDR suggested that public-utility holding-company abuses might be corrected. In fact, the President would have preferred to abolish the nefarious business altogether, for so much of it had rested on paper values with no relation to the realities of actual production. The entire business community rallied to the defense of the holding company "as if it were the ark of the American covenant." The Administration's bill, they charged, would destroy capital and credit; there would be bankruptcies; and millions of poor widows and orphans holding stock in utilities would face absolute penury. Never had so many corporations acquired so deep a concern for the welfare of the unfortunate.

Flooded with thousands of telegrams, Congress passed a diluted bill. A subsequent Senate investigation revealed that the telegrams were totally counterfeit. The corporate infighting had been vicious and dirty. One of the utility industry's staunch defenders was Howard Hopson of Associated Gas and Electric; several years later he was to go to jail for fraud. Ultimately, the best the Administration could secure was a compromise that allowed public-utility holding companies to remain if they could demonstrate that the underlying operating firms could not survive without them. In other words, part of the layer cake was left standing.

And so business revived its faith in itself. In the first one hundred days of FDR's regime, reform could be swift precisely because businessmens' claim to dominance had expired in the ashes of the Depression. No one believed in them any longer; in 1933 they did not believe in themselves. One entrepreneur had hoped that God would forgive him for having voted for Hoover. But the mood of humility did not last long. Reverting to time-honored postures, businessmen could not forgive Roosevelt for having saved them from extinction. They behaved like drowning men who attack their rescuer. When the SEC commissioners came to visit the Stock Exchange in New York, employees and brokers were asked not to boo them. A descendant of a distinguished gunpowder-making family pledged to spend his money inside the country as an expression of concern over the plight of the nation. *Fortune* deplored the fact that it cost forty thousand dollars to introduce a young lady to society. And J. P. Morgan predicted that civilization would founder if the leisure class were to be destroyed. (By the leisure class he meant all those persons who could hire servants.) There remained a sharp contrast between the six-figure salaries of the potentates and the $22.50 per week earnings of laborers fortunate enough to have jobs.

By 1934 the business community was in firm opposition to the New Deal, and it was by no means loyal. To the businessman, FDR headed a totalitarian state representing, according to Herbert Hoover, a "stupendous invasion of the whole spirit of liberty." Fostered by reckless third-rate professors, the New Deal was dictatorship gone berserk. It was destroying American self-reliance, though the self-reliance of the nineteen-twenties was not mentioned. John J. Raskob complained bitterly that Negroes on his plantation in South Carolina were refusing to work because the Government had given them easy jobs. The Liberty League was formed to foster the views of the rich and to channel opposition to the New Deal. Its goal was to teach regard for the rights of individuals and to compel the Government to exercise respect for private enterprise. About two-thirds of the newspapers were virulently hostile to Roosevelt and his Administration. Even the proposal in 1936 to introduce social security was grist for the propaganda mills of business. Warnings were placed in pay envelopes charging that workers would never see their withheld money again. Only the people supported Roosevelt, and in 1936 they made it clear whom they wanted as President and what they expected him to do. Meanwhile, the New Deal was dragging business into the twentieth century, screaming and unwilling.

CHAPTER 17 The Corporate Takeover

The post World War II period in American business has been a success story of revival and seemingly endless prosperity. When the nation entered the War, the Depression had been buried in its bones like a never-ending fever. The vast outlays occasioned by the war effort had engendered a repressed demand and unused purchasing power that exploded after 1945 with such force that all the dour predictions of the economists proved groundless. In the early nineteen-forties the population had grown to 137,-000,000; twenty years later, there were 180,000,000 heads to count. In the same period, the gross national product went from $230,000,000,000 in real dollars to $500,000,000,000. The result was a marked increase in per-capita real income. Steel production jumped in the two decades by more than a third, aluminum output was up ninefold, oil production doubled, almost twice as many automobiles were now on the road, and expenditures for housing had increased by 60 per cent. The United States became a wonder in the world: a perpetually prosperous nation.

Yet two persistent problems gnawed at its vitals: income distribution remained lopsided, so that not everyone shared in the newly attained paradise, and stability kept teetering on the knife-edge of recession. While the sort of poverty that had been so pervasive in the thirties had clearly diminished, America seemed unable to grapple with the hard core: the rural poor, the Negro and other ethnic minorities, the aged, and the low-paid workers. The income line that marked off the lowest fifth in the income scale was $2,400 in 1950; but, said the Department of Labor, it required $3,700 to support a family of four on a "modest but adequate budget." In 1935 the lowest fifth got 4.1 per cent of total income; in 1950 the lowest fifth got 4.8 per cent; in 1967, the figure was virtually the same. In the same years the richest fifth's share hovered between 44 and 45 per cent. There had not been much substantial change in relative patterns of distribution. Whatever improvement there had been stemmed from an upward shift in the entire scale. Meanwhile, poverty was threatening to become a chronic ailment.

For even during the postwar booms, full employment remained an unattainable goal. There were three recessions—in 1948–49, 1953–54, and 1957–58—each of which left behind a residue of unemployed, until by mid-1961 the unemployment rate reached almost 7 per cent, a staggering figure for a prosperous economy. Moreover, the unemployed were now at the bottom of the manpower pool, where stagnation was buttressed by lack of skills and lack of education. It was said that changes in technology were enforcing new educational requirements that the unemployed did not possess. Then, in the nineteen-sixties, whatever impact technological changes may have generated was submerged in the exigencies of war, this time in Southeast Asia. Aggregate demand, stimulated by war outlays, sharply reduced the unemployment rate. Nevertheless, vast needs for roads, hospitals, schools, and sheer environmental quality remained unfilled, despite alarums raised among concerned persons. There was ample reason for such alarums, for Lake Michigan had begun to die of pollution, and people in the cities were gasping as smog replaced air. But when government sought to enforce corrective regulations, or to insist on safety in automobiles, certain business elements were sure to cry out in dismay.

Meanwhile, business itself was acquiring attributes of elephantiasis. A company that had had assets of $250,000,000 in 1949 would have needed $375,000,000 to hold on to its ranking a decade later. In the nineteen-sixties, annual sales of $1,000,000,000 were not unusual. In 1968 there were more than one hundred industrial firms with sales in excess of $1,000-000,000; almost fifty banks had deposits exceeding $1,000,000,000; there were almost thirty insurance companies with assets of over $1,000,000,000; sales of twenty merchandising firms went above that figure; and more than thirty utilities showed assets that allowed them to join the circle. Indeed, the sales of one corporation, General Motors, were equivalent to almost 3 per cent of the gross national product.

Large corporations so dominated the economy that the welfare of the nation was now largely dependent on their success. Some argued from numbers—after all, there were still at least 5,000,000 enterprises in the United States—the big fellows did not account for everything. But such arguments ignored the patent fact that most of these enterprises were far too small to exert any weight in the balance. Some 2,000,000 firms could be found in retailing, the last refuge of the individual entrepreneur, who in any case was being displaced by the giant department store and large supermarket operator. Indeed, the 500 largest industrial firms had sales in 1969 equivalent to almost half the gross national product, a gain of some 8 per cent over 1962. Of all the active enterprises in the United States only about 2,500 could be counted as economically significant, and these were controlled by no more than one-tenth of 1 per cent of the recorded stockholders. More and more, the major economic activity of the nation was being sustained by the large corporations.

Moreover, new faces began to appear among the billionaires. As Ferdinand Lundberg has remarked, there was room at the top in postwar America. J. Paul Getty, one of the newer oil-rich magnates, was reputed in 1969 to be the world's wealthiest man. He had made his first million dollars in 1916 at the age twenty-three as an oil wildcatter, but an inheritance of $15,000,000 that grew over the years to $700,000,000 constituted the foundation of his fortune. In the nineteen-thirties, when prices were low, he began to buy into the Pacific Western Oil Company and Tidewater Associated Oil. Within a few years, an involved sequence of stock purchases brought him control of Tidewater, despite opposition from the Standard Oil people, whom he succeeded in outwitting—no small feat. In 1937, he secured control of another sizable firm, Mission Development Company. Getty now holds almost 80 per cent of Getty Oil, which in turn controls Mission; the latter holds majority shares in Tidewater and Skelly Oil. The combined value of Getty, Skelly, and Tidewater is well over $3,500,000,000. Though his companies are not as fully integrated as other large oil firms, Getty manages to hold his own, ruling his empire quietly from a mansion near London. In the manner of an old-fashioned entrepreneur, he has avoided publicity and politics.

Other oil magnates have been less retiring about political affairs. H. L. Hunt, whose wealth has been estimated at around $500,000,000, has sponsored numerous right-wing political ventures, some of them close to the lunatic fringe. Hunt approaches the Henry Ford paradigm, subsidizing radio programs that broadcast sentiments redolent of the red-necked, spittoon-filling, Fundamentalist, cracker-barrel philosophy of the Ku Klux Klan. His subsidiaries are funneled through a number of foundations whose purposes have not yet been questioned by the Internal Revenue Service. Hunt has been rather tight-fisted with outright political gifts, even to the Republican party, which for him may not be far enough to the right. Yet when oil-depletion allowances are even mildly threatened, as in the early days of the Kennedy Administration, Hunt's largesse to the opposition seemed ample enough. The Hunt philosophy appears to be a variant of nineteenth-century Know-Nothingism, in the modern version of which all Presidents after Coolidge have been wild-eyed radicals.

Supplementing Hunt's politics were those of Clint Murchison and Sid Richardson, also Texas oil millionaires. To be sure, their views were not so extreme as Hunt's, but they occupied the right spectrum nevertheless. Murchison and Richardson started with buying and selling oil leases, and by the nineteen-thirties had built up the Southern Union Gas Company and American Liberty Oil Company, both of which were later sold at handsome profits. Murchison's business interests were quite diversified, branching into insurance, transportation, and banking. When Robert Young sought help in wresting the New York Central away from the Vanderbilt interests in the nineteen-fifties, Murchison and Richardson joined in with dispatch. In 1962, Richardson's $70,000,000 foundation disbursed $14,500, hardly a munificent sum. Yet the foundation enabled him to claim a reduction of 14 per cent in maximum-tax rates. Hugh Roy Cullen, who died in 1957, leaving $200,000,000, was another of the genre. He had gone into the oil business in 1917, but remained a nineteenth-century businessman, opposing the New Deal, unions, and reciprocal tariffs. Oil-depletion allowances, of course, were entirely acceptable to him.

To find a contrast to the Hunts and Cullens, one may examine the career of Everetts Lee DeGolyer, a man of scientific achievements who came to be known as the "father of American geophysics." A trained geologist and engineer, DeGolyer revolutionized techniques of the search for oil, applying scientific methods to a study of oil-dome characteristics. Although himself an oil magnate, DeGolyer had an impressive list of publications, lectured at various universities, and served for a while as professor of geology at the University of Texas. Had he not spent so much of his time in scholarly pursuits he would have been an even wealthier man than he was.

But by the nineteen-sixties, the personal touch was no longer the dominant motif in American business. It was the impersonal corporate entity that was to set the tone of the economic environment. And the corporation was to grow by acquisition, swallowing other corporations like an anaconda. The merger became the classic American way of building an industrial empire. In Europe, where the cartel had usually been employed, some concession was made to individual corporate identity. But here businessmen preferred to buy out their rivals, taking over plants and assets *in toto* and fusing disparate enterprises into new and wonderfully complex organizations. Bringing together plants, financial structures, and selling apparatuses, the merger, which became something of an imperative in American business, was largely made possible by the ineffectiveness of the antitrust laws. These laws, sufficient for controlling loose arrangements, such as trade associations, were unable until 1950 to place any restraint at all on merger activity. A Clayton Act amendment in that year made mergers which tend "substantially to lessen competition" legally dubious. Of course, the question of when competition was *not* reduced in an industrial combination was difficult for a jurist to decide, as is illustrated by the ruling of Federal Judge W. J. LaBuy, who dismissed antitrust charges against du Pont, General Motors, and United States Rubber. This distinguished jurist held, among other things, that there was no proof that du Pont controlled General Motors, even though at times it was voting 51 per cent of the stock at stockholders' meetings.

The first great merger movement took place about 1898 to 1904. The underlying factors in this wave included a rapidly growing market for mass-produced goods, thus irrevocably destroying the century-old grip of local parochial monopolies and markets. When these became national in scope, a smaller merchant or manufacturer might no longer expect to retain leadership at home simply because he held a locational advantage. For this he had to thank the fantastic growth of cheap transportation facilities. In addition, technological advances inexorably increased the ratio of fixed to variable costs. The businessman suddenly faced the problem of idle capacity and overhead. The first solution was a price war calculated to destroy his rivals; but such a war only created a dilemma, for the ensuing cutthroat competition threatened to wipe out everyone. And so there came a realization that "live and let live" should be the ideal rule. Even better, some thought, would be "living together as one," for then anxieties concerning mavericks who might willy-nilly cut prices could be entirely eliminated.

The kind of forces that were joined during the first wave of mergers was epitomized by the spectacular case of the United States Steel Corporation. After 1904, the American public, giving vent to its traditional hostility toward corporate bigness, began to clamor for a breakup of the trusts. Businessmen themselves were calling for a temporary halt in empire building, not merely to digest what they had already absorbed, but also to gather strength for the expected economic storms: these broke out in 1907. Then came World War I.

A favorable climate for a second wave of mergers was created by postwar optimism. Professional promoters, discovering that capital was readily available, prepared to turn an easy profit. From 1919 to 1921 mergers were initiated, either through holding companies or outright consolidations, expressly for the purpose of taking advantage of a bull market in securities. New companies meant new stocks, and in a rising market a handsome gain could be easily recognized. So far as industry itself was concerned, the major motivations for mergers stemmed either from a desire to establish vertical combines, thereby ensuring a regular supply of raw materials, or from a need to rationalize sales and marketing operations.

By 1926, the third-wave period, a number of new industries—motion pictures, public utilities, radios, automobiles—had reached a state of economic maturity. But the business community did not hesitate to subject them to reorganization, combination, and merger. Nor did they cease with the onset of the Depression. From 1932 to 1938, according to a Federal Trade Commission report, there were numerous consolidations in which the outstanding feature was the absorption of small firms by large ones. In the steel industry, during this time, firms with $3,000,000,000 in assets swallowed firms worth $217,000,000; in auto accessories, $377,-000,000 in assets took over $28,000,000; in oil $832,000,000 absorbed $42,000,000.

The greatest merger movement of all occurred in the nineteen-sixties, yet curiously enough, an affluent society paid it little mind. In the post-World War II period, the FTC found that there had been about seven hundred to eight hundred mergers a year. Between 1940 and 1947 more than 2,500 firms with total assets of over $5,000,000,000 disappeared: this was equal to 5.5 per cent of the total assets in manufacturing industry in 1943. Yet all this was merely a prelude to the wave of mergers that has reached its peak in recent years. Large corporations have been literally hunting for new industrial conquests. In 1967 there were almost three thousand mergers, an increase of 25 per cent over the previous year. It was estimated that more than $14,000,000,000 was spent on mergers in that year. Such firms as Litton Industries and IT&T have with notable success fed on all sorts of companies. It seemed that the desire to be big could not be suppressed.

The mergers were made easier by offering convertible securities, rather than cash, on which capital-gains taxes would have had to be paid. Moreover, attractive dividend rates inhibited conversion and protected the remaining common stock from dilution. And so the McDonnell Company, a military aircraft firm, took over Douglas Aircraft, and Ling-Temco-Vought acquired Wilson and Company, a meat packer. A further harvest could be garnered by splitting up the acquired properties and offering to the public portions of the stock on each part. Ling-Temco-Vought not only dismembered Wilson in this way but toyed with its own properties as well. The procedure was called "redeployment of assets."

There was little doubt that businessmen welcomed mergers, particularly the inside managers who kept expressing a concern with growth. Managerial interest appeared to focus on maximizing size rather than profit, thereby insuring control of the market. Pious expressions of faith in the Smithian "unseen hand" notwithstanding, rigorous price competition remained the bane of their existence. The urge to monopolize has not been the sole motivation for mergers. Frequently a profitable firm would buy up unprofitable ones for the purpose of acquiring tax losses to balance against accumulated gains. Tax benefits have been the major consideration in at least 10 per cent of the mergers of small firms and in at least 25 per cent of the large firms. Some older firms bought younger ones to take over new inventions and ideas; sometimes the motive for a merger was euphemistically described as "diversification," or the need to produce a fuller line of items. Whatever the immediate reason, the basic acquisitive urge was to achieve a dominant position in their field. The merger movement basically was a struggle for greater market strength, with personal ambition playing a not insignificant part. The natural consequence was to create monopolistic industrial structures.

Small firms were frequently willing to let themselves be hooked because the bait was so attractive. Such firms, while having a good salable product, may also have insufficient working capital. The merger of General Mills and O-Cell-O, a small sponge company, was a case in point. The latter, whose annual sales approximated $3,500,000 compared with General Mills's yearly gross of $480,000,000, was founded by three young men, previously du Pont engineers, who within a few years had built up a fairly respectable business. When they finally allowed themselves to be taken over, they were given thirty thousand shares of General Mills stock. This was about 1.4 per cent of the total, a significant chunk in a company where the largest single block was but 4 per cent. The profit on the deal amounted to $1,700 for every $100 originally invested and was subject to tax at capital-gains rates, which are considerably lower than ordinary income levies.

That concentration in industry is increased by such mergers would seem to be self-evident. George Stigler, a fairly conservative economist, said once that not one steel company had been able to add as much as 4 per cent of ingot capacity through attracting new customers, implying thereby that the greatest part of growth was to be explained by merger, consolidation, and asset purchase.

Yet the Government in the nineteen-sixties seemed reluctant to hinder the merger movment, despite the fact that some of the mergers were of a wildly improbable sort. Thus, RCA, a leading manufacturer of communications equipment and operator of the National Broadcasting Company, bought control of the Hertz car rental agency, creating a most curious combination. Aware of the torpidity of the Antitrust Division of the Justice Department, businessmen in the late nineteen-sixties decided to merge while the merging was good. The Justice Department, for its part, concluded that prosecution was not necessary, since a mere legal scowl had called off a number of undesirable merger plans. A case in point was the delay in the proposed merger of IT&T with the American Broadcasting Company, a stall that impelled IT&T to back out of the arrangement. Nevertheless, it appeared that the purpose of antitrust was not to insure "free competition" but to enhance the growth of corporations by directing attacks on them into ceremonial channels. An occasional governmental foray simply made bigness respectable. Thus antitrust entered into the mythology of American business.

As a matter of fact, antitrust never did halt the march toward bigness. There is little proof that governmental action ever reduced concentration in any sensible way; on the contrary, monopoly in the widest sense increased despite the "concern" of government. All that could be said is that legal action, or the threat of legal action, influenced the shape that mergers have assumed (that is, asset versus stock purchase, or outright amalgamation versus integration). Little effect has been exerted on prices, output, or employment policy. Whatever the form, there has been an undeniable tendency toward control from the center. In many ways, this has been due to the legal philosophy that underpinned antitrust; all too often, real collusion, or behavior close to conspiracy, had to be demonstrated to justify intervention. Yet price maintenance and restricted production can be achieved without actual collusion. Price leadership, "moral suasion," and mutual understanding among giant rivals were all acknowledged social forms for establishing monopolistic control, yet in such instances it was virtually impossible to discover conspiracy within the meaning of the law.

The simple fact was that antitrust had been a failure. The Sherman Act had been emasculated by judicial interpretation, and by 1920, it was useless. The Clayton Act fared no better. The only thing that could be said for antitrust was that it inhibited outright monopoly; business potentates thought it the better part of valor to let a few small rivals stay put. Some critics have suggested that changes in corporation law, taxes, and the patent system could create incentives for industrial giants to disgorge their subsidiaries. Whatever the merit of these notions, the merger movement has continued unabated.

During the nineteen-sixties the most dramatic merger development was the growth of conglomerates, combinations of firms operating in disparate fields. The term was derived from geology, where it refers to a mass of heterogeneous material. To some critics it implied that "those who run this new-fangled kind of corporation don't know what they're doing." As the trend accelerated, operators began to talk of "emerging" conglomerates and "mature" conglomerates, as if the slow process of geologic time had been speeded up. In reality, the form was nothing new; Andrew Mellon had done it all long before Wall Street started to talk about Litton Industries and Ling-Temco-Vought.

But the conglomerates grew bigger and the mergers more numerous. Steel companies bought TV stations, credit companies absorbed computer manufacturers, railroads acquired apparel makers, petrochemical firms purchased airlines, and hotel chains took over helicopter factories. Increasingly, mergers came to involve companies that had no economic or other logical connection. The FTC estimated that four-fifths of the mergers in 1967 were conglomerate. The agency was concerned that the movement might in fact increase concentration: at any rate, it appeared that conglomerates enhanced economic power. It was dubious that the growth of such companies reflected improvements in products: they reflected, rather, the attraction of empire building. The hunger for acquisitions was assuaged by plunging into debt or issuing new securities to buy up other corporations. Of course, such flotations made the conglomerates the darlings of Wall Street.

One of the more spectacular conglomerates was the one engineered by James J. Ling, a high school dropout, who began with a modest electrical business to build an empire, Ling-Temco-Vought, worth more than $2,000,000,000. His Ling Electronics, which went public with the aid of a Dallas banker, acquired Temco Electronics and Missiles, Altec, and several other firms in 1960. Borrowing $10,000,000 one year later, Ling added Chance Vought, an aircraft and missile manufacturing company with assets of $195,000,000. In 1967, another conglomerate, Greatamerica, which controlled insurance firms, an airline, and a bank, was brought into the combine. In all, Ling carried through more than thirty mergers after the acquisition of Chance Vought. The technique was always the same: a purchase of majority control with borrowed cash, followed by a transfer of the victim firm's outstanding shares in exchange for Ling-Temco-Vought securities. Most of the debt is then transferred to the new subsidiary. Ling lives as well as any Texas oilman, with a home constructed like a roadside motel, estimated to be worth $1,500,000.

The technique for taking over another firm often resembles an old-fashioned proxy fight or corporate raid. The conglomerate would tender an attractive offer for a bloc of the victim's stock. Brokers would then move in to purchase as much as they could on the open market and resell to the hungry conglomerate; the prospective takeover might be fought off with counterbids, complaints to the Government, press releases, and letters to stockholders urging them to hold the line. Of course, the result is frequently to drive up the price of the stock sufficiently to discourage the conglomerate. Likely prospects for a takeover kept their ears tuned for rumors and unusual activity in their stock. Or they watched the columns of the *Wall Street Journal* and the financial pages of *The New York Times* for takeover bids to be announced, as required by the Securities and Exchange Commission in the interest of full disclosure. Yet most companies that have attracted the lustful glance of others were unable to resist being raped; their only defense was to merge with a friendly suitor, on the theory that seduction was more acceptable. Thus, Sinclair Oil resisted the blandishments of Gulf and Western Industries only to lie down with Atlantic Richfield. Power seemed to be in the hands of the attackers.

Much of the growth has been based on the expansion of paper. There was some doubt that earnings had been really enhanced by the mergers. The operators were arguing that conglomeration had a synergistic effect on earnings, that the whole was greater than the sum of the parts. But as the underlying units in most of these combinations were left to their own devices, just as they were before they had been absorbed, ordinary arithmetic still held—two plus two equaled four, not five. It was clear that the new corporate setup was simply a matter of enhancing the price of the parent stock on the market. Manipulation of price-earnings ratios by generating "growth" and "distributing" risk over a larger number of subsidiaries drew in the new lambs of the nineteen-sixties. The Wall Street wolf was now more sophisticated, but his teeth were still shiny and sharp.

Some were saying that the new conglomerates were frauds, as ever more acquisitions had to be carried through to bolster the "income" of the parent company. Complex financial operations accompanied the mergers with pyramids of paper involving new convertible securities. The "pooling of interests" was sufficient to send the price of stocks skyward like a space missile, without any change in management, production, or marketing. So long as the ratio of stock prices to earnings was low, the parent could create the illusion of having grown rapidly. Reorganizations and new securities added to the merger craze. Fancy terms were applied to new acquisitions: the purchase of a wire firm provided a "synergistic steel fabricating resource base"; a motel chain became a "leisure-time division," with the parent company announcing that it intended "to be a leader in the coming travel revolution." Gobbledygook was by no means limited to government bureaucrats.

Hanky-panky with financial statements became a favorite tool in all the financial legerdemain. Indeed, the SEC and the New York Stock Exchange, as well as the more prudent security analysts and accountants, began to question the accounting methods of the conglomerates. To some accountants, conglomerate financial statements disclosed more of a credibility gap than they did earnings pictures. A whole new galaxy of securities was having a strange impact on corporate profit-and-loss statements. The conglomerates were reluctant to show the extent of dilution in earnings stemming from convertible securities, the usual form of financial paper employed in carrying through acquisitions. While some companies, to be sure, were candid in their reporting, many others were "long on fancy artwork, dramatic charts and high-flown language, but short on information." One device was to restate the operating results of companies subsequently acquired in making a before-and-after comparison, thereby inflating apparent earnings.

The theory behind this kind of accounting was described as "pooling," on the ground that a merger was like the coming together of two rivers. One professor of accounting, who had practiced for more than three decades, confessed that there was many a conglomerate report he could not decipher. Was it essential that all the assets of a merger be commingled, as in a pool? Or should they be treated simply as an acquisition, with some losses incurred on occasion? But adjustments for such losses would be painful, because earnings could be reduced and the write-off would not usually be tax-deductible. Yet corporate officials argued that their companies had to be judged as a whole, or, as one accountant said, "like chop suey." Such juggling was described by a cynic as "the difference between a young lady who may have an occasional affair and a nymphomaniac."

One professor of accountancy was disturbed by the prospect that the pressures for "growth" generated by conglomerates would ultimately seduce the more prudent old-line companies into employing "balance sheet razzle-dazzle to please stockholders." Companies following traditional accounting practices feared that their stocks would be dumped by mutual funds and other institutions fascinated by prospective increases in earnings, even though such increases might have been engineered through liberal depreciation and dubious inventory practices. In any case, the attempt by conglomerates to force the price of their stocks up led to complicated financial maneuvering. A Harvard Business School expert commented after reading a Ling-Temco-Vought prospectus, "I've read it twice and still don't understand it. Of course, I only have a Ph.D. and teach at Harvard. On the other hand, I'm sure a lot of widows and orphans understand it."

Companies not eager to be raped by conglomerates were defending their honor by devising other accounting tricks. By altering record-keeping methods they hoped to show better earnings than current practice would ordinarily allow. Thus, they might induce investors to hold on to their stock rather than take a conglomerate's convertible security in exchange. The major device was to decelerate depreciation write-offs: instead of depreciating quickly during the early years of the life of equipment, the defenders were taking their time and applying a straight-line deduction over the full period that installations would be in operation. This method reduced immediate depreciation cost and made profits look greater. Thus one steel company that was not anxious to surrender its chastity to some lustful conglomerate was able to jack up the price of its stock from fifty dollars a share to fifty-five dollars. But of course, the accelerated depreciation was still applied for tax purposes, since that would cut tax liabilities. The newer methods were displayed only in reports to stockholders.

Accountants and analysts were not the only ones who were puzzled. Economists were uncertain how these combinations would affect the economy, nor could they say what the effect on competition might be. Some were arguing that bringing together disparate firms would not restrict competition; others said that sheer economic power could submerge the functioning of the market. For one thing, a conglomerate could keep the number of companies competing in a market from increasing. It could "outspend and outdare" a one-product rival; it could survive the failure of one of its items more easily; it could use its enormous buying power to compel suppliers to purchase from one of its subsidiaries. Some economists were not disturbed: to them market power and bigness were like obesity and pregnancy; the conditions were different and required different treatment. Yet it could not be denied that a conglomerate was much less subject to the influences of the market than a company producing a single commodity. Nor were antitrust guidelines very clear. The Supreme Court had specified in 1964 that it would not approve mergers that extended market power. Where acquisition was substituted for direct entry into competition, the court withheld its blessing. The FTC promised a detailed study of the situation. Yet the mergers continued unimpeded, sans logic. There was a growing suspicion that it all paralleled the paper expansion of the nineteen-twenties.

Interestingly, the Nixon Administration appears willing to joust with the conglomerates. In March, 1969, the Justice Department decided to move against Ling-Temco-Vought in an effort to divorce from it the Jones and Laughlin Steel corporation, the nation's sixth largest steel company, which had been ensnared by the Ling-Temco-Vought octopus. Ling-Temco-Vought had acquired no less than 63 per cent of the steel firm's shares by an exchange of bonds, stocks, and warrants, as well as by outright purchase. But as of late 1969 the case had not yet come to court, and the Justice Department had agreed to let Ling-Temco-Vought acquire additional Jones and Laughlin shares, so long as it held no more than 81 per cent. This ratio, however, represented a victory for Ling-Temco-Vought, since 80 per cent control was needed in order to consolidate tax statements, an accounting device that would save the parent company about $25,000,000 a year in taxes. Moreover, it would allow Ling-Temco-Vought to shift debt obligations to Jones and Laughlin, a tactic that the conglomerate described as "redeployment."

It appeared that the Justice Department's sudden antitrust vigor was tempered by a sympathetic concern for Ling-Temco-Vought's financial well-being. On the other hand, the conglomerates were hinting darkly that the Justice Department was attempting to protect old line Republican leadership in the major industries from a takeover by newcomers. The fact was that antitrust action against conglomerates did not develop until Jones and Laughlin, B. F. Goodrich, New York's Chemical Bank, Great American Insurance, and Pan American World Airways were threatened. Basically, the parties in the battles were the old establishment and the *nouveau riche*.

In any case, the conglomerates did not seem to be overly disturbed by renewed antitrust action. Moreover, they had their defenders who argued that much good had come of the search for "investment values," a search that was shaking up otherwise complacent managements. One conglomerate protagonist hoped that the Federal Government would not overreact "to give undue protection" to the corporate *status quo*.

True enough, some conglomerates have stubbed their toes on occasion. For example, Northwest Industries gave up a seven-month battle in 1969 to take over B. F. Goodrich, giving some cheer to old-line corporations. It was the first time since 1965, when conglomerates began to display their voracious appetites, that one had met its comeuppance. Until then they had seemed invincible.

Goodrich appeared to be just the right sort of victim. The one-hundred-year-old rubber company had been an indifferent profit-maker in recent years. Its profits had increased only about 2 per cent a year since

1958, while its rivals—Goodyear and Firestone—had been gaining about 8 per cent a year. Goodrich management was conservative and cautious, as befitted a firm headed by a prudent economist. The ratio of debt to equity was small, suggesting an unwillingness to tap capital markets. Its capital structure made the company a relatively attractive one for a conglomerate takeover. It was paying out too much in dividends; its investment in equipment in relation to labor costs was too low; and it was losing a significant portion of the tire market to Goodyear.

Northwest Industries, headed by Ben Heineman, had taken over the Chicago and Northwestern Railroad in 1956 and had not only made the trains run on time, but had actually extracted a profit from the expiring railroad. The Chicago and Northwestern became a holding company in 1967, then merged with the Philadelphia and Reading Corporation, a small conglomerate. Heineman had tried once before to take over Goodrich, in 1968, but had failed. Then came the final battle in January, 1969. On the twentieth of that month Heineman bid for every Goodrich share that was tendered. Goodrich publicly called the offer "reckless," but privately resigned itself to a new management. Northwest held 5 per cent of Goodrich shares and Loew Theaters, associated with Northwest, held another 2.5 per cent.

But Goodrich responded with three law firms, two public relations experts, two investment banks, and one accountant, all of whom prepared glowing forecasts of the company's future that were directed to Goodrich stockholders. A deal was worked out with Gulf Oil to acquire some of the latter's properties for stock, locking up 5 per cent of Goodrich stock in Gulf's safe. In March, Goodrich bought the Motor Freight Corporation for some 55,000 shares of Goodrich stock, thereby further diluting Northwest's holdings. Besides, as Motor Freight's routes ran close to Chicago and Northwestern, Goodrich contended that any shotgun marriage with Northwest would have to be approved by the ICC. As a last line of defense, the election of directors was staggered, so that even if Northwest acquired a majority of the shares it could not gain control of Goodrich until 1971. Then came shots from the Justice Department directed at Northwest, and while the conglomerate survived the antitrust attack, the price of its stock began to slide. Goodrich stock also fell, but by this time, Northwest had lost heart. Further, it could not dispose of its Goodrich stock without a rather substantial loss, as its January tender offer had been in the 60's while the price now was in the 30's. Old-time managements throughout the country were sleeping more soundly.

Ling-Temco-Vought also has had its problems. Earnings expectations in 1969 were not fully met. The company had blamed a strike at Jones and Laughlin, where an arbitrator awarded incentive pay scales that were higher than anticipated. Other subsidiaries were having raw-materials problems, Braniff Airways was overstaffed, interest rates on short-term debt had been unbearable, and antitrust suits were depressing the price of Jones and Laughlin debentures. All this meant more redeployment for Ling-Temco-Vought—or reorganization—to shake up the management staffs of its subsidiaries and also to see what could be done by way of tax savings. In any case, Ling-Temco-Vought still had its antitrust suit—it was just possible that the court would decide that a conglomerate *is* a threat to free competition.

More upsetting was that the buffeting conglomerate shares were getting in the stock market. By the middle of 1970 their glamor had been tarnished, and conglomerates no longer seemed to be the "highest form of creative capitalism." It was discovered that they were not more efficient than other corporations, that earnings per share were not always as high as anticipated, and that growth was not unlimited. Indeed, all that had happened was the absorption of more and more firms making conglomerates larger and fatter than ever. But the promised profits failed to materialize, except in a few really well-managed companies. And, as Wall Street brokers had been pushing conglomerate shares onto a gullible market, the sudden recognition that there was more puff than profit in a conglomerate led to some sickening collapses in stock values. The parallel with the nineteen-twenties was most disconcerting.,

Corporations also became transnational in character. American firms developed manufacturing facilities overseas, coming to play a significant role in the economic life of the countries concerned. Not only was it necessary to establish relationships with foreign governments, but it also became more difficult for government policy in the United States to have any effect on such corporations. These included IBM, which produced three-fourths of the world's computers; Standard Oil of New Jersey; General Motors; Ford; and Alcoa. One authority has estimated that by the end of the century the world economy will be dominated by some two hundred large corporations responsible for the greater part of world industrial production. For all transnationals, domestic and foreign-based, investments had risen from $15,000,000,000 in 1940 to about $100,000,000,000 a quarter of a century later.

For some companies, foreign investments were even more important than domestic operations. In 1962 the Singer Sewing Machine Company, for example, drew 52 per cent of its sales from overseas, and 65 per cent of its assets were in foreign nations. Colgate-Palmolive's foreign subsidiaries supplied 54 per cent of total sales, and Europe was a more important market for Standard Oil than the United States. There was concern that such developments would upset the balance of payments, despite the inflow of dividends, and that the huge flow of transactions internal to the transnationals would escape whatever controls the Government might wish to exercise through monetary or fiscal policies. When General Motors decided to halt shipments of cars from Australia to Japan, leaving the latter to its California plants, Australia was confronted by Japanese imports without any car exports to counterbalance the inflow. When Ford and General Motors decide in Detroit to curtail either German or English car shipments to the United States, they can easily generate resentment. Moreover, foreign nations discover that their economic plans may be frustrated by the sheer power and flexibility of the transnational corporation. In self-defense, foreign nations may have to control (through an instrumentality such as the Common Market) the investment plans and capital movements of international corporations. Some of the American-based firms believe that employing nationals in their foreign subsidiaries will minimize hostility. But this does nothing to modulate their impact on foreign economies.

Here, corporate power was often expressed through control of prices. Most major industries had long since become oligopolistic, that is, dominated by a few. The rigidities in price structure that oligopolies introduced were bound to have a harmful effect on the consumer. A case in point was the drug industry, which had been subjected to close scrutiny by the late Senator Estes Kefauver. The industry's advertising had been directed to nonprice features, with emphasis on brand names, though it had been long known that advertised drugs were substantially cheaper when sold under their generic or chemical names. The Senate investigation disclosed, for example, that cortisone derivatives used in the treatment of arthritis were ten times more expensive when sold under brand names rather than generic names. A pill that cost 1.5 cents to make was sold to patients for 3 cents, a twentyfold jump. Drug manufacturers excused themselves by observing that the price was still less than the cost of a milkshake. Further, promotion and advertising costs, they explained, were quite heavy: in one company, these averaged 32.5 cents out of every sales dollar. And when a drug was controlled by a patent, the price to the consumer really mounted. Drug companies encouraged doctors to prescribe only brand items distributed through "detail" men, a trade euphemism for salesmen.

Though the price of a drug might be no more than the cost of a candy bar, for older persons on meager pensions three pills a day amounted to an expensive sweet tooth. The manufacturing cost of one antidiabetic tablet was $13.11 per thousand: the druggist paid $83.40; it went to the patient for $139.00. The pyramiding of markups was more than tenfold. As it was a patented item, there was nothing for the patient to do but pay the bill. Senator Kefauver disclosed that foreign drugs had markedly lower price tags. With such a price structure profit rates were astronomical. *Fortune's* list of the five hundred leading industrials showed that some drug companies enjoyed a 38 per cent rate of return on invested capital: the average for the entire list was 9.5 per cent.

At the same time other industries were insisting on government subsidies, demonstrating that businessmen were still not in the least shy about seeking government aid. An outstanding example was the merchant marine, the industry that builds, sails, and mans ships flying the American flag. Annual government subsidies to the industry averaged $400,000,000 a year in the postwar period. Since 1936, when the present subsidy law was passed, total aid to the merchant marine had come to $4,000,000,000. Yet, as one writer remarked, it was only a leaky ship that the nation had purchased, for the simple fact was American vessels could not compete with those of other nations. The share of foreign trade carried in American bottoms had plummeted from a high of 68 per cent in 1945 to 7 per cent in 1963. As far back as the nineteen-thirties, congressional investigators had demonstrated that the subsidy system merely supported inefficiency and corporate corruption. For all its outlay, when it came to meeting the logistical requirements of the war in Vietnam, the Government had to call back old ships long since retired to mothballs. Why was such a situation tolerated? The reasons could be traced to the great political weight and the strenuous lobbying of the industry, often in tandem with the unions.

Increasingly, the conviction has grown that the corporation has become a system of private government structured along hierarchical lines very much like a totalitarian state. Lacking constitutional guidelines, many threatened to become lawless. Their economic power and strength, and the strength of the nation, rested in the hands of a few thousand men in control of the corporate bureaucracy. Indeed, in ranking the major United States corporations and governments by size of income or revenue, there were about eight private corporations that followed the Federal Government before any of the fifty states were reached.

In recent years a relatively small oligarchy from the same milieu, whose members deal almost exclusively with each other, and possess no ownership relation of any sort, have come to represent *the* power center of the corporation. Hence the hope expressed by some corporate defenders that the corporation could be "constitutionalized" to make it responsive to the wishes of its "members," the stockholders, was a rather vain one. In fact, it became technically difficult to impose a proper exercise of the corporate franchise. The National City Bank once listed fifty-six large corporations with more than 50,000 stockholders each, and twenty-seven with more than 100,000. Democracy in the ordinary meaning of the word would simply become chaos. The very diffusion of stockholdings make government in the usual sense impossible. Even the 5 or 6 per cent of stockowners who held the bulk of outstanding shares were too numerous to manage the corporations effectively, for they still numbered over a 1,000,000 persons. Thus, despite some concentration in stockholdings, dispersion was sufficient to create a passive attitude. Further, most stockowners were much too concerned with prices on the exchange to be genuinely interested in running a corporation. Besides, political analogies holding stockholders to be the ultimate source of power were false, as stockholders were not the ones governed in a corporation. Rather the governed were the direct participants in the economic and industrial activities dominated by the corporation; they were mainly workers and suppliers. It was here that government within the corporation began.

The passive nature of the stockholders allowed control to be held by a managerial corps. Sometimes more direct devices were employed, as in the case of the Sears, Roebuck pension plan. Nor did voting rights given to future pensioners in similar arrangements in Standard Oil, Union Carbide, or the Celanese Corporation affect the continuing control of managerial insiders, for there would have had to be some unity of purpose and some sort of bloc voting for a real change to take place. The likelihood of this ever occurring was dim.

Robert A. Gordon, a leading economist, once demonstrated that majority ownership was the *least* common mode of control in the larger nonfinancial enterprises. Minority control was most typical in more than half the cases he studied, while stock dispersion was so widespread in another 34 per cent of the cases that management was able to do quite as it pleased.

Might increased common-stock purchases by financial intermediaries—banks, insurance companies, invesment trusts, mutuals, and pension funds—have led to a new kind of finance capitalism? In fact this was unlikely. True, most of the $30,000,000,000 or so of the stockholdings of these institutions were concentrated in a few hundred blue-chip issues. Such investments stemmed mainly from a need for safety and a good yield. In almost all instances, those who ran the financial intermediaries transmitted their proxies to incumbent managements without question. If they disliked what management was doing, the stock was simply sold on the exchange. This often did more to rattle a board of directors than a threatened proxy fight.

Of course, managers do frequently own stock in their own corporations, yet Gordon's data showed that all the members of his boards of directors, plus all corporate officers, held only about 2 per cent of the voting shares in their firms. In only 20 per cent of the companies studied did management hold more than 10 per cent of voting stock. This did not mean that officers had no financial stake in their corporations, for 1 per cent of $200,000,000 in outstanding shares is $2,000,000, and at a 5 per cent yield this could bring a neat $100,000 per annum. The executive did indeed have a keen financial interest in his organization, even though he didn't "own" it. He thus had sufficient reason to welcome the control provided by the modern corporation; when other stockholders tried to rebel, he was apt to view their action as a peasants' revolt to be crushed.

This was the reality of the corporation: noncorporeal property, proxies, and the centralization of power. We had now a managed economy in which the central question was: for whom is the managing done? Obviously not for those subject to the power of the archon, the man at the top. His rule led rather to a system of commands and internal sanctions which created a tightly knit operational code. As a result, the oligarchs had successfully disfranchised the mass of stockholders and, unless restrained by the countervailing power of a labor union or a government agency, were able to injure workers, suppliers, and customers. And such countervailance was not always forthcoming: as in the case of the electrical conspiracy, countervailance often occurred after the damage had been done.

The malefic power of the corporation was most clearly exposed in its relationships with the consumer and his family. Here countervailing power was utterly absent. Here producer and consumer proved to be unequal antagonists. One possessed unbounded economic horizons; the other was severly limited as to what he could do, dependent on the sale of labor services, and subject to ailment and accident. One produced commodities of dubious quality; the other had to buy what was available. One was a paragon of efficiency; the other a backward practitioner of the art of spending money. One had vast financial resources at its command; the other, despite the availability of installment credit, suffered from serious economic disability. One invested in the latest physical equipment; the other was frequently unable to make proper provision for human capital. One could build new plants in the suburbs; the other had to accept such services as the city offered, and these were usually inadequate. Yet it was the consumer who was supposed to be the beneficiary of whatever the corporation did. In reality, the consumer had long since lost his sovereignty and his supposed capacity to influence the social and economic order. Estranged from the sphere of production by technology, he had long since forgotten what property meant, which itself had been attenuated to the point where it no longer had substance.

Large corporations had come to control a significant part of the economy and of society. Indeed as society became increasingly dependent on the corporation, the latter's independence was correspondingly increased. Corporate directives and decisions acquired the force of law, as accommodation to that law became the quintessence of adaptability. Self-appointed corporate guardians emerged, responsible only to themselves. Whatever motion they generated in their capacity as corporate managers became a way of validating their own exercise of power. It was all that corporate managers required.

CHAPTER 18 The Age of Space

According to Henry Ladd Smith, an historian of aviation, the story of air transportation was very much like that of the railroads, though somewhat telescoped in time. Both businesses had pioneers and heroes, and both had adventurous innovators who, after revealing the true potentials of their enterprises, were then skillfully squeezed out by hungry promoters. In air transport, there was the same march to consolidation and big business and the same robber-baron ruthlessness as had occurred in nineteenth-century railroading.

Although the Wright brothers, Orville and Wilbur, had demonstrated the practicality of heavier-than-air flight in 1903, the airplane was for a long time considered little more than a toy. As with most technological innovations, the origin of the airplane could be traced to early experiments. In the eighteenth century, Sir George Cayley had demonstrated the principles of aerodynamics; William Henson built a motor for a flying machine in the nineteenth century; and Otto Lilienthal and Samuel Langley attempted actual flight. But these efforts were not successful, and Simon Newcomb, an eminent mathematician, "proved" that flight was impossible. The Wright brothers remained unconvinced; working out their own aerodynamic tables, they built a machine at Kitty Hawk, North Carolina, where the winds were stronger than anywhere else in the country, and flew for as much as forty yards. Thus the day of the birdman dawned on the sand dunes of the Carolinas.

Nevertheless, the Government evinced scant interest. By World War I there was little growth to show that a new industry had been born; not until combat possibilities were demonstrated and bombs tossed from airplanes by hand did the United States Government awaken to the intriguing prospects of flight. The war brought on a crash program to build flying instruments, but it contributed little to either winning the war or advancing aviation. By the time of the Armistice, the Government had spent almost a billion dollars on airplanes, with little to show for its sudden enthusiasm. Of the sixteen firms that were given wartime contracts, only six really knew how to build planes. Further, the first of several scandals in aircraft erupted: a committee headed by Charles Evans Hughes censured aircraft companies for behavior tantamount to fraud. Immediately after the war, all contracts were canceled, and the nascent industry collapsed. Production dropped from 14,000 planes in 1918 to 260 in 1920. As there was no commercial market, the future looked bleak indeed.

The strongest company was Glenn Curtiss in Buffalo; Glenn Martin held on desperately in Cleveland; an order to recondition 50 wartime airplanes for the Army saved Boeing in Seattle. New companies were initiated by seemingly foolhardy entrepreneurs. A Navy order helped Donald Douglas gain a foothold in Los Angeles, and W. B. Stout began to build all-metal planes, precursors of Ford's famed trimotor, the *Tin Goose*. By 1925 aircraft output had gone up to 780 planes.

What the industry needed was Government help. That was provided by the initiation of subsidies for air mail. The Post Office Department had pioneered with air-mail service, but flight had not been much of an improvement, if any at all, over railroads. Experiments were conducted with night flying, but safety requirements were still lacking: there was virtually no inspection of aircraft, there was a paucity of skilled pilots, airports were few and far between, airways had not yet been charted, and there was as yet no adequate nationwide weather service. Flying was still in its era of daring and heroism.

Finally, in 1925, the Kelly Bill authorized the Postmaster General to let contracts for air mail. Now the aircraft builders, most of whom also controlled the early carriers, could have a chance for profit. So did the Wall Street promoters, and under the guise of introducing order into a chaotic infant industry, they began to maneuver for control. As with the railroads, the major technique was sponsoring consolidation and mergers, a device for squeezing out the maverick and the recalcitrant. The first major combination brought together Boeing Aircraft, Boeing Air Transport, and Pacific Air Transport in 1929, eventuating in United Aircraft and Transport. This signaled Wall Street's entrance into the industry on a significant scale: the underwriter was the National City Bank. Pratt and Whitney and various motor manufacturers, propeller companies, and makers of light private planes were also drawn into the fold. The moving spirit was F. B. Rentschler, whose brother happened to be president of National City. A large slice of the capitalization of the 2,500,000 shares of common and the 1,000,000 shares of preferred went to the banking firm.

Hayden Stone of Boston and Bancamerica teamed up to merge Curtiss–Wright, Eastern Aircraft, Ford Instrument, and General Aviation into

North American. The Aviation Corporation (AVCO) entered the picture in a big way in 1929, with Juan Trippe as its principal figure. Trippe had started in the industry after graduation from Yale with an air-taxi service on Long Island. Later he formed Eastern Air Transport, then merged with Colonial Airways, carrying mail from New York to Boston. Vanderbilt help played no small part in Trippe's rise to the top. In 1927 Trippe managed to secure landing rights in Cuba, thus laying the foundation for his Pan American Airways. He moved up and down South America, working out landing agreements and deals with local airlines. By the nineteen-thirties he was pushing across the Pacific toward Asia. Meanwhile AVCO was emerging as one of the octopuses of airlines by buying up airports, engine plants, airplane factories, and instrument companies. Subsidiaries were created out of subsidiaries until the maze was impenetrable.

In 1929 the value of aviation stocks reached $255,000,000; the future had a rosy hue, only to turn dark gray as the stock market collapsed. Detroit Aircraft, a major airplane builder, disappeared in 1931. North American and AVCO both had difficulty weathering the financial storm. Yet slowly air transportation was becoming established. By 1939, output reached 5,800 planes, of which 3,600 were for commercial use. It was now evident that the gathering clouds of war in Europe would mean an expanded market for the industry, signaling the end of its depressed condition. Some $85,000,000 worth of British and French war contracts was a powerful stimulant, and American entry into the war heralded maturity for the industry. It was asked to build in one year as many planes as had been produced in all the years since Kitty Hawk. With the Government's help and with the start of the "contract state" facilities were vastly expanded. Even Henry Ford, erstwhile pacifist, got into the act, making engines for Pratt and Whitney.

However, air transport, rather than aircraft building, proved to be the most fascinating aspect of the aviation story. Prior to the New Deal both were usually subsumed in a single company. At first the profit came chiefly from air-mail contracts. As fees were based on weight, the airlines were barely interested in passenger service, and many lines did not even bother to install seats. Only those lines lacking a Government contract were to make special efforts to carry human cargo. Interest in the airlines was aroused by Charles Lindbergh's solo flight across the Atlantic in 1927. Stocks boomed, though often the speculators did not know what they were buying. One stock that benefited from the craze was the Seaboard Airline, a railroad from New York to Florida; the speculators thought the name was sufficient. Airlines with contracts mailed telephone books back and forth and sought out heavy parcels to increase the weight carried. One line shipped Christmas cards weighing a shade under the prescribed postal limit, making a profit of nine cents per card.

In 1928, Walter F. Brown became Hoover's Postmaster General and promptly made himself dictator of the aviation industry. He wanted transcontinental lines with feeder routes, and to foster such an empire, one that would be controlled by private industry, he handed out air-mail contracts only to those companies he thought could do the job he wanted. Brown forced companies to extend their lines, even when they were not ready to do so, and he granted contracts by "negotiation" rather than by bid, as specified by Congress. A shotgun marriage was forced through between Transcontinental Air Transport and Western Air Express to create Trans World Airlines. The Postmaster General had thought such a merger would be desirable. Illegal terms were inserted into advertisements for bids in order to exclude "independents," those lines in disfavor with the Post Office Department. Mail routes were parceled out at "spoils conferences" in Washington, dubious meetings in the light of the antitrust laws. When TWA was given an award in 1930, the Controller General declared it to be illegal, as a rival's bid had been lower. It was rumored that TWA had been helped by the presence of Herbert Hoover, Jr., on its payroll. Whenever an independent opposed these high-handed methods, it was simply bought out by the favored companies, as in the case of E. P. Halliburton, a tough Oklahoma oilman, who was bought off for $1,400,000, although his airline assets were not more than $800,000.

A few years later came the reaction. James Farley, the new Postmaster General, charged that air-mail contracts had been given to a favored few who then used their funds for "wild stock speculation." Moreover, he alleged, the contracts had been illegal, airline executives had destroyed evidence when inquiry threatened, and collusion had resulted in payments of more than $78,000,000 to the airlines between 1930 and 1933, although the actual service rendered had been but 40 per cent of that sum. Fulton Lewis, Jr., a reporter for the Hearst newspapers, discovered that Eastern Air Transport had been awarded a contract on a bid of eighty-nine cents a mile, while another firm—friendly to Lewis—had offered to carry mail over the same route for twenty-five cents a mile. When a congressional committee began to look into what seemed to be a corrupt mess, Lewis made available all kinds of sordid facts to its investigators. The rigging of bids and stock manipulation were only minor aspects of the entire tale.

It was more than FDR could take, and in February, 1934, he ordered the cancellation of air-mail contracts. The airline industry had behaved as wantonly as a streetwalker, and for the Puritans of the New Deal its disreputableness was unbearable. Pending new arrangements, Roosevelt ordered the Army to take over the air mail. The outcry by business and editorial writers was loud and bitter. Responsibility for several crashes was placed at the Administration's door, though the Army actually was doing a commendable job in delivering the mail. Of ten Army pilots killed at the time, only four died while in the mail service; the others crashed while in training or en route to their posts.

Under the new legislation, independent operators such as Tom Braniff were given a chance at the mails. Braniff had been one of those kept out by former Postmaster General Brown; his unceasing efforts to get a slice of Government business finally succeeded under the New Deal. Transport was separated from manufacturing by the new regulations, and the names of many firms were gravely changed from "ways" to "lines." Some of the less virtuous airline executives were blacklisted, but for the most part, one could observe no sharp break in management continuity. AVCO spun off American Airlines; United Aircraft was dissolved to emerge as United Airlines; TWA was separated from North American; and General Aviation gave birth to Eastern Airlines, which had the lucrative New York to Florida run. The new lines also included Braniff, National, and Northeast. Normality seemed to prevail by 1938, as new technological advances, such as retractable landing gear, wing flaps, and the controllable pitch propeller, made flying somewhat safer. By that time World War II was ready to cast its shadows. But it was the sort of darkness in which aviation could thrive and prosper.

Another war-born instrument of great significance today is the computer. It goes back to the work of Howard Aiken, who, as a graduate student at Harvard in 1937, tried to devise a machine that would solve polynomials. The International Business Machines Corporation, happy to lend its support, provided a team of four high-powered engineers, and the Automatic Sequence Controlled Calculator—Mark I—was unveiled in 1944. Mark I was an electromechanical machine with more than 760,000 parts, including a bewildering array of switches, wheels, relays, and cams, and 500 miles of wire. It was completely automatic, as it could follow instructions fed into it by a programmer. It had an input unit that utilized punched paper tape, a memory unit, an arithmetic unit, controls, and an output device—components now found in all digital computers. But it was rather slow: addition and subtraction took one-third of a second, multiplication five seconds, division sixteen seconds, and computing a logarithm to twenty decimal places took the unconscionable time of one and one-half minutes.

About a year before Mark I had been completed, scientists at the University of Pennsylvania started to construct an electronic computer that was to make the older machine as archaic as a water wheel. Dispensing with telephone relays and other electromechanical components, J. P. Eckert and John Mauchly put together eighteen thousand vacuum tubes and related equipment that could do the same switching and circuit operations as Mark I but in about a millionth of a second. Their machine, known as ENIAC (Electronic Numerical Integrator and Calculator), was able to perform five thousand additions per second. Completed in 1945, it was used to compile firing tables for ballistic trajectories, a prime war need. There were some inherent difficulties in it, however. The memory capacity was small, there were bottlenecks at both input and output stages arising from the higher speed of the arithmetic unit, and the circuitry was such that each problem required rewiring and replugging, causing frustrating delays. It was evident that something new and different would have to be built.

One day in 1944 a member of the Pennsylvania group, Herman Goldstine, met John von Neumann, the eminent mathematician, who had been working on computation techniques for solving certain partial-differential equations related to the atom bomb, and told him what Eckert, Mauchly, and he were doing. Neumann immediately associated himself with the project in a fruitful collaboration that led to EDVAC (Electronic Discrete Variable Automatic Calculator). Neumann became a confirmed believer in the computer's usefulness, especially for numerical methods to solve problems once thought beyond the scientist's capabilities. The major innovations in EDVAC, which was not completed until 1952, were the use of the binary number system, a much larger memory or storage capacity, and instructions placed into the machine itself. The basic operations were now part of the circuitry: the tedious business of plugging and unplugging each time a new problem was to be solved could be avoided.

The growth of computers has indeed been one of the marvels of modern technology. Mark I begat ENIAC, which begat EDVAC, which begat EDSAC, a machine that placed both instructions and data into the memory unit; then came RAYDAC, a second cousin to UNIVAC I. SEAC, BIZMAC, FLAC, MIDAC, and DYSEAC quickly followed, all utilizing the basic EDVAC storage idea. Mark III was born in 1950, and OARAC, a close relation, arrived three years later. The descendants increased in biblical fashion—some had no names, only numbers, but ORDVAC begat AVIDAC, and after ILLIAC came MANIAC I. A third generation of computers was created, surpassing the older vacuum-tube and solid-state systems with magnetic thin-film memories and microminiaturization, but there were some who thought that MANIAC might be an appropriate name for them all, as they had stemmed mainly from the demands of war. (In fact, while ENIAC and EDVAC were being built, rumors that they were gigantic white elephants were deliberately circulated so that enemy curiosity would be deflected.)

Since 1950, when it was thought that about a dozen large-scale machines would satisfy the requirements of science and business for years to come, the commercial electronic computer has grown to the multi-billion-dollar level. In 1963, 4,789 commercial computers costing more than $2,000,000,000 were installed, with similar outlays for programming or "software." By 1965, the total number of computers in the United States had reached 25,000; four years later the count was almost 70,000.

The giant in the industry, with sales in 1968 of almost $7,000,000,000, is IBM, which traces its origins to Herman Hollerith's Tabulating Machine Company. Hollerith was a Census Bureau statistician who devised mechanical tabulating equipment for the 1890 population count. The 1880 census had taken over seven years to complete, and the bureau was in a panic. Hollerith came to the rescue. In 1900 he produced an automatic electric sorter that handled punched cards at the rate of three hundred a minute, as well as a tabulator and key-punch machine. Three years later, Hollerith went into business for himself and began to squabble with the Census Bureau over rental fees and patent rights. Progress has been such that, in 1960, fifty statisticians and a battery of computers did the work it had taken four thousand statisticians to do in 1950. Today IBM has installed three-fourths of the computers in the world—more than ten times the number of its closest competitor, Sperry Rand. As one business magazine observed, "As a company, IBM is probably more pervasive in its influence on the way business is done than any in history. Its products, preceded by squads of salesmen and flanked by corps of educators, are changing the whole fabric of management structure in business and altering the basic methods used in science and engineering."

IBM owes its present industrial preeminence to Thomas J. Watson, a tearful sentimentalist and superb salesman who firmly believed that his frequent perorations to his employees stemmed from divine inspiration. As one biographer has said, his conception of business was compounded of mysticism, evangelism, and a sublime faith in himself. Under Watson, IBM became a paternalistic company that produced the archetypal organization man who blandly regurgitated Watson as the ultimate in human wisdom.

Watson was not the founder of IBM; it was created by Charles R. Flint, a nineteenth-century business buccaneer who was as adept with a merger and in watering stock as J. P. Morgan. Flint had been a gunrunner, a double agent in banana-republic revolutions, and an organizer of the U. S. Rubber Company. In 1911 he set up the Computer-Tabulating-Recording Company as an umbrella for a number of firms that manufactured counting and weighing equipment, among them Hollerith's Tabulating Machine Company. Computer-Tabulating-Recording was capitalized at $6,500,000, a figure that was twenty-five times the combined assets of all of its subsidiaries. In time, Watson became an officer of Computer-Tabulating-Recording.

A descendent of a Scotch-Irish family that had migrated to the United States in the eighteen-forties, Watson was born in upstate New York in 1874. He started his business career at an early age peddling pianos and organs through the rural northern tier of the state, later drifting to Buffalo, where he tried his hand at several other selling jobs. The experiences were to enhance a native skill in convincing others that goods of dubious quality were desirable. Eventually, Watson went to work for the National Cash Register Company—The Cash—becoming its most successful salesman. Indeed, so successful was he that John H. Patterson, The Cash's chief, assigned him to the task of intimidating rival firms. Patterson was determined to create a monopoly in the cash-register business, an objective that was advanced by harassing competitors with lawsuits to the point where they caved in. Watson lent a willing hand to this dubious practice, eventually capturing the used machine business for Patterson.

Though Watson was to remain with Patterson for over a decade, he never really got along with that industrial pirate. Patterson's treatment of his subordinates was strange—he was evidently jealous of the more successful ones—and one day Watson was to find his office locked. Yet he was not fired; indeed, by 1910 he had been elevated to general manager. But trouble was brewing: in 1912 Patterson, Watson, and several other officers were indicted for criminal conspiracy under the antitrust laws, and amazingly enough they were convicted. Like some later industrialists, Patterson, though himself in the dock, turned on Watson and fired him. He had done too good a job.

Without work, Watson looked up Flint, whom he had once heard give a talk at a Chamber of Commerce meeting. He was hired by Computer-Tabulating-Recording at a salary of $25,000 a year plus a share of the profits. For ten years, from 1914 to 1924, Watson labored for Computer-Tabulating-Recording, the perfect embodiment of the man in the gray flannel suit. Meanwhile, he became acquainted with George F. Johnson of the Endicott-Johnson shoe firm, from whom he learned the ways of industrial paternalism. At Computer-Tabulating-Recording, he was primarily concerned with building the sales force, a task he fulfilled with evangelical fervor. Company psalms were composed to foster the proper spirit, and employees were expected to be duly appreciative of management's efforts. But when adversity struck in the depression of 1921, many of the faithful were laid off.

In 1924, Watson became head of Computer-Tabulating-Recording, promptly changing its name to IBM. His action reflected a determination to reshape the company in his own image, and he was most successful in it. Sales increased and the value of the company's stock began to soar. There was no boss in IBM other than Watson; anyone who thought differently was committing a sin, "something like inducing carnal fantasy in a state of grace." There was but one leader and his followers were to walk in his shadow chanting,

> With Mr. Watson leading
> To greater heights we'll rise
> And keep our IBM
> Respected in all eyes.

A sign with a single word "Think" began to appear in all the company's offices and on all its desks; on occasion, a prankster would alter the "n" to an "m" or place the sign inside a toilet door with a comma after "Think" followed by "too." Before World War II employees were exclusively male WASPS, as Jews, Catholics, Negroes, and women were thought to be incapable of intoning the master's wisdom with the proper cadence. It was only after the war that some IBM research centers might be described at times as "Israel West." But the discipline and organizational mystique were never lost.

For some time during the late nineteen-forties and early nineteen-fifties, IBM made only electromechanical machines. The momentary lapse in judgment was underscored in 1948, when IBM saw the Census Bureau install Sperry Rand's UNIVAC, the first electronic computer. There was little doubt that the future was an electronic one. IBM quickly developed its numbered machines: 650, 701, 702, 704, and 705. By 1956, it was far ahead of its competitors. The transition from ordinary sorters and tabulators, used in relatively simple statistical and accounting tasks, to computers for scientific laboratories was not difficult. During the same period, the huge monolith that the elder Thomas Watson had built was decentralized by his son, who took control in 1956. Nevertheless, the corporate structure remained so complex that a distinct management committee was required to settle disputes between divisions. Not counting the World Trade Corporation, which handled overseas business as a wholly owned subsidiary, there were the Service Bureau, Electric Typewriter Division, Supplies Division, Federal Systems Division (selling equipment to Uncle Sam only), a sales division with 190 branch offices, a division for small and medium-sized data-processing systems, another for large systems, a components division, and, understandably, a research and development division. A later reorganization added the Industrial Products and Real Estate Divisions.

The emphasis has shifted from handling past data, like accounting and statistical reports, to current-information processing. The latter is the basis for "integrated systems" design, a technique intended to give the corporate officer more effective control of the business heap on which he sits. In computer jargon, the objective is to provide "real-time processing" of data so rapidly that the results are available in time to influence the process itself. In effect, the flow of information is utilized to influence events before they have passed by. This information, the businessman believes, will supply the control that supposedly eludes him.

The computer business is attractive enough to tempt others to encroach on the giant's domain, but so far they have only nibbled at the borders. None of the seven or so companies trailing IBM could really expect to displace it in the calculable future. But they were all enthusiastic and hopeful. At the start of 1963, Sperry Rand reported a large order backlog for its UNIVAC; General Electric enjoyed an almost 50 per cent sales increase over the previous year; Minneapolis-Honeywell had the highest sales-rate increase for computers in its history; RCA shipped 280 systems in 1962, an increase of 155 over 1961; Burroughs' deliveries went up from 5 systems to 70; and National Cash Register's equipment was so well received that it could require that its neophyte salesmen be college graduates. Orders for computers continued at a rapid pace.

IBM's rivals have not only imitated its sales, service, and "customer education" methods, but they also introduced faster computers with automatic-translation accessories, and attempted, at the same time, to exploit specialized markets. They have offered a bewildering variety of machines: high-speed data-handling equipment that makes possible short-wave transmissions of voice communication in the form of digits; computers that punch cards, transfer data, process, and print simultaneously; and flexible machines designed to accommodate various sorts of peripheral equipment, like tape transports and printers.

The biggest customer, of course, is the Federal Government, which has provided about half the business. The Budget Bureau estimated that total direct Federal outlays for data processing in fiscal 1964 were more than $800,000,000 and that this figure would triple by 1970. In 1963 Uncle Sam used almost 1,300 computers, as against 730 in 1961. It was a nice chunk of business; all the manufacturers have sought contracts with the Defense Department, Atomic Energy Commission, National Aeronautics and Space Administration, National Science Foundation, Institutes of Health, Census Bureau, Labor Department, Post Office, and Veterans' Bureau. In fact, the decision to pursue Government business, especially in scientific fields, enabled one of the smaller companies, Control Data Corporation, to expand with astounding rapidity from a few engineers in 1957 to 3,200 employees and $50,000,000 in sales in 1963. Control Data's emphasis has been on scientific applications for selected customers, 70 per cent of whom are among the agencies just listed. Because as much as two-thirds of the cost of a computer system may be invested in accessory equipment like readers and devices that move tape past sensing and recording heads, the company decided in 1963 to make its own. And, as is usual in successful firms, Control Data has acquired its portion of affiliates: the Bendix Computer Division, Cedar Engineering, Meiscon Corporation, and Electro-Facts (a Dutch instrument maker) have come under Control Data's expanding corporate umbrella.

Business in America was not enough, however, so the companies also went rushing overseas. In late 1963, two Australian government agencies granted an $8,500,000 order to Control Data, whose salesmen traveled 9,500 miles to underbid six other United States and British competitors. IBM had to stage a computer performance contest with a Swedish manufacturer to win a $10,000,000 contract with the Swedish Government. American computers were installed in a Ghanaian university, in a department store in Colombia, in Hong Kong, Japan, and Bombay. Although the overseas market has accounted for but one-fourth of domestic sales, it has been estimated that it will equal them by 1975. IBM's foreign sales have increased at twice the rate for installations here, and by 1970 are expected to match domestic volume. The Netherlands Automatic Information Processing Research Center has estimated that computer installations in the Common Market nations grew from 135 in 1958 to 985 by the end of 1961, with 950 on order but not completed. The center predicted 9,500 computers at work in the six European Economic Community countries alone by 1971. Of course, the appeal of computers and automation in these areas arises from labor shortages. In West Germany, for example, thousands of workers from Italy and Spain were imported to get critical work done. Process control appears essential to the viability of Western European economies.

By 1964, it was evident that American manufacturers were dominating the international computer market. Since 1960 American computer concerns had built or bought more than twenty manufacturing plants around the world, in addition to making numerous sales and licensing agreements. IBM's overseas earnings in 1964 were $124,000,000 on sales of $933,000,000. United States companies accounted for about 70 per cent of all overseas installations, a figure that was bound to be increased by General Electric's acquisition of the commercial data-processing interests of Olivetti in Italy and the Compagnie des Machines Bull in France. Although American companies have made large investments overseas, they do have to contend with nationalist sentiments: de Gaulle was able to prevent General Electric's original takeover attempt on Machines Bull and IBM has had difficulties producing its 360 system in Japan, where the government prefers to have computers built by domestic firms. Nevertheless, IBM is still the leading computer-maker in Japan, holding more than 40 per cent of the market.

The American companies, of course, by no means cultivated virgin soil overseas. Resident computer makers had their own national prestige to defend, and so IBM, Control Data, and RCA confronted the competition of English Electric, Machines Bull, Olivetti, and Telefunken. Despite the battle for markets, or perhaps because of it, cartel arrangements were started. Machines Bull, which had developed financial problems in 1963, was not unwilling to be in with General Electric for 20 per cent of its stock. But Charles de Gaulle's sense of *la gloire* led him to veto the General Electric proposal; the Americans had enough fingers in French business already. But as there was no other solution for Bull's financial distress, the General had to relent, to the shouts of the stockholders, "Long live the Yanks." And so Bull got a new lease on life, and another American company had penetrated the French market for computers at the relatively low cost of about $43,000,000. General Electric quickly followed up this coup with a deal for the Olivetti computer interests in Italy, thus becoming the second largest factor in European data processing. It seemed that IBM's hold on overseas business was to be loosened somewhat.

The intercompany connections were manifold and complex. Elliott-Automation, a large British firm, made one-fourth of its products under license from National Cash Register and other American computer makers. While International Computers absorbed Britain's EMI, Ltd., and Ferranti, Ltd., computer operations, Bull across the channel established a joint research-and-development program with Compagnie Générale de Télégraphie Sans Fils to dominate the French sector of the industry. The Banque de Paris et des Pays-Bas controlled Sans Fils and had a major interest in Bull's financial structure. Compagnie des Compteurs, which made the American Packard-Bell process computer in France under a licensing arrangement, was also controlled by the Banque de Paris. Sans Fils, in turn, had under its corporate wing a French firm that marketed the Thompson-Ramo-Wooldridge computer. In Japan, Minneapolis-Honeywell worked through Nippon Electric, Sperry Rand through Oki Electric, and RCA through Hitachi. RCA also had a licensing tie-in with Siemens & Halske in West Germany. The hands of the computer makers intertwined across the seas.

The techniques of selling computers do not differ sharply from those employed for marketing other kinds of industrial equipment. The only need is to demonstrate that a computer can reduce costs, despite the high initial investment. Institutional advertisements will ask, "What are the costs of getting out routine paper work? How many people are tied up in these operations?" It is strongly hinted that the work force, even in offices, can be reduced. The seller may have to make a fairly detailed survey of the prospect's operations before submitting a proposal. These preliminary investigations can be rather expensive for the vendor, but it is all part of the product's being sold or leased. Vendors often prefer to lease their equipment, for such an arrangement extracts more money from the client. The Air Force for example, had to be reminded by the Government's General Accounting Office that it could save almost $1,800,000 by purchasing certain leased data-processing components outright. The larger companies, like IBM, train their salesmen to be specialists in data processing in one or more major industries, with the result that they are not just old-fashioned drummers but "sales engineers." Even fashion appeal is not overlooked: a machine may come in several color schemes; the customer has his choice of Roman-gold and earth-brown, surf-green and sea-green, or steel-gray and marine-blue. Light and dark "values" are also available. And to make the whole assemply ultra chic, the seller may furnish a list of decorator ideas "coordinated" with the color selected—fluorescent lamps, floor coverings, tables, telephones, and wastepaper baskets.

Yet trouble seemed to be brewing for IBM as it came under fire from a number of sources. Control Data, which had become a major competitor by 1968, sued under the antitrust laws, charging IBM with monopoly and violations of the Sherman Act. This suit was followed by another by Data Processing Financial and General which asked the court to break up IBM's vast holdings. And the Government, beginning to scrutinize the giant, contemplated an antitrust suit in the waning days of the Johnson Administration. So large had IBM become that a $2,700 investment in its stock in 1914 would have been worth some $18,000,000 by 1968. But it was unlikely that the flurry of antitrust actions would be more than a nuisance to the company: it seemed invulnerable.

When Dwight D. Eisenhower left the White House in January, 1961, he warned in his Farewell Address against the growing influence of the "military-industrial complex." Although the speech had been written by Malcolm Moos, later president of the University of Minnesota, the mere fact that it was acceptable to the President was significant enough. Said Eisenhower, "[The] conjunction of an immense military establishment and a large arms industry is new in American experience . . . we must not fail to comprehend its grave implications [and] we must guard against the acquisition of unwarranted influence, whether sought or unsought, by the military-industrial complex. The potential for the disastrous rise of misplaced power exists and will exist." The warning was most appropriate, for, as the outgoing President had predicted, the military-industrial complex did soon become large enough to exercise the power he had feared.

Yet the alliance between the military and business had been evident in earlier years. Their ties were particularly noticeable in World War I when the economy had become sufficiently industrialized to provide fertile ground for their growth. The demand for a maximum war effort at the time led to a relaxation of the antitrust laws and a mitigation of the hostility to business that had been displayed in the years before the war. Some businessmen showed a seemingly selfless patriotism by serving as dollar-a-year men to help the Government win the war. A Council for National Defense was formed on the assumption that business could supply all the material that was needed; moreover, firms were anxious to demonstrate that they could govern themselves during the national crisis. Yet it was not uncommon for the dollar-a-year men to make certain that war contracts were directed to their own firms or those of their colleagues; there was a threat that business would repeat its behavior in earlier wars. Congress finally delimited such practices in contract awards when it passed the Lever Act. Still, even the distinguished members of the War Industries Board often found it difficult to separate public and private interests. Not until 1918 did the Administration decide to avoid appointing potentially embarrassing businessmen to the board. By then the war was almost over. Nevertheless, much of the military procurement remained under the control of businessmen; the threatened chaos was hidden by the arrival of Armistice Day.

At present the parallel with procurement in World War I seems close enough to warrant warnings such as those expressed by Eisenhower. The background was supplied by the space-and-technology race with Russia after Sputnik I. Space exploration became a surrogate for war and a gambit in international diplomacy; it served to force the arms expenditures of both the United States and Russia higher and higher. Each time the Soviets put a man into space the American military had an attack of fever. At any rate, the armed services had ample excuse to agitate for larger appropriations, even though the new hardware sought often became obsolete from a purely technological standpoint. Industries in a position to supply the esoteric equipment discovered a splendid opportunity to keep themselves in the black through the Government's readiness to provide funds for "research and development." And numerous communities that had come to rely on the prosperity generated by the Cold War made the plea that their economic health depended on outlays for space and the advanced military technology.

In 1948 defense budgets had dropped to a reasonable level of some $12,000,000,000. The Korean conflict lifted outlays on defense to more than $50,000,000,000; despite the efforts of President Eisenhower, and later of Secretary of Defense Robert McNamara, to be realistic, there seemed to be no way of stemming the rising tide. Then, with Vietnam, the total came close to $80,000,000,000. From 1950 to 1959 alone, total procurement for defense was estimated at $228,000,000,000. In fiscal 1967, half the defense budget, or $39,000,000,000, went for prime military contracts, providing the sinews that wove together the fabric of the military-industrial complex. Half of these expenditures went to some thirty-four firms, among them McDonnell Douglas Corporation, General Dynamics, General Electric, United Aircraft, AT&T, General Motors, Westinghouse, Ling-Temco-Vought, Raytheon, Bendix, and IT&T. The payroll for the armed services in the United States totaled more than $17,000,000,000. Over three-fourths of the congressional districts had one or more military installations. The whole country had a vested interest in what had become a contract state.

By the late nineteen-sixties some 22,000 prime contractors and 100,000 subcontractors relied heavily on defense business; more than seventy-five industries could be classified as Department of Defense-oriented; more than 50 per cent of the income of plane manufacturers and shipbuilders came from government contracts; and about 5,300 cities and towns depended on at least one defense plant that did business with the Pentagon. Defense agencies maintained about 5,500 bases and camps around the country, plus nine arsenals employing 57,000 workers. The trough was vast enough to keep everyone well fed.

Yet there were petulant cries from some congressmen that their districts were being treated unfairly; others complained that Texas, President Johnson's home state, was receiving a disproportionate share of Government business. When McNamara closed forty-five installations in 1964, saving some $475,000,000 a year, he received more than 150 telephone calls from angry congressmen in one day. Key members of Congress pleaded that the people back home, especially in their own districts, should not be hurt. The Georgia congressional delegation included the chairmen of the House and Senate Armed Services Committees; there were more military installations in Georgia than anywhere else. When still another new base for Georgia was proposed, a general quipped, "One more base will sink the state." Supported by representatives from South Carolina and Louisiana, who occupied strategic committee spots, southern politicians made sure that their region would have more than just a fair share of military installations. Where materiel was purchased also concerned Congress: its members often arranged for special treatment for plants back home. Defense became a more complicated, if not a more sophisticated, version of old-fashioned pork-barrel politics.

During his tenure as Secretary of Defense, McNamara did manage to withstand much of the military-industrial pressure. When finally forced to shift over to the World Bank in 1968, he observed that he had won 98 per cent of the battles with the military; indeed, he had been the only Defense Secretary who had ever been able to impose civilian control over the sprawling Pentagon empire. With the military and defense contractors chomping for a greater bite out of the public purse, McNamara did exercise a tight and somewhat restraining leash. For fiscal 1969 the armed services called for an outlay of $100,000,000,000; McNamara cut it back to $80,000,000,000. The three services mounted a furious public-relations campaign to convince Congress and the public that the nation's security was in jeopardy. Of course, interested businessmen were sympathetic to Pentagon views. Lobbying activity was carried on through the Pentagon's "legislative liaison" office, which has enjoyed a budget of almost $4,000,000. This was thirteen times the outlay of the largest private lobbyist. Pentagon lobby men were said to have organized Congress "like a Marine Corps landing."

All this was grist for the profit mills of the defense contractors, who secured the bulk of their business through negotiated agreements. From 1961 to 1967 the top fifteen defense suppliers obtained more than half of the Pentagon's business. These included Lockheed, General Dynamics, McDonnell Douglas, Boeing, United Aircraft, Raytheon, and Ling-Temco-

Vought. To insure favorable treatment, the firms stressed "good personal relations" and contributed heavily to the Navy League, the Air Force Association, and the Association of the U. S. Army. One contractor who was in danger of losing his bid induced an admiral friend to stall the decision. Another got the Secretary of the Air Force to overturn an unfavorable Pentagon response. Reliance on retired service officers to help maintain "good personal relations" was as essential as it was widespread. In 1959 more than 1,400 retired officers with the rank of major or higher were employed by defense contractors. In 1968, according to Senator William Proxmire, there were 2,072 retired officers on the payrolls of the top hundred defense contractors, holding more than $26,000,000,000 in military contracts or 67 per cent of defense outlays. The leading ten companies employed more than half the retired officers, all of whom had been at least colonels or Navy captains. Although retired officers were prohibited from soliciting their branch of the service, it was reported that 90 per cent ignored the regulation.

Indeed, the defense-oriented industries had become so embedded in the entire complex that they would have been unable to cultivate civilian-product markets even had they wanted to. When defense cutbacks took place on occasion, the industries were at a loss as to what to do; it seemed that the only way to return to life in a peaceful world was to seek comfort in a conglomerate. Nevertheless, advocates of defense cutbacks argued that there was too much fat in the military-industrial complex. If procurement for long-range attack weapons and antisubmarine weapons was reduced, no harm would come to a reasonable defense effort, they argued. Moreover, a considerable amount of manpower for other purposes would be released. Further, assuming that the Vietnam commitment could be liquidated, anything over $40,000,000,000 for overall defense seemed little short of waste. Of course, extremists argued that even the $40,000,000,000 was waste.

The space-and-defense industries' contribution to economic growth had long since reached the point of diminishing returns. Employing exotic materials and esoteric production methods, these industries were frequently inconvertible coin: they failed to display the sort of relationship to the rest of the economy that was characteristic of earlier defense efforts. In peacetime many of them would be useless. For example, only once in the years 1950–55 did the aircraft industry sell as much as 30 per cent of its product to civilian customers. With their sales and marketing experience so limited, it was not surprising that defense firms (most of whose industrial capacity was due to Government subvention anyway) feared defense-budget cutbacks, for they knew how to politic and bargain with one big customer only.

And this was not quite the same thing as knowing how to carve out a slice of domestic sales.

Where could the airframe industry, to take it as a representative example, go for nondefense business? Commercial aircraft? That would bring in about $200,000,000 a year, hardly enough to pay expenses. Prefabricated homes? With a potential of 1,500,000 units annually, the industry might secure $850,000,000 a year. If there were bridges to build or if building of the much-needed rapid-transit systems was undertaken, perhaps another $500,000,000 or so a year could be recaptured. Yet even with all of this, only 60 per cent of the airframe industry's sales capacity could be replaced.

After World War II many aircraft manufacturers shifted halfheartedly to canoes and power boats and stainless-steel caskets, and subcontracted for musical-instrument manufacturers, but firms like General Dynamics, skilled only in high-cost, high-specification operations, had great difficulty in adapting successfully to big-volume, low-cost, low-quality production. True, some companies were helped by such gimmicks as loss carrybacks to offset past taxes, which enabled them to latch on to more profitable firms— and here again the Government became an underwriter. There was little opportunity to apply the modern techniques of military production— techniques that require parts to be assembled in dust-free, vibrationless plants with devices constantly tested, temperature and humidity carefully controlled, and precision machinery of the kind achieved only by computer calculations—to normal factory production. For concerns geared to modern military production, abolition of the Cold War meant sad obsolescence— until the space program came to the rescue.

From a purely economic standpoint, the disappearance of these industries would not have been a great calamity. Their technology was so special that the income they created in other sectors of the economy—the Keynesian multiplier—was considerably less than the amount that flowed from the old-line industries. It was estimated that about $22,000,000,000 of direct military purchases in 1958 generated another $44,000,000,000 of indirect demand—a multiplier of 2. But meanwhile, the arms mix underwent rapid change, and with virtually every alteration in defense strategy (from surface weapons to missiles, from airframes to electronics, from simple logistics to complex "subsystems"), the capital share in military spending went down; it moved from about 75 per cent in 1951 to 47 per cent in 1962. In consequence, the defense industry multiplier was now probably a good deal less than 2.

A further result of the stress on these exotic industries had been the loss of overseas hard-goods markets: machine tools, for example. More-over, the distorted geographical distribution of defense contracts influenced the pattern of industrial location in ways that could, in the absence of advance planning, result in chaos when cutbacks occurred. Many towns in the South rely almost exculsively on military installations. In Los Angeles almost 200,000 workers drew paychecks in 1962 from three aircraft com-panies. In Wichita, 72 per cent of the work force was employed in making planes and missiles. In the states of Kansas, Washington, California, Connecticut, and Arizona, anywhere from 20 to 30 per cent of manufactur-ing employment was in ordnance, electronics, aircraft, missiles, and ships— the leading industries in the military-space complex. Disarmament would unquestionably leave many localities in these areas as destitute as the ghost towns in western movies.

The National Aeronautics and Space Administration was admonished several times by Congress to spread its share of the business, but most of it still went to the West Coast and the South. Of the $2,700,000,000 NASA spent in fiscal 1963, California received 30 per cent, 28 per cent went to three southern states, and only 1 per cent to all of New England. The Pentagon explained—and with some justice—that its contracts had to be placed where prior investment had been made in research and where the higher skills for making the new weaponry could be found. Thus, the increasing need for technical competence and scientific components in-creased the insulation of the space-and-defense sector from the rest of the economy.

Since 1920, research-and-development expenditures have increased at a phenomenal rate, rising 400 per cent in relation to the national income, while output per man-hour in the economy as a whole hovered steadily around the old norm of a 2 to 4 per cent gain per annum. Not only has there been no perceptible relationship between research and development and economic growth, but the latter may have been inhibited by just the sort of research demanded by the military. Missiles and shooting for the moon may have enhanced our international prestige, but they have added little to the ordinary goods and services needed by an expanding popula-tion. Even worse, space-and-defense research had become a parasite on the rest of the economy, for it fed upon some of the best talents of society. The old-fashioned scientist who might have invented a gadget that could in-crease output per capita was now an engineer on a team project construct-ing a component for the trigger of a space vehicle.

Military and space technology, in short, moved farther and farther away from industrial research, to the point where the possibility of communication between them had all but disappeared. Indeed, how could such skills as preparing a research proposal or designing space instruments or planning "component development" be transferred to production for civilian markets? While there had been some products, such as cordless shavers, resulting from successful transfer, these were exceptional. There were few, if any, civilian counterparts for nuclear warheads, supersonic planes, and the rare materials that went into spaceships. The very habits of the scientists and engineers involved were wrong for civilian production. They were concerned only with performance—"Tell the front office to worry about cost"—and they were accustomed to producing prototypes of machines while eschewing standardized methods. The inescapable conclusion was that spillover from defense production to civilian life was almost nonexistent.

The outlays on research and development, which once had been an important source of economic growth, were being directed more and more to noncivilian endeavors. While in some years during the nineteen-sixties as much as $16,000,000,000 of Federal money was channeled to space-and-defense research and development, less than .002 per cent was spent for civilian purposes. And it was estimated that less than one-fourth of private research and development outlays was aimed at improving civilian productivity. The rest was given over to securing larger Government contracts.

The increasing power and influence of the military-industrial complex was illustrated by the decision in September, 1967, to build a "thin" antiballistic missile system. McNamara had long resisted the system, supposedly directed at China, on the grounds that it would be unreliable and inordinately expensive. Since $2,400,000,000 had been spent in the previous ten years on researching the system, many companies had acquired a vested interest in it. It was said that at least fifteen thousand firms would benefit from the thin system, including General Electric, Sperry Rand, Raytheon, and General Dynamics. A million persons in 172 congressional districts would gain employment. One Wall Street concern commented that the Pentagon's go-ahead signal would "shake the money tree for electronics companies." The stock in those corporations that were apt to benefit most —Raytheon, Aerojet General, and Sperry Rand—went up almost at once. The space-and-defense pork barrel was vastly enriched.

As a result, some seventy-five mutual funds shifted a total of $90,000,000 from other holdings to electronic shares. Such was the immediate direct gain that grew out of the extraordinarily heavy pressure that had been applied to McNamara. Only nine months before he had acceded to the ABM enterprise, McNamara had advised the Senate that it was a dubious venture. Indeed, the Pentagon admitted that the country had spent $20,000,000,000 since World War II on a variety of missile systems that soon became obsolete. The military value of the systems had quickly dropped to zero, the social waste was enormous, but private profit had been quite handsome. The only contribution had been to help escalate the Cold War. The basic fact that had been obscured in all the furor was that the initial cost of $5,000,000,000 for the thin ABM system opened a Pandora's box that would eventually cost $40,000,000,000 to $70,000,000,000.

Furthermore, the Pentagon's fear of Soviet intentions was flatly controverted by the National Intelligence Estimate, a consensus view stemming from the work of the Central Intelligence Agency, State Department, and other experts who denied that Moscow had any first-strike plans—the official Department of Defense concern—nor was there any evidence that the Russians were adopting such a policy. Not even the Air Force, which habitually viewed the Soviet threat with great alarm, was prepared to make a first-strike argument. Nevertheless, the Pentagon, represented by Melvin Laird, Nixon's Secretary of Defense, urged that the ABM system, increased by the Republicans from $5,000,000,000 to $7,000,000,000, be adopted. Congressional opposition, however, was quite strong: one senator described the ABM system as "a defense in search of a mission." The Administration was prepared to provide that mission.

Another furor arose when the Department of Defense approved a multi-billion-dollar contract to General Dynamics for the TFX fighter plane. Most of the technical advisers had argued that the order would eventually reach $6,500,000,000, provide 1,700 standardized planes for the Air Force and the Navy, and yield 20,000 jobs. The charges and countercharges became so venomous that Congress decided to investigate. It discovered the usual cabal of Pentagon and business interests boiling in a caldron of intense lobbying and political pressure. General Dynamics planned to build the aircraft in Texas, so opponents promptly dubbed it the LBJ plane. The Navy, horrified at the thought that it might share equipment with the Air Force, sought to suppress at least its part of the contract. It was clear that the Navy would not cooperate with any contractors not on its list of favorites. Its agonized posture before Congress finally paid off when the Senate Armed Services Committee ditched the Navy's share of the TFX, or the F-111, as it had come to be called. Immediately Grumman, McDonnell Douglas, Ling-Temco-Vought, and North America activated plans for the

Navy version of the fighter plane. They had all had a long-standing harmonious relationship with that branch of the Pentagon.

In any case, it was evident that one of NcNamara's major errors had been the TFX. There were signs that the outgoing Johnson Administration might want to cut its losses—the cost of the planes had reached several billion dollars—and retreat from the whole business. But the Republicans decided that the TFX, or F-111, was to become "one of the foundations of our air supremacy," despite the fact that it had proved to be somewhat less than a howling success in Vietnam; indeed, the TFX had had to be grounded shortly after its arrival in that unhappy battlefield. Quite simply, the plane had turned out to be a failure, and at $6,000,000 each, a rather expensive one. The only winner in the imbroglio, which would have been comic were not its aftermath filled with tragic consequences, was General Dynamics, the plane's manufacturer. General Dynamics had become the country's largest defense contractor with $2,200,000,000 in contracts for fiscal 1968 alone. The original cost of the TFX was set at $3,000,000 per plane; by 1968 the price had more than doubled.

Had it not been for the TFX, General Dynamics would have gone into bankruptcy in 1961. Losses on its civilian plane business had cut its working capital below the minimum required by the company's bankers, who then helpfully reduced this minimum. Then General Dynamics was saved by the TFX contract in 1962. When the Navy's share was canceled, General Dynamics' profits went into a tailspin, dropping from $36,000,000 in the first nine months of 1967 to $9,000,000 in the same period a year later. The TFX affair revealed more than any other episode in the military-industrial chronicle the degree to which the Pentagon bureaucracy had coalesced with its business counterpart. The main purpose of the contract had been to rescue the largest company in the defense complex from financial disaster. As one writer put it rather bitterly, "Billions which could do so much for poverty are squandered to maintain these favorite Pentagon clients on the military relief rolls in the lush style to which they have become accustomed." Joining the Pentagon's rolls was not difficult when one of General Dynamics' former presidents had been a Secretary of the Army and a member of its law firm had served as Deputy Secretary of Defense. With such friends in court, it was not surprising that the company could obtain the contract, despite the fact it had been underbid by Boeing Aircraft. Not the least of the persuasive arguments that impelled the Pentagon to overrule the Boeing bid was the fact that the then Vice-President of the United States, and later President, happened to be a resident of the state in which General Dynamics had its principal office.

The supersonic transport project, though ostensibly planned for civilian purposes, gave further evidence of the technological gravy-train that had been fattening corporate enterprise. The idea for an SST capable of traveling at three times the speed of an ordinary jet goes back to 1961. But once more private industry nudged the Government to pay for something it might have undertaken itself. As it turned out, the United States was to put up $6.50 for every $1.00 that the private companies might invest in developing an SST. It was all reducible to the age-old proposition: let the government assume the risk and industry take the profit. By 1968 development costs had reached $1,500,000,000 of which the Federal budget paid $1,300,000,000. Before the SST could become operational it appeared likely that Washington would have to fork over another $3,000,000,000.

Many were asking, "For what?" The plane would be longer than a football field and would need two hundred miles of air space just to turn around. A landing would require closed-circuit television, and huge airports able to accommodate the monster would have to be built. There was a widespread suspicion that the SST had been little more than make-work, for the idea was first suggested when space-and-defense companies feared there might be little defense work to count on. The SST was hailed as a perfect substitute, for the subcontracting would total $30,000,000,000 spread over forty-six states. One congressman looked at the project as a way of "sharing the wealth." With 50,000 jobs for prime contractors, 100,000 jobs for subcontractors, and another 100,000 jobs to be stimulated by the multiplier effect, the SST became America's version of pyramid building.

The interested companies—Boeing, General Electric, Republic Aviation, Fairchild, and others—engaged in polite blackmail by threatening to purchase the European version of the plane if the project were not approved, thereby endangering our balance of payments. Aside from the fact that it was an empty threat, the truth of the matter was that the American taxpayer could not possibly get his money's worth by paying for an SST. Though it would cost triple the price of the conventional jet plane, the SST's practicable speed was actually only twice as great. Moreover, the problem of sonic boom, which poses a threat to health and property, has not been solved. Yet so intense was the pressure by industry—with the military standing by grinning like a Cheshire cat—that Congress was finally lobbied into the project. But before the Government could break even, about six hundred SST planes would have to be sold; there was serious question that the market could absorb that many. An SST would gulp fuel in huge quantities, increasing operating costs many fold; the traveler would have to pay premium fares for the privilege of getting to the other side of the continent for a second cup of coffee before lunch. As one writer remarked, the taxpayer had been conned into buying a super-sleek pig in a poke.

The Comsat project was another venture of the space age that illustrated the influence and power of the complex against which President Eisenhower had cautioned. AT&T was able to outmaneuver and outlobby the aerospace companies that had also sought to dominate communications via satellites. In the end, the telephone interests secured a stranglehold on the new system with dollars that came from the taxpayer. The conflict was fierce and intense, straining the alliance between Government agencies, communication companies, and the space industry. The practicability of sending messages through space had been demonstrated by the Army Signal Corps when it bounced radio signals off the moon in 1946. In 1958 the Air Force sent back a recorded Christmas message from an orbiting satellite. The possibilities of expanding telephone communications via satellite had been demonstrated, and AT&T was determined to clasp the business to its corporate breast. But there was the aerospace industry that also wanted a slice of the pie, for it had been responsible for the underlying technology.

In 1959 AT&T audaciously requested the National Aeronautics and Space Administration for full and exclusive rights to the space-communications business. It offered to build the system itself at a cost of some $400,000,000, without indicating, of course, that telephone subscribers eventually would have paid the bill. NASA refused at first, but the seduction was not difficult to consumate, and two years later AT&T was franchised. The aerospace companies, reacting as though they had been the ones suffering rape, insisted that ownership of communication satellites should be shared. In the ensuing imbroglio, the Federal Communications Commission, which also had a voice in the matter, ruled out domestic carriers and equipment manufacturers as possible part-owners in the space system. Thus the independents were frozen out by administrative fiat, while small individual investors were excluded by the high initial price of the shares in the new communications satellite company that was formed to rule the outer airwaves. The debate in Congress became so involved, and the AT&T thrust toward absolute monopoly so obvious, that several of the more liberal senators staged a filibuster. Then while the debate in Congress raged, Telstar was shot into space to present America with a *fait accompli*. AT&T's joyous advertising forgot to tell a startled public that its satellite had been pushed into orbit by Government-issue rocket boosters. With the subsequent formation of Comsat, AT&T promptly acquired 29 per cent of the stock, enough to give it a major voice, if not outright control, in the quasi-public corporation.

New millionaires inevitably arose out of the military-industrial complex. Scientists in universities—especially chemists, physicists, and engineers—established their own firms, many of which were later absorbed by prime contractors with handsome gains to the founders. A Dr. Arnold Beckman began making scientific instruments in his garage, and a few years later was reputed to be worth over $60,000,000. The High Voltage Engineering Corporation, founded by D. M. Robinson, soon reached a sales level of $20,000,000 a year. The Massachusetts Institute of Technology alone spawned some three hundred post war companies, 80 per cent of which managed to survive the difficult first few years.

The classic tale of business success in the age of space concerns the Thompson-Ramo-Wooldridge firm, started under the beneficence of the contract state by Simon Ramo and Dean Wooldridge, two obscure space scientists. Air Force favors and Government contracts made them wealthy enough eventually to allow them to turn over the conduct of their business to others. Ramo and Wooldridge had been advisers on a missile contract held by General Dynamics. A subcontract to evaluate the design of an ICBM placed them at the center of activity. Astute politicking brought Ramo and Wooldridge a contract to supervise General Dynamics' missile work. Within a few months the company that had been formed for the purpose had thousands of workers under its wing. Corporate legitimacy was provided by a merger with Thompson Products, an established automotive-parts supplier. Ramo and Wooldridge each invested $6,750, receiving 51 per cent of voting stock in the new company. Pacific Semi-Conductors was added, enabling Thompson-Ramo-Wooldridge to move into computers, transistors, and general communications. Buildings were financed by borrowing from the Thompson employee pension fund, but it was all quite riskless, since Ramo and Wooldridge could insure Air Force contracts as a base for operations.

By 1957 sales had reached $43,000,000 a year; Pacific's losses provided tax offsets, so that from 1953 to 1957 no taxes were paid on earnings. In 1958 a reorganization was carried out in which Thompson-Ramo-Wooldridge stockholders received almost $17,000,000 as their equity. Ramo and Wooldridge had run their modest $13,500 investment up to $6,200,000. Despite a palpable odor of scandal in the original Air Force-Ramo-Wooldridge arrangement, the facts were never brought to light. By 1963 Thompson-Ramo-Wooldridge had become a $500,000,000 corporation, engaging in half Government and half private business. Even the Army and Navy favored it with contracts, even though the company had started as an Air Force darling.

These were the elements of the contract state, the newest manifestation of the world of business. As H. L. Nieburg, an astute observer of these matters has noted, the Government contract became a major corporate device, rivaling tariffs and taxation as an instrument for shaping that world. There was question whether a firm doing 90 per cent of its business with the Federal Government was really a private venture. Cost-plus contracts, a frequent lack of specifications, and the absence of sufficient controls to protect the public interest placed a heavy burden on the body politic. As the Air Force could not match the Army in procurement experience, it turned increasingly to private sources to fill its needs. Broker specialists evolved (America's version of the *tolkachi* of the Soviet Union) who could manage contracts, deal in paper, and bring interested parties together. Yet the whole complex proved to be frightfully inefficient. In the fifteen years from 1953 to 1968, the country had invested almost $9,000,000,000 in fifty-seven military contracts that were subsequently canceled. A prime example was the B-70 bomber, which cost $1,500,000,000 before it was canceled in 1967. The Navajo and the Snark, two jet-powered missiles, had cost about $1,400,000,000 before cancellation in 1957 and 1962. The Skybolt missile, junked in 1963, cost $440,000,000; the Rascal, abandoned in 1958, cost $448,000,000; and the F-111B, the Navy's share of the TFX, accounted for $200,000,000 before it was dropped.

The Government's direct role in managing the new technology was drastically reduced, to be replaced by the contractor, a new species of sophisticated businessman who soon displayed all the virtues of the older corporate breed. The sole difference was that the new men of power had the inside track to the public trough, and there seemed no way to shunt them aside so long as the Cold War and a fascination with space dominated the American spirit. As Seymour Melman has said, these new men of power had developed an ideology that sought to maintain and extend their control of the military-industrial complex. It became an ideology based on the notions that the health of the nation is dependent on economic growth, even if that growth provides few goods and services for the common man; that the alternative programs foregone can be provided out of other resources (a belief patently contradicted by the absence of any meaningful alternatives); that "spillover" helps the civilian economy (although such spillover has yet to become significant); and that military and defense outlays are a means of stabilizing the economy. It was an ideology that reflected the condition to which the latest stage of America's business civilization had brought the nation.

BIBLIOGRAPHY

AARON, D., ed., *America in Crisis*. New York, 1952.

ABELS, J., *The Rockefeller Millions*. New York, 1965.

ADAMS, J. T., *Our Business Civilization*. New York, 1929.

————, *Big Business in a Democracy*. New York, 1945.

ADAMS, W., and GRAY, H. M., *Monopoly in America*. New York, 1955.

ADELMAN, M. A., *A. and P.* Cambridge, 1959.

AITKEN, H. G. J., ed., *Explorations in Enterprise*. Cambridge, 1965.

ALBION, R. G., *The Rise of New York Port*. New York, 1939.

ALDEN, J. R., *A History of the American Revolution*. New York, 1969.

ALLEN, F. L., *Lords of Creation*. New York, 1939.

————, *The Great Pierpont Morgan*. New York, 1949.

————, *The Big Change*. New York, 1952.

————, *Only Yesterday*. New York, 1957.

ANDREANO, R., ed., *The Economic Impact of the American Civil War*. Cambridge, 1962.

————, ed., *New Views on American Economic Development*. Cambridge, 1965.

APPEL, J. H., ed., *Business Biography of John Wanamaker*. New York, 1930.

ARCHER, G. L., *History of Radio to 1926*. New York, 1938.

ARNDT, H. W., *The Economic Lessons of the 1930s*. London, 1944.

ARRINGTON, L. J., *The Great Basin Kingdom*. Cambridge, 1958.

AVERITT, R. T., *The Dual Economy*. New York, 1968.

BABCOCK, G. D., *History of the U. S. Rubber Company*. Bloomington, 1966.

BAILYN, B., *The New England Merchants of the 17th Century*. Cambridge, 1955.

————, ed., *The Apologia of Robert Keayne* (reprint). New York, 1965.

————, *The Ideological Origins of the American Revolution*. Cambridge, 1967.

BAIN, J. S., *Barriers to New Competition*. Cambridge, 1956.

BAKER, L., *The Guaranteed Society*. New York, 1968.

BALTZELL, E. D., *An American Business Aristocracy*. New York, 1958.

BARCK, O. T., JR., and LEFLER, H. T., *Colonial America*. New York, 1958.

BARITZ, L., *The Servants of Power*. Middletown, 1960.

BARRETT, W., *The Old Merchants of New York City*. New York, 1963.

BAXTER, W. R., *The House of Hancock*. Cambridge, 1945.

BAZELON, D. T., *The Paper Economy*. New York, 1963.

————, *Power in America*. New York, 1967.

BEARD, C. A., *An Economic Interpretation of the Constitution*. New York, 1913.

————, *Economic Origins of Jeffersonian Democracy*. New York, 1915.

————, *The Economic Basis of Politics*. New York, 1922.

————, and BEARD, M. R., *The Rise of American Civilization*. New York, 1933.

————, *America in Midpassage*. New York, 1939.

BEARD, M., *A History of the Business Man*. New York, 1938.

BEARDSLEY, H. M., *Joseph Smith and His Mormon Empire*. Boston, 1931.

BENDINER, R., *Just Around the Corner*. New York, 1967.

BENNETT, H. H., *We Never Called Him Henry*. New York, 1951.

BENSON, L., *Turner and Beard*. New York, 1960.

BENTLEY, A. F., *Makers, Users and Masters*. Syracuse, 1969.

BERG, I., ed., *The Business of America*. New York, 1968.

BERLE, A. A., *Power Without Property*. New York, 1959.

————, *The American Economic Republic*. New York, 1963.

————, and MEANS, G. C., *The Modern Corporation and Private Property*. New York, 1933.

BERNSTEIN, B. J., ed., *Towards a New Past*. New York, 1968.

BERNSTEIN, I., *The Lean Years*. Boston, 1960.

BERNSTEIN, M. H., *Regulating Business by Independent Commissions*. Princeton, 1955.

BINING, A. C., and COCHRAN, T. C., *The Rise of American Economic Life* (4th ed.). New York, 1964.

BIRMINGHAM, S., *Our Crowd*. New York, 1967.

BISHOP, J. L., *A History of American Manufactures from 1608 to 1860*. Philadelphia, 1864.

BJORK, G. C., *Private Enterprise and Public Interest*. Englewood Cliffs, 1966.

BOLLES, A. S., *Industrial History of the United States* (1881, reprinted). New York, 1966.

BOORSTIN, D. J., *The Americans: The Colonial Experience*. New York, 1958.

————, *The Americans: The National Experience*. New York, 1965.

BRADY, R. A., *Business As A System of Power*. New York, 1943.

BRAMSON, R. T. L., *Highlights in the History of American Mass Production*. Detroit, 1945.

BRANDEIS, L. D., *Other People's Money*. New York, 1932.

BREBNER, J. B., *The Explorers of North America*. London, 1933.

BRIDENBAUGH, C., *Cities in Revolt*. New York, 1955.

————, *Cities in the Wilderness*. New York, 1960.

BRIGHT, A. A., JR., *The Electric Lamp Industry*. New York, 1949.

BRODIE, F. M., *No Man Knows My History*. New York, 1946.

BRODY, D., ed., *Industrial America in the Twentieth Century*. New York, 1967.

BROOKS, J., *Business Adventures*. New York, 1969.

BROWN, R. E., *Charles Beard and the Constitution*. Princeton, 1956.

BRUCHEY, S., ed., *The Colonial Merchant*. New York, 1966.

BUCK, S. J., *The Granger Movement*. Cambridge, 1913.

BUNZEL, J. H., *The American Small Businessman*. New York, 1962.

BURLINGAME, R., *Backgrounds of Power*. New York, 1949.

———, *Machines That Built America*. New York, 1953.

———, *Henry Ford*. New York, 1957.

BURNS, J. M., *Roosevelt: The Lion and The Fox*. New York, 1956.

BURR, A. R., *Portrait of a Banker: James D. Stillman*. New York, 1927.

CADMAN, J. W., *The Corporation in New Jersey*. Cambridge, 1949.

CAMERON, E. H., *Samuel Slater: Father of American Manufacturing*, Freeport, 1960.

CARNEGIE, A., *The Empire of Business*. New York, 1902.

———, *Autobiography*. New York, 1920.

CARR, A. Z., *John D. Rockefeller's Secret Weapon*. New York, 1962.

CARR, W. H., *The du Ponts of Delaware*. New York, 1964.

CASH, W. J., *The Mind of the South*. New York, 1941.

CATTERALL, R. C. H., *The Second Bank of the United States*. Chicago, 1903.

CHALMERS, H., *The Birth of the Erie Canal*. New York, 1960.

CHAMBERLAIN, J., *Farewell to Reform*. New York, 1932.

———, *The Enterprising Americans*. New York, 1963.

CHAMBERS, C. A., *Seedtime of Reform*. Ann Arbor, 1963.

CHANDLER, A. D., JR., *Henry Varnum Poor*. Cambridge, 1956.

———, *Strategy and Structure*. Cambridge, 1962.

———, ed., *Giant Enterprise*. New York, 1964.

———, ed., *The Railroads*. New York, 1965.

———, and BRUCHEY, S., and GALAMBOS, L., eds., *The Changing Economic Order*. New York, 1968.

CHAPMAN, C. C., *Development of American Business and Banking Thought*. New York, 1936.

CHILDS, M. W., and CATER, P., *Ethics in a Business Society*. New York, 1954.

CHINARD, G., *Thomas Jefferson: Apostle of Americanism*. Boston, 1929.

CHOMSKY, N., *American Power and the New Mandarins*. New York, 1969.

CLARK, I. G., *Then Came the Railroads*. Norman, 1958.

CLARK, J. M., *Social Control of Business*. New York, 1939.

———, *Competition as a Dynamic Process*. Washington, 1961.

CLARK, V. S., *History of Manufactures in the United States*. Washington, 1916.

CLARK, W. H., *Railroads and Rivers*. Boston, 1939.

CLEMENS, R. A., *The American Livestock and Meat Industry*. New York, 1923.

CLEVELAND, F. W., *Corporations on Trial*. Belmont, 1964.

———, and POWELL, F. W., *Railroad Promotion and Capitalization*. London, 1909.

COBEN, S., and HILL, F. G., ed., *American Economic History*. New York, 1966.

COCHRAN, T. C., *Railroad Builders: 1845–1890*. Cambridge, 1953.

COCHRAN, T. C., *The American Business System*. Cambridge, 1957.

———, *Basic History of American Business*. Princeton, 1959.

———, *The Inner Revolution*. New York, 1964.

———, and BREWER, T. B., ed., *Views of American Economic Growth*. New York, 1966.

———, and MILLER, W., *The Age of Enterprise*. New York, 1942.

COLE, A. C., *The Irrepressible Conflict: 1850–1865*. New York, 1934.

COLEMAN, J. R., ed., *The Changing American Economy*. New York, 1967.

COMMAGER, H. S., *The Search For a Usable Past*. New York, 1967.

COMMONS, J. R., *Documentary History of American Industrial Society* (1909, reprinted). New York, 1958.

———, *History of Labor in the United States*, 4 v. New York, 1918–1935.

CONRAD, A. H., and MEYER, J. R., *Studies in Econometric History*. London, 1965.

COOKE, J. E., ed., *The Reports of Alexander Hamilton*. New York, 1964.

———, ed., *Alexander Hamilton: A Profile*. New York, 1967.

COREY, L., *The House of Morgan*. New York, 1930.

———, *The Decline of American Capitalism*. New York, 1934.

———, *Meat and Men*. New York, 1950.

CUSHMAN, R. E., *The Independent Regulatory Commissions*. New York, 1941.

DAGGETT, S., *Chapters in the History of the Southern Pacific*. New York, 1922.

DANHOF, C. H., *Government Contracting and Technological Change*. Washington, 1968.

DANIELIAN, N. R., *AT&T: The Story of Industrial Conquest*. New York, 1939.

DAVIS, D. B., *The Problem of Slavery in Western Culture*. Ithaca, 1966.

DAVIS, J. P., *Corporation* (reprint). New York, 1961.

DAVIS, J. S., *Essays in the Earlier History of American Corporations*. Cambridge, 1917.

DEGLER, C. N., ed., *Pivotal Interpretations of American History*. New York, 1966.

———, *The Age of the Economic Revolution, 1876–1900*. Glenview, 1967.

DESTLER, C. M., *American Radicalism, 1865–1901*. New London, 1946.

———, *Roger Sherman and the Independent Oil Men*. Ithaca, 1967.

DEVOTO, B., *The Year of Decision*. Boston, 1943.

DEWEY, D. R., *Financial History of the United States*, 10th ed. New York, 1928.

———, and HOLDSWORTH, T., *The First and Second Bank of the U. S.* Washington, 1910.

DEWING, A. S., *The Financial Policy of Corporations*, 3rd ed. New York, 1934.

DIAMOND, S., *The Reputation of the American Business Man*. Cambridge, 1955.

———, *Creation of Society in the New World*. Chicago, 1963.

———, ed., *The Nation Transformed*. New York, 1963.

DICKSON, H., *The Story of King Cotton*. New York, 1937.

DODD, P. A., *Financial Policies in the Aviation Industry*. Philadelphia, 1933.

DODGE, G. M., *How We Built the Union Pacific Railway* (reprint). Denver, 1965.

DOMHOFF, G. W., *Who Rules America?* Englewood Cliffs, 1967.

DORFMAN, J., *Thorstein Veblen and His America*. New York, 1934.

————, *The Economic Mind in American Civilization*, 5 v. New York, 1946–1959.

DORIAN, M., *The du Ponts from Gunpowder to Nylon*. Boston, 1962.

DRUCKER, P., *The Concept of the Corporation*. New York, 1946.

DU BOIS, W. E. B., *Black Reconstruction 1860–1880*. New York, 1935.

DUTTON, W. S., *Du Pont*. New York, 1942.

EARLE, E. M., ed., *The Federalist*. New York, 1941.

EAST, R. A., *Business Enterprise in the American Revolutionary Era*. New York, 1938.

————, *John Quincy Adams*. New York, 1962.

ECKENRODE, H. J., and EDMONDS, P. W., *E. H. Harriman*. New York, 1933.

EDWARDS, G. W., *The Evolution of Finance Capitalism*. New York, 1938.

EDWARDS, W. B., *The Story of Colt's Revolver*. Harrisburg, 1953.

EELLS, R., *The Meaning of Modern Business*. New York, 1960.

————, *The Government of Corporations*. New York, 1962.

————, and WALTON, C., *Conceptual Foundations of Business*. Homewood, 1961.

EISENSTADT, A. S., ed., *American History: Recent Interpretations*, 2 v. New York, 1962.

EMMET, B., and JENCK, J. E., *Catalogues and Counters*. Chicago, 1950.

ENGLER, R., *The Politics of Oil*. Chicago, 1961.

EPSTEIN, R. C., *The Automobile Industry*. Chicago, 1928.

FEIS, H., *1933: Characters in Crisis*. Boston, 1966.

FERGUSON, E. J., *The Power of the Purse*. Chapel Hill, 1961.

FINE, S., *Laissez Faire and the General Welfare State*. Ann Arbor, 1956.

FINN, D., *The Corporate Oligarch*. New York, 1969.

FISHER, M., *Workshops in the Wilderness*. New York, 1967.

FITE, E. D., *Social and Industrial Conditions in the North During the Civil War*. New York, 1910.

FLEXNER, J. T., *The Traitor and the Spy*. New York, 1953.

FLYNN, J. T., *God's Gold: Rockefeller and His Times*. New York, 1932.

————, *Security Speculation: Its Economic Effects*. New York, 1934.

————, *Men of Wealth*. New York, 1941.

FORBES, E., *Paul Revere and the World He Lived In*. Cambridge, 1942.

FORTUNE, *Fortune's Favorites: Portraits of Some American Corporations*. New York, 1931.

————, *The Space Industry*. Englewood Cliffs, 1962.

Fox, D. R., *The Decline of Aristocracy in the Politics of New York*. New York, 1919.

Freeman, R. E., ed., *Postwar Economic Trends*. New York, 1960.

Friedman, M., and Schwartz, A. M., *A Monetary History of the United States*. Princeton, 1963.

Fuller, R. H., *Jubilee Jim*. New York, 1928.

Galbraith, J. K., *American Capitalism*. Boston, 1952.

————, *The Great Crash: 1929*. Boston, 1954.

————, *The Affluent Society*. Boston, 1958.

————, *The Liberal Hour*. Boston, 1960.

————, *The New Industrial State*. Boston, 1967.

Gates, P. W., *The Illinois Central Railroad,* Cambridge, 1934.

————, *The Farmer's Age*. New York, 1960.

————, *Agriculture and the Civil War*. New York, 1965.

Genovese, E. D., *The Political Economy of Slavery*. New York, 1965.

Gibbon, H. A., *John Wanamaker*. New York, 1926.

Giddens, P. H., *The Birth of the Oil Industry*. New York, 1938.

————, *The Standard Oil Company of Indiana*. New York, 1955.

Gilbert, J. W., *The History of Banking in America* (1837, reprint). New York, 1967.

Ginger, R., *The Age of Excess*. New York, 1965.

Glaab, C. N., and Brown, A. T., *A History of Urban America*. New York, 1967.

Goldman, E. F., *Rendezvous With Destiny*. New York, 1952.

Goldston, R., *The Great Depression*. Indianapolis, 1968.

Goodman, G., *Government Policy Toward Commercial Aviation*. New York, 1944.

Goodman, W., *All Honorable Men*. Boston, 1963.

Goodrich, C., *Government Promotion of American Canals*. New York, 1960.

————, *Canals and American Economic Development*. New York, 1961.

Gordan, R. A., *Business Leadership in the Large Corporation*. Berkeley, 1961.

Gort, M., *Diversification and Integration in American Industry*. Princeton, 1962.

Goulden, J. C., *Monopoly*. New York, 1968.

Govan, T. P., *Nicholas Biddle*. Chicago, 1959.

Grace, E. G., *Charles M. Schwab*. Bethlehem, 1947.

Gras, N. S. B., *Business and Capitalism*. New York, 1939.

————, and Larson, H. M., *Casebook in American Business History*. New York, 1939.

Graubard, S. G., ed., *Perspectives on Business*. Boston, 1969.

Grayson, T. J., *Leaders and Periods of American Finance*. New York, 1932.

Green, C., *Eli Whitney and the Birth of American Technology*. Boston, 1956.

Greenslet, F., *The Lowells and their Seven Worlds*. Boston, 1946.

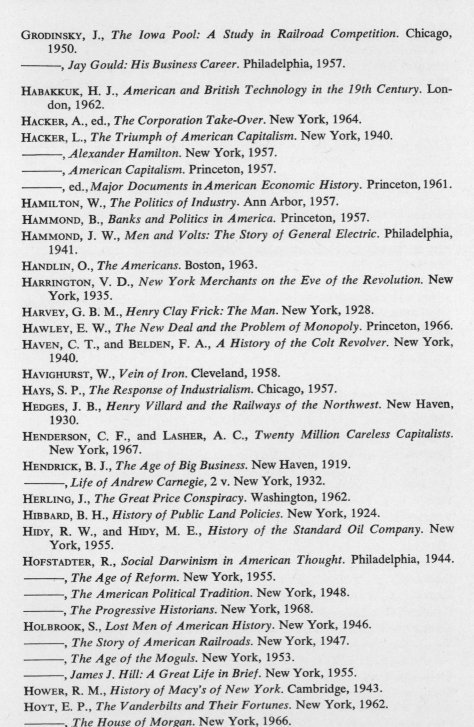

GRODINSKY, J., *The Iowa Pool: A Study in Railroad Competition.* Chicago, 1950.

——, *Jay Gould: His Business Career.* Philadelphia, 1957.

HABAKKUK, H. J., *American and British Technology in the 19th Century.* London, 1962.

HACKER, A., ed., *The Corporation Take-Over.* New York, 1964.

HACKER, L., *The Triumph of American Capitalism.* New York, 1940.

——, *Alexander Hamilton.* New York, 1957.

——, *American Capitalism.* Princeton, 1957.

——, ed., *Major Documents in American Economic History.* Princeton, 1961.

HAMILTON, W., *The Politics of Industry.* Ann Arbor, 1957.

HAMMOND, B., *Banks and Politics in America.* Princeton, 1957.

HAMMOND, J. W., *Men and Volts: The Story of General Electric.* Philadelphia, 1941.

HANDLIN, O., *The Americans.* Boston, 1963.

HARRINGTON, V. D., *New York Merchants on the Eve of the Revolution.* New York, 1935.

HARVEY, G. B. M., *Henry Clay Frick: The Man.* New York, 1928.

HAWLEY, E. W., *The New Deal and the Problem of Monopoly.* Princeton, 1966.

HAVEN, C. T., and BELDEN, F. A., *A History of the Colt Revolver.* New York, 1940.

HAVIGHURST, W., *Vein of Iron.* Cleveland, 1958.

HAYS, S. P., *The Response of Industrialism.* Chicago, 1957.

HEDGES, J. B., *Henry Villard and the Railways of the Northwest.* New Haven, 1930.

HENDERSON, C. F., and LASHER, A. C., *Twenty Million Careless Capitalists.* New York, 1967.

HENDRICK, B. J., *The Age of Big Business.* New Haven, 1919.

——, *Life of Andrew Carnegie,* 2 v. New York, 1932.

HERLING, J., *The Great Price Conspiracy.* Washington, 1962.

HIBBARD, B. H., *History of Public Land Policies.* New York, 1924.

HIDY, R. W., and HIDY, M. E., *History of the Standard Oil Company.* New York, 1955.

HOFSTADTER, R., *Social Darwinism in American Thought.* Philadelphia, 1944.

——, *The Age of Reform.* New York, 1955.

——, *The American Political Tradition.* New York, 1948.

——, *The Progressive Historians.* New York, 1968.

HOLBROOK, S., *Lost Men of American History.* New York, 1946.

——, *The Story of American Railroads.* New York, 1947.

——, *The Age of the Moguls.* New York, 1953.

——, *James J. Hill: A Great Life in Brief.* New York, 1955.

HOWER, R. M., *History of Macy's of New York.* Cambridge, 1943.

HOYT, E. P., *The Vanderbilts and Their Fortunes.* New York, 1962.

——, *The House of Morgan.* New York, 1966.

HOYT, E. P., *The Guggenheims and the American Dream*. New York, 1967.

————, *The Goulds*. New York, 1969.

HUGHES, J. R. T., *The Vital Few*. Boston, 1966.

HUMPHREY, G., *Stories of Our Great Inventions*. Indianapolis, 1927.

HUNT, F., *Lives of American Merchants*, 2 v. (1856–58, reprint). New York, 1969.

JAHER, F. C., ed., *The Age of Industrialism in America*. New York, 1968.

JAMESON, J. F., *Privateering and Piracy in the Colonial Period*. New York, 1924.

————, *The American Revolution Considered As a Social Movement*. Princeton, 1926.

————, ed., *Essays in Colonial History*. Freeport, 1966.

JANEWAY, E., *The Struggle for Survival*. New Haven, 1951.

JAY, A., *Management and Machiavelli*. New York, 1967.

JENKINS, J. W., *James B. Duke: Master Builder*. New York, 1927.

JENNINGS, W. W., *Twenty Giants of American Business*. New York, 1953.

JOHNSON, A. M., and SUPPLE, B. E., *Boston Capitalists and Western Railroads*. Cambridge, 1967.

JONES, P. d'A., *The Consumer Society*. Baltimore, 1965.

————, ed., *The Robber Barons Revisited*. Boston, 1968.

JOSEPHSON, M., *The Robber Barons*. New York, 1934.

————, *The Politicos*. New York, 1938.

————, *Edison: A Biography*. New York, 1959.

————, *Infidel in the Temple*. New York, 1967.

KAHL, J. A., *The American Class Structure*. New York, 1957.

KANE, R. M., and VOSE, A. D., *Air Transportation*. Dubuque, 1967.

KAPLAN, A. D. H., DIRLAM, J. B., and LANZILLOTTI, R. F., *Pricing in Big Business*. Washington, 1958.

KARIEL, H. S., *The Decline of American Pluralism*. Stanford, 1961.

KAUFMANN, C. B., *Man Incorporate*. New York, 1967.

KEFAUVER, E., *In A Few Hands: Monopoly Power in America*. New York, 1965.

KELLER, S., *Beyond the Ruling Class*. New York, 1963.

KENNAN, G., *E. H. Harriman: A Biography*, 2 v. Boston, 1922.

KENNEDY, E. D., *The Automobile Industry*. New York, 1941.

KENNEDY, G., ed., *Democracy and the Gospel of Wealth*. Boston, 1949.

KIRKLAND, E. C., *Men, Cities, and Transportation*, 2 v. Cambridge, 1948.

————, *Business in the Gilded Age*. Madison, 1952.

————, *Dreams and Thought in the Business Community*. Ithaca, 1956.

————, *Industry Comes of Age*. New York, 1961.

KOCH, A., and PEDEN, W., ed., *Life and Selected Writings of Thomas Jefferson*. New York, 1944.

KOHLMEIR, J. M., JR., *The Regulators*. New York, 1969.

KOHT, H., *Driving Forces in History*. Cambridge, 1964.

KOLKO, G., *The Triumph of Conservatism*. New York, 1963.

———, *The Roots of American Foreign Policy*. Boston, 1969.

KONEFSKY, S. J., *John Marshall and Alexander Hamilton*. New York, 1964.

KRANZBERG, M., and PURSELL, C. W., JR., ed., *Technology in Western Civilzation*, 2 v. New York, 1967.

KROOS, H. E., *American Economic Development*. Englewood Cliffs, 1966.

KUHN, J. W., and BERG, I., *Values in a Business Society*. New York, 1968.

LAIDLER, H., *Concentration and Control in American Industry*. New York, 1931.

LANE, C. D., *American Paddle Steamboats*. New York, 1943.

LANE, F. C., and RIEMERSMA, J. C., ed., *Enterprise and Secular Change*. Homewood, 1953.

LANE, W. J., *Commodore Vanderbilt*. New York, 1942.

LARKIN, O. W., *Samuel F. B. Morse*. Boston, 1954.

LARSON, H., *Jay Cooke, Private Banker*. Cambridge, 1936.

LARSON, J. A., *The Responsible Businessman*. New York, 1966.

LEECH, H., and CARROLL, J. C., *Armour and His Times*. New York, 1938.

LEFF, G., *History and Social Theory*. London, 1969.

LEKACHMAN, R., *The Age of Keynes*. New York, 1966.

LEUCHTENBERG, W. E., *The Perils of Prosperity*. Chicago, 1958.

———, *Franklin D. Roosevelt and The New Deal*. New York, 1963.

LEUPP, F. E., *George Westinghouse: His Life and Achievements*. Boston, 1918.

LEWIN, L. C., *Report from Iron Mountain*. New York, 1967.

LEWIS, O., *The Big Four*. New York, 1938.

LEWIS, R., and STEWART, R., *The Managers*. New York, 1961.

LIPSET, S. M., and BENDIX, R., *Social Mobility in Industrial Society*. Berkeley, 1959.

———, and HOFSTADTER, R., ed., *Sociology and History: Methods*. New York, 1968.

LIVINGSTON, J. A., *The American Stockholder*. New York, 1958.

LLOYD, H. D., *Wealth Against Commonwealth*. New York, 1894.

———, *Lords of Industry*. New York, 1910.

LUNDBERG, F., *America's Sixty Families*. New York, 1937.

———, *The Rich and the Super-Rich*. New York, 1968.

LYNCH, D., *The Concentration of Economic Power*. New York, 1946.

LYND, S., *Class Conflict, Slavery, and the United States Constitution*. New York, 1967.

MCCLOSKEY, R. G., *American Conservatism in the Age of Enterprise*. Cambridge, 1951.

MCDONALD, F., *We, The People*. Chicago, 1958.

———, *Insull*. Chicago, 1962.

———, *E Pluribus Unum*. Boston, 1965.

MacGill, C. E., *History of Transportation in the U. S. Before 1860*. Washington, 1917.

Machlup, F., *The Political Economy of Monopoly*. Baltimore, 1952.

MacLauren, M., *Rise of the Electrical Industry During the 19th Century*. Princeton, 1943.

Mahoney, T., *The Great Merchants*. New York, 1955.

Marris, R., *The Economic Theory of "Managerial" Capitalism*. New York, 1964.

Martin, J. C., and Dyer, E. L., *Edison, His Life and Inventions*. New York, 1929.

Marvin, W. L., *The American Merchant Marine*. New York, 1902.

Mason, E. S., *Economic Concentration and the Monopoly Problem*. Cambridge, 1957.

————, .ed., *The Corporation in Modern Society*. Cambridge, 1959.

Mazlish, B., ed., *The Railroad and the Space Program*. Cambridge, 1965.

Means, G. C., *The Corporate Revolution in America*. New York, 1962.

————, *Pricing Power and the Public Interest*. New York, 1962.

Meyers, M. G., *The New York Money Market*. New York, 1931.

Miller, J. C., *Origins of the American Revolution*. Boston, 1943.

————, *Alexander Hamilton: Portrait in Paradox*. New York, 1959.

Miller, F. T., *Thomas A. Edison*. Philadelphia, 1931.

Miller, W., ed., *Men in Business*. Cambridge, 1952.

Mills, C. W., *White Collar: The American Middle Classes*. New York, 1951.

————, *The Power Elite*. New York, 1956.

Minnegerode, M., *Certain Rich Men*. New York, 1927.

Mirsky, J., and Nevins, A., *The World of Eli Whitney*. New York, 1952.

Mishan, E. J., *The Costs of Economic Growth*. London, 1967.

Mitchell, B., *Rise of the Cotton Mills in the South*. Baltimore, 1921.

————, *William Gregg: Factory Master of the Old South*. Chapel Hill, 1928.

————, *Industrial Revolution in the South*. Baltimore, 1930.

————, *Depression Decade*. New York, 1947.

————, *Alexander Hamilton*, 2 v. New York, 1957.

————, *A Biography of the Constitution of the United States*. New York, 1964.

Mitchell, W. C., *Business Cycles and Their Causes* (reprint). Berkeley, 1959.

————, *History of the Greenbacks* (reissue). New York, 1960.

Moley, R., *The First New Deal*. New York, 1966.

Moloney, F. X., *The Fur Trade in New England*. Cambridge, 1931.

Monson, R. J., Jr., and Cannon, M. W., *The Makers of Public Policy*. New York, 1965.

Montague, G. H., *Trusts of Today*. New York, 1904.

Moody, J., *The Truth About the Trusts*. New York, 1904.

————, *The Railroad Builders*. New Haven, 1919.

————, *Masters of Capital*. New Haven, 1919.

MOORE, B., JR., *Social Origins of Dictatorship and Democracy*. Boston, 1966.

MOORE, J. H., *Andrew Brown and Cypress Lumbering in the Old Southwest*. Baton Rouge, 1967.

MOORE, W. E., *The Conduct of the Corporation*. New York, 1962.

MORGAN, D. L., *The Great Salt Lake*. New York, 1942.

MORGAN, H. W., ed., *The Gilded Age*. Syracuse, 1963.

MORISON, S. E., *Builders of the Bay Colony*. Cambridge, 1930.

———, *Maritime History of Massachusetts* (reprint). New York, 1961.

MORRIS, L., *Postscript to Yesterday*. New York, 1947.

MORRIS, R. B., *Government and Labor in Early America*. New York, 1946.

MYERS, G., *History of the Great American Fortunes* (reprint). New York, 1936.

———, *The Ending of American Hereditary Fortunes*. New York, 1939.

NELSON, R. L., *Merger Movements in American Industry*. Princeton, 1959.

NETTELS, C. P., *The Emergence of a National Economy*. New York, 1962.

NEU, I. D., *Erastus Corning: Merchant and Financier*. Ithaca, 1960.

NEVINS, A., *The American States During and After the Revolution*. New York, 1924.

———, *The Emergence of Modern America*. New York, 1927.

———, *John D. Rockefeller*, 2 v. New York, 1940.

———, *Study in Power: John D. Rockefeller*, 2 v. New York, 1953.

———, and COMMAGER, H. S., *A Short History of the U. S.*, 5th ed. New York, 1966.

———, and HILL, F. E., *Ford: The Times, The Man, The Company*. New York, 1954.

———, *Ford: Expansion and Challenge*. New York, 1957.

———, *Ford: Decline and Rebirth*. New York, 1963.

NEWCOMER, M., *The Big Business Executive*. New York, 1955.

NIEBURG, H. L., *In the Name of Science*. Chicago, 1966.

NORTH, D. C., *Growth and Welfare in the American Past*. Englewood Cliffs, 1966.

NOYES, A. D., *Forty Years of American Finance*. New York, 1909.

OBERHOLZER, E. P., *Life of Robert Morris*. New York, 1903.

———, *Jay Cooke*. Philadelphia, 1907.

O'CONNOR, H., *Mellon's Millions*. New York, 1933.

———, *Steel, Dictator*. New York, 1935.

———, *The Guggenheims*. New York, 1937.

———, *The Astors*. New York, 1941.

———, *Empire of Oil*. New York, 1955.

O'CONNOR, R., *Gould's Millions*. New York, 1962.

ORLANS, H., *Contracting For Atoms*. Washington, 1967.

OZANNE, R., *A Century of Labor Management Relations at McCormick and International Harvester*. Madison, 1967.

PAINE, R. D., *The Ships and Sailors of Old Salem*. Boston, 1908.

PARADIS, A. A., *The Hungry Years*. Philadelphia, 1967.

PARKER, W. N., ed., *Trends in the American Economy in the 19th Century*. Princeton, 1960.

PARRINGTON, V. L., *Main Currents in American Thought*, 3 v. New York, 1927–30.

PASSER, H. C., *The Electrical Manufacturers: 1875–1900*. Cambridge, 1957.

PEARSON, H. G., *John Murray Forbes: An American Railroad Builder*. New York, 1911.

PEASE, O. A., *The Responsibilities of American Advertising*. New Haven, 1958.

PHILLIPS, V. B., *Life and Labor in the Old South*. Boston, 1929.

PORTER, K. W., *John Jacob Astor: Business Man*, 2 v. Cambridge, 1931.

———, *The Jacksons and the Lees*. Cambridge, 1937.

———, and LARSON, H. M., *The History of the Humble Oil and Refining Company*. New York, 1959.

PROUT, H. G., *Life of George Westinghouse*. New York, 1922.

PURSELL, C. W., JR., *Readings in Technology and American Life*. New York, 1969.

PYLE, J. G., *Life of James J. Hill*, 2 v. New York, 1917.

RAE, J. B., *American Automobile Manufacturers*. Philadelphia, 1959.

———, *The American Automobile*. Chicago, 1965.

———, *Climb to Greatness*. Cambridge, 1968.

RANDALL, J. G., *Civil War and Reconstruction*. New York, 1937.

RATNER, S., ed., *New Light on the History of Great American Fortunes*. New York, 1953.

RAUCH, B., *The History of the New Deal*. New York, 1944.

REAGAN, M. D., *The Managed Economy*. New York, 1963.

REDLICH, F., *History of American Business Leaders*, v. 1. Ann Arbor, 1940.

———, *Essays in American Economic History*. New York, 1944.

———, *History of American Business Leaders*, v. 2, 3. New York, 1951.

REID, S. R., *Mergers, Managers, and the Economy*. New York, 1968.

RIEGEL, R. E., *The Story of the Western Railroads*. New York, 1926.

ROBERT, J. C., *The Story of Tobacco in America*. New York, 1949.

ROBERTSON, R. M., and PATE, J. L., ed., *Readings in U. S. Business and Economic History*. Boston, 1966.

ROCHESTER, A., *Rulers of America*. New York, 1936.

ROCKEFELLER, J. D., *Random Reminiscences of Men and Events*. New York, 1909.

RODGERS, W., *Think: A Biography of the Watsons and IBM*. New York, 1969.

ROE, J. W., *English and American Tool Builders*. New York, 1916.

ROHAN, J., *Yankee Armsmaker*. New York, 1935.

ROSE, A. M., *The Power Structure*. New York, 1967.

ROSSITER, C., *Conservatism in America*. New York, 1955.

ROZWENE, E. C., ed., *Ideology and Power in the Age of Jackson*. New York, 1964.

RUSSELL, C. E., *Haym Solomon and the Revolution*. New York, 1930.

SATTERLEE, H. L., *J. Pierpont Morgan*. New York, 1939.

SAUM, L. O., *The Fur Trader and the Indian*. Seattle, 1965.

SCHACHNER, N., *Alexander Hamilton*. New York, 1946.

——, *The Founding Fathers*. New York, 1961.

SCHLESINGER, A. M., SR., *The Colonial Merchants and the American Revolution*. New York, 1918.

——, *New Viewpoints in American History*. New York, 1922.

SCHLESINGER, A. M., JR., *The Age of Jackson*. Boston, 1945.

——, *The Crisis of the Old Order*. Boston, 1957.

——, *The Coming of the New Deal*. Boston, 1958.

——, *The Politics of Upheaval*. Boston, 1960.

——, and WHITE, M., ed., *Paths of American Thought*. Boston, 1963.

SCHUBERT, P., *The Electric World*. New York, 1928.

SCHUMPETER, J. A., *Business Cycles*, 2 v. New York, 1939.

SCHWARTZ, B., *The Professor and the Commissions*. New York, 1959.

SEAGER, H. and GULICK, C. A., *Trust and Corporation Problems*. New York, 1929.

SELIGMAN, B. B., *Main Currents in Modern Economics*. New York, 1962.

——, *Most Notorious Victory: Man in an Age of Automation*. New York, 1966.

SELIGMAN, E. R. A., ed., *Encyclopaedia of the Social Sciences*, 15 v. New York, 1933.

SHANNON, D. A., ed., *The Great Depression*. Englewood Cliffs, 1960.

——, *Twentieth Century America*. Chicago, 1963.

——, *Between the Wars: America 1919–1941*. Boston, 1965.

SHANNON, F. A., *The Centennial Years*. New York, 1967.

SHARKEY, R. P., *Money, Class, and Party*. Baltimore, 1959.

SIEPMAN, C. A., *Radio, Television, and Society*. New York, 1950.

SIMONS, A. M., *Social Forces in American History*. New York, 1911.

SIMONSON, G. R., ed., *The History of the American Aircraft Industry*. Cambridge, 1968.

SMITH, H. L., *Airways*. New York, 1942.

SMITH, H. N., ed., *Popular Culture and Industrialism*. New York, 1967.

SMITH, R. A., ed., *Corporations in Crisis*. New York, 1963.

SORENSEN, C. E., *My Forty Years With Ford* (reprint). New York, 1962.

SOULE, G., *Prosperity Decade: 1917–1929*. New York, 1947.

——, *Economic Forces in American History*. New York, 1952.

STAMPP, K. M., *And The War Came*. Baton Rouge, 1950.

——, *The Peculiar Institution*. New York, 1956.

——, ed., *Causes of the Civil War*. Englewood Cliffs, 1959.

STAMPP, K. M., *The Era of Reconstruction*. New York, 1965.

STEGNER, W., *Mormon Country*. New York, 1942.

STEHMAN, J. W., *Financial History of the A.T.&T. Company*. Cambridge, 1925.

STEINDL, J., *Maturity and Stagnation in American Capitalism*. Oxford, 1952.

STERN, P. M., *The Great Treasury Raid*. New York, 1964.

SUMNER, W. G., *The Financier and the Finances of the American Revolution*. New York, 1891.

SUTTON, F. X., and others, *The American Business Creed*. Cambridge, 1956.

SWADOS, H., *A Radical's America*. Boston, 1962.

———, ed., *Years of Conscience*. Cleveland, 1962.

SWANBERG, W. A., *Jim Fisk: Career of an Improbable Rascal*. New York, 1959.

SWARD, K., *The Legend of Henry Ford*. New York, 1948.

TARBELL, I., *The History of the Standard Oil Co*. New York, 1904.

———, *Life of Elbert A. Gary*. New York, 1933.

TATE, A. O., *Edison's Open Door*. New York, 1938.

TAYLOR, G. R., *The Transportation Revolution: 1815–1860*. New York, 1951.

TEBBEL, J. W., *The Marshall Fields*. New York, 1947.

TOLLES, F. B., *Meeting House and Counting House*. Chapel Hill, 1948.

TRESCOTT, P. B., *Financing American Enterprise*. New York, 1963.

TROW, C. E., *Old Shipmasters of Salem*. New York, 1905.

TUGWELL, R. G., *FDR: Architect of an Era*. New York, 1967.

TURNER, F. J., *The Frontier in American History*. New York, 1920.

TYLER, P., ed., *Airways of America*. New York, 1958.

UNGER, I., *The Greenback Era*. Princeton, 1964.

VAN DOREN, C., *Benjamin Franklin*. New York, 1938.

———, *The Great Rehearsal*. New York, 1948.

VEBLEN, T., *The Theory of the Leisure Class*. New York, 1899.

———, *The Theory of Business Enterprise*. New York, 1904.

———, *Absentee Ownership and Business Enterprise*. New York, 1923.

VER STEEG, C. L., *Robert Morris: Revolutionary Financier*. Philadelphia, 1954.

VILLARD, H., *Memoirs*, 2 v. New York, 1904.

WARNER, W. L., *The Corporation in the Emergent American Society*. New York, 1962.

———, and ABEGGLEN, J. C., *Big Business Leaders in America*. New York, 1955.

———, and others, ed., *The Emergent American Society*. New Haven, 1967.

WARREN, H. G., *Herbert Hoover and the Great Depression*. New York, 1959.

WASSON, R. G., *The Hall Carbine Affair*. New York, 1941.

WEBB, W. P., *The Great Plains*. Boston, 1931.

WECTER, D., *The Saga of American Society*. New York, 1937.

WEIDENBAUM, M., *The Modern Public Sector.* New York, 1969.

WEINSTEIN, J., *The Corporate Ideal in the Liberal State.* Boston, 1968.

WEISS, L. W., ed., *Cases in American Industry.* New York, 1967.

WELLER, D. L., *The New Haven Railroad: Its Rise and Fall.* New York, 1969.

WHITNAH, D. R., *Safer Skyways.* Ames, 1966.

WHYTE, W. H., JR., *Is Anybody Listening?* New York, 1952.

WIEBE, R. H., *Businessmen and Reform.* Cambridge, 1962.

WILBURN, J. A., *Biddle's Bank.* New York, 1967.

WILDES, H. E., *Lonely Midas: The Story of Stephen Girard.* New York, 1943.

WILLIAMS, E., *Capitalism and Slavery.* London, 1964.

WILLIAMS, W. A., *The Contours of American History.* Cleveland, 1961.

WINKLER, J. K., *John D. Rockefeller: Portrait in Oil.* New York, 1929.

———, *Morgan the Magnificent.* New York, 1930.

———, *Incredible Carnegie.* New York, 1931.

———, *The First Billion: The Stillmans and the National City Bank.* New York, 1934.

———, *The du Pont Dynasty.* New York, 1935.

———, *Five and Ten: The Fabulous Life of F. W. Woolworth.* New York, 1940.

———, *Tobacco Tycoon: The Story of James Buchanan Duke.* New York, 1942.

WRIGHT, E., ed., *Causes and Consequences of the American Revolution.* Chicago, 1966.

WYLLIE, I. G., *The Self-Made Man* (reprint). New York, 1966.

YOUNG, A. F., ed., *Dissent: Explorations in the History of American Radicalism.* DeKalb, 1968.

INDEX

ABOUT THE AUTHOR

Ben B. Seligman is Professor of Economics and Director of the Labor Relations and Research Center of the University of Massachusetts. Before coming to the university in 1965 he spent many years as an economist in the labor movement, most notably with the Retail Clerks International Association. He has written and edited seven books and has authored more than one hundred papers, articles and reviews for such journals as *Dissent*, *Commentary*, and the *New Leader*, as well as for professional journals, including the *American Economic Review, Journal of Economic Issues, American Journal of Economics and Sociology*, and *History of Political Economy*. Professor Seligman received a Guggenheim Fellowship in 1967 and the Distinguished Alumnus Award of Honor from Brooklyn College in 1968.